BLUE COLLAR DOCTOR

An Adventure in Living

Dr. E. Jeff Justis

Copyright © 2014 E. Jeff Justis
All rights reserved.
ISBN-10: 1500125733
ISBN-13: 978-1500125738

DEDICATION

To Louise (Lisa) Mayo Rollow Justis

To Sally VanDervort Strain Justis

And to Catherine Ann Justis
Jeff Rollow Justis
Louisa Justis Garrido
Steven Frederick Strain
Kim Justis Eikner

CONTENTS

BLUE COLLAR DOCTOR

Acknowledgments   vii

PART I

	Introduction	3
	The Last Suture	3
1	Beginning	7
2	First Flight	12
3	War Games	20
4	Senior Year	24
5	Friends	30
6	College	38
7	Cruising	50
8	Medical School	59
9	Flying	70
10	Externship	81
11	Rite of Passage	90
12	Graduation	105
13	Internship	110
14	Gun Runner	133
15	Lisa	143
16	Appalachia	155
17	Air Force	172
18	A Cold Christmas	190
19	Campbell Clinic	195
20	Germany	218
21	CONUS	249
22	Memphis (Alpha and Omega)	262

23	Anything but a Broken Heart	270
24	The Back Room	283

PART II

	Introduction	289
	Beginning Again	289
1	Sally	291
2	Life's Log Book	294
3	Honeymoon	302
4	Back to Work	306
5	Care Medico	313
6	Day to Day	319
7	Hand Surgery	323
8	Practice	327
9	The Project	337
10	Politics	342
11	Return to the Dominican Republic	347
12	Bicentennial – 1976	350
13	The Voyage	352
14	Friendships	360
15	Flying Adventures	363
16	Air Force Reserves	370
17	A Full Life	375
18	The Second Big Adventure	389
19	The Experimental Experience	395
20	Routine Adventures	399
21	Return to Germany	402
22	One More Flight in Europe	404
23	Family Affairs	406
24	The Next to the Last Chapter	418

ACKNOWLEDGMENTS

My youngest daughter, Kim, who never got to know her mother, Lisa, inspired me to write about our lives before and just after her birth. Cathy, my oldest daughter, suggested a vignette format and has encouraged me to continue writing. Linda Jones of the Campbell Foundation provided much needed editorial advice. I am indebted to my family, friends, colleagues, mentors, and patients, who have brought richness to my life.

PART I

INTRODUCTION

The Last Suture

I walk down the white-tiled hall toward the operating room. My short-sleeved, green scrub suit fits loosely and comfortably; shoe covers, a cap and mask complete the uniform. A nurse approaches, dressed similarly, but her figure pleasantly fills her scrub suit, and her mask provides a mystique that adds to the appeal of these able operating room assistants.

"You're in room two, Dr. J. Jeannie will be your scrub tech. I wish I could be with you." She smiles as she brushes past.

I push open the door to the number two O.R. suite. "I see I'm lucky this morning —I've got a whole room full of S.Y.T.'s!" I joke.

Jeannie's blue eyes sparkle above her mask.

"I hope *I* still qualify as an S.Y.T.," Martha, the nurse anesthetist, comments as she adjusts the heart monitor. I am happy to have her managing my patient's anesthesia; her experience is mirrored in the fine wrinkles at the corners of her eyes.

"You sure do." I continue the light-hearted banter that has characterized these last few years before my retirement. Mary, our circulating nurse is busy setting up the instrument table.

"How about me?" she asks, her dark skinned eyes smiling above her mask.

"You *know* I include you."

My patient, gray hair strands peaking out under her head cover, is lying quietly with her right arm outstretched on a "hand table." Her left arm is supported by an arm board, with an intracath and plastic IV infusion set taped to her forearm.

"What is an S.Y.T.?" She looks up at me.

"Well, you *are* one! Sweet Young Thing—that's what a S.Y.T. is," I reply.

She laughs and the nurses giggle. My patient doesn't seem to resent my sexist approach.

I pick her right hand up from the hand table and gently palpate her wrist. "Has it been bothering you much lately?"

"It sure does; I can't do anything without my fingers going to sleep. Just yesterday I tried to write a letter and…"

"These three fingers tingle a lot don't they?" I rub my fingers over her thumb, index and middle fingers; all three feel dry to touch. "Well, we're going to stop that."

"I hope so, but I'm a little scared – you won't hurt me will you?"

"Not a bit. Martha is going to fix your arm so you won't feel a thing," I reassure her.

I walk out to the scrub sink as Martha begins putting in the arm-blocking anesthetic.

The pungent odor of the antiseptic soaps, Betadine, Phisoderm, and Hibeclens fills my nostrils as I begin scrubbing my hands and forearms, wandering away from the sink and dripping great globs of brown Betadine foam across the floor. Norma is behind me with a mop.

"We can always find you by your leavin's," she jokingly complains.

"Bet you wish I'd stand still. You know, I've always had trouble being still. My mother called me a wiggle worm."

"Well we can confirm that, but we love you anyway."

I've always been fortunate to have people around me who accept my idiosyncrasies, and with few exceptions I respond in kind.

I elbow through the swinging door back into the operating room. Jeannie hands me a towel then holds up a sterile gown. Mary, the circulating nurse, ties the gown in the back as I place my hands into the number 9 latex gloves offered by Jeannie.

Rachmaninoff's Concerto No.2 is playing softly over the built-in stereo system. Some surgeons are all business and don't want music or other distractions but I work best in a relaxed atmosphere. I look over the shiny, stainless steel instruments that have been laid out for me and reflect for a moment on all the new high-tech monitors and machines that are at my disposal. I think about my patient and how she has put herself in this intimidating place out of trust. She had met me in the office only weeks before, but in that meeting I gained her trust enough that she is here now, ready for me to violate the integrity of her skin to try to solve a problem that has disabled her. I marvel at her faith in me. The haunting fear I had felt in the beginning of my path toward a medical career is now only a memory, however vivid. I also marvel at these wonderful, patient ladies who have assisted me in the operating room. They are always ready to help cranky doctors, egotistical surgeons, and an occasional incompetent do the best for the most important one in the room—the patient. I will miss them.

Everything is ready. Jeannie and I place drapes over the patient, leaving her arm uncovered on the sterile table. We sit. I lightly prick the patient's palm with a needle.

"Do you feel anything sharp?" I ask.

"Nothing," she replies, "and I don't want to either."

"You won't," I reassure.

I pick up the scalpel and following the palm crease near the base of the thumb make an incision through the skin. There is no active bleeding, because we are using a tourniquet, but tiny vessels are visible in the subcutaneous fat. I am confident of the anatomy, having gained familiarity with the secrets beneath the skin through experience. The deep transverse carpal ligament glistens white and is tough as it yields to the knife. Upon opening the carpal canal, the contents bulge slightly, and we protect the median nerve as the incision is lengthened. Finally, with Jeannie's help, the ligament is stretched open with retractors exposing the nine tendons and median nerve. This most important nerve for the normal sensation and fine motor function of the hand has been under pressure because of its entrapment in a space too small and its proximity to tendons that are perhaps swollen from overuse. Today, through the functioning of my own median nerve, her median nerve will become unrestricted and function as intended. A check of each tendon reveals some adhesions that have formed from the chronic inflammatory reaction that may accompany carpal tunnel syndrome. The wound is carefully irrigated with saline to flush out debris.

"You want your usual suture don't you, doctor?" Jeannie asks as she places the small needle in the jaws of the needle holder.

"Yes 'ma'am 602 Stainless —I wonder if anybody's going to use up my suture. I tried to teach the residents how to use this type."

Jeannie laughs. "They never could get the hang of it. Some of the residents would get so frustrated when it kinked and twisted out of control."

I place the first suture through the skin edges and loop in the first tie. Using my left index finger and thumb to hold the forceps and my little finger to control the suture, I proceed to place a neat running line of sutures—"whip stitching" as I jokingly refer to this type of closure.

"You know this is my last case," I announce with slight hesitation. I apply a dressing and splint to the patient's forearm.

"I can't believe it," one of the nurses replies. "We don't want it to be."

"It's hard for me to believe, too. But it's time. I need a change and it's best that I give up the surgery."

All my hospital friends have known about my plans, and I believe they are genuinely distressed at the finality of this day.

I finish my final surgery and walk down the white-tiled hallway, maybe for the last time. I think back on the forty years that preceded this day—from that first prideful day in September of '53.

It has taken a long time to get to this position of confidence and to this level of surgical skill, but I think this is when I should give it up. I'm leaving with the knowledge that I'm still doing a good job—not after the confidence and skill begin to fade, as it will. I push through the swinging doors of the surgical suite, pass the lobby, exit into the chilly December air, and enter into a new life.

BEGINNING

There's magic in that white lab jacket, or so it seems—as I sprint toward the Wittenberg building for my first class in medical school. The white coat tails flutter behind me in a gentle breeze—wings for my hopes and dreams. I know that being a doctor is a part of my special destiny, but I am unsure why and not a little intimidated by the prospect. What has brought me to this place and time? Can I know what is ahead? Can I succeed in this undertaking?

For years I had assumed that I would become a dentist, as had my father, but as a youngster, visiting my dad's office in the Exchange Building, I can remember distaste for the antiseptic smells and sounds of a dental office. Curiosity led me to peruse the thick medical and dental books in my dad's private office, but the slight sense of nausea that crept over me on seeing a photograph of a bloody procedure prompted me to retreat into my own fanciful world of mechanical things—the submarine I was going to build—a new bomb device—a new airplane. These were war years. Building models, learning how to spot enemy aircraft, and thinking of ways to fight the Japanese and Nazis were immediate concerns; besides, at age 10 or 11, I didn't need to worry about my reactions to the world of biology.

It was about this time in my life that my dad, prompted by my professed desire to emulate him, began to tell everyone, "This is my son, Jeff; he's planning to become a dentist," or later, "This is my son, Jeff; he's going to enroll in pre-dental school," or, on inquiry, "He made up his own mind; he doesn't have to go to dental school but he wants to." So after several years, I didn't question my own doubts. Even when something occurred that made me want to turn completely away from the biological, I always assumed that someday, somehow, I would no longer have to be concerned. That assumption never came true.

Recess in the ninth grade at Pentecost-Garrison was an active time for a class of thirty to thirty-five boys. Some were testing how fast they could run or how far they could jump from a swing. Others were climbing all over the monkey bars. Suddenly, I heard a scream from one of the younger boys on the playground who had slipped from the bars and landed on his outstretched arm.

"My arm! My arm! Oh — oh —oh —my arm!" He screamed over and over. A chill came over me when I saw him grab his left elbow, which was bent backward.

I'm going to be a dentist — maybe I should help him, but what should I do? WHAT CAN I DO...WHAT CAN I DO?" I was screaming on the inside. I was a boy scout, I had to do something, but I couldn't move. I was frozen.

About that time one of my classmates, a large boy, W.G., who had been elected president of our class and seemed to have a confidence I could only dream of having, began to calm the injured boy, getting him to cradle his broken arm against his side. Soon a teacher drove her car out onto the playground, and W.G. helped the youngster into the car and rode with him to the hospital. Several days later, with his arm appropriately splinted, the young victim bragged about how calm he was and that getting his arm set "wasn't all that bad." W.G. was, of course, the hero and I was left with a sense of guilt at not being able to overcome my own fear enough to do something. Even at that early time in my life, I was developing an unrealistic sense of purpose and expectancy. For years, seeing W.G. would trigger that same sense of inadequacy I had felt on the playground. At a party, decades later, I saw W.G., a balding, obese, dyspneic, businessman and I was finally able to let go of that childish feeling of inferiority.

In grammar school, I was not particularly interested in medicine (as opposed to dentistry) but perhaps my sense of guilt at inaction on the playground was a result of my own exalted expectations.

I was a questioning youngster and would embarrass my parents because of my interest in science— *Popular Science* and *Popular Mechanics* being my primary source books. Once after Sunday school, our large, black-robed Presbyterian preacher looked down at me as I blurted out the question of questions.

"If God is all powerful and all knowing, then who made God?"

"Well — young man — you see — well — God is Love," he replied, somewhat taken aback by my audacity.

His answer didn't satisfy me and only added to my curiosity. I had little patience with accepting on faith. Even then I wanted to figure things out for myself.

Once I wrote a report in which I made a statement about man being related, through a distant ancestor, to the great apes. I don't remember learning this in school and neither of my parents held this view. I was, however, convinced of the logic of evolution (most likely because of my addiction to *Classic Comics*), but I had broken my teacher's heart. Across the top of my paper in bold red letters she had scrawled, *OH NO!* I had sinned — I was unrepentant.

High school opened many doors to me. Although I did not want to leave home, the lack of educational opportunity in Memphis had prompted my parents to encourage me to go to a preparatory school. Most of my friends from Pentecost-Garrison were also going away to school, and I suppose it was easier to acquiesce than to push to remain in a local high school. So I was soon on my way to Virginia and Woodberry Forest School.

My impression of most youngsters in high school then as now is that education is not a high priority and that learning is okay as long as it doesn't interfere with fun and games. Not so at Woodberry. Traditionally, college is the place for questioning and doubting and absorbing new ideas, but at Woodberry my college education began in the tenth grade.

I don't remember being especially inspired toward a medical career at Woodberry but science courses intrigued me, and aeronautics was one of my favorite classes. Mr. Lord was the teacher who introduced us to the physics of flight. As a part of his course a field trip to Gordonsville Airport was planned. He even arranged a short flight for those of us who had parental permission. Ah, there was the rub! There is no predicting what direction my life would have taken if my parents had allowed me to fly at that time. As it was, being denied only stoked the fire of my desire.

Shop training, taught by Mr. Rogers, introduced me to metalworking, and mechanical drawing and art classes were significant in my development. This blue collar, hands-on work was just what I needed since I was away from my shop for nine months of the year. At home my father and I had built a 12 x 12 ft. workshop out of concrete blocks to replace my first workshop that was built from crate material that a neighbor had given to me when I was ten.

As a child and adolescent, I avoided unstructured situations, because I feared not being in control. Once when I was a boy scout, I was asked to give the scout motto in front of parents and scout leaders. I started, "A scout is honest, courteous -- uh -- a scout is -- is..." I couldn't get the rest of it out. Everyone was waiting. I was mortified. Someone in the wings whispered and finally, in a shaky voice, I uttered the rest of the words. A few years later at Woodberry, I was asked to give a report in English class. Someone in the back of the room had made a funny comment that got me tickled. Every time I opened my mouth to give the report I would start to giggle. I couldn't stop and finally the teacher told me to sit down until I had control of myself. That embarrassment furthered my resolve to avoid uncontrollable situations as much as I could. Perhaps this played a role in my choice of an occupation. Physicians and especially surgeons strive to maintain control of every situation. Even the uncontrollable emergency is quickly transformed into a structured situation through the formalities of the emergency room or operating room.

The desire to become a physician grew slowly through exposure to several books. *Giants in the Earth* cultured an independent spirit. *The Magnificent Obsession* was a romantic beacon, but I identified with Martin Arrowsmith and especially Andrew Manson in the *Citadel*. These thoughts were my secret, however, because everyone knew I was going to be a dentist. I was so convincing to myself and to others that to this day some friends of my youth still think I studied dentistry.

FIRST FLIGHT

It's sometimes difficult to know oneself and to accommodate two seemingly different personalities. On the one hand, I am a romantic – in the classic sense of the word. Wuthering Heights and Jane Eyre immediately come to mind, and the idyllic desert island paradise of Swiss Family Robinson pulls me inward toward tranquility. On the other hand, I am intrigued by science and discovery and the world of adventure. Perhaps flying helps me bridge these extremes. As a child I had experienced flight—at least in my imagination.

Jumping off the yellow school bus, I ran up the gravel driveway as fast as my ten-year old legs could carry me.
"Annie! Annie! Has it come yet? Has it come?"
"Law! Young Jeff you sho' is wanting dat package bad."
"I can't wait to get it, Annie Lou. I can't wait."
Only Christmas Eve could rival the anticipation I felt. Ever since I saw the cockpit depicted on the back of a Kellogg's Rice Krispies box, I knew I had to have it. It was my destiny.
"It ain't come yet. Maybe you'll see it in the afternoon mail."
I remember how Christmas Eve was torture. The excitement and anticipation conspired to keep me awake and sleep was the only thing that would let the time pass. Oh, how I wished the time would pass.
I hugged Annie's wonderful black neck. "Where's mama?"

"She shoppin. She say be sure you do your homework."

"Aw, Annie. I don't need to do it now. I got all day."

"She say you better do it before supper. It's three-thirty now."

"Three-thirty! Stella Dallas is on. I'll get my book."

....AND NOW – STELLA DALLAS, BACK STAGE WIFE... the radio announcer intoned with enticing drama...*WILL STELLA BE ABLE TO HELP HER HUSBAND GET A PART IN BART'S NEW PLAY? CAN SHE OVERCOME BETH'S ANGER? STAY TUNED....*

I fumbled through my arithmetic book, with my ears tuned to the radio. *I wish Annie could read. She could help me get through this. Maybe I can teach her some day.*

"Annie would you like me to teach you to read?"

"Law, young Jeff, I 's too old. You know dat."

"Naw you're not Annie. See you hadn't got any grey hairs." I ran my fingers across her jet-black hair.

"Yeah, I *is* old."

"Won't you let me try?"

"Maybe — maybe some day."

"I want to try to teach you anyway."

*....AND NOW THE GREEN HORNET DEFENDER OF TRUTH AND THE AMERICAN WAY...*The radio announcer introduced the next show to the music of Flight of the Bumblebees. That was one of my favorites, but so was Sky King and Superman and Batman. I guess I liked all the afternoon shows.

"You doin' your homework?"

"Yeah, Annie."

I wrote my multiplication problems in one column and then next to it I filled in the answers. *Let's see nine times seven is, nine times seven is...I hate the multiplication table. Nine times eight is...is.* I added up nine eights, *that's right—seventy-two. Let's see nine times seven—heck.*

......WILL THE GREEN HORNET SURVIVE HIS FRIGHTFUL FALL FROM TEN STORIES? TUNE IN TOMORROW, SAME TIME, SAME STATION TO FIND OUT...

I loved the afternoon radio. That's why I was always glad to come home after school if only I didn't have homework. Dad said I had to learn the multiplication table. He had trouble with math, but he wanted me to be better. I didn't need to be better; I wanted to be like him.

"What time is it, Annie?'

"Bout fo-thirty."

"I better check the mail then."

Every afternoon for a week, I had expectantly opened the mailbox. I tried everything I knew to alter reality. *Maybe if I can kick the same rock all the way to the street, it'll be there. Today, I'll try holding my breath 'til I get to the mailbox. I'm gonna do it. I'm gonna do it—I'm Superman.* My lungs were about to burst. *I'm almost there.* I touched the mailbox. "Whew." I sucked in the sweet air and stood by the box a few seconds, breathing deeply before I opened it.

"It's here!" Expectation was rewarded. "It's here!" I grabbed the letters in one hand and with the other reached for the brown paper-covered box. It was bigger than I thought. The package filled the mailbox in width and length and was thick as my hand. I ran back up the drive.

"It's here, Annie! It's here!"

"Law, young Jeff, slow down."

I bounded up the stairs to my room, a pine-paneled gable room over the garage, and carefully unwrapped my package.

YOU CAN BE A PILOT
Learn to fly with your Kelloggs' Cockpit Kit
Instruction Manual Included
How to fly an Airplane

I placed the main instrument panel on a table, unfolding the cardboard side pieces. The throttle control really worked – and the instruments all had little arrow pointers that could be turned. The control stick fit in an accordion fold of cardboard fastened to the floor piece. Two rudder pedals with pleats really moved as I stepped first right then left.

Flying is easy if you understand a few basic principals. I read. *The control stick is used to control pitch and roll. The rudder pedals are used to control the yaw.* Pictures helped me understand these terms. *The throttle controls power. To take off, advance power, push the stick forward to raise the tail. Move the airspeed to 60 mph then gently pull back on the stick and you will be flying....*

I am ready. The room vanishes. My left hand is on the stick, my right hand on the throttle and my feet rest on the rudder pedals. "Cleared for take-off," the tower controller issues clearance.

I move the controls gently. Acceleration pushes me back in my seat and the wind increases against my face as I push forward on the throttle. I pull back on the stick, and in that magic moment, I am lifted above the ground. My house falls away beneath me, and I make lazy circles high above the trees in my yard. I am with the birds now. I am free. I am flying.

"Jeff! Jeff! JEFF!"

Suddenly, I was back in my room. My mother was leaning through the doorway to my room.

"Hi mama, come look. I want to show you my airplane."

"That's nice, honey."

"Look—let me show you how it works. I'm learning how to fly."

"I see! Have you done your homework?"

"Almost."

"Well, you'd better finish."

"Aw, mama. I want to fly some more. Mama, I'm not playing! I'm really learning to fly."

"Uh huh."

"You believe me, don't you? You believe I can fly, don't you?"

"*Some day maybe you can. I'm not sure I want you to, but someday maybe you can.*"

She was right. She didn't want me to learn to fly.

Thousands of hours later, thinking of that first flight of my imagination, I recalled a sense of awe and wonder often lost in the pressures of the present.

It was not until 1950, at the age of seventeen, when I finally was able to experience the wonder of flight outside of my imagination, and the reality was no less than I had ever dreamed.

My good friend, Hugh Humphreys, invited me to spend spring break cruising the Bahama Islands aboard his dad's yacht, "The Humko." The yacht was a fifty-foot, ocean-going vessel and was used to entertain customers of the Humko Company, a successful vegetable oil refinery started by Herbert Humphreys and Hugh Kopold. Hugh and I rode the train south from Virginia to Miami where we met Mr. and Mrs. Humphreys, their new son, Herbo, Lynn and Leslie, Hugh's younger sisters, and the six-man crew.

I was a bit smitten by Lynn Humphreys and did my best to impress her with teenage machismo. I even dissected an eye of a barracuda that we had caught while trawling and described the anatomy I had just learned in biology class at Woodberry. Everyone commented on how they were sure I would become a doctor. In spite of the obvious impression I had made on Lynn, I could only hope that our hands would touch as we stood together at the mahogany rails watching the sun turn red in the western sky. I could not get up enough courage to move my hand closer much less put my hand gently on hers as I wanted to with all my heart. What I would have done had she grabbed my hand, I can only guess, but if my heart had beaten any faster, I'm sure the boat would have shuddered. Alas, too soon the ship's bell called us to dinner. Thus, my shipboard romance was only consummated in my teenage imagination.

The cruise was in every sense an adventure and provided me with my first experience in breaking through the racial prejudice that was so much a part of my Southern heritage. Several years had passed since I had felt the glare of white eyes when I offered a black lady my seat on a full city bus in Memphis. I had been taught to be a gentleman, and it seemed only right that I should defer to age. As I stood beside her, sensing the hatred aimed at her and at me, I felt that universal conflict between the desire to conform and one's conscience. So when The Humko anchored off the North Coast of Andros Island in the Bahama Islands, I had the opportunity to view racial acceptance first hand. The governor of the island, a heavy-set black man who was educated at Oxford and spoke with a beautiful British accent, was invited for dinner on board the Humko. He delighted us with stories of shipwrecks and pirates and invited us ashore for a banquet at the governor's mansion the following evening. As we sailed away from Andros, no one aboard cared what color the governor was — only that he had become our friend.

We sailed under darkening clouds toward Bimini and noticed anxious exchanges between the captain and crew and Herbert Humphreys. Hugh, who was quite knowledgeable of the sea, said a storm was coming, and it was uncertain whether we could make it to the mainland in time to catch the train back to Woodberry. Missing any classes was undesirable, because there was always the threat of summer school if all work was not successfully completed by the end of the school year. The captain said he would make one attempt to cross the Gulf Stream and if unable to do so would return to Bimini.

The Humko listed in the churning water, climbed the swells, and slammed down hard as we tried to cross the sixty or so nautical miles to Florida. Wilda Humphreys cradled Herbo in the cabin below. The girls stayed on the bridge, but Hugh and I held on to the forward rail, letting the spray sting our faces and feeling the exhilaration of riding the waves in the face of nature's fury. But even this fifty-foot yacht could not continue this way, and soon we put into a lee port on Bimini Island.

Although Hugh and I would have enjoyed trying the crossing again, time was short, and when we learned that Hugh's dad was considering chartering an airplane to get us back to Miami, excitement grew once again.

If I had doubts about my future career in dentistry, there was no doubt that I wanted to fly more than anything else. Although I cannot confirm it, my mother said that the first word I uttered was "airplane" as one passed overhead. Sometimes on Sunday afternoons we would go to the airport, and my desire to fly grew with each visit. One day we saw a large sign that proclaimed: **Airplane Rides - $5.00**

Please—Please—Please! I had begged. My dad relented, but my mom hesitated. "Suppose something happens. Look how small that plane is," she worried. My dad tried to reassure her. I remained quiet—I wanted to fly. As we moved closer to the ticket counter my mother finally decided it was too dangerous, and my dad didn't argue. I never got over that disappointment, but it fueled my desire and I knew that someday I *would* fly.

The next morning, in clearing skies, my excitement grew with each step as we approached the imposing Grumman Widgeon, sitting high on her retractable wheels on the hard packed sand of Bimini Bay. Hugh encouraged me to sit next to the pilot since he had flown before and knew that I had not. Hugh was selfless like that, and although our paths separated in coming years, I always considered him to be my best friend.

I buckled into the co-pilot's seat and intensely absorbed every movement of the pilot's hands. He moved levers forward, flipped switches, and turned valves to start the Pratt & Whitney's on each wing. The groan-puff-groan-puff-rrrump of the starting sequence gave way to a thunderous roar as the big engine on my right vibrated to life. The prop blast brought the smell of av-gas and oil into the cabin and the low pitched rumble of the radial engine added to the mystique, and I felt I was a part of this machine. The pilot powered up the left engine and the big machine began moving. I kept my side window open as the pilot taxied down the beach toward the water. The hull of the amphibian slid into the blue bay, and the wheels splashed the cool water through the open window across my arm and face. I hardly noticed in my wonder. The pilot retracted the wheels, shut the cockpit windows, ruddered into position and pushed the power levers forward. Both engines roared in response, and we began to plow through the water, slowly at first, then skipping the waves until we planed across the water faster and faster. Compressed between water and wing, thin air gained substance, and reacting to the downward flow created by accelerating molecules over the camber of the wing, the machine, a lumbering mass on land or water, lifted gracefully from the bay and climbed quickly over the gulf stream toward Miami. I was ecstatic. I had dreamed of flying, yet even the dreams fell short of the reality. I *knew* I was destined for this. I only *thought* I was destined for medicine.

A little over a year remained of the days of learning and confusion referred to in our country as "high school." I had so frequently said that I was going to be a dentist that I believed it myself, yet there were doubts. Like many boys of my generation I stood in awe of my father, but like adolescents of any generation I needed to break free—to prove myself in the world. War and the trappings of military life attract many young men at this vulnerable time of their lives. The young fight wars with no experience at war. If they survive the horror, they may become leaders, avoiding future horror by position or responsibility. I was registered for the draft during the Korean War, and I remember wishing I would be drafted so that I might put off what I considered a life decision filled with uncertainty. However, I was either too fearful or too smart to volunteer—perhaps both.

WAR GAMES

A summer breeze cools the screened-in porch of the Snowden House Bed and Breakfast Inn at Horseshoe Lake, Arkansas. Sally and I sip wine as we wait for dinner.

"This place holds a lot of memories for me," I say, looking toward the lake. "In fact, right out there—just beyond the pier—is where we blew the bottom out of a boat."

"How'd that happen?" Sally asks.

"Teenage adventurism, I guess! I think I was eighteen at the time."

Bayard Snowden's uncle invited him, Hugh Humphreys, and me to spend a weekend the summer of 1950 at Horseshoe Lake. Happy Snowden, Bayard's cousin, also had invited one of her friends. We got tired of swimming from the pier, so we pulled out an old wooden flat-bottomed fishing boat and fitted it with an outboard motor. Since only three could sit in the small boat at a time, we alternated riding and watching from the pier.

"Hey, I've got an idea!" Bayard said as we began to discuss ways to make the afternoon more interesting. "I've got some cherry bombs. Let's see what they'll do in the water."

"Yeah, let's try 'em."

The girls stood back as a lighted cherry bomb was hurled from the pier. BOOM! A large geyser plumed up from the lake spraying us with a cooling mist in the hot summer sun. The girls screamed in delight and we were pulled in our imagination back to the Great War that had not long before ended.

"Let's put on a show for the girls!"

"That'll be neat."

We three boys got in the boat with a supply of cherry bombs. Bayard was in the bow with the ammunition. Hugh was in the middle seat, and I was at the helm. We started an attack run at the pier turning at the last minute, spraying a sheet of water over the excited girls.

"Watch out — they're firing at us!" Hugh shouted as Bayard heaved a bomb forward. I turned the boat just in time to avoid the explosion. The geyser of water fell over us as we passed the near miss.

Our torpedo boat zigzagged through the churning water, dodging everything the enemy could throw at us. Then it happened. A bomb was thrown straight ahead. I steered the boat closer than ever to where the bomb was dropped. I was just beginning a short evading turn when—**WHAM! BOOM!**—the bomb exploded right under our boat. The front end bounded up at least two feet out of the water.

"Hey we've got a leak!" Bayard shouted. Water began pouring through the bottom where a plank had been pulled loose by the explosion.

"She's filling fast, Jeff!" Hugh exclaimed as I began heading the crippled vessel toward shore. The water was over my ankles, and the little outboard motor was struggling to push the rapidly filling boat closer to land.

The girls ran toward us to help, and just as the bow of the boat slid onto the muddy bank, the stern with the motor and me sank into the shallow water.

"Help me get this motor loose."

The outboard bubbled and choked to a stop.

"Boy that was close."

"Yeah! But we made it."

"We were afraid for you," one of the girls said and, of course, for three teenage boys that made the whole adventure worthwhile.

The next morning, with our mishap fresh on our minds, we repaired the boat and cleaned the motor then used the boat as a platform to swim offshore.

"Hey, Jeff, look."

Just as I turned toward the voice, Bayard slapped his hand obliquely into the water sending a spray right into my face.

Instinctively, I threw my left hand toward the surface and just as my palm made contact, I felt my watch—a waterproof Mido—slide over my hand and plunge into the water.

"I've lost my watch you guys. Help me find it."

"Where'd it go in?"

"Right in line with the pier—about 20 feet out. Should be right here," I said, treading water.

Hugh and Bayard both dove down but could see nothing in the murky lake water.

"I think my uncle has a diving bell," Bayard said. "Let's go look."

We found the large cast iron bell with a glass view plate in a storage shed. A long rubber hose attached the bell to a hand-powered air pump.

"This is great," we agreed as we loaded the heavy bell shaped diving helmet into the boat.

"I'll be first," Bayard said. Hugh and I carefully placed the heavy bell on his shoulders. Hugh pumped as Bayard sank out of sight. There was much bubbling and commotion and then Bayard popped to the surface without the helmet.

"Couldn't see anything and the helmet's too heavy," he said breathless from his dive. Two of us followed the air hose to the helmet resting on the muddy bottom and hoisted it into the boat.

"Let me try it," I said. They lowered the helmet onto my shoulders. The unpadded iron pushed down hard, and I was glad for the buoyancy of the water as I let the helmet push me to the bottom.

My feet sank six inches into the mire, and I struggled to remain upright under my top-heavy load. I could see nothing but brown. Holding my hand up to the glass, I could just see my fingers six inches away. *My watch is lost for sure*, I thought as I tried to lean over enough to see the bottom of the lake. Suddenly, the helmet rolled off. Gasping, I propelled myself to the surface.

"I don't think there's much use in looking."

"Well let me go down one time just to see what it's like," Hugh responded. We realigned the boat with the pier after retrieving the diving gear and helped Hugh into the helmet. We pumped air for Hugh as bubbles danced in the water. Suddenly in the midst of the bubbles Hugh popped to the surface.

"I found it!"

"You're joking! I can't believe it!"

Hugh held out his hand over the boat and there was my stainless steel Mido watch.

"But how?"

"Well, I never saw it, but when I went down on my knees in the mud, I threw my hand out to catch myself and felt something hard in the mud. It could've been a rock, but as I closed my fingers around it, I knew I had something else."

We all agreed it was a miracle. The girls were appropriately impressed—a fact that heightened the satisfaction we felt at the end of an adventure filled summer weekend of war games.

SENIOR YEAR

The sound of a train whistle evokes conflicting emotions. On the one hand there is the excitement of travel and exploring new places. On the other hand, there is the aching memory of being separated from my family.

I stood silently in the cool September evening at Buntyn Station on Southern Avenue. Too soon the oscillating headlight cut through the darkness, and the ground shook under my feet as the rumbling diesel locomotive with its string of Pullman cars screeched to a metallic halt. Leaving home was always hard for me, although I adapted to the Woodberry Forest environment as well as any first-born son or only son was likely to do.

"Come on, Jeff, the train's leaving," Hugh called.

I hugged my mom and dad, grabbed the handrail, and pulled myself aboard the Southern Railroad Sleeper.

The conductor showed me to my seat, which he and the other Pullman workers were in the process of converting into upper and lower berths. I was happy to have a lower bunk, because I could watch the lights of farmhouses and cars pass in the night until they blurred and flickered out in my sleep.

The onset of homesickness was always delayed by activity as when Hugh and John T. and Walk suggested that we go to the club car. I was ready to join them. I did not drink nor did Hugh, but I remember one time that John T., who was actually a little younger than I and in the class behind mine in school, announced that he was going to have a drink. He ordered a cocktail.

"Are you sure you're old enough?" The bartender was suspicious.

"If I am old enough to fight a war, I'm old enough to drink." John T. was referring to the Korean War, which was in full bloom in 1950.

Rules were somewhat relaxed on the train so John T. got his drink, but we all knew that if the authorities at Woodberry found out that would be grounds for expulsion.

Hugh and I were perhaps a bit too judgmental. John T. later became a respected businessman and representative of his church. Hugh and I remained teetotalers until college. I succumbed, however, to peer pressure my senior year at Woodberry and joined (with my parents permission) the Smoking Club. I admired Hugh for his strength of character during those years in prep school, but the college life and freedom was too much even for Hugh, and alcohol became a controlling factor for much of his adult life.

Especially during my senior year, I was haunted by self-doubt. To everyone else and to my parents, I was certain of my future and announced it freely.

"Yes, I'm going to follow in my dad's footsteps."

"Well you'll have some big shoes to fill!"

"You'll probably be president of the Dental Society like your dad."

I responded with a smile but always felt a lingering uncertainty. I didn't *want* to be president of anything; I didn't *want* to have the same friends my dad had; I didn't *want* Dad making my decisions.

"I wish I would get drafted," I thought aloud, responding to my own thoughts.

"What did you say, Jeff?" Hugh asked as the train sped along the darkened tracks to the northeast.

"Oh I guess I was just thinking out loud. I was just wishing I didn't have to make so many decisions this year— you know—college applications and all that."

There are so many factors that influence our decisions that one may wonder where free will really comes into play. Parental influence always is in competition with peer pressure, and if the latter is stronger at a young age, then that influence itself is immature and an adolescent may follow his peers into ill-advised activities. But with strong parental influence, I continued down the path I had so often announced, all the while harboring doubts and daydreaming of a different life—my life.

Crawling into that lower bunk on the Pullman car of the Southern Railroad, I peered through the window at the lights and dreamed of the romance of medicine in the time of Martin Arrowsmith or the adventure of flight with Charles Lindbergh and hoped, with the rumbling persistence of the train, that someday my dreams might be fulfilled.

I have fond memories of my senior year in high school. On Saturdays my friends and I walked the winding road through the woods to Cube's country store. Over a Coke and an ice-cream sandwich we'd laugh at each other's silliness or discuss the more serious business of girls.

"You know that girl who comes with the guy delivering milk from town Saturday afternoons?"

"Yeah, I know the one."

"Well, I saw her doing it with him in the woods last week."

"You did? How? Where?" Everybody was interested.

Charley filled in the details as we let our eighteen-year-old imaginations enhance this Boccaccio's tale. I'm sure that poor girl wondered why for months young boys would stare, whisper, and giggle every time she came on campus.

I participated in several sports activities in high school. Most were individual activities such as track (I was pretty fast at the 220 yard dash but ran out of steam trying the 440 yard run) and tumbling (I enjoyed doing flips until I bent my right middle finger backward; that proximal interphalangeal joint has been thicker ever since). I did well in soccer also—anyone can kick a ball, and the organization of the game is not as rigid as in football—but I am remembered by many of my classmates for two things: the post office and my gum machines. To earn some spending money I worked as Assistant Postmaster at the Woodberry Forest Post Office, sorting mail, filling out money orders, posting packages; in general, learning to respect the routine work done every day by postal workers. My gum machine venture was the result of seeing an advertisement in *Popular Science* Magazine. I purchased three with which I hoped to make my fortune. The good people of Orange, Virginia indulged my entrepreneurial venture by allowing me to place the machines in several stores. Each Saturday I would remove the week's take, give the storekeeper his share, and refill the machines with gum or peanuts. In my nickel-operated machine, I carefully placed prizes near the outside of the glass globe as an enticement. The other machines were penny- operated.

"Hey, Shylock, are you counting your pennies again?" My friends would tease me when they saw me hovering over a mound of pennies. I learned soon enough that it takes a *lot* of pennies to make a fortune. Before graduating I sold my "business" to a younger, less jaded, budding entrepreneur.

Attendance at Chapel was required several times during the week and, of course, church was mandatory on Sunday. I always considered myself to be spiritual and personally reflective, but I was sometimes embarrassed by the public display that was often necessary in an Episcopal Church. Kneeling, ritualistic recitation, and the boring Communion were endured but not enjoyed. Rarely did a sermon inspire me, so my daydreams often carried me out of the church into the fields and woods that were there to be explored.

Charlie Yarbrough and I often hiked along the Rapidan River, talking about the Civil War and the possibility of finding some secret cache of old guns or gold hidden in the rocks. Ante-bellum homes were all around Woodberry. In fact, the "Residence", home of the headmaster, was built in the late eighteenth century. One Sunday afternoon we stumbled across an abandoned graveyard hidden in a dark woody thicket. In whispered tones we read the names and dates on the vine-covered tombstones and imagined the lives of those who had once walked here before us. The past was viewed through the mists of romance and always seemed to have a quality of tranquility—not the uncertainty and turmoil that characterized the teenage spirit.

Although I loved history in the abstract, I had difficulty remembering dates and with only weeks remaining before graduation, I flunked, along with Martin Baker, my last history exam. The pressure was on and having to study for a re-examination dulled the excitement of the upcoming festivities. Nevertheless, I managed to get through the trauma and passed the re-examination qualifying with a "C."

The girl I had invited to the prom was a thin, blond young lady whose affect was a bit flat, and I remember her not being very exciting. She had invited me to several functions in Memphis so I was reciprocating. In all fairness, however, she was appreciative and I did my best to show her a good time. Only once or twice more did our paths cross during college and nearly thirty-five years passed before I saw her again, this time as a patient. She had tried to commit suicide by slicing her wrist, but only succeeded in severely damaging the tendons and median nerve. When I walked into her hospital room, I saw a frail, edentulous, wrinkled old lady in place of the girl I had dated at the prom. "Oh Jeff, I don't want you to see me like this," she said to me. "I don't want you to think of me this way; I made a mistake—I had too much to drink and ...." I felt sorry for this young woman grown old. I felt like a space traveler who returns to find those left behind older than he. The years had not been kind to her. She was embarrassed to be there as if I had learned her deepest secrets and could no longer remember her as she was in the innocent years.

The Graduation Ceremony with its pomp and circumstance was under the trees beside the chapel. My grades placed me in the top 25%, but because of my close call with History, I did not win any honors. We felt sorry for Walk J., because he was going to have to attend summer school before receiving his diploma. The elation of finally completing high school and of looking forward to new adventures was tempered by the realization that we were passing through a door that, once closed, could never again be opened. Perhaps this realization accounted for the few damp eyes and prolonged hand shakes with friends we might never see again. We were all taking diverging paths of varying lengths and could only look back in our memories and imaginations.

FRIENDS

Robust and energetic is the way I remember Hugh, not the cosmetic, still form before me. I turn away, afraid that this view will in some way adulterate memories of long ago.

"Come on, Jeff, we need to keep going or we won't make it to the shelter," Hugh shouted to Bobby and me as we struggled to keep up with his self-imposed fast pace along the Appalachian Trail.

At Davenport Gap we had unloaded our gear, said farewell to the motel owner who was kind enough to help us get to the Gap and to drive our green Dodge back into Gatlinburg. We had arrived late in Gatlinburg and found a cabin motel off the main drag. The proprietor was a friendly, graying gentleman who seemed impressed with our respectful way of speaking: "yes sir", "no sir", and "thank you." He agreed to keep the Dodge until we returned about a week later.

We were seventeen and beginning an adventure. To hike the entire Appalachian Trail from Maine to Georgia was our initial goal, but time and money constraints subdued our ambitions and we settled upon a more modest endeavor. Our destination was Newfound Gap, 30 miles to the southwest.

Hugh and I both attended Woodberry Forest, and Bobby was in Baylor military school near Chattanooga. We three had shared several adventures in the past: exploring the Wolf River bottoms behind Hugh's home; camping out at Norfolk Lake in Arkansas, and sporting around town in Hugh's restored Model T Ford. The green Dodge used on this latest adventure was another of Hugh's rebuilt cars. Although his father was quite wealthy and could have bought him any new car, he insisted that Hugh work for what he got. This work ethic was also a part of my upbringing: "If you will fix up an old car its yours, but I won't buy you a new one," my father would say. To this day I take greater pride in the ability to fix something than in the ability to own something.

"Dad says we can use the Dodge to go to Gatlinburg, but we'll have to agree to some rules," Hugh said as we began plans for our summer trip.

"Sure, Hugh, anything." Bobby and I knew we couldn't get a car to make the trip. I had a Model A Ford that I had been working on, but the engine had a cracked block and the mechanical brakes were unreliable, and Bobby was only able to use his folk's car occasionally.

"Dad wants us to promise not to go over 50 miles per hour and not to drive over 40 at night," Hugh said.

None of us thought that would be a problem. There were no expressways in the early fifties and the two-lane highway to Gatlinburg didn't inspire one to great speed. We each took turns at driving, and we watched each other's speed. Some argument and confusion developed when I attempted to pass a truck along the way. As we struggled alongside a large semi, trying to maintain the magic number 50, it seemed the truck was trying to keep pace. We never were going to pass—then just as a head-on collision with an approaching car seemed eminent, I sped up and cleared the truck.

"You shouldn't have tried to pass!" Hugh scolded

"Yeah," Bobby agreed.

"We'll never get there if we don't try to pass these trucks," I responded.

"But we promised not to go over 50!"

I knew they were right on a moral principle, but from a practical viewpoint I had my doubts. Nevertheless, when I think of contemporary society, especially its youth, with its lack of a strong moral stance and sense of self-discipline, I marvel at the responsibility shown by three teenagers alone on an adventure in those halcyon days.

At Davenport Gap, we entered the leaf-canopied Appalachian Trail. I inhaled the fresh green smell of the woods that beaconed us into the wild. Our backpacks each weighed fifty pounds, and as we began our hike the gradual slope of the initial trailhead belied the struggle not far ahead. I remember the discomfort in my neck as the backpack straps pulled down on my shoulders, aggravating a "crick" I had developed overnight in the cool motel cabin. Hugh took the lead and Bobby and I alternated trailing last. Hugh had been told that he had a heart murmur and an enlarged heart, but apparently any concerns doctors had expressed for his exercise tolerance never slowed him down. In fact, on this trip, he seemed determined to be the first one up the mountain.

I would have liked to pass Hugh, but the pain in my neck and weight of my pack resigned me to a slow trudging climb as the trail became steeper in the thickening woods. Heavy breathing and a pounding heart interfered with our perception of peace in the forest, but when we rewarded ourselves with a rest, and leaned back on our packs, the forest spoke with gentle rustling leaves and calling birds.

We reached our first campsite late in the afternoon. Spaced every five miles or so along the Appalachian Trail in the Great Smokey Mountains National Park, the campsites were cleared areas off trail with three-sided shelters and a stone pit for cooking. The shelters were floored with wire mesh about two feet above ground level. For extra comfort, we layered leaves and pine needles under our sleeping bags on the wire. The first day's climb was our hardest and shortly after finishing our baked beans and hot chocolate all three of us were asleep.

We were awakened in the damp predawn chill by the loud rattling of tin cans. With our flashlights we saw a large black bear sniffing and pawing one of our backpacks. Only then did we remember that a cardinal rule in the Smokies is that food should be hoisted off the ground by a rope over a limb or put in bear proof containers—certainly not left on the ground or slept with.

We shouted, **"Shoo! Shoo! Scat bear!"** Hugh grabbed a frying pan and started beating on it with a spoon. The bear stopped his rummaging and looked directly at us as if to say, "What are you people doing?" He snorted loudly and shuffled off into the woods. A torn backpack, several dented cans, and scattered marshmallows were punishments for our carelessness.

As the sun began to warm the morning, we lit a fire for breakfast. We did not bring dried camper's food or war surplus k-rations but were well supplied with bacon, eggs, bread, and assorted canned-goods. Our breakfast smelled delicious to us—and to our bear friends. Soon two more bears entered the scene. One left because of the noise we were making, but the other stood half hidden behind our lean-too.

"I'm gonna try to get a close up," I announced as I pulled a small "Kodak" from my backpack. "You all keep his attention." I quietly began to make my way around the opposite side of the shelter to sneak up on our visitor.

"Be careful. You remember what the rangers say about these bears," Hugh cautioned.

I think I always enjoyed doing something no one else was doing or something that could best be done alone. Certainly my later life choices: flying, skiing, scuba, wood working, mirrored my proclivity for individual accomplishment.

This bear, smaller than our first visitor, was absorbed in what Bobby and Hugh were doing and didn't notice my self-perceived stealthy Indian approach. I was probably three feet behind him with my camera ready when—WHOMP—he suddenly spun around, raised himself up and threw his front paws hard onto the ground—nearly on my feet.

We had startled each other. The primal fight or flight hormones surged through our bodies. I suspect his impulse was more fight and mine was more flight. We both retreated, however, preferring peaceful co-existence to confrontation.

We, saw many bears along the trail the following days, but no others approached us closely—word undoubtedly having circulated in the bear community to watch out for those crazy-acting teenage boys!

Using a trail map to navigate the Appalachian Trail, especially in the Smokies, is not difficult but there are pitfalls. Occasionally, a fork in the trail will be confused with an uncharted trail. Just before stopping for our lunch snack one day we started down a trail that continued downward a lot longer than our map indicated it should. Still, Hugh and Bobby who were up ahead thought we should keep going. Although we would occasionally become separated on the trail, we always managed to get together during rest stops and if one of us lagged behind too much, we would shout our presence. None of us wanted to be left alone in the woods, so each of us assumed responsibility for the other—as good soldiers, scouts, and comrades should. I sensed we were going in the wrong direction. "Listen!" A faint murmuring sound soon became the roar of a mountain stream thundering over boulders as we approached and finally pinpointed our position on the map.

"We're here," Bobby said indicating a point a full two miles off the trail and at least five more miles from the next campsite.

"I'm sorry. I'm sorry I led you all down this way," Hugh apologized, even though Bobby and I had made the same error initially.

Hugh was that way. If he expressed friendship it was because he was a friend, and if he was apologetic it was because he was truly sorry. If he said he was going to do something, he would. In a word, he was honest.

"Well, we need to get going if we're going to get to the next camp," Bobby reminded us. Since I was last down this trail, I decided to lead the way back.

"Let's go," I said as I hoisted my backpack, grabbed a stick, and started the uphill climb to the main trail. The crick in my neck was no longer bothering me.

There's something about being ahead that inspires one to stay ahead. I puffed and pushed and forced each step to the next, climbing agonizingly toward my goal. I was determined that Hugh and Bobby would not pass me but was mindful that I must not lose the trail—a reminder of the responsibility of leadership. Finally, the crossroad appeared and I wearily slipped out of my pack and leaned against a log.

As Bobby and Hugh came into view, I shouted, "What kept you? I've been here forty-five minutes. Let's keep going."

They saw how hard I was breathing as I feigned getting up to hike again; we all burst out laughing. We rested a long time.

"You know, we're not going to make it to the next shelter," Hugh sighed.

"I know," Bobby replied, looking at his watch. It was nearly four o'clock.

"Let's just plan to camp on the trail and stop before dark," I said, as we looked at the map. "How 'bout this knoll about a mile and a half farther up?"

We agreed to this plan and were glad to find a smooth enough area on a treeless "bald" to set up our three-man tent. We were in a cloud on our high perch and could find no dry wood. As hard as we tried, using all the Boy Scout skills at our disposal and too many of our matches, we could not light a fire.

"Too much wind."

"Too wet and too little oxygen." I was the one planning a scientific (medical or dental) career, so I provided the latter excuse.

Needless to say, we ate a cold dinner, which did not help the chill we felt. Our sleeping bags absorbed the mist and the wind whipped our tent, making sleep difficult. Cold and miserable at first dawn, we welcomed the new day. Without breakfast we hiked silently to the next shelter where we could finally build a fire and cook up some hot chocolate and savor the marshmallow topping in relative warmth.

Later we took time to explore off trail areas. Climbing around rock faces and onto jutting ledges, we reveled in our freedom. As we hiked toward our goal of Newfound Gap, our stamina improved and lookouts provided breathtaking panoramic views of the valleys and lakes of East Tennessee. Eagles and hawks soared effortlessly in the cloudless sky. We felt that we were one with nature. All the conflicts and doubts of a teenage life seemed insignificant in this place. We were happy.

Only once in our thirty-mile hike did we meet other people. The last shelter before reaching Newfound Gap was shared with some young men of dubious character. It seemed they were more interested in avoiding the draft than in enjoying the beauty of the Smokies. The three of us were eligible for the draft, of course, but deferment for college was possible and a strong motivator to maintain acceptable grades. However, I don't think any of us would have tried to avoid the draft had we been called. In fact, I was secretly hoping to be drafted to avoid having to make up my mind about the future direction of my life. Sometimes it's more frightening to take responsibility for life decisions than to allow events to mold those decisions. But, who wants to give up freedom of choice – even if we choose unwisely!

Later, as the trail descended toward Newfound Gap, we passed by an area filled with Rhododendron and wild flowers. The sweet scent and forest quiet prefaced a time years later when I would propose marriage to Lisa. I wanted to show her a bit of the trail three boys had ventured upon in a youthful past.

We burst upon the Gap unshaven and unwashed after six days on the Appalachian Trail. Our good manners and courteous demeanor were unconvincing to the majority of sightseers driving to and from this famous landmark.

We almost despaired of finding transportation back down the mountain to Gatlinburg when we spotted two rather seedy looking men getting into their even seedier looking car. They were more than willing to give us a ride, and we were all too willing to accept. It was almost a fatal mistake – more dangerous than any bear or snake or high precipice in the Smokies.

As soon as we pulled out of the parking area the wild eyed driver, flashing a snagle-toothed grin, offered us a swig from a paper sacked bottle handed over the front seat. We declined.

"Don't you guys drink?" The red-faced, uncombed man in the right seat asked us.

"Well – uh – not now – we'll wait till we get home," one of us replied.

None of us drank but we didn't want to sound like prudes. We sometimes had that problem even with other friends. If you didn't smoke or drink or "burn rubber" you weren't "in," and to *say* you didn't do these things was prudish.

Our redneck friends passed the bottle back and forth several times, while we careened down the mountain toward Gatlinburg, slinging us side to side in the rear seat. It seemed to the three of us that these guys were trying to straighten some of the hairpin curves on the road, perhaps, we feared, killing us in the process.

Needless to say, we survived that exciting end to our adventure, and later, after a hot shower, we savored a fresh cooked dinner for the first time in six days at our cabin in the foothills of the Great Smoky Mountains.

Graduation from high school and attendance at separate colleges sent the three of us on divergent paths. We remained friends but were never again as close as when we hiked the Appalachian Trail. We saw each other rarely. Months, then years passed; memories crowded out memories. Then Hugh's great heart gave out and only the memory of his steady determined stride up from Davenport Gap remains for Bobby and me.

COLLEGE

You see a wrecked car on the side of the road; you would:
1. *Seek assistance by calling for the police.*
2. *Go to the wreck to help out.*
3. *Pass the car, assuming help was on the way.*

When I contemplated the answer for this question on the aptitude test, I consciously tried to pick the answer that I thought a Martin Arrowsmith or an Andrew Manson would choose, for these men were my heroes in medicine. If this were to be my career, then certainly I must have the same qualities of perfection I perceived in them.

Although I had recently wished for the draft to save me from decision-making, I nevertheless applied for a deferment that would allow me to continue pre-dental studies and eventually dental school as long as I maintained an adequate grade point average. I was aware of the benefits of the officer corps versus the enlisted ranks; undoubtedly some of this awareness was generated by watching war movies and discussions I had with older classmates—veterans attending college on the G.I. bill.

Initially, I signed up for a pre-dental course of study at Southwestern-at-Memphis, a liberal arts college replete with gothic arches, tree lined paths and a great faculty. The medical units at The University of Tennessee, Memphis, only required two years of undergraduate study in 1951 and because of the Korean War needs, the dental and medical schools were each graduating around fifty students four times a year. I was happy to be home in Memphis, and Southwestern had great appeal; the campus was an architecturally unified, variegated stone, gothic complex; sports activities were secondary, and most important to me it was co-educational. It was pleasant sitting next to girls, their perfume tickling my senses, and in biology class, especially, it was nice to be asked, "Please, Jeff, can you show me how to—ugh—pith this frog"........ "Please help me dissect this earthworm." I was a willing advisor.

But in organic chemistry class that summer of '51 I got my first real shock in undergraduate school. I understood nothing that Dr. Webb was explaining. A few days later, after consulting with my advisor, I enrolled in inorganic chemistry to better understand the basics. It seems I had inflated the knowledge I had gained at Woodberry Forest—at least in chemistry class.

Freshmen at summer school were more or less in limbo, caught between the exuberance of having finally graduated from high school and the let down brought on by the dominance of upper classmen, the intimidation of the required curriculum, and uncertainties in dealing with the opposite sex. Orientation parties helped, but it took me a bit longer to become comfortable since I lived at home.

"Hi, I'm Jeff Justis," I said as I shook hands with a blond headed, friendly-appearing young man standing near the doorway to the basement "rec room" of Fischer Hall.

"I'm Charles Diehl. Are you enjoying yourself?"

"Yes, I am," I answered. Then awkwardly, "I'm a freshman. What class are you in?"

"Well, you see, I teach—English," the professor said with a smile.

"Oh—uh—uh—I thought you—you see—I—I…" I was flabbergasted. I was embarrassed, although I need not have been, since Charles Diehl, who at that time was in his early forties, was rather flattered by my innocent approach. He was the son of the former president of the college and an excellent English teacher. Years later, we laughed about that incident.

In those early days of summer school, I met a fellow freshman, also, coincidentally, named Charles from Union City in northwestern Tennessee. He had short blond hair, was thin and two inches taller than I. I had met him at a freshman get together and when he suggested that we take in a movie, I accepted, happy to have a friend with whom to share the newness of college life. During most of that summer, I found it easy to go along with Charles and one or two other freshmen I had met.

One weekend I drove with Charles to his home in Union City where his widowed mother, Mary Howard, lived. She was extremely doting and lavished a great deal of affection and food on us. Charles was the dutiful son with his mother, and he enjoyed his overindulged relationship with her, but away from her, he was somewhat rebellious. I recall how, after leaving a movie, we drove with some local girls to a dance hall at least 30 miles away. I was a little uneasy in those days before seat belts; we sped along dark country roads then bumped onto gravel side roads and finally turned into the rutted parking area of the Crystal Palace. The barn-like structure vibrated with 50s music. Smoke permeated the stale air, offending my nose, and there was an aura of fear as older guys ("red necks" we would say) intimidated anyone they didn't like—who, of course, was everyone else. As I remember, we had cokes, danced one or two slow dances (the only kind of dancing I knew) and left.

In her ingratiating way, Mary Howard insisted that I come back to visit. I had enjoyed the weekend, but I had other things I wanted to do. Charles was adamant, though, which made me feel uneasy. I had always been uncomfortable in situations in which I was not in ultimate control, but because I was unwilling to be rude or insensitive to other's feelings, I often felt trapped. These feelings were to recur many more times with Charles and later in medical school with other dependent friends.

Later, it was Charles who, at that time was more worldly than I, introduced me to beer. On the outskirts of Memphis there were many establishments that catered to the young crowd, including those who were underage as was I. It didn't take long for the pitcher of beer to have its effect and soon I had to lean on Charles as he helped me navigate to his car.

I visited Charles once or twice more, but as the summer progressed my circle of friends expanded, and I began to feel that Charles' demand on my time was excessive. Once, another friend, Lee, and I had arranged to go to a movie together. When Charles called to see if I could go with him, he became upset. This was disquieting, but I could not be responsible for anyone's happiness but my own. Then I began to hear rumors. "Don't you know he's queer?" someone said and I couldn't believe it. Having gone to an all boys' school, I was surprisingly naive about such matters. Calling someone a "queer" was just like calling someone a "sissy" or, in the war years, "a Jap,"—it was an insult, with little thought as to the true connotation. Nevertheless, Charles' possessiveness was a concern.

When summer school ended, pledge week began. In high school, I had belonged to the "Smoking Club" with my parent's permission (convincing them that smoking was certainly better for you than drinking. How we can fool ourselves!) This was my social club as there were no fraternities at Woodberry Forest. During my senior year, we began to talk about the various fraternities in college and some opinions or prejudices began to form: "Pikes! Oh they're all funny — maybe queer. ATOs – they're too brainy. SAEs – they're all jocks." At any rate, we had a week to sort things out. We were "rushed" from one party to the next.

"Jeff, you're the kind of guy we need." A large, rather pompous young man extolled the virtues of his particular fraternity. The implied exclusivity was there as he mentioned "Southern heritage" and the "*right* kind of person." I did not agree with his blatant prejudice even though legal and immoral segregation remained entrenched in the South

In the end, I chose a fraternity that had a greater proportion of athletes than the others because of two fellow freshmen I had met, Lee Weed and Billy Callicott. We had a good time together, without the uncomfortable sense of obligation I had developed with Charles.

Once I had chosen and been accepted by SAE. The group would often sit together in a row during mandatory chapel at this Presbyterian College of Southwestern at Memphis. Charles had chosen another fraternity, but as we lined up for chapel it was obvious he wanted me to sit with him.

"You're still my friend aren't you, Jeff?"

"Sure, Charles, but I want to sit with my new friends. I like a lot of friends."

"But I *need* you to sit with me."

I felt terribly uncomfortable. I didn't want to hurt his feelings, but...

As we walked into the hall, I didn't know what I would do but when my other friends filed into a row of seats I followed and Charles continued forward alone. He looked back from several rows ahead with a strange, anguished look on his face. I felt sad for him, but suddenly, I felt free. I knew I could finally be with whom I pleased without a burden of guilt.

For the remainder of my college years, Charles remained only a speaking acquaintance; if we ever had anything in common (and I question that) we had even less after I had joined SAE. Years later, on a trip to Knoxville to look at potential internship locations, I saw Charles for the last time. He was studying law at the University of Tennessee and, as if to explain something to me, he said, "I have finally discovered who I am. I think I can be happy now."

This puzzled me, but in the years to follow, I heard that he had moved to New York and joined the gay community. He has since died.

I enjoyed my association with the fraternity, Sigma Alpha Epsilon. For someone who professed an independent spirit, I must have enjoyed the security of some group association or I would have avoided a fraternity altogether.

Part of the experience of college is the enhancement of socialization skills, and fraternities may contribute in a positive or negative way. The initiation process is an interesting phenomenon in which those that are "in" see how intimidating they can be to those who are "out." There was no physical "hazing" in the fraternity I chose, but psychological badgering was the accepted standard at Southwestern. In fact, the institution participated by acquiescence in freshman week during which all male freshmen wore beanies and all female freshmen wore bonnets—a mildly humiliating form of hazing.

Playing the game as expected seemed the easiest path to follow. In fact, I can remember holding back on laughing at several upper classmen trying to intimidate me through verbal abuse.

"You are the stupidest freshman I've ever seen; don't you know you're supposed to carry your books on your *head?*"

The fraternity hazing was actually more educational. We had to memorize much of the history and secret facts about SAE.

"Quick, Pledge, give me the names of the founding fathers?" I was asked as I entered through the thick wooden door of the SAE fraternity house located on fraternity row.

"When was Nathan Devote born?"

"Who is the Eminent Supreme Archon?"

We learned facts, which certainly would have no lasting meaning in our lives, because we wanted to, because we wanted to be "in." We wanted to be a part of this particular group of individuals. This desire to be "in" was more socially acceptable, perhaps, and less dangerous, but not much different from the desire of a disadvantaged youth of today to join with a local gang.

Chimpanzees and humans exhibit a need for close contact within the group but there is also a need for space and one may occasionally observe a lone individual in either species self absorbed—yet happy. As I remember my feelings at the time, I enjoyed group activities but was happiest when I could retreat to my workshop to construct a wooden album cover for the fraternity house or later to build and install some kitchen cabinets. Thus I could obtain recognition without exhibiting public prowess in athletic activities.

Final initiation night was a set up, and I knew it, instinctively or by observation. The idea was to have each pledge come before the council to be judged. My pledge group consisted of about six, but I can only remember Lee Weed and Billy Callicott and Rodney Field. We were lined up outside the house but within hearing distance of the activities inside. We could hear questions shouted in rapid succession, accusations of previous infractions of "fraternity" rules, castigation of character, and finally: "You're out! Get out!" We heard a door slam and saw the first pledge running from the house into the night—a rejected soul.

At last it was my turn and I played the role expected. I was contrite, despondent, and ashamed as I stood before the Council, their faces almost cracking in the candlelight as they tried very hard to make me think they were rejecting me. Appropriately downcast I pushed through the back door.

One of the brothers whispered, "Run around the east end of the ATO house and then walk quietly back here from the other side and be quiet."

Soon the six of us were gathered together and ushered back into the meeting room, the lights were turned up and all the brothers shouted: "Congratulations to our new brothers! *Phi Alpha—Phi Alpha—Phi Alpha.*"

Our pretentious sadness could now turn to the happiness of being accepted—we were "in."

By large university standards the Tennessee Zeta Chapter of Sigma Alpha Epsilon was quite small. Although many of the members were varsity athletes, the college insisted that academics remain first and foremost. I participated in intramural sports activities including touch football and soccer. I even won in a gym contest in rope climbing. Hand over hand, without leg assistance,

I shimmied up the rope to touch the metal clamp at the very top of the gym, reveling in the shouts of encouragement and praise from my frat brothers. I've always had good upper body strength. Unfortunately, in my later years, although the upper body strength may be nearly the same, the lower body presence is somewhat greater, and I strongly doubt my present rope climbing capabilities.

As I mentioned, I helped the fraternity in ways that better suited my personality: building cabinets, repairing the pool table, among other things; it was in part because of this that I met Mr. Johnny. Mr. John Rollow's picture was, in fact, prominently displayed in the SAE house since he was a most respected alumnus of the chapter.

Mr. Johnny, as he was affectionately called by everyone on campus including the President, Peyton Rhodes, was the engineer of the college and responsible for the maintenance of every structure and all of the grounds. He and his family lived on campus in the "Gate House" and to the chagrin of his wife, Louise, he was on call twenty-four hours a day. The admiration everyone felt for him was genuine and when I learned that he could, as he said, "fix anything but a broken heart," I decided to associate with "Mr. Johnny" as much as I could. Of course, of all his accomplishments, none could compare to the one that would forever influence my life, fathering Louise Mayo Rollow. I began working for him as an assistant before I met Lisa who, I was to learn, had great admiration for and devotion to her father. I learned to weld with him, and I developed a sense of self-confidence in all things mechanical and electrical. One time we were replacing a large fuse in the main power line to the physics building. Using a long grappler we eased the six-inch long fuse toward its receptacle.

ZAP...BANG. Sparks flew and the concussion reeled us backward on our heels.

"Guess we need to find the short in the circuit before we try *that* again," Johnny said laconically.

"I'll never try to replace that size fuse by hand—that's for sure," I observed.

With Johnny, no job was impossible—it just took the right engineering. Later, Johnny asked me to replace some damaged molding on one of the heavy oak doors at the entrance to the dining hall. We found some scrap oak and Johnny was going to set me up in the campus shop to do the work. Being confident in my own woodworking abilities, I suggested I could do the job in my own shop quicker. I think I impressed him when I returned later in the day with the molding I had shaped and had it in place within a short period of time.

Sometime during my freshman year, I began to wonder if dentistry was the career I truly wanted to pursue. Sometimes classmates, in observing me in biology class would say, "You are pre-med aren't you?" At first I said, "No! pre-den," then I started saying, "I'm not sure—maybe medicine—maybe dentistry."

Although I was in a liberal arts college, it seems that I did not really consider all the possibilities for life's work in making my decisions. Had aviation not intrigued me as long as I could remember? Did I not savor every magazine or book about flying? Adventure books had been a staple of my reading diet as a youngster, and flying adventures had especially filled my imagination. So why did my consideration of a career not include aviation? Was it fear of getting too far out of line? My dad had always said, "Get a profession!"

Brought up poor in the small town of Dyersburg, he learned that professionals had a better life, and although the term "professional" applies to anyone making a living at a single skilled pursuit, my dad, encouraged by his mother, narrowed the term to include medicine, dentistry, and law. "What about engineers?" I would later ask.

"They have to work for someone else."
"What about teachers?"
"They really have a hard time financially."
"Preachers?"
"If you really wanted to do that."
"Pilots?"

"You get an education first—then maybe you can fly."

So I guess it's no wonder I narrowed my own choices in spite of my love for aviation, my mechanical aptitude, uneasiness with some aspects of medicine, and shyness in dealing with people.

I remember acute discomfort during my first public speaking class. Having been told that I needed such a course to be effective as a doctor, I nonchalantly enrolled and without any recognition of anxiety joined the class. I was taken aback when Professor Hill announced that each of us in turn should give an extemporaneous talk about ourselves. As each student proceeded to talk, I found myself becoming increasingly anxious. I was breathing rapidly; my heart was pounding, and my palms sweating. I was almost paralyzed when my turn came and I had to hold on to the desk to steady myself. My voice was shaky, my lips trembled and my talk was mumbled. I had not expected such a reaction in myself, and the fear of that loss of control was to haunt me the rest of my life.

The event so disturbed me in that freshman year that I discussed it with my psychology professor, Dr. Lewellen Queener. He suggested hypnosis. I was willing to try anything and in a quiet classroom we began.

"Concentrate on this one spot on the blackboard—relax, and think of resting—think of peace and quiet— think of sleep—sleep…," he droned on and on and all the while I was thinking, *yes I'll relax—but I'm not sleepy—well I'll shut my eyes—but I'll not go to sleep—I don't want to hurt his feelings—I'll pretend I'm asleep.*

And so for the next ten minutes, I listened to him tell me how I would not be uncomfortable in public speaking class or standing before people and how I could do so without fear or anxiety. It was nice to hear but it did no good whatsoever. There would be no easy fix to this problem or to any other problem I might have in the years to come.

But in that time I discovered that I could project a persona that was not necessarily who I really was. I could pretend to be hypnotized rather than have Dr. Queener fail. I could even slant my aptitude toward medicine while harboring doubts.

It was ironic that, although there was so much in the world to interest me, I was purposely and systematically narrowing my choices. With no fanfare and without discussing it with my parents, I obtained the necessary papers from UT Memphis and registered for medical school. I didn't realize until later that dual registration was not allowed. (I had registered in Dental School shortly after beginning summer school at Southwestern.) The university did not find out about this for nearly two years.

There are many things I remember with fondness about those college years: participating in "All Sing" during which I learned the principles of harmony, acting as Johnny in *Frankie and Johnny* (no lines), playing touch football for the fraternity, and drinking beer.

Drinking beer! I had started smoking in my senior year of high school but during college I got the idea that if I were going to be a doctor I ought to give up smoking and I did. Drinking was not allowed on campus, so most of the drinking was done in one of the many darkened jukebox parlors that populated Memphis in the early fifties. Drive-in restaurants also served beer and one of the benefits of fraternity membership was that brothers over twenty-one could get beer for those of us who were younger. Going out with the guys was a bachelor's Saturday ritual, but dating some girls who did not approve of drinking kept many of us from abusing alcohol. In those days (and perhaps it should still be so today) the girls were the keepers of the moral standards. Their behavior and expectations kept the testosterone-saturated males under some semblance of control.

Socials and dances on campus were usually fun, and I remember how proud I was that my first cousin, Bill Justis, and his band were playing at a college dance. Some of the fellows would leave the dance for a while and return in a somewhat more jovial mood. Obviously, they had been nipping the bottle in the parking lot. Someone must have thrown an empty bottle into the back seat of my car. When my dad spotted it there later, I had some explaining to do. I was innocent, but it certainly looked bad. I did not drink hard liquor, however, so my explanation was accepted.

I had a crush on Imogene Myers, a cute blonde from Mississippi, and dated her occasionally. She was in love with Bobby, however, in spite of the fact that he had a medical disability, a congenital cardiac abnormality. Some of us who did not understand the nature of mature love were confused by this seemingly incongruous relationship.

According to my college advisor, I needed to continue my studies during the summer after my freshman year in order to have sufficient credits for dental or medical school. I would only have a six-week break. My parents were discussing a trip to Europe during that time, but I was more interested in staying home and being with my new friends until they suggested that my old friend, Hugh Humphreys go with us.

The details were worked out and in June of 1952, Hugh and I, with my parents, boarded the S.S. United States on her maiden voyage.

CRUISING

The theater is dark. A clinical movie shows in vivid reds the detailed extraction of a deeply impacted molar. As the sound of the suction machine echoes and the sight of flowing blood fills the screen, I feel weak. I imagine the blood flowing from my brain onto the screen just as my knees buckle. I sit hard on the seat behind me. I bend over and feel the return of warm blood to my head reviving me. I'm sweating, but I'm alright—or am I? A wave of guilt passes over me. How can I be a doctor—any kind of doctor—if I react this way? I flat out deny it. It could be something I ate. It'll never happen again. Fear takes its turn—but what if it does happen again—maybe I shouldn't be a doctor. Maybe I shouldn't have bought that microscope.

The essence of the teen years is one of rebellion and conflict. One rebels at the status quo and at conventional wisdom, and there is always the need to express one's individuality and independence. So, for my middle-aged parents (my dad was in his late fifties and my mom in her late forties) to take on two teen-aged boys was an act of courage.

Perhaps Hugh and I sensed that and responded appropriately by following the rules. We were rewarded by the freedom to adventure on our own, which included exploring the great aluminum transport carrier and cruise ship: The S.S. United States. Now in mothballs, the ship was designed to be rapidly converted into a troop carrier in time of war. She was the fastest ship of her size afloat, and we were proud to be on board during her 1952 maiden voyage during which the previous transatlantic crossing record was broken.

I would have been satisfied with further exploration of the engine room, the radar dome, the bridge, or with silent contemplation of the great blue sea that surrounded us and the vault of crystal bright stars that pricked the black void above. There are those who truly want to be alone and then there are those who want to be alone—with someone else. If that is a contradiction, then it must be a source of conflict within my own personality.

Standing by the rail one evening, I became aware of a pleasant fragrance—a smell not of the sea but of—a girl. The loner was pulled from his contemplation of the universe toward the source of such enticement.

"Hi! I'm Jeff Justis."

"I'm Barbara and this is my sister, Debra."

The ice was broken, connections were made: "I'm in pre-dental school, but I may go into medicine..."

"I'm a sophomore at Vassar..."

Much small talk ensued and my desire to be alone faded. So from about the second day of the cruise Barbara and I sought each other's company. Hugh seemed to like Debra so the four of us enjoyed our association on the all too short Atlantic crossing. As shipboard romances go the only commitment made was to see each other on the return voyage, yet there was some sense of loss for me at our final parting later in the summer.

We docked at Southampton England, disembarked and waited for the ship to unload the Chevrolet my dad had shipped over as cargo.

There was a certain amount of boredom riding in the back seat of that Chevrolet during a five week tour of Great Britain and Europe. Hugh and I would read (until told by the tour guide parents in the front to "look at that cathedral; see that castle ruin; look at that glorious mountain"). Occasionally, we would talk but mostly we thought or planned or imagined a world of our making.

We couldn't wait to stop for the evening at Llandudno, Wales; the bags were quickly unloaded. Hugh and I began a climb—the evening's adventure—to the top of a steep mountain just to the west of our hotel. We managed to find adventure at the most mundane locations, but we always returned by mealtime. My dad liked to repeat a story he had told many times; after being told to go easy on ordering from a rather expensive menu, he overheard us complaining that we weren't getting enough to eat and that we "sure would be glad to get back on board ship so we could order two steaks if we wanted to." Thus is the appetite of two teenage boys.

The Lake District brought out the romantic in me. From high school days I had liked poetry, and I think Wordsworth was always one of my favorite poets. Here near Rydal Mount, I found a "field of Golden Daffodils" and leaned against the old stone wall that separates man from man.

In Dusseldorf, Germany we visited a dental acquaintance of my dad. Six years after the end of World War II, bomb damage was evident throughout Germany, and Hugh and I were intrigued by the large crater in the doctor's backyard and his stories of unexploded bombs and of the horrors of nighttime incendiary bombing. Obviously he and his family had been victims—but of whom? Of our relentless bombing or of the regime that had pushed Germany into the aggression that led to the war in the first place? Or were they victims of their own apathy or their own prejudice? We Americans were on top of the world after the war. We had fought the good fight—the moral fight. A Hitler would never dupe us; we would never allow prejudice to produce laws designed to subjugate another race. Or could we?

One evening we were late arriving in Heidelberg and most of the hotels were full. My parents found a decent Gästehaus; Hugh and I stayed in the guest room of a German family recommended by a hotel. We climbed the open steps of a half destroyed apartment house. We looked out through the torn brick walls toward the hills of the Black Forest and, although we laughed at my mother's concern for our safety, we secretly wondered about the structural integrity of this bombed out building.

Later in the trip, a failure to obtain reservations resulted in our spending the night in the lobby of a very large hotel in Naples, Italy. I remember feeling a little embarrassed although now I honestly can't remember why. Such is the self-consciousness of the teen years.

Hugh's goal on the trip was to investigate, for possible purchase, Mercedes Benz, Volkswagen, and Citroen automobiles. He had been given the responsibility of picking the best car for the price. As it ended, he was torn by his desire for the quality of a Mercedes and his considerable conscience which, properly enhanced by telephone conversations with his father, resulted in his not getting anything. Hugh's conscience was big enough for both of us but unfortunately later in life was more than he could handle and the conflict required too much solace from alcohol.

My goal was to find a microscope. Dental school (and at that time secretly—medical school) required the use of a microscope. Even in that early postwar period, Germany's reputation for precision optical equipment was unsurpassed. I was quite proud when I found a Binocular Leitz Microscope in a beautiful mahogany case. Leafing through the instruction manual, I imagined myself searching for the definitive pathogen as had Andrew Manson in the *Citadel*.

Our tour ended in France. An international dental meeting in Paris was the original purpose of the trip. Hugh had no reason to be interested, and I had no excuse not to be interested. After all, I was going to go to dental school wasn't I? So for one full day I was to be in the pit so to speak. I was to be introduced; I was to be assured many times that I wanted to be a dentist.

"He's made the decision himself."

"Boy you've got some big shoes to fill." Dentists from all over the world would say to me as they patted my dad on the back. I was proud of him, but I did not have a desire to compete with him on his turf. I wondered through the exhibits and that sense of mild nausea I experienced earlier in my dad's office returned with the smells of antiseptics and acrylic and amalgam. The movie they showed of an impacted molar being extracted left me wondering if I could even be a doctor, but I managed to put the incident behind me. I'm quite sure, however, that I never seriously considered dentistry again after that, but for another year that would be my secret.

Hugh and I met a dentist's son, Earney, who was staying at the same Parisian hotel—the Intercontinental. He was probably twenty-one, and to us a bit more sophisticated.

"Say, I've been doing some investigation about things to do around here," Earney said with a knowledgeable tone in his voice.

"And it's not just going to museums either. If you think that the Folly's was good, you ought to see the Hot Cat Club."

We had been to the Folly's the night before—standard tourist fare for new comers to Paris—risqué by American standards but according to Earney "we haven't seen anything yet."

My parents had offered to take us out on the town with them, but Hugh and I said we would go with Earney. We were not sure what he had in mind, but the prospect seemed a bit more exciting.

A short cab ride later we were in the nightclub district or, should I say, the "red light" district. What a surprise when we entered one club frequented by Americans and saw my parents. We all had a laugh, but soon we made our excuses and began walking from one noisy club to the next. Girls of the evening followed us down the street with enticement of great pleasure. Hugh and I had not been drinking but Earney had and soon, through clouded judgment, accepted the invitation of one of the more persistent and I must say, attractive of the girls.

"Come on, guys, come with me."

"Naw! We're not interested."

"Aw, come on. At least wait for me," Earney pleaded.

"You must come and see my place," the young lady protested. I'm sure she was looking for more business.

"Okay, we'll come wait for you, Earney." Hugh and I relented.

Just about a block away was a row of narrow, two-story houses, stone-fronted with green shutters obscuring any light from within. We were ushered into the parlor. Three large overstuffed chairs covered with red velvet sat in three corners of the room. A coffee table contained several showgirl magazines and stairs leading to the upper floor exited one corner near a passageway to the kitchen.

"See you guys later." Earney said as the crimson-dressed young lady who probably was no older than I, but whose hard life had taken a toll, pulled him by the hand up the stairs and out of sight.

Hugh and I sat silently with our own thoughts. We were tempted. What young man wouldn't be? The biological imperative was certainly there. The problem, however, was in the details—the messy details—the fear of disease—the lack of discipline.

"No thank you." Hugh said in his most polite voice to the young lady who had just led a sheepish Earney down from his encounter with a real Parisian lady of the evening. She was trying to entice us both.

"No, I don't think so," I said, and to keep from hurting her feelings I added, "at least not tonight."

Earney said nothing and Hugh and I respected his silence. Perhaps there was passing envy of Earney, but more likely there was a sense of gratitude at having retained some strength of will.

The next evening Hugh and I decided to go alone, not back to the red light district but to a jazz club near the Champs d'Elisses.

Bobby Short was playing and although we didn't realize it then, he was and is a noted Cole Porter performer. I've heard him many times since and his voice always evokes pleasant memories of that evening near the end of our tour when Hugh and I sat before his piano listening to him sing into the early hours of a Parisian summer morning.

Returning from Europe to begin summer school at Southwestern, I felt a bit uncomfortable when I was asked about my summer vacation.

"Man, I wish my folks were rich," was the usual response to my explanation.

"They're not rich! My dad's a dentist—he saved his money."

This was certainly factual but the perception was that anyone going to Europe during college must be very well off. I did not want to be that different from my peers and tended to down play my prep-school education and any show of money. Of course, there were many with more money and my resentment of their ostentation reinforced my desire to play down the many privileges life had handed me. Even then I was more comfortable wearing the blue collar—symbolically if not actually.

After the uncomfortable incident in the Public Speaking course, I noticed that some of my classmates who had to work to pay for their tuition or who had served in the military, for example, had the most self assurance when speaking in public. I envied their confidence. I needed a handicap; was it not their disability or their struggle that provided them with a self-confidence that I seemed to lack? Only with advancing age and experience have I come to realize that everyone has some burden with which to deal, and the successful individual is the one who not only accepts his own limitations but also appreciates his unique talents and continually tries to improve that which is good.

My sophomore year was a good year. I no longer suffered the uncertainties of pledging a fraternity for I was "in." SAE provided community service at Christmas by delivering presents to an orphanage. The unsolvable plight of these youngsters recalled that tugging homesick feeling I had experienced in summer camp many years before, but for me that feeling was transient; I was fortunate to have parents who provided stability in my life.

Southwestern (now Rhodes College) was a liberal arts college and although a few pre-den or pre-med students may have thought that they needed more science, I was personally happy to study literature and philosophy. In fact, if I have a regret about my college education, it is that I did not stay for four years. I would have enjoyed the opportunity to learn more of the humanities. After all, not only do practicing physicians need understanding of the human condition, but most (unless we die before retiring) will have more need in later years for greater understanding our own humanity than we will for our scientific backgrounds.

Exactly when and where I first met Lisa, I cannot recall. While I was working with Johnny Rollow, it seems that Lisa was just there and I was infatuated. She was elected Miss Southwestern and was the sweetheart of SAE. She was, I was certain, unattainable, but in the late summer of 1952, without having even dated her formally, we became friends. When Johnny and Louise invited me to come to "Maddox Bay" for a weekend (Lisa would, of course, be there), I jumped at the chance. It was a wonderful weekend. Mrs. Rollow cooked the best roast and biscuits and gravy I had ever had. In the balmy, late summer evenings Lisa and I would sit on the rear deck of the houseboat quietly talking of many things. I, of course, could not say what was really on my mind. I could only dream as I lay in my room alone that Lisa would be thinking of the same thing.

Sometime in the spring of 1953, I received a call from the registrar of the University of Tennessee.

"Mr. Justis, we've been getting our applications sorted for acceptance and we find that you are registered in Dental School *and* Medical School."

"Yes ma'am," I replied.

"You can't do that," she said rather sternly.

"I – I can't?"

"That's right, you have to drop one or the other or you'll be disqualified on a technicality."

"When do I have to decide"?

"I'll give you until Monday."

It was Friday! Decision time! I was not ready. The weekend was spent in anxiety, trying to weigh the pros and cons of these life-altering choices. It finally came down to a wish not to disappoint my Dad. My mother would be pleased with either choice, but deep down (although he would proclaim otherwise) my dad would have liked to see me enter dental school—to follow in his steps. I wanted to chart my own path, however, so on Sunday evening I reluctantly approached Dad with my decision softening the blow by reasoning that it would be easier to switch to dental school after three to six months of medical school than vice versa. Although disappointed, Dad was accepting, and throughout his remaining years to age ninety-nine, he never expressed anything but pride in what I had chosen.

Another choice became necessary when I was formally accepted into medical school. I could begin the first semester in July of 1953, with only two academic pre-med years at Southwestern or I could go to summer school, completing three years pre-med and enter the first quarter of medical school in the fall of 1953.

Somehow, I did not feel confident in launching my medical career in less than three months. I did not have the self-assurance of Andrew Manson—yet. Surely that would come. Another factor that played a part in my delaying medical school was, of course, my infatuation with Lisa. During the summer, I made her a what-not shelf of walnut, but because of her increasing popularity and my perception that she enjoyed the lime light (a perception that was untrue as I was to learn after we were married) and because of my own discomfort with any kind of public display, whether it be speaking or assertion, I seemed to fall into the background of Lisa's life. Instead of being close before I entered medical school, Lisa was with her sister in Clarksville much of the time, and I steeled myself to study and to the course I had chosen.

MEDICAL SCHOOL

"Ease in the throttle all the way. Push the stick forward—not too much— ease back..." the words melt into the roar of the engine. I am holding the stick in my right hand, my left hand moves the throttle forward but am I doing this or is Charlie Pugh controlling the plane from the backseat? I dare not let go to find out. The ground falls away and—and—I am flying. I am really flying. I am really going to be a doctor and I am really flying!

*A*nxious anticipation. These two words summed up my feelings as the September date of my first class at the University of Tennessee Medical School approached. There was the anxiety of uncertainty. Was I making the right decision? Would I be able to live up to my inflated ideal of the "great physician?" Could I accomplish this goal? Yet, I was eagerly anticipating the new adventure ahead.

Books and basic equipment for anatomy: forceps, scissors, and a scalpel were purchased. Then there was that wonderful white lab jacket—the feel of it—even the fresh smell of it—its aura embodied all the mystique of the healing arts.

"I'm going to be a doctor! I'm really going to be a doctor!" I almost shouted the thought as I approached the Wittenberg Building and bounded up the stairs to the second floor classroom of Gross Anatomy, the first course taught to freshmen medical students (and for some – the last).

DR. E. JEFF JUSTIS

The smell of formaldehyde filled the stairway and halls, I found myself in line with fifty fellow students. Each of us was ushered through the class doorway to be personally greeted by Dr. Simon Brucsch.

"Mr. Jeff Justis, welcome to Anatomy one," he said as he intently scrutinized my face comparing it with his class roster photographs. From that day and for many years later, he knew by name every member of every class he taught. Some say he remembered details of every student he taught until the day he died in 1994.

"Gentlemen and ladies," Dr. Bruesch began his orientation lecture "today you will begin a career in which you will have to learn a new language. Your vocabulary will have to expand by at least twenty-five thousand new words. Many old concepts will have to be discarded as new meanings and thought processes are learned. It is a daunting challenge, and yet I have confidence that each of you, with proper attention and work, will meet that challenge."

Then he began a detailed lecture on the integument. He outlined our first dissection of the cadaver, assigned five students to a table and, after a short break, led us into the dissection lab.

For better or for worse, my career in medicine was about to begin. And for each student entering that lab, his or her perception of the human body and of life was to change forever. One cannot enter the hallowed ground of a fellow creature's body without recognizing one's own frailty. It is difficult to put aside the knowledge that this still form—this wrinkled, naked, yes, grotesque body was once a living, breathing, sensate human being.

Here the compartmentalization of emotion, often seen in the too busy physician, begins. Here, we must set aside a natural revulsion. Here we must make light of our feelings. We must not let emotion stand in the way of science and later we must not let emotion prevent us from dealing effectively with disease and dying and fear in those who entrust themselves to our care.

For some of my classmates, this dichotomization seemed to come easily or naturally.

"Let's call him George," Aubra said.

"Let me make the first cut," Lloyd suggested.

I felt unsure, but if I acted confidently, surely I would be confident. The five of us at table number twelve shared a common goal, and we each discussed that freely; we supported each other in the learning process. Each of us also had common fears but these we kept to ourselves and thus, although common, these fears were ours alone to bear.

"Jeff, it's your turn to dissect—here's the scalpel."

Suddenly that old feeling crept into my consciousness—that feeling of slight nausea in my dad's office—that feeling of weakness and loss of control on watching a bloody tooth extraction.

"No! Not here—not now! Not when I'm just starting this!" I thought as I struggled against this intrusion.

"Wait a minute," I said as I bent down to tie my shoe. The blood rushed to my head and with a sense of relief, I was finally able to stand and, although a little shaky, I managed to incise the skin properly and even identify the cutaneous nerves without cutting them.

I felt good that afternoon, having overcome my initial reaction to our cadaver. Over the years, I've learned that this response is not rare among medical students and for some, myself included, is associated with a fear of failure and often is precipitated in situations of perceived lack of control. To take the first step into the unknown alleviates some of the fear of the unknown and with each step knowledge is expanded and anxiety lessened.

Ed Lindsey exuded confidence, and I was a little envious. He had been a practicing optometrist for ten years and at age 33 was one of the oldest students in my class. He was in my dissecting group. When he found out we lived close by each other, he suggested that we car pool. At first, I demurred. I wanted my independence, the ability to come and go as I pleased, and after my experience with Charles in college, I didn't want to feel tied or obligated to anyone. But Ed was persistent, and since he was married I knew the arrangement was for school not social convenience. Over the years the arrangement was a good one, saving us both money and along with some other students providing study help with difficult classes—especially biochemistry.

I found medical school demanding but in many ways quite logical and understandable. Memorizing the terms and relationships in anatomy was easier through visualization than trying to learn the formulas and cycles in biochemistry. Embryology was interesting to me because of my infatuation with evolutionary principles. I could see the development of gills that mirrored our phylogenetic past and the almost indistinguishable appearance of the embryo of other mammals compared with the human embryo.

"That's a good looking microscope you've got," a smiling student across the table of embryology lab remarked one day.

"Thanks. I got it in Germany last year."

"Do you live in town?" he asked and before I could answer added, "I'm staying at the Phi Chi house and I'm trying to find someone with a car."

"How come? I've got a car, but Ed and I car pool together." I didn't want him to think I had a car available all the time.

"Well, I'm trying to get someone to take me to the airport Sunday. I've got a flying lesson. By the way, my name is Frank Farris." Frank had short blonde hair, a medium build, and thin nervous hands.

Flying lessons! In medical school? How? Why? I had to know more.

"Yeah. I soloed in Knoxville. U.T. had an aeronautics course, and taking flying lessons was part of that course."

"Boy! That sounds great. I've always wanted to fly but I figured I'd better finish medical school first." And I really believed that; I was brought up espousing delayed gratification. "Don't waste your money on junk. Save it so you can buy something nicer later on," I was told many times by my parents. And, of course, "Get a good education first, *then* you can do some of those things you want to do." However, one can put off desired goals so long that no time remains for achieving those goals. Perhaps that thought prompted my willingness to take Frank to the airport the following Sunday.

Frank wanted to check out in an airplane so he could fly locally. He was the only son of a very nice and affluent Rogersville, Tennessee family who did not seem to put any restrictions on the fulfillment of his desires. And in the end, I think that overindulgence in self-gratification was the ultimate cause of his demise. But that sad part of this story will come later.

I sat on the faded brown couch in the office of Memphis Flying Service on Winchester just east of Memphis Municipal Airport. It was late fall, 1953. Mrs. Oxley was busy behind the counter. Frank was already in the air in a faded yellow Piper Cub. I looked out the window at the blue sky and wished I had gone to a University that offered such a wonderful course as aeronautics. I had missed my best opportunity at Woodberry Forest when my mother would not give her permission for an orientation flight as part of that school's "Introduction to Aeronautics" class.

Just then, Charlie Pugh, one of the senior flight instructors, entered the small office. He had a decided limp; I was to learn later he had an artificial leg, the result of a crop dusting accident.

"You the fellow who brought Frank out for his lesson?"

"Yeah, I'm Jeff Justis," I said, standing to shake Charlie's hand.

"Before he went up with Joe he mentioned you might want to take lessons too."

"Oh, I guess I want to and I will someday; I just can't afford it now."

"How come?" Charlie asked. "It doesn't cost much and it doesn't take much time – just an hour a week, that's all." He smiled. "How much you got in your pocket?"

Today's aviation community could sure use some of Charlie's salesmanship ability.

I was going along with his banter and pulled out my wallet. "Ten dollars is all I've got," I replied, thinking that with the plane, lessons would surely cost more than that.

"Come on, I'll give you your first lesson."

I was excited but a little reluctant. "I may not be able to keep up the lessons once I start," I said hesitating.

"Aw! You'll find a way." Charlie was prophetic.

We walked out to a blue and white Aeronca Champ, waiting, it seemed, to capture my mind and spirit. The little high wing plane sat with its nose in the air and its rear resting on a diminutive tail wheel. I had always been intrigued by—the smell—the sounds; but there was no mystery, for I had read everything I could about flying and airplanes. I imagined I could already fly. He asked me a few basic questions, showed me what to look for during the preflight inspection, demonstrated how to hold the brakes and turn on the magnetos, and cautioned me not to push the throttle in once the engine started until we were ready to fly.

"Switch off!" Charlie shouted from in front of the propeller.

Charlie manually turned the prop over two or three times. Then he shouted, "Contact."

I flipped the magneto switch to **both on** and shouted back, **"Contact."**

With that Charlie flipped the propeller hard. The little sixty-five horsepower Continental engine popped and rumbled to life. The prop blast burbled around the windscreen and into the window reviving memories of my very first flight in the Bahama Islands in 1950.

Charlie climbed in the rear seat and fastened his seat belt. "Let's go," he said, "ease forward on the throttle—that's it—now use your rudder pedals—not too much—don't over control—zigzag so you can see where you're going."

At first, I seemed to be turning too fast, then jerking back in the other direction, but slowly I got the hang of it, and by the time we had taxied to the north end of the grass strip, I had the little craft under a semblance of control.

"Now follow through with me," Charlie ordered as we lined up on the runway having checked the engine and looked for traffic.

I couldn't believe it; I was at the controls as the ground dropped beneath us. I was fulfilling two dreams at once, flying and becoming a doctor, but at the same time there was a question of confidence. Could I become the physician I felt I should become and could I become the pilot of my dreams?

"Don't over control—use your feet when you're banking to turn—watch your altitude."

There was so much to keep up with in three dimensions, and it seemed everything had to be done at the same time.

That first lesson left me a little drained and with less confidence in my innate ability to fly, but the challenge had been accepted, and I knew that I must continue. I told Frank to keep my lessons a secret for now, but we agreed that every week or so, we'd come back to the airport. In those days, there was little formal ground school. Just talking with one's instructor before and after the flight seemed sufficient; after all, flying the airplane is what counts. Except for an occasional glance out the window at an aircraft flying overhead during class, my entrance into the field of aviation did not interfere with my medical studies. In fact, I believe that my ability to escape the realities of every day existence through my trysts with the mistress of the sky aided my ability to persevere through medical school. I can remember rewarding myself after a difficult week of studying or after a fatiguing exam with a trip to the airport and a peaceful flight over the fields and woods of north Mississippi.

The University of Tennessee Medical School was organized on the quarter system. During World War II there was an increased need for physicians, and graduating over two hundred doctors a year required four classes of about fifty students. In the first year, each class lost as many as twenty-five percent of the students. Some simply dropped back a quarter to start over; others "laid out" a quarter to work or do other post graduate work. Although all of us may have, at times, questioned our decisions to attend medical school, a few were so overwhelmed by the amount of work ahead and great expectations that they dropped out never to return. There may even have been a deliberate attempt on the part of the faculty to intimidate by implication so that only the most determined would persevere.

Monte R. was in my dissecting group, and although I and one or two others had experienced some initial queasiness in anatomy, he felt that his revulsion in anatomy and his lack of basic understanding in biochemistry was a clear signal that medicine was not the path he should choose. He later became a pharmacological representative (detail person). If he had continued, I think he would have been a good physician, but perhaps it is better for someone to consider what might have been than to become embittered and disillusioned in the often-demanding responsibilities of medical practice. It takes time, but one must learn to accept his limitations along with his gifts.

The first six quarters were considered to be preclinical. "Why in the world do we need to know the Krebs Cycle?" Lloyd would ask.

"Beats me!" Ed replied.

"It's necessary to understand metabolism when you study diseases such as hyperthyroidism," Professor Morrison would explain to the unconvinced.

"But these sensory skin nerves—why are they important? They're so small—we'll never need to know that when we see patients."

We couldn't wait to get out of the basic sciences and begin dealing with real patients. It is only when one actually does begin to deal with patients or when one actually does surgery on a living human being that the need for basic knowledge in physiology and anatomy and yes, even physics becomes painfully clear. Then and only then does one wish to learn again the basics that one was so eager to leave behind.

Although the anatomy lab was on the second floor of the Wittenberg building, the side-facing windows opened onto higher ground. One bright day several classmates and I decided we'd take a break (the professor said he had to leave but would return in a hour), so one by one we dropped out of the window, walked across the quadrangle and across Union Avenue to the Rexall Drug Store for a soda. When we got back we found the windows closed, and we could see a few laughing faces peering down at us. We ran around to the front of the building into the main hall. Just as we opened the door to the stairway, the adjacent elevator opened and there stood Dr. Bruesch. He said nothing. The next day, however, he seemed most interested in the progress (or lack of it) of our dissection. We applied ourselves a lot harder to make up for our excursion. In the time allotted for anatomy, there really was little time to waste.

Once over the initial anxiety and self-doubt, I rather enjoyed most of my classes. Occasionally, as a class, we would visit a clinic or emergency room for clinical orientation. Some of my classmates even worked in an emergency room and bragged about sewing up a wound; I wondered if I could do the same. Later, Pathology Class tested my resolve. Sitting in an amphitheater with a fresh corpse lying naked upon a stainless steel table, I once more experienced that uneasy feeling reminiscent of public speaking and my first experience with a cadaver.

Man! I thought I was over this—why, why—come on—settle down, I talked myself into a little more peace. *It always happens in a new situation; I'll get over it. I'll get over it.*

"Mr. Justis, what am I going to see if I cut down right here?" Professor Tebeaux brought me back to reality. He had made a long, irreverent incision from the base of the neck to the lower abdomen and was beginning a transverse limb of the incision on the right.

"I – I – I think the liver should be there."

"What's this then?" Tebeaux asked as he reached in and lifted a hand full of small intestines out of the open wound, allowing them to slither onto the table. Everyone laughed; I felt better.

"Yes, the liver's here somewhere – under these guts. Here 'tis."

We each came closer to appreciate the difference between our formaldehyde soaked cadaver and this fresh specimen. *Now we're getting somewhere—fresh specimen—that's it—separate the emotional from the scientific—compartmentalize. Don't think of that body as a human being, recently vital, but as a specimen—to be probed and cut and investigated.*

It's a trick all physicians learn; some learn to repress the emotional aspect of dealing with the sick and dying so well that they become cold and unfeeling in their practices. Others, unfortunately, turn to alcohol or drugs to dull the inner anxieties they feel so acutely. The fortunate few find a middle ground, retaining a sense of humanity yet functioning in surgery in a skilled detached manner, no longer having to sense each needle's prick or incision's pain.

I doubt if any physician's career can be totally free of self-doubt, anxiety, and concern (sociopaths may not make the best physicians although some, I fear, are well known).

For me it would not have been healthy to live with these feelings beyond the workday so I learned early how to escape. Since childhood, a workshop was such a place of escape. Having received a power jigsaw from my Uncle Everett at about ten years of age, and a lathe for Christmas at twelve, a workshop was already a part of my life. In college I had built my mother two wing chairs and two corner cupboards; it seems I always had some project. Admittedly, while planning a piece of furniture, my mind might wander from the medical studies at hand, but in general, I was able to find time to keep up in class and reward myself with an afternoon in the shop when I completed a study assignment. And then when I entered my alter career of flying, that activity provided another avenue of escape from the realities of life that the study of medicine forces upon us.

I was slowly developing a philosophy in which my white-collar career, the necessary obligation, was balanced by the more physical blue-collar life of woodworking and flying. I never felt a desire to escape from flying or woodworking back to medicine but the reverse certainly was and remains true.

Socially, medical school provided interesting contrasts with undergraduate school. For one thing, there were many married students, and in a class of fifty there were only two females. Pledging one of the two medical fraternities was basically a matter of expressing interest. A few of the upperclassmen I had met and most of my class friends were in Phi Chi Medical Fraternity so I followed suit. The fraternity house was home to many out-of-town students and had, I was to learn, a reputation as a den of iniquity. This reputation was not entirely undeserved.

"You coming to the house party tonight Jeff?" Aubrey asked with a twinkle in his eye.

"Yeah, I guess so. What's the occasion?"

"They're having a special program—it's closed door."

Closed door? I was curious so after the last class Friday I drove over to Waldron Street, climbed the wooden front porch steps of the Victorian Mansion that was the Phi Chi house, pushed open the cast brass doors, and entered the den. Loud music filled the back hall as the accumulating crowd of tomorrow's physicians eagerly pushed through the double doors into the ballroom. The dimly lit room reeked of smoke and a hint of formaldehyde from the numerous lab jackets.

"Gentlemen! May I have your attention! Please! Through special arrangements with Mr. Johnson our favorite pharmaceutical tech rep we have got a SHOW for you!! One word of caution—keep this to yourselves; our alums might not approve, especially since they weren't invited." The fraternity president continued as shouts from the floor began.

"Let's get it on!"

"Bring her out."

"Let's see what she's got."

"Okay, okay—go ahead Joe," the president responded as he signaled the dark suited man seated by a record player. Bump and grind music began as a scantily clad gal in her thirties slipped on stage from behind a curtain. There was Pandemonium as she danced and flirted about the ballroom.

I found myself wondering about her motives and her life. Was her companion her manager or her husband? Did she have children she was trying to support? I had a feeling of embarrassment not just for myself but also for these future physicians. My embarrassment peaked as one of the rather obese upperclassmen began stripping his clothes in concert with the dancer. Hoots and shouts and laughter filled the house. Disillusionment again. It was a reminder that even in this revered profession in which one is entrusted with the life and well being of another human being there are all the frailties of humanity. Where then, can one find the perfect physician?

FLYING

I live in two worlds: the world of medicine, which demands discipline and devotion to the science and art thereof, and the world of aviation, which, for survival, demands the exercise of good judgment. Once the technique of flying an aircraft is mastered, the art of flying through the use of good judgment becomes paramount. I presumed parallels in aviation and medicine then; I know the similarities now.

Flying was my secret life known only to Frank and a few classmates.

Bob Suber asked one day, "When are you going to take me flying?"

"Just as soon as I solo." I hardly considered that such a flight would be illegal. I was gaining more and more confidence in my flying ability with each lesson and after eight hours of instruction with Charlie Pugh, I was surprised one afternoon when he said, "Let me out at the hangar and you go do a few landings by yourself."

Am I ready? I questioned myself. *I know I can do it—I can.*

I remember the sense of elation I felt as the wheels lifted from the grass runway of Memphis Flying Service on my first solo flight.

"I am really flying," I shouted to the wind. After two or three acceptable landings, I taxied up to the hangar and shut down the engine.

"Pretty good," Charlie allowed, "now, give me your student certificate."

"What student certificate?" No one had told me I needed a student certificate to solo. Charlie told me to get one and come back next week and not tell anyone I had soloed.

Dr. Mallory Harwell gave me the physical exam for a student certificate, and I can remember his words of encouragement, "Stick with your flying—not only will you gain joy in your life, but it can be useful in the practice of medicine." Dr. Harwell was a respected local pilot and physician and for years used an airplane to commute to and from Osceola, Arkansas where he provided medical service to that community.

Armed with my student certificate, I returned to the airport the following week. Unfortunately, Charlie was not around so one of the other instructors had to fly with me. He was not satisfied with my performance, and I had to fly with him two more weekends before he let me solo —the second —but first legal time.

Once I had soloed, I began to enjoy this newfound freedom more than any other sport or extracurricular activity. I studied hard but lived for my free time. Occasionally, especially with daylight savings time, I could spend a couple of hours at the airport after class during the week. My confidence in my ability to continue medical school grew as my confidence in my flying abilities increased with each flight hour. The difference was one of comfort. In medical school, I was under scrutiny all the time, a situation that, even to this day, makes me quite uncomfortable. In flying, on the other hand, I was testing myself against the laws of nature.

Bob Suber expressed confidence in my ability along with a great desire for me to take him flying. In those days we practiced off airport landings, and my instructor (a former crop duster) and I had touched down on many flat fields in the area. It was best to scout a field for stumps or ditches, and although I had flown over an especially enticing green field near Germantown, I drove out to walk its length prior to an upcoming bit of youthful foolishness.

Bob and I arranged the time and scheduled the Piper Cub for an hour. Mrs. Oxley certainly would have disapproved of my secret plan had she known, for more than once Mr. Oxley had to truck out an airplane damaged in an off airport landing by an inexperienced student.

After take off I flew south for quite a few miles before turning east and then back north toward my rendezvous. I spotted Bob's car near the field. I made a low pass and seeing nothing in the way came back around, slipping close over the bordering trees to land in a rougher-than-expected polo field.

Bob was a big man and as he got into the front seat of the cub, a moment of anxiety passed over me at the thought of clearing the shrubs at the far end. I taxied back as close to the woods as possible, turned around, and opened the throttle full. The sixty-five horses struggled to pull the craft forward—inches—then feet—a little faster still. I let the tail come off the ground just a little and held it there. We accelerated—the hedgerow loomed—I eased back on the stick and we were flying, clearing the hedge. We climbed over fields of green and brown that now are covered and swallowed by the tract houses of an overburdened city. The thirty-minute flight was uneventful and we landed near his car. He waved as I took off, climbing rapidly—much relieved of Bob's weight.

Mrs. Oxley did not seem at all suspicious, but Mr. Oxley did seem to notice a greater amount of grass caught in the axle of each wheel. No damage was done but the sense of guilt at having disobeyed the rules furthered my resolve to avoid the exercise of such poor judgment in the future. I think I can say now that I have, to the best of my ability, tried to follow the rules since that time in 1954.

I continued to gain in confidence and skill in both flying and medical school during 1954. I dated a number of girls that I had met as a result of being in the medical field. Student nurses were young, attractive, and available. Lab technicians, assistants, and even female medical students provided abundant opportunity for the single male medical student. It seems that when I left Southwestern, I left that social sphere behind; unfortunately, that included my secret love—Lisa. I had heard that she had become engaged to a fraternity brother, Tom Tosh. He was, of course, on the football team; thus my worry about not being a "jock" was justified. From then on I harbored no serious intention of having any long-term commitment and rather enjoyed dating a number of different girls with one possible exception. I was intrigued by the slight limp I detected in the gait of the thin young lady walking ahead of me one day between classes. I caught up with her.

"Hi, what class are you in?"

"Oh, I've just started. I'm in the first quarter." She smiled and introduced herself. "I'm Marianna M."

I was one quarter ahead of her at that time and dated her off and on all during medical school; I visited her in Florida in 1957. She is a fine person and I truly enjoyed her company but was never prepared to consider marriage. After the Florida trip in 1957, our paths separated, although I still think of her as a friend.

In undergraduate school my good friends and fraternity brothers, Lee Weed, Billy Callicott, and I had gone to movies together. Similarly, on the few Saturday nights in which nothing was going on, one or two of my anatomy lab partners and I would meet for a movie then stop by one of the many beer joints around Memphis. There was no liquor by the drink at that time, so most people brown bagged their liquor, but we were usually satisfied sharing a pitcher of beer at La Rosa's or The Pig and Whistle. I always enjoyed the camaraderie but occasionally my mind flashed back to college and that sense of being trapped by someone too demanding of my time. Once, after driving him home after a movie, a friend wanted to keep talking instead of getting out of the car. I was anxious to leave but he persisted, explaining that he wanted me to be his close friend. I mumbled: "I like a lot of people but I need to go home; I've got to study!" I said, as my anxiety increased.

"Can't you stay?"

"No!" I said firmly. I was quite relieved when he finally got out of the car.

Perhaps I should feel guilty for my homophobia, but at that time in my life I felt threatened by closeness with other men. Maybe that is the American male's burden; he can live a lifetime emotionally isolated, his only confidant being his wife if he is lucky. Women, on the other hand, seem to share an easy closeness with other women.

The blue collar to me signifies an active, participatory, life. I enjoy the feeling of control in operating a tractor, heavy equipment, an airplane, or a machine—any machine. It is a hands-on approach that allays anxiety by action. But there is another side of me—contemplative, reflective. Flying seemed to bridge these apparent extremes, for on the clearest of days, with the great Mississippi extending north and south to the horizon and the rice elevators of Arkansas rising white from the flat green paddies near Stuttgart, all my self doubt and worry vanished, and I was literally on top of the world. If I never experienced a sense of awe and wonder at the great unknowns in a church, I never failed to sense a connection with the *Great Whole* while suspended on molecules of air during my flying career.

In early 1954, the Sunday Commercial Appeal listed an ad that caught my attention. There usually were interesting ads in the airplane section of the classified but most were for airplanes much beyond my means and were seemingly there as an enticement.

Forty horsepower, two seat Taylorcraft
$350.00. See at Wilson Field

Three hundred fifty dollars! I can afford that.

"Frank, how about going in fifty-fifty on an airplane?" I asked after impulsively phoning the Phi Chi house to speak with Frank Farris.

"Well, let's look at it first," he suggested. Later that day we drove to Wilson Field about five miles southeast of Memphis Flying Service.

Harry Wilson was an early Memphis area aviator. Having flown during World War I he was a part of the pre-depression boom. His small airport had been making money, servicing and maintaining the biplanes of the Barnstorming era. Then, during the Depression he lost his investments but was able to hang on to the airport and a few airplanes abandoned by owners who were unable to maintain them. The experience marked him forever; all of his business dealings were cash only; he would never sell an asset unless his price was met; his office building, begun years before, remained an unfinished shell. The concrete block building had a flat, tar-papered roof..

"Some day I'm going to build an observation deck on top," Harry was fond of saying. A smelly couch with shredding upholstery lined one wall. A glass-fronted counter filled with dusty relics of aviation stuck out toward the middle of the room and streaked glass windows looked out onto the grass east-west runway. When we opened the sagging door, several of Mr. Harry Wilson's numerous cats scampered out of the way. We introduced ourselves and found Harry to be a friendly, grandfatherly gentleman whose pessimism concerning the future of the economy and aviation in particular was founded on his own experience during the Depression and later with the collapse of one of his hangars during a storm.

"Yeah, I'll show you the Taylorcraft; the fabric's not too good but should last a couple more years."

We explained that we wanted to build up a little time so that we could get our private licenses.

The faded blue Taylorcraft sat in tall grass; the mower had left her in her own bed for most of the past six months. However, with prompting from Harry Wilson and a few pulls on the prop she came to life still tethered to the ground.

This could be our *own* airplane. We told Mr. Wilson we would return with cash on Monday afternoon. I had a tight schedule that day, but after getting $350.00 from the bank I drove back to Wilson Field with the money. Harry had arranged for an instructor to check me out and after a few takeoffs and landings, I was on my own. The forty horsepower, single magneto, Continental engine was sluggish compared to the Cubs and Champs I had been flying, and the Taylorcraft was slow to accelerate in the grass of Wilson Field. The hedgerow loomed ahead but was cleared by several feet. Frank paid his share, and we both flew in our quest for the forty hours required for a private license. However, progress over the ground was snail paced and we wondered if cross-country training would be possible in this airplane. A decision to buy another airplane was made easy one day when the fabric on a section of the wing of the fading Taylorcraft rolled up like a window shade. Through airport gossip, we learned of a Luscombe for sale at West Memphis. For nine hundred fifty dollars we could have a silver, high-winged, all metal bird and, boy, would she fly fast! Back to the bank for more birthday money, I was not feeling the least bit guilty because I was continuing in my medical studies and averaging in the top twenty percent of my class. Sure, I might have been able to earn higher grades had I devoted more time to studying, but I was beginning to realize that a personal sense of well-being required variety in my life. I could not remain focused on one endeavor to the exclusion of those activities that provided wonder and beauty in my life.

Ed Lindsay was privy to my aviation adventures and served as a more experienced mentor since he had flown B-29s near the end of World War II.

"Sure, I'll help you get the Luscombe from West Memphis over to Wilson Field," he volunteered as we drove down Union toward the medical school later in the week.

Since neither Frank nor I had our licenses yet, Ed's offer was appreciated since the airplane had remained at West Memphis after we had been checked out.

We were late to Pathology class the day we finalized the paperwork on the purchase and as we tried to slip into our seats the professor said, "I sure hope you two have a good excuse!"

"Yes sir—we've been buying an airplane!" we said in all innocence.

Amidst the resounding laughter in the classroom, we sat demurely as the professor's jaw dropped; nothing else was said—just a slow shaking of his head—medical students buying an airplane!

The next Saturday Ed climbed into the left seat of the Taylorcraft. He was rather obese and spilled over into my seat. I managed to climb in and close the door after hand propping the engine. Ed was the expert so I let him fly. Just as we started an agonizingly slow climb from the runway toward the hedges at the end, the single magneto misfired once—then twice. The hedges grew larger in the windscreen and I wondered if we'd clear them. A few leaves slapped at the wheels but we continued our climb—the forty horses struggling against the constraints of gravity.

Ed was an experienced pilot of heavy iron but was inexperienced in small airplanes; he was beginning to question his decision to help me in this adventure. After a somewhat bouncy landing at Brewer field in West Memphis, I thought I should fly with Ed in the Luscombe. I was an inexperienced student pilot proposing to check out a B-29 pilot! But Ed seemed nervous after his landing in the Taylorcraft, so when we started the Luscombe and began taxiing for take off he over-controlled a bit and we almost dropped into a ditch. The take off was acceptable and we turned left to come back around in the pattern. Usually, I decreased power to idle opposite the point of intended landing to curve gently around in a descent to landing. But Ed, as in his training, used too much power in his approach and came in quite high and fast. I sat there wondering if Ed could salvage this landing as the wheels touched down over half way down the runway. The highway crossed just north of the north-south runway on a levee type embankment; cars and trucks zoomed past in front of us and I knew I had to do something. I jammed the throttle forward as I shouted "I've got it." The craft shuddered and bounced into the air; the embankment was just ahead; I eased back on the stick and our wheels cleared the pavement by inches. Ed's hand was shaking as he lit a cigarette; we realized how lucky we were that a car or truck did not come along at the same time we were passing over the highway.

"Maybe, I shouldn't try to fly this thing," Ed announced.

"Aw try once more." I showed him how slow the Luscombe could fly in safety. He did better the second time and after several more landings regained his confidence and took off alone to fly back across the river to Wilson field. I followed in the Taylorcraft. Several weeks later we were able to sell that fabric-covered airplane for nearly the same price that we had paid. Ed did not fly with me anymore after that incident; he told me later that he felt quite confident in flying military aircraft but preferred more power and speed than general aviation had to offer. Many ex military pilots never flew again after the war—probably because of similar feelings and a basic insecurity in the lack of discipline found in civilian aviation.

I had confided to my Dad that I was learning to fly but we both thought that telling my mother would cause her unnecessary worry. She never asked directly what I was doing all Sunday afternoon when the weather was perfect for flying. Perhaps she didn't want to know. If she had any suspicion, however, all questions were answered Christmas Eve, 1954. I was in the workshop completing a music stand I was making for my aunt.

"Jeff, come in the house. I want to talk to you." There was insistence in my mother's voice as she pushed open the shop door. Before I could reply she had turned on her heels and stormed back to the house.

"What in the world?" I thought as I rather sheepishly came out onto the porch. My dad was unusually subdued.

"What does this mean?" She handed me a section of the newspaper.

There, under a column entitled "Memphis Aviation News," I read: *Jeff Justis and Frank Farris have just soloed in their new Luscombe 8A.*

I gulped. "Well, you see, I—uh—when you get an airplane—you—uh—you have to be checked out in it before you can fly by yourself."

"You mean you have been flying? How long?"

"About a year," I replied quietly.

"And *you* knew about this all the time?" My mother stared in disbelief at my father who was sitting rather uncomfortably on the couch.

"We didn't want to worry you," he said finally.

"Well you two are something! I don't know what I'm going to do with you!" She stormed out of the room.

We were definitely in trouble, my dad and I, and we were especially good to my mother over Christmas and New Years. Although she has never forgotten "the worst day of my life," as she recalled, she has, if not forgiven, then accepted the "fait accompli" of my aviation career.

Navigation in those days was strictly by pilotage; by continually referring to maps and ground and by following a constant compass course, disorientation was rare. Nevertheless, a week or so later, when I embarked on my first solo cross-country flight, I was careful to follow the line I had drawn on the map.

Where is that railroad track? I should have crossed one already. Then I saw a clear-cut line in the woods; the abandoned track was barely discernable. Each mile traveled gave confidence for the miles to go and soon my first cross-country was consigned to my logbook.

I earned my private pilot certificate in February 1955. Frank obtained his shortly thereafter, and we were then ready to use the Luscombe for travel adventures. My dad did not hesitate to fly with me. In fact I flew him to Springfield, Missouri for a dental meeting at which he introduced me as his brother—a tongue in cheek effort to deny his age.

One Sunday when dad was out of town, I talked my mother into coming to Wilson Field to see my airplane. Reluctantly she sat in the side-by-side two place Luscombe and eventually consented to a short flight. Harry Wilson hand propped the engine and we taxied onto the grass runway. My mother held to a frame member, her knuckles blanching, with her right hand hand and clutched her seat with the other. She was not enjoying this but remained quiet. Then as I pushed full throttle and we began bouncing across clumps of grass and the wheels left the ground, I heard her say,

"Let's go back!"

"Mom, just look at the fields and trees." I pleaded.

"Let's go back!"

"Don't you want me to take you over our house?"

"Let's go back!"

"Can't I just circle the field once or twice?"

"Let's go back!"

And so I landed and so ended my mother's first flight.

She has flown commercially since that time, and she even flew with me one other time (from Holly Grove, Arkansas to Memphis), but any love for aviation my mother may have had was given over to me fully on the day of my birth.

EXTERNSHIP

The window overlooks a large hay field bordered at the far end by trees, waving gently in the late spring breeze; it is a scene in sharp contrast to the tension of the operating room. I had often dreamed of doing surgery in such a place, but alas the modern approach is toward more isolation—more sterility—not just biological but emotional sterility as well.

In medical school, the clinical Quarters were approaching and spring of 1955 was to be my "six-X" or "lay out quarter." I suppose we could have used the time as a vacation but most of us felt we needed some experience in clinical medicine. We were weary of histology, bacteriology, embryology, and biochemistry. We wanted to deal with real people—with patients. There were some local opportunities available, the John Gaston and St. Josephs to name a few, but these larger facilities also had interns and residents who were eager to learn and would not be likely to let some lowly extern (as medical students were called) do anything. So Frank Farris and I settled on the small Rutherford County Hospital in Murphreesboro, Tennessee. He drove my car and I flew the Luscombe landing at the paved local Murphreesboro airport. We were welcomed to the two story brick hospital by the young administrator, Marvin, and assigned quarters in the hospital. Later we were befriended by Mrs. Wall who worked in the administrative section and whose nephew, Pat Wall, lived with her. Pat was a youngster then but has subsequently become a Dean of Admissions, and later Dean of the medical school at the University of Tennessee. I remember good meals with Mrs. Wall and later a few parties at her home across the street from the hospital.

We were introduced as "Doctor" to patients and staff. I supposed everyone was saying "Student Doctor,"—but the "student" was silent. I doubt, however, that the word "Doctor" instilled any more confidence when the patient saw the white-jacketed youth before him.

As luck would have it, I was assigned to the emergency room that first night. I was grateful for an experienced, kind nurse who recognized my anxiety when a lady was brought in with a long gash across her knee. I had practiced suturing on a cadaver but never on a living, breathing human being. Like a black shadow, self-doubt enveloped me.

"Here, doctor, take this syringe and block the wound with Novocain." Florence Nightingale coached me through my uncertainty.

The patient had been complaining as the nurse had cleansed the wound prior to the use of a local anesthetic. Once I had finished injecting the anesthetic the patient became silent and rested, and I marveled at my ability to relieve pain through such a simple act. I gained a bit of confidence.

"Doctor, here is your suture." My nurse all but guided my hand as I placed, carefully, perhaps too carefully, that first suture. *Am I too deep? Should I go farther from the edge?* Slowly the gaping wound was brought together; the oozing flow of bright, red blood began to subside, and I had been able to convert chaos into order—an unstructured wound into a structured repair. I had done it. I had overcome my self-doubt, albeit with help from Florence Nightingale.

The staff doctor stopped by to check the patient. I had done well he said, but I should be careful not to tie the sutures too tightly. I was beginning a process that would change a self-doubting young man of twenty-two into a medical doctor – perhaps not the Andrew

Manson or Martin Arrowsmith of my imagination, but a doctor of some skill and confidence.

Although Frank and I had mutually agreed upon Rutherford County Hospital for our layout quarter, we saw surprisingly little of each other during those three months. For one thing, Frank seemed to favor internal medicine or general practice and I leaned more toward surgery. In retrospect, my personal choice was probably because of the mechanical or hands-on aspect of surgery. The attraction must have been strong for it persisted in spite of my early aversion to blood and, I was to learn, in spite of the intimidating loss of control suffered under the staff surgeons to whom I was assigned. Surgeons as a group tend to be self-directed, in charge people and although the instrument throwing, cursing, red-faced stereotype can still be found, he (or she) is now more likely to be asked to retire from surgery by his peers if such behavior cannot be altered.

"DR. JUSTIS. REPORT TO THE OPERATING ROOM IMMEDIATELY – DR. JUSTIS..." The pager was insistent.

"Dr. Robinson wants you now – you better get scrubbed." The operating room supervisor greeted me as I entered the lounge to change clothes. I had known there was a case that afternoon with Dr. Robinson, an abdominal hysterectomy, but I thought I would be called before it started.

"G'damn it, Justis! Where have you been? Get over here and hold these retractors." Dr. Robinson was a large man. He was gruff even when not in surgery, but with the tension of a case his green eyes fired exasperation at me from the red sweating forehead that showed above his mask. I could scarcely hold the retractors correctly. "Pull—pull! G'damn it! G'damn it! Don't pull so hard you'll tear the damn gut! Sponge—SPONGE! I can't see a G'damn thing. I'm trying to peel this uterus off the gut and I can't see."

I could do nothing right it seemed. I wanted to walk out. I wanted to forget this—yet I stayed.

"Justis break scrub and put another pair of gloves on. Get under the sheets and stick your finger in her rectum so I can see where her gut is up here."

I got down on my knees and pulled the drape sheets up enough to crawl under. I couldn't see but I felt my way to her perineum.

"Come on Justis — get in the rectum."

"I'm trying; here; is that it?"

"G'damn it can't you tell the difference between a vagina and a rectum? Get in the g'damn rectum. Okay you got it – now stay there."

I could feel him working over my finger as he dissected the uterus off the distal colon and rectum. I hoped he would not slip with the scalpel, but in spite of his abrasiveness, he was a good surgeon.

With the resection of the uterus complete, Dr. Robinson seemed to relax.

"Let's take a break. Gertrude! Is she stable?"

"She's just fine," Gertrude, one of the better nurse anesthetists, replied, glaring over the drapes at the head of the table.

Dr. Robinson and I stepped over to the large picture window that was unique in this operating room. Dr. Robinson pulled his mask down and with this gloved hands lit a cigarette. I had stopped smoking while at Southwestern because that habit did not fit with what I felt a doctor should be. But I was content for a few minutes to enjoy the peace.

"Let's get going, Justis! Here, you close."

We had changed gloves and now this gruff surgeon was actually letting me place sutures to close this patient's wound. Dr. Robinson and I worked together on many occasions during my three months at Rutherford County and although he continued to castigate me, and shout and cuss, he was letting me do more and more—and I was learning. Being abused, I concluded, was just part of the sacrifice expected of an apprentice!

Dr. Williams was a younger surgeon who was not as intimidating as Dr. Robinson. Having served in the military, he wore combat boots to the operating room and was more interested in talking about his experiences during the Korean War than he was in the case at hand.

"You know, Justis, there's no calling greater than being a combat soldier!"

"You mean that's better than being a doctor?" I was a bit disillusioned by his statement.

"Well, there are similarities, but in medicine we often don't have a clear objective. You know we can remove a cancer – but what's the use if the patient dies anyway. Now, the combat soldier has but one objective—to kill the enemy and if he does that well—then, there's nothing like it."

Dr. Williams' sociopathic leanings were apparent. Technically, he performed surgery adequately but compassion was not one of his best points.

Darlene, the "angel of death," was a nurse anesthetist of uncertain qualifications. Observing her made me acutely aware of the risks assumed by unsuspecting patients in many rural hospitals during the fifties. Dr. Robinson would not work with her but Dr. Williams often laughed about her patients who, during recovery from anesthesia, began to violently shake.

"That's just the pentothal shakes," she would claim.

"I don't care about that as long as the patient wakes up," Dr. Williams would often say.

I was helping him with a routine appendectomy one day. The patient was a large muscular black man in his twenties. We were beginning to close the wound when Dr. Williams noted there was little bleeding and the blood was rather dark.

"How is everything up there, Darlene?"

"Oh, I think its okay; I'm just having trouble bagging him – that's all."

"Check his blood pressure."

"Well I can't do that and bag him too!" The "angel of death" seemed more frustrated than concerned.

"Justis you finish and I'll check him."

"There is no blood pressure," Dr. Williams said after a few minutes, "and no heart beat."

"Well, I can't help that!" The "angel" replied. "He must have had a reaction."

"Yeah! A reaction to no oxygen!" Williams sounded upset – then – "Oh well, we lost one."

I felt helpless and somehow responsible. After all I was a part of the procedure; I was there when this healthy young man died. Suppose I had been the operating surgeon, what would I have done? Perhaps what I learned was that reputation, either good or bad, is earned and that we must choose, in so far as possible, the best people available for the benefit of our patients.

"Come on, Justis; let's go tell the family." I dreaded that necessity and, in the years since, I have never been able to comfortably tell someone of a loved one's death or other traumatic news without emotional lability.

With an air of authority and with his combat boots clicking rapidly down the hall, Dr. Williams burst into the patient's room to the startled faces of the patient's mother, brother, and wife, as well as several cousins.

"Well, Joe was sicker than we thought. We did everything we could but we lost him."

"Oh Lord Jesus! Oh Lord Jesus—Oh, Lord—Oh Lord!" Each black face in that room was contorted with grief and disbelief.

I choked back my own emotions. Dr. Williams went on to explain how the appendicitis must have poisoned his system. If I had told the family that the "angel of death" in the form of an incompetent nurse anesthetist had contributed to this loved one's death, would the loss have been less? In the end, all I could do when Dr. Williams turned to leave, was to put my hand on the mother's sobbing shoulder and whisper in a broken voice, "I – I'm sorry."

Who then would be worthy of my admiration: the hard nosed abusive surgeon who had the patient's best interest at heart and who was able to empathize with his patients, or the easy going "combat surgeon" who could shed any emotional burden as easily as he could fire an M-16? This was but the beginning of a repertoire of experiences that would shape and mold me in my quest to become a physician.

There were rumors that the young administrator of the hospital and his wife were having marital problems. I didn't think much of this until a slight blonde-haired girl struck up a conversation with me during a Saturday party at Mrs. Wall's home just across the street from the hospital. We were attracted to each other and although I was a bit uneasy when she whispered, "He might come by," I acquiesced when she suggested we step out on the back porch.

"Who?" I asked.

She didn't answer and while sitting on the back steps with this attractive, somewhat passionate young lady, at that moment I really didn't care.

The passion of the moment was suddenly shattered by the screen door banging open behind.

"Jean! Come home now!" The hospital administrator was glaring at both of us. He grabbed her by the arm and pulled her through the doorway. I didn't say anything; I didn't know what to say. I was embarrassed. I stayed out on the back porch quite a while after the administrator and his wayward wife had left.

"Hey you almost got yourself in trouble, there, didn't you, Jeff?" one of the orderlies commented.

"That gal's dangerous," someone else added.

Apparently I wasn't the first young man around the medical community to have been taken in by her charms.

I was happy for a little escape Sunday and headed to the airport. I'm not sure why Frank didn't fly as much as I did. Perhaps he was a bit uneasy. He always seemed nervous and when sitting his foot would be in constant motion. He "fiddled" with the controls when flying and never seemed to relax and enjoy the flight. Of course, his reluctance was my gain, and I was able to plan flights most any free weekend.

DR. E. JEFF JUSTIS

I was to be in Hugh Humphrey's wedding in Louisville, Kentucky and flew the Luscombe to Bowman Field. We had just installed a wind-driven generator and our first two-way radio so I was filled with a sense of excitement as I called Bowman tower for landing clearance. I delighted in relaying details of my flight to the bridesmaids and other young ladies of the bridal party, but at the reception I began to feel somewhat feverish and by the time I got to the hotel, I was sick with an acute tonsillitis. The next day I knew I couldn't fly but thought surely I would be better the next day. I awoke still suffering chills and fever, and pleaded with a pharmacist for some antibiotics—after all, I was halfway to becoming a doctor. No luck. The hotel sent a doctor to the room at my request. He was skeptical at first but when he peered into my throat and saw my swollen tonsil he agreed with my diagnosis and handed me some Erythromycin samples. Twenty four hours later I was better but not in condition to fly. I called Hugh who had spent his honeymoon in Louisville and was staying with Patty's parents. He and Patty insisted that I stay with them, and for many years Hugh took great delight in telling everyone how I had been with them on their honeymoon. I recuperated and soon was able to fly back to Murphreesboro to the relief of Frank who had to cover for me during my longer-than-expected absence.

With some soreness remaining in my throat, I accompanied Dr. Schmidt, a general practitioner, on rounds the day after I returned to the hospital.

"Looks like you've got a peritonsilar abscess, Mr. Brown," Dr. Schmidt explained to the anxious patient in room 16. I swallowed hard feeling the pain in my own throat.

"We need to open that and I believe we can do it right here if you're willing."

Without anesthesia?

"Open your mouth and try to hold still." With that, Dr. Schmidt took a scalpel with a number eleven sharp-pointed blade and thrust it quickly into the abscess. The patient jerked back and cried out in pain. He then began to spit blood and pus; he gagged and I gagged. Surely there was a better way.

The patient's room was not a controlled environment nor is the site of an accident. I knew I could not be comfortable in such uncontrolled situations. As the years have passed, I have come to realize that the structured environment of the operating room and the control of a patient's pain helped my confidence in dealing with the many anxiety-provoking situations faced by physicians.

After three months at Rutherford County Hospital, I was ready to face the clinical years at medical school. I realized that I could sew up a wound, and I was grateful to the emergency room nurse, my Florence Nightingale, for having been understanding of my anxieties and helping me through them. Still, my vision of the great and confident physician remained in contrast to my own sense of inadequacy, although I realized I had taken a few faltering steps toward my goal.

RITE OF PASSAGE

Each challenge and anxiety that I overcome is accompanied by the fervent wish that subsequently I would no longer have doubts and concerns. Yet life seems to be a rite of passage, a gauntlet of fears, of real or imagined problems that, once negotiated, require us to enter a new passage. Once we learn to accept this as inevitable, we can rejoice in the beauty of the countryside before and after each tunnel through which we must pass. Gratefully, the older I become the shorter the tunnels seem and the more appreciative I am of the wonder of life.

Back at school, we were finally assigned to clinics and to the various medical and surgical services. As a second or third assistant in surgery, I was constantly reminded of the hard-nosed personality that can be seen in many surgeons. As in many life situations abuse begets abuse. I was determined to break that cycle if I were to become a surgeon. However, completing medical school was my only goal at this point and a decision toward specialization would come much later. General practice had an appeal and experiences with "my family" provided me with the gratification of being appreciated.

Each of us in the family practice clinics was assigned a family for whose medical needs we would be responsible. My family, the Anderson's, lived in a three-room apartment in a midtown housing development. Mrs. Anderson, a frail woman in her forties, was disabled with diabetic neuropathy. One 10-year old daughter was rather anemic and had many allergies, but the two boys, twelve and thirteen, were happy and healthy. Once a week I visited them in their apartment in Lauderdale Court to give Mrs. Anderson a shot of Vitamin B-12, check her urine for sugar and acetone, and check the kids. I genuinely enjoyed playing my role as physician. I was on call for advice they might need and for emergencies. One Saturday I got a call from a frantic Mrs. Anderson.

"Oh, Dr. Jeff, Helen's been hit by a car and they've taken her to St. Joseph's. Please help her if you can—I can't get over there and, Lordy, I need to know how she is."

"I'll go right over. Try not to worry and I'll call you later."

I found out that Helen had a closed fracture of the tibia midway between the knee and the ankle and that one of the residents from Campbell Clinic was coming over to take care of her. I had attended a few orthopaedic lectures but had no experience in dealing with orthopaedic problems. On the way to the hospital, I recalled my childhood feeling of helplessness in dealing with an injured classmate and had to repress that underlying fear of failure, of not living up to self imposed expectations that had haunted me as long as I could remember and would probably be with me as long as I lived.

I followed Helen as she was being rolled into the fracture room. There was a large sink against the right wall next to a counter stacked with plaster and padding material. Helen was frightened, but relaxed when I held her hand and the nurse began administering the anesthetic. Leon Hay, the orthopaedic resident, gently lifted the child's leg from the splint. The break became obvious as the limb bent at an abnormal angle. I could hear the grinding of bone ends and then, as I held her knee off the side of the table as directed by Dr. Hay, the grinding crepitance transmitted to my own hands.

"I hope we can get this reduced closed," Dr. Hay said as he pulled with increasing force against my counter traction.

Click—click—gr—gr—grate resounded in the small room. I felt uneasy but managed to continue my effort in pulling up on the child's knee.

"There—we got it," Leon said. "Now let's don't lose it—hold perfectly still."

As the plaster was applied we could relax. X-rays showed a good reduction, and I was able to call Mrs. Anderson with the good news. At that point in my medical career, I did not give orthopaedics much thought and did not imagine that some day I would become a "bone setter."

I was able to help "my family" through a few more crises and gained their affection and appreciation. At Christmas I took a bundle of presents to them and received notes of appreciation for several years after my graduation. I always felt, however, that I had gained so much more than I had given and for the first time understood that deep sense of pride in doing something as a physician for fellow humans. So the learning process continued—not only in medicine but also in flying and in life.

It was around this same time in medical school that Granddad, my dad's father, William Justis came to our house one Sunday for dinner. He had just driven from Dyersburg in his car, a 1939 Ford Coup, loaded with combs, brushes, and many other sundries. At 92, having been a traveling salesman all his life, he treated his customers as his friends and they reciprocated with affection for Will Justis.

After dinner he went to rest, excusing himself by saying, "I'm kind of tired," as he made his way to the closed-in porch just off the living room.

I went to the carport and had started to work on my car when: **"Jeff, Jeff, come quick!"** my mother shouted from the kitchen door.

I ran inside to find my dad leaning over granddad who was face up on the couch. Dad was distraught but sensible. "I've seen folks die before—I think granddad's dead," he said, choking back tears.

I grabbed my medical bag and with that symbol of medicine, the stethoscope, listened to granddad's chest for any sign of life.

"I'm afraid he's gone, dad; I'm so sorry. We both loved him." I felt needed by my dad in that situation. I, who had needed his support during my childhood, was now in a position, through medical training and increasing maturity, to provide comfort to him. It was a watershed moment.

Throughout medical school Ed Lindsey and I continued to car pool and to study together occasionally. Ed was somewhat of an entrepreneur and dictated class notes into a sound-absorbing microphone adapter for tape recording. He was quite a sight mumbling into the large black cylinder (about twelve inches long and six inches in diameter) during class, but in spite of teasing everyone was quite happy to get a copy of Ed's notes.

There were several members of my class that were older than the majority. This didn't seem to matter during the pre-clinical years; we were all struggling to learn the material. But in the clinical years when the art of medicine, the art of dealing with people and gaining a patient's confidence, becomes important, the age difference gave an edge to those over thirty.

Ed especially excelled in OB/GYN. The patients loved him. He worked at St. Joseph's Hospital on weekends and told us about the many deliveries he had done. There were many babies being delivered at the John Gaston Hospital in the fifties, and as students we were given a lot of responsibility in monitoring patients in labor. We even learned how to administer nitrous oxide anesthesia. It was a trial by fire for me (and for my young patient) while holding a mask over her face, muffling the screams: **"Lord Jesus help me! Help me! Oh Jesus, please help me! Don't put that thing on me!"**

The OB resident shouted, "Put the Nitrous on four and the oxygen on two, Justis, and hold the mask on her face."

The woman screamed, "Oh Jesus, oh Jesus, it's coming, it's coming!"

"Hold the G-damn mask on her face, Justis."

"I'm trying, I'm trying."

Then with a final prolonged "Jeeeeesus Lord—Thank you Jesus," the baby was pushed also screaming into the world. I decided then that anesthesia would probably not be my specialty.

It was a hard three-month rotation, as I recall, because we worked in shifts. Eleven to seven was the worst for me. I had to go to work when I was usually getting ready for bed. During one such shift I was assigned to watch a young "primip" through her labor. She had started about thirty minutes before I arrived so I felt I was in for a long evening.

Between her pains, which at first were coming every 15 minutes or so, she was resting quietly. She was unmarried as were many of the John Gaston OB patients and only a little over fifteen years old.

"Oh, oh, ohoooooo Jesus," she began with the onset of a contraction.

"Just breathe easy through your mouth—easy," I said as she squeezed my hand. *I'd better check her dilatation.* I slipped on rubber gloves. *Two centimeters—we've got a way to go. It's gonna be a long night.*

Contractions were more frequent now and so were calls to Jesus. *Still two centimeters; how come she's not dilating?* I was just about to call the resident to help me figure out the lack of progress when my patient began a particularly loud "Lordy...... Jeeesus, Jesus, **Jeeeeeeeeeesus.**" As I reached down to once again check her dilation, a hairy crown began to form in her birth canal and with a great shove and shout, the whole baby squirted onto the bed and into my hands. Then a nurse appeared and we tied off the cord and delivered the placenta. Calming down after all the excitement, I picked up my first delivery, a primip precipitation, and, feeling his two centimeter fontanel, realized that what I had been assuming was the cervix was the baby's own skull. Well the young mother was happy in spite of the fact that her "doctor" had let her precipitate right in the labor room. And I decided against one more area of specialization.

Later when we were assigned to a specialty with specific hours (ophthalmology) there was some free time during the day. I offered to help Lynn Hamilton and Bill Doak in an engineering endeavor. Lynn had conceived of an all steel unsinkable barge in which we could cruise the mighty Mississippi. Made of one eighth inch thick steel, the vessel was about sixteen feet long and four feet wide with integral air compartments doubling as seats. A welding shop on Madison Avenue fabricated the monster under our watchful eyes over a three- or four-week period. Launch day arrived and I furnished the trailer to move the barge to a ramp on President's Island. Slowly we backed the trailer down the ramp.

"Hold it," Lynn shouted.

The ramp was too steep and instead of floating free the aft end of our barge was plowing into and under the water. After considering our options we slid the boat off the trailer onto the ramp, then with much grunting and pushing we finally shoved the barge sideways into the water and it floated. With three of us in the boat and with a small outboard on the aft end, water splashed over the gunwale whenever we encountered the wake of a passing boat. No problem! The exuberance of youth overcomes all obstacles. We navigated out of McKellar Lake onto the Mississippi River, hugging the shore, avoiding passing barges and after six hours, with our gasoline supply running dangerously low, we managed to deliver the boat to the Yacht Club on Mud Island. Tired and somewhat disappointed in the performance of our creation we nevertheless celebrated that night at a downtown pub. We never used the steel barge after that and Lynn finally sold it to a local fisherman before we graduated. Perhaps it found some utility as a cattle feeder or planter for I doubt any nautical function.

As medical students we were, of course, low on the hierarchical ladder, and we could expect to be chewed out on a daily basis. Residents castigated the interns for some infraction and in turn the interns came down on the students. I recall the indignation I felt when I was blamed for not completing a CBC (complete blood count) on a patient for whom the test had been ordered early that morning. It made no difference to the irate intern that I had checked the chart prior to his writing the order and that I had not been notified.

In surgery, as I had learned at Murphreesboro, tension can lead to explosive outbursts and, to an objective observer, rather childish behavior. Surgery requires maintaining control at all times. The surgeon cannot allow his hands to shake in fear of the knife's potential, and when an unexpected bleeder suddenly spurts a stream of blood onto his glasses and mask he must respond quickly with applied pressure and a clamp. With a vulnerable patient, his body open to the world, the surgeon, unless a sociopath, feels the weight of responsibility for this fellow human. Since frustration and anxiety build up and cannot be vented on the helpless patient, the nurses, students, interns, and others down the ladder from the responsible surgeon receive the full force of pent up emotion. Certainly not all surgeons react in this way; some become silent while others delay their response, and their wives or children become helpless recipients. Although a surgeon's personality may lead him into specialization, the type of surgery performed may in itself influence the surgeon's personality. Life-threatening procedures obviously produce a greater degree of tension in the operating surgeon than, say, orthopaedic surgery or hand surgery. A surgeon is fortunate when he chooses a specialty that allows him to practice his art with satisfaction and equanimity.

With one's every move under scrutiny and with the pressure of trying to avoid mistakes building during the week, it was healing for me to drive south on tree-lined Mount Moriah Road to Winchester, then past green fields and woods to turn in through a hedgerow into the gravel parking area of Wilson Field.

Now, this whole area southeast of Memphis is overfilled with houses and people. Then, there was the peace of the country and an eccentric god-fatherly, Harry Wilson. He would talk of the old times and the depression and how bad things were then and in the present. My perspective was different, because I had an airplane. When the Luscombe lifted from the turf, I was on top of the world, in charge of my own fate, with no responsibility except to my airplane and myself. It was and is a great escape.

One warm spring afternoon, I was securing the aircraft when a young lady approached with a smile. "Hi, I'm Wanda. I just wanted to see your airplane. Harry's a friend and he said you would show me."

"Yeah, I'm Jeff." Wanda was interesting. She was mature in her behavior and appearance. In fact, I believe she must have been nearly forty years old. She feigned interest in everything about the airplane, sitting in the cockpit with her skirt pulled up above her knees while I showed her how the control stick worked. She moved her legs provocatively when the stick moved side to side. Before I knew what was happening we had agreed to meet later that Saturday at a local nightspot. After she drove off to get ready, I casually mentioned our upcoming meeting to Harry.

"I would be careful if I were you," Harry said in his best grandfatherly tone.

"What do you mean?" I asked innocently.

"You just better be careful. That gal's got a reputation as a man chaser."

I wasn't sure, at age 22, if such a warning should be taken as a warning at all but, over the next several months of an on-again, off-again liaison, I realized the shallowness of our relationship and was happy to leave Wanda behind when I finished school and moved to Knoxville.

Meanwhile, I continued to date Marianna; she remained my best friend throughout medical school and during my internship until our parting in Havana, Cuba in 1957. One long weekend I flew Marianna to Mobile, Alabama to visit her mother. As we climbed through a layer of puffy white scattered clouds banking to remain in the clear, I sensed her watching the pleasure my face exhibited.

"You really enjoy flying, don't you Jeff?—And I love you for it."

I reached for her hand but I was embarrassed. I just could not seem to respond with the same degree of love for her. Perhaps I was threatened or afraid that I could not walk away as I had been able to with other girls I dated. Perhaps there was a lingering feeling that I should not give up on the one true love I had left at Southwestern.

Between quarters, we often had a week before new classes or assignments began. With a valid private pilot's license and a shared airplane, Frank and I decided to fly to New Mexico to visit Ben McCartney whose father was in general practice in Farmington. I had actually flown very little with Frank and that trip, in which we alternated flight legs, was to be a test of my patience. Frank was a nervous individual. In class, the floor vibrated synchronously with his foot in constant motion up and down. Even in the airplane, he would fly with his feet off the rudder pedals in uncoordinated flight. The ball indicated a constant "slip" and the ride was uncomfortable at best. At least on approach to land he assumed more control and I never felt that safety was compromised. Another annoying habit he had was to fly out of trim. He trimmed nose down so he would always have to maintain some back pressure on the control stick; thus whenever his attention was diverted, the craft would enter a shallow dive and lose altitude. Each leg of the flight was about two hours long, and I always looked forward to my turn in the left seat.

Finally, we arrived in New Mexico, flew through passes, low over mesas, maintaining a maximum altitude of 10,000 feet above sea level. At that, the little 65 horse power Luscombe was giving all she had as we passed over the area south of Farmington.

We spent a few days sightseeing and following Dr. McCartney on his rounds. I was intrigued by the variety and challenges of family practice and still harbored dreams of my own "Citadel" inspired world. On the day of departure, the wind was gusting from the west and on the way to the airport, Frank seemed especially anxious.

"I don't feel good about this," he said nervously. It was his turn as pilot in control.

"Why don't you let me fly." I said. "I don't mind a little wind."

He calmed down a little. I felt better being in control and my confidence grew. Farmington Airport's runway is quite long but is perched high on a Mesa with a precipitous drop at each end and I think this, too, intimidated Frank. After run-up I taxied onto the runway and eased the throttle forward. The Luscombe accelerated slowly in the thin air but finally became airborne in a very slow climb from the airport elevation of over 5000 feet toward 10,000 feet. We turned toward the southeast to skim across the flat mesas once again. Frank relaxed as he realized that his premonition was unfounded, and I marveled at the stark and desolate beauty of the southwestern United States passing 500 feet below our wings.

Ready or not, graduation was approaching, but sometime during the tenth quarter, I developed some swollen lymph nodes in my neck with associated general malaise.

"Infectious mononucleosis, that's what you have," announced Dick Wooten after a blood test.

Rest was the treatment and it nearly resulted in my having to repeat the quarter. Fortunately, I had kept my grades high enough and was able to keep up by studying during that six weeks of enforced rest so that I was able to obtain full credit.

One of my classmates, planning a general practice in Mississippi, announced that he was not going to take an internship. When he graduated he would have a license to practice medicine and surgery and that is exactly what he intended to do. The rest of us considered the internship to be an opportunity to really "do something." We had heard embellished stories of how a staff doctor had let an intern take out a gall bladder from start to finish or how another intern had shown such competence that he had been allowed to operate unassisted. Many of my classmates decided to remain at the John Gaston. Although a little intimidated at the prospect, I set out to find an internship with a reputation of challenging the interns with more responsibility. Frank was undecided, so during one of our inter-quarter breaks we used the Luscombe to investigate various programs. Nashville General was our first stop and was very similar to the John Gaston, a large charity institution. There were many residents and for that reason I was not interested. The next morning, we flew over the Cumberland Plateau, landing at Island Home Airport. Knoxville General was a dilapidated early twentieth century hospital with tall ceilings, thick molding, and large paned windows, often opened in the days before air conditioning. The facility was obviously in need of repair, but the interns were basically running the hospital, and I knew there would be a great opportunity to put into practice some of the things that I had learned over the past three years. Frank was not interested, probably because Knoxville was so close to his home in Rogersville. On obtaining an application from the administrator, I learned that the hospital was to close in December of 1956 and that all the patients would be transported to a new facility being completed across the river, the University of Tennessee Memorial Research Center and Hospital. There would be no residents initially. I was intrigued and might have stopped looking at other facilities; however, I had agreed to the flight and the next day we left for Washington, DC. The Appalachian Mountains were not much of a challenge compared to the high country of the Rockies, and we easily negotiated the valley between Knoxville and Roanoke and through the beautiful Shenandoah Valley and out onto the coastal plains cut by the Potomac River. Believe it or not, in 1956, we landed at Washington National Airport (Reagan) in our small craft, using a single-tower frequency to transmit and a low frequency tunable receiver. Our wind-driven generator and battery provided just enough power to communicate within ten miles of the airport.

DC General was like all big city general hospitals, somewhat impersonal and, to me, unattractive. Frank for some reason liked it. We stayed at the Phi Chi House at Georgetown, and he was impressed by what some of the interns had to say.

The Aircraft Owners and Pilots Association headquarters was located in Bethesda, and I was more interested in visiting the headquarters than in spending more time at the hospital. I met Max Karant who was a founder and president of that organization; I became a member on that day and I have retained my membership ever since.

I was growing tired of looking at internship programs but I enjoyed the flying. We flew directly over Washington DC, diverting around the White House and Washington Monument; our only concern was with the sights below and our check points in pilotage navigation. Once we had cleared the immediate airport area, the radio was turned off and not used again until we approached our next point of landing: North Philadelphia Airport with Philadelphia General next on our agenda.

We were invited to watch a bronchoscopy from an observation area in one of the many operating rooms. The thoracic surgery resident was having a particularly difficult time passing the bronchoscope in a coughing, struggling patient. The topical anesthetic was inadequate and the resident was venting his frustration on the helpless patient.

"G-damn it, if you don't hold still I can't do this procedure. Hold still!"

How do you expect the patient to suppress his cough reflex while you're jamming that tube down his throat? Why don't you give the anesthetic more time?

The resident persisted and finally the scope was passed although the patient continued his retching and now, silent coughing. Although in my career I have had very few truly uncooperative patients, most will respond to a physician's empathy. The patient should feel that he or she has some control and that the physician will listen and respond. If something we do hurts, we should be willing to slow down or stop or change the way we are approaching the problem. In orthopaedics, one must occasionally manipulate a fracture without anesthesia, especially in children in whom a general anesthetic is an unacceptable risk or in whom an injection is more feared and painful than the manipulation. However, the rule should be to limit such procedures to those in which a quick, single movement will correct the deformity. Repeated manipulation or procedures during which the surgeon may have to intermittently cause pain, necessitate anesthesia. Even deep injections into joints or bursae should be preceded by a local anesthetic so that the large needle and its movement will not be felt.

The last leg of our internship adventure required a flight up the East Coast past the Statue of Liberty and out Long Island to Zahn's Airport. Again, I remember the freedom in flight of those days, the ability to over fly areas that today are restricted by regulated air space and the requirement to remain in constant contact and in radar control.

We found our way to the Long Island Railroad Station and soon, we were in Manhattan. We located a small hotel near Grand Central Station. We did not hesitate to use the subway system, and I can recall no fear as we roamed through areas of New York City that today would intimidate an armed Bernard Goetz.

Frank went off on his own to visit Bellevue and Columbia the following day (I had already decided that I would not be interning in New York City); I visited the American Wing of the Metropolitan Museum of Art. The eighteenth century furniture that I had learned to appreciate through my early furniture making efforts impressed me. In fact, I was thrilled to see a gate leg table for which I had measured drawings. The inspiration stayed with me until 1960 when I was able to begin construction of a reproduction of that table.

That evening, we wandered along 42nd Street looking for a place to eat. An inviting looking menu at a small bar did not overcome the uncomfortable atmosphere (at least for me) of this obviously gay hangout.

"The sooner we get out of here, the better," I said, before we even sat down.

"Aw come on, let's eat." Frank was insistent.

"No, I'm leaving." I did not like getting into a situation in which I was uncomfortable and I did not like the feeling of being controlled. "I'll see you at the hotel; I'm tired and we've had a long day." I was determined, so Frank acquiesced.

Later, after dinner at the hotel when I said I was returning to my room, Frank said that he felt like walking and would see me later. I waked up early the next morning ready to begin the long flight home. I had seen enough to realize that I would not be happy interning anywhere out of Tennessee, and I was tired of dealing with Frank. I wanted to leave when I was ready.

"Frank, get up," I shouted. It was 9:00 am. He didn't budge. "Wake up, we have got to head home."

He moaned. "I was up late last night and I need to sleep."

"Come on, I'll do the flying. Let's get going."

Finally, he dragged himself up, and with few words passing between us we commuted to Zahn's Airport. Frank was so groggy that he sat quietly as I planned the flight and preflighted the airplane. Once in the air, he slept and I could be alone with my thoughts and with my own appreciation of the landscape below. Partnership with Frank had allowed me to own an airplane but I was already figuring out a way to buy out Frank's interest. I had hoped that Frank would not choose to intern with me not only because I wanted the airplane for myself but also because I was becoming more and more impatient with Frank's manner. The flight home was uneventful, and soon the remaining clinical work and classes occupied an increasing amount of time.

I was accepted for an internship at the UT Hospital in Knoxville. Frank, who had chosen Washington DC General, agreed to sell me his half of the Luscombe for $625, an amount that I was to pay him over a six month period. In 1954 we had paid $475 each for this airplane that would become a Classic by the 90s and would probably sell for nearly $20,000.

Studying for the Tennessee Medical Board's examinations brought anxieties to the fore for all of us. After all, what good was a medical degree if we were not licensed in the state to practice. Each of us approached studying in a unique way. I wanted to get my homework over with, especially on weekends so that I could use the good daylight hours for my woodworking or flying. Even for important exams, I would try to study on a scheduled basis but at 11:00 or 11:30 pm I was usually ready for bed. My married classmates and I were compatible in that respect but some students, many of whom lived in the Phi Chi House, felt that they must study all night if they were to pass. They took amphetamines to remain awake. Unfortunately, more than one would "crash" at an inappropriate time. For Frank this may have been the beginning of his experimentation with drugs that would lead to his tragic fall. For the most part, I was becoming more comfortable in traversing the road that I had chosen. I was learning to accept the fact that perfection was an illusive goal and better left to the imagining of great authors.

I succeeded in gaining confidence in my ability to assist effectively in surgery and suture lacerations, but I would be reminded of my old fears by being assigned to give a report to the class, for example, or by having to assist in a difficult case with a castigating surgeon. Would I ever be totally at ease in this endeavor? Somehow, I was able to accept self-criticism in my flying and woodworking and to retain equanimity through control. Perhaps this was my problem with medicine and with any public display. I feared a loss of control. In spite of this I was soon to graduate and the elation that accompanied this prospect was, in itself, confidence building.

GRADUATION

As I look out over the vast expanse of sea, my mind falls back many years to that day, December 17, 1956, fifty-three years to the day from the "First Flight" at Kitty Hawk by the Wright Brothers. It was a milestone for me. Through education and experience my perspective forever changed; life and sickness and death had new meaning.

What a great day! I purchased an "MD" tag for my car and would install it after the ceremony. My uncle Everett had even come to the airport one Sunday to letter *'The Medic'* on the cowling of the Luscombe. There had been a popular TV program in the 50's entitled, "The Medic" and I had thought it very appropriate that my airplane carry this symbol of my new career. As new physicians, we were proud of the title "Doctor." We wanted to be of service and prepare ourselves to assist at accidents or whenever called upon. I'm not sure when the change began, but in today's society, there are few physicians who display "MD" on their vehicles. Unlisted telephones are more common and Samaritan laws were required to entice doctors back to accident sites or to the aid of a fallen stranger. Now some physicians refuse treatment to patients with AIDS. In the home, care is relegated to nurses and technicians, and the pursuit of the dollar has replaced the pursuit of excellence and the higher calling of personal patient care. Did the physician's unwillingness to come to the ER even when not officially on call eventually lead to the patient's disaffection or did the disaffection of the public and lack of appreciation fuel the physician's lack of concern? Few physicians in the latter part of the twentieth century have escaped some sense of bitterness over what has been lost or perhaps what has been given away. Perhaps, then, it is appropriate that in officialdom "provider" has replaced the revered title "Doctor."

But, on that glorious day in mid December, when I stood with the Class of 1956 to recite the Hippocratic Oath, I wished for nothing more than to live up to my image of the good physician.

Lisa had recently given her engagement ring back to Tom Tosh, and I called to invite her to my graduation. She remained my secret love, but she responded as a friend. I was happy for her friendship although I yearned for more than that. She had obtained a job at Kennedy Hospital in the Microbiology Lab after returning from New Orleans where she had been working on her Master's Degree in Microbiology. She never completed that program in large part because of the harassment of a professor at Tulane. I was about to begin a new adventure as an intern, and we both must have felt that to kindle dormant flames at this juncture would not be wise. In addition, I was preparing for a final fling before settling into the hard work of internship. A classmate, Freddie Lansford and I planned to fly to Florida after Christmas. He was going to intern in Chattanooga, so I could easily drop him there on the way back to Knoxville. I had to report for intern duty in Knoxville on January 1, 1957. Freddie knew several girls at Daytona Beach and promised that I would have a date. I was looking forward to this escape after three years and three months of medical school. Soon many ties would be broken as they are at every fork in the road of life in which each of us takes a new direction.

Frank came by the house on his way to Rogersville and Washington DC. He had graduated number one in his class and had seemed elated on the day of graduation. When he came into the shop that December morning, he seemed subdued, perhaps depressed. We talked briefly about the payments I would make for the airplane. Then he said, "Jeff, there is something I want to tell you. I don't want you to tell anyone else."

"I won't, Frank." I had no idea what he was going to say. Although we had known each other for over three years, I really did not know much about Frank. I had always thought that his parents over indulged him and I knew that he had a nervous affect. He had dated a mutual friend, the daughter of a Memphis dentist, but had just broken up with her and except for the flying trips we had taken together we did not socialize very much. Most of my socializing was spent with Wanda, Marianna, Betty, and Shirley to name a few.

"You know," he continued, "I have always had a strong sex drive."

What's he telling me this for? I wasn't at all sure I wanted to hear more.

"I think I may be homosexual. I just wanted you to know."

Why? Do you think that this will make me think better of you? I thought back to my college days and to the first quarter of medical school when friends had made me quite uncomfortable in what I considered unreasonable demands on my time and attention. Then I recalled a visit to Rogersville a year before to look over the town as an eventual practice site. Frank was visiting his parents and I flew up for the weekend. We toured the east Tennessee area, climbed Roan Mountain and I was pleased to meet his grandfather who owned a hardware and automotive supply store. I bought, at wholesale cost, a professional Black and Decker UniDrill that made the whole trip seem worthwhile. I was ready to start back on Saturday as I had planned but at the insistence of Frank's mother, I agreed to another home cooked dinner as long as I could leave Sunday morning. Frank kept saying, "I wish you would stay," and I began to get that uncomfortable feeling of not being in control. On Sunday, I found myself being pulled from one place to the next. All the while, I was insisting that I had to leave that day. I did not want to hurt Frank's or his family's feelings but late in the afternoon, I prevailed and was reluctantly taken to the grass strip just south of town.

"It's getting dark and you won't be able to take off," he insisted as we drove up to the barn near the south end of the strip.

"Oh yes I will." I replied. I had obtained night experience in cross-country flying with Lynn Armour prior to obtaining my private license so I was legally qualified. There was one problem however. The grass strip had no lights. The sun had set and there was no moon. "Let's drive down the runway then back to this end," I insisted.

Frank did as I suggested as I scanned the runway for obstacles or potholes. At the far end was a fence, and I would be taking off in the opposite direction toward the last glow in the western sky. I checked the Luscombe carefully. My flashlight had fresh batteries and after a quick "goodbye, thanks for the hospitality," Frank obliged by hand propping the Luscombe as I switched both magnetos "on" and the little continental engine popped to life. By holding the flashlight out the left window and by setting the throttle and steering with the rudder pedals, I inched down the runway towards the fence at the far end. Occasionally, a rabbit jumped out of the way and I could see a few cows on the other side of the fence that marked the end of the runway. I had arranged for Frank to park at the other end with his headlights aimed down the runway. I turned the Luscombe around with a blast of prop wash, startling a few cows in the process and saw two rather dim headlights about 2,000 feet away. I stowed the flashlight, checked the engine, checked the controls and pushed the throttle full forward, accelerating slowly into the blackness. I kept the craft heading directly for the lights ahead. There was no other reference. I eased the tail off the turf and as I sensed the weight transferring to wing, I pressured the control stick back gently. The roughness of the ground gave way to the glassy night air and I passed over Frank's car climbing to the west and home. I was glad to be free and in total control once again. *Friends can be a real pain.*

And now, he's telling me something about himself I would prefer not to know. Perhaps I should consider it a compliment that I should be so trusted. "Well—I guess that's your business," I said after a pause.

"I just wanted you to know—since we're friends. I thought maybe you would understand," he said.

I failed to understand at that time; but now I can accept the fact that some humans are biologically predisposed to homosexuality. I didn't know it at the time but he had deeper emotional problems. We shook hands and Frank left for his year of internship. I would see him only four more times in the years to come and would hear of his tragic descent into the darkness of mental illness.

INTERNSHIP

Alone with my thoughts, I fly northeast up the Cumberland Valley toward Knoxville and the beginning of a new venture. It is one thing to be legally referred to as "Doctor Justis", but quite another to do something for or to another human being that may help or hurt. "First—do no harm" is an overwhelming responsibility. Am I ready? I worry, but just as landing is a necessary part of the flight, so facing each day is a necessary part of life.

Four of my classmates, Don Wallace, Aubra Branson, George Barker, and "Durbo" Harrison were also going to intern at the University of Tennessee Memorial Research Center and Hospital. I was fortunate enough to have been given a 1956 Chevrolet as a graduation present from my parents but now I had the problem of getting a car *and* an airplane to Knoxville. George (or Bub as we called him) Barker volunteered to drive my car to Knoxville, because he had no other means of transportation.

As a final expression of freedom, Freddie Lansford, who was to intern in Chattanooga, and I left for Daytona Beach the week after Christmas. We flew the Luscombe to Tuscaloosa, Tallahassee, Jacksonville and south down the silver strip of Florida's east coast to Daytona Beach. We basked in the sun, roasted marshmallows on the beach, and duly impressed our dates, "Yes, we are real doctors now and my airplane is appropriately named The Medic."

Moonlight romance on the beach, dancing in several of the numerous night spots that in later years would draw the young from colleges at spring break filled our evenings and too soon it was time to head back north and begin the serious business of putting into practice all that we had learned in medical school.

George had made it to Knoxville in my Chevrolet and by the time I had tied the Luscombe down on the ramp at Cherokee Aviation on McGee-Tyson Airport, he was there.

"Man, we've got to get us some dates for tonight. It's New Year's Eve", Bub said.

"Yeah, that'd be great but where and how this late?" Actually, I had been looking forward to a quiet New Year's after my week in Daytona.

"Let's call the nurses dorm when we get home," he suggested. "Home" for the next year was to be an early twentieth century, two-story frame house on the University of Tennessee campus converted into a dormitory for use by the single interns and residents at the hospital. Since the hospital was new, the residency programs were not established, so George and I shared the house with Joe Crumley who had finished his internship and surgery residency and who was optimistic enough to start training in orthopaedics before a formal training program was approved.

"Sure, come on over and we'll see. We can't promise anything, though." The young lady at the nurse's dorm several blocks away at least hadn't said "no." George and I showered and dressed and were trying to be gentlemen. We were ushered into the first floor reception room of the University Nurse's dorm. A young lady, watching TV, volunteered to go upstairs and tell Jill and Donna their dates had arrived. In a few minutes two nicely dressed young ladies came down and after we introduced ourselves and they checked us out, they agreed to go out for a short while. We would have to have them back at the dorm by midnight or they would be in trouble with their housemother. We agreed and all of us had a good time at the *Lantern,* one of the many nightclubs on the outskirts of Knoxville. I never dated Jill again but was happy that we had spent the evening together because otherwise it would have been a lonesome New Year's Eve.

Knoxville, in 1957, was in a dry county except for 2.8% beer, but in practice the law made little difference because federally stamped alcohol was readily available and only a "phone call away." Pizza delivery was unheard of then, but an articulate gentleman, after a phone call, would quickly deliver a paper sack covered bottle of scotch or Jack Daniels right to the door of our "house."

At the hospital, I was assigned to the Medicine Floor during the first three months, and although there were three or four staff doctors supervising my work, I soon realized I had to assume a great deal of responsibility for the patients under my care. There were no medical residents, so I answered directly to the staff. I learned the sliding scale to monitor and treat diabetic patients. Diabetic acidosis was a common admitting diagnosis. It seemed to me that "cures" in internal medicine were rare. With the exception of antibiotic treatment for specific infections, we were just holding off the inevitable in advanced hypertension, emphysema, heart failure and other chronic diseases.

We slept in the hospital when we were on call (often 12 hours on then 12 hours off) and one night I was awakened with an emergency call from the nurse on the Medicine Floor. "You'd better come quick! Mr. Johnson can't breathe."

"I'll be right there." I said as I slipped on my white "bucks." We wore scrub suits all the time so in a few minutes I was in Mr. Johnson's room. His presumptive diagnosis was diphtheria, and now before my eyes he was turning blue from lack of oxygen as the diphtheroid plaque blocked his trachea.

"Get me a tracheotomy set, *stat*," I shouted. I wanted to call the staff for help but there was no time. Mr. Johnson was struggling to breathe. I had only seen one tracheotomy as a student and I hoped I could remember the landmarks. I didn't need any local anesthetic as my patient had lost consciousness by the time I made a midline incision just below the cricoid cartilage. There was a "whosh" of air as I incised the trachea and spread it open with a hemostat.

Mr. Johnson's chest expanded with life-giving air. I tied the tracheotomy tube in place and stayed in the room a long time to be sure all was well. I felt then that if I did nothing else worthwhile in my medical career, the gratification from helping this one patient was worth all the struggle and anxiety that had gone before.

"One of the student nurses is in room 410—a Miss S," the chief floor nurse told me one morning near the end of my medical rotation. "You need to work her up for Dr. Smithfield."

That was another thing I didn't like about medicine—the workups. The past histories were usually complex and with many patients the review of systems precipitated a litany of complaints. What a pleasant surprise when I saw Miss S. Shirley was a pleasant twenty-year-old with long black hair and a sensuous smile.

It was difficult to adhere to all of the precepts of the Hippocratic Oath while attempting to perform even an abbreviated physical exam. Fortunately, her complaint was of a sore throat and swollen glands and her diagnosis was that of a disease I was all too familiar with—infectious mononucleosis, resolving. I would see much of her in the months to come.

Surgery rotation was to be exciting, since I was leaning in the direction of specializing in the surgical arts. I was more comfortable seeing the result of something I did immediately than in the delayed gratification necessary in the medical management of a problem. An additional enticement was the mechanical nature of hands-on work. If the medical profession could be so categorized then internists are white-collar workers and surgeons are blue-collar counterparts.

The staff surgeons were generous to me and many of the young interns in letting us do many of the cases we worked up. Gallbladders, appendectomies and hemorrhoidectomies were "ours." Hemorrhoidectomies were not particularly sought after, however, and abscesses were especially avoided. One Saturday, however, no one else was available as a thin, very sick diabetic patient was rolled into the OR with what apparently was a perirectal abscess. We drained a foul smelling, purulent mass to the left of this man's rectum, but within hours the patient's temperature spiked to 105 degrees and the crepitance of subcutaneous gas could be felt under the bluish discolored skin of his buttock, hip and left thigh. Necrotizing fasciitis secondary to anaerobic streptococcus is deadly, especially in diabetics. Hurriedly, the staff doctor and I took the patient back to the OR for debridement. As we incised the skin, necrosis from vascular compromise was apparent. We cut away dead skin and fascia exposing muscle. The damage was extensive – down the thigh to the knee and around to the umbilicus on the abdomen. We were skinning this patient alive. As a youngster I had been impressed by a painting in Mexico of a martyred Saint who was being skinned alive. At least our patient was under anesthesia.

"He may not make it, Justis", Dr. Schmidt said as we applied dressings to the massive wound. "If he lives, we'll have to do multiple skin grafts to get this wound covered." Subsequently, the patient's post operative course was consistently down hill and four days later the combination of diabetic vasculitis, septicemia, and fluid imbalance took it's toll and our patient was saved from further surgery by his death.

I was quite proud of my accomplishments in surgery; I had gained in confidence and was not intimidated by the staff. Dr. Rothstein was a new general surgery resident who had been culled from a northeastern residency program that utilized the pyramid system. Even though the UT program was not yet approved, he came for the experience. He didn't stay long.

"Where the hell is Rothstein", Dr. Jones shouted to the OR supervisor. "This is his case and he's late. Come on Justis, you'll do this resection."

Gratefully I had read the surgery text the night before and was able to intelligently describe a bowel resection for diverticulitis. As we donned our gowns and gloves, Rothstein burst through the door.

"I – I'm sorry I'm late," he said breathlessly.

Dr. Jones didn't even look up; it was not the first time Rothstein had been late. "Here Justis, you do the case." Dr. Jones handed me the scalpel.

Rothstein finished scrubbing and came into the OR suite. If he was expecting to do this case he was disappointed, because as soon as he came up to the table Dr. Jones said, "Here. You hold the retractors for Dr. Justis—it's his case now."

Later during my surgical rotation my Dad visited the hospital during a trip to Knoxville for a dental meeting. He was able to observe as I did an appendectomy with Dr. Jones supervising. I think the pride he felt at that time washed away any residual misgiving he may have had about my choice of medicine over dentistry.

Meanwhile, my social life continued on the weekends and nights when I was not on call at the hospital. Some friends said later that I should have known or suspected. Be that as it may, when I stopped by the hospital pharmacy one day to check on a patient's prescription, the petite, redheaded pharmacy tech intrigued me with her questions about flying, obviously a subject I was eager to discuss. One thing led to another and before I knew it, we were planning a flight together the following Saturday.

"Do you want me to pick you up at your house?" I asked as we discussed our "date."

"No," she said rather emphatically. "I'd rather meet you at the airport." Perhaps I didn't want to know more, so I didn't ask any questions.

Late Saturday afternoon, I was checking out the Luscombe when Betty arrived dressed in a rather form-fitting sweater and slacks. It was all I could do to concentrate on the job of being sure the plane was ready for flight. Once airborne for a lazy flight over the valley and lakes southwest of Knoxville, I relaxed a bit in spite of the tremendous distraction that occupied the right seat of that Luscombe. As I maneuvered the craft in gentle turns she pressed her thigh against mine, and the smell of her perfume further intoxicated me. Flying under such circumstances certainly had to be unwise, although unlike the rules relating to alcohol or drugs, the Civil Air Regulations made no mention of flying under the influence of a rather sexy young lady.

I did get the plane safely on the ground, however, and was invited to follow her home. She said she had made some arrangements and wanted to fix my dinner. It bothered me that she wanted me to park a block from her house and that later she rushed to the front of the house to check on some noise she heard.

"What are you so jumpy about?" I asked rather naively.

"Well, he's not supposed to be in town, but he might come back early."

"Who?" I asked.

"My husband, that's who."

"You mean—you mean—you're married?"

"Yes! I thought you knew. I don't wear a ring 'cause he and I don't get along so well. He's too jealous. All my friends know."

"Well —I—I didn't," I stammered.

Here I was again caught in an uncomfortable situation, yet somehow I rationalized, *Hadn't she wanted to fly with me? Hadn't she invited me to her home for dinner?*

"So what if he comes." I said rather foolishly. "You can tell him I'm just a friend can't you?"

"You don't know Jim. He comes from Harlan, Kentucky; they're clannish up there. If he found you here he'd bring his cousins to Knoxville to get even with you."

"Maybe I'd better leave now," I said as I imagined the potential problems I could face.

"You might as well stay for dinner now," she said as she pulled the lasagna from the oven.

I didn't want to seem ungrateful, and I didn't want to show the nagging fear I was experiencing, so I ate the dinner, said goodbye, and drove back to my quarters.

I kept one eye on the rearview mirror and more than once imagined a car full of Kentucky rednecks closing from behind, vowing to avenge a jealous husband.

I avoided the pharmacy for several days but was brought back to reality by a call from the administrator's office. "Dr. Justis, there's a man in my secretaries office who claims you've been messing around with his wife. Is that true?"

I explained that I didn't know she was married when we went out and that I had no intention of seeing her again, and I certainly didn't want to confront her husband. The administrator protected his intern the best he could and apparently convinced Betty's irate husband that I would not be a threat to him. I learned later that Betty had used me to spark his jealousy, apparently deriving some perverse pleasure in those antics. Rumors persisted that Betty's husband wanted revenge.

I confided my fears to Aubra Branson, and he immediately suggested that I protect myself with a firearm. I was certainly not a violent person and cannot conceive of ever being an aggressor—especially if armed, but I could, at that time and now, conceive of defending myself if necessary.

So I filled out the required state forms and purchased a .22 caliber Colt target pistol. Don Wallace, a gun enthusiast, and I occasionally went target shooting, and I kept the gun hidden away just in case. I have it to this day.

The triangle misadventure gradually faded in significance as the dreaded imagined "redneck's revenge" never occurred and Betty channeled her energies on other young men to keep her husband fired with jealous rage. It was a dangerous game, and I had learned a valuable lesson.

I would be certain that any young lady I went out with in the future was not married. Later, I was to discover that even that precaution might not be sufficient.

I was alone in a dark sky. Landing at night especially without a landing light gives one the same feeling as descending into a bottomless pit. The runway lights provide guidance to the black hole that must be the runway. Maintain a gentle rate of descent with partial power, feeling gingerly for the squeak-squeak of the tires. Then apply slight forward stick pressure and keep the plane tracking down the runway on its two main wheels until finally the stick can be brought full back holding the tail wheel onto the Tarmac. A "wheel landing" is the only way to land at night without a landing light. To attempt a "three point" landing is to guess at the height above the dark pavement: too low and a bounce is inevitable; too high and a stall with loss of control might result in damage to the airplane—or worse.

I'm not sure what prompted me to work toward a commercial pilot's license during my internship. It was not a matter of trying to fill spare time for there was precious little of that. Rather it was the realization that with two hundred hours of flight time in my logbook, this accomplishment was within my grasp. I did not want a commercial license restricted to daylight flying only but I needed five hours of night cross country experience to get an unrestricted license; coincidentally, the written portion of the Florida State Medical Board Examination scheduled in Gainesville in the spring of 1957 provided a good excuse for a long trip. Stamina was no problem at age 24, so a day working in the emergency room seemed no obstacle to an all night adventure.

"You're what?" an incredulous emergency room nurse exclaimed when I told her my plans.

"Yeah – I'm leaving in a few minutes for the airport. Want to go?" I was being nice. Actually I preferred to make the flight alone. Besides, there was this girl in Daytona, but that's another story.

"No. Aren't you afraid to fly after dark?" Her eyes expressed concern. "How do you find your way?"

I told her how navigating by the towns and highways at night was often easier than in daylight because each town stood alone like a cluster of stars in a dark sky and that airport rotating green and white beacons could be seen for miles. There were, in 1957, a few remaining lighted airway markers and even a few low frequency ranges. Listening for the dot-dash and dash-dot signals that blended into a single sound gave rise to the old expression of "flying the beam." Of course, in those days, the single radio in my Luscombe 8A was used primarily for communication with control towers and with CAA radio facilities now called flight service stations. I did not have an instrument rating and all of my navigation was by reference to the ground.

"Good luck," my friend said and at about 6:00 p.m. I drove to the airport to begin my adventure.

Dusk filled the valley before me as I guided the small aluminum craft toward Chattanooga. This part of the flight was relatively easy because the valley between the Smokies and Cumberland Plateau funneled all the ground traffic and lights toward Look-Out Mountain. After refueling at Lovell Field, I departed in the dark for Fulton County Airport near Atlanta. In today's aviation environment, landing or taking off without a landing light can become an emergency procedure. But in 1957, in my small craft, a landing light would have been a luxury. The wind-driven generator barely maintained my battery charge when the navigation lights were on and I routinely turned off my radio once away from the airport traffic area. Taxiing slowly and occasionally using a flashlight held out the left window to spot the edge of the taxiway seemed reasonably prudent at that time.

Past Look-Out Mountain the mountains give way to rolling hills and fewer ground lights so I was careful in comparing my map with what I could see below and ahead. There was a high overcast so the darkness of the night was complete, and only the comfort and security of this cabin—this womb as it were—kept the sense of isolation from being oppressive.

Flying over the darkened earth a pilot considers the possibility of engine failure but reasons that through training and practice for such contingencies, he can survive such an event. I had invested in a set of three "Kilgore" parachute flares and had practiced the 360-degree overhead approach that would be required to pick a field and make an emergency landing. Of course, I prefer trusting the reliability of the power plant to the reliability of surplus flares that could at worst explode in my hand or at best fizzle their way to the ground below me. Nevertheless, the thought of having an option provided some comfort in the darkness that surrounded me.

Soon enough the tell tale glow of a great city reflected on the clouds; then discrete lights broke through the darkness as I decreased power and lined up with the runway at Fulton County. It was nearly ten o'clock and to the south, I could see an occasional lightning flash brightening the overcast. Thunderstorms, beautiful in their awesome power, are to be given a wide berth by a wise pilot much as an Alaskan trapper would avoid direct confrontation with a Grizzly.

"You're going out again?" The lineman was ready to go home, but was kind enough to fuel the Luscombe before leaving.

"I'm going to check the weather," I replied, "but I plan to go on to Florida."

"You in a hurry?"

"No, I'm just trying to get some night experience."

It was obvious he wouldn't consider doing what I was doing. "Need to see where I'm going," he muttered.

There's an overcast at seven thousand with scattered imbedded thunderstorms. They're more prevalent along the coast but they seem to be decreasing in intensity, the *CAA* station manager read from his Teletype report. *Visibilities are running ten miles or better so I doubt that you'll have any trouble getting to Tallahassee. Just stay away from those thunderstorms,* he warned.

Most of the men working in the CAA "shacks" were extremely helpful and friendly, especially those working the night shift.

"You be careful. I'll open your flight plan for you once you take off," he offered.

A flight plan wasn't required but made sense. Someone would know I was overdue if I did not arrive at my destination, and the Civil Air Patrol could be called into action to begin a search. Otherwise, an aircraft could remain hidden for months under an unbroken canopy of forest or swamp.

The lighted outline of Atlanta came into view once again on climbing out to the South. *Keep a steady compass heading and watch for checkpoints.* If you know where you are when you start and you can see the next ground reference point, navigation over long distances becomes a one-step-at-a-time exercise. The trick is to pick reliable and easily distinguished checkpoints. Towns and lighted airports are the best; prominent highways and lighted towers help. But railroads and rivers at night are hard to spot unless a train with its oscillating headlight happens along its track or the moon reflects on a meandering river or lake.

What was that? A flash illuminated a dark mass several miles ahead. The few ground lights in the area seemed to disappear under a dark, broad shaft extending from the overcast to the ground. Another flash. *A rain column! I'm glad I saw that. I'd better deviate to the east.* I was having a smooth flight so far but knew that venturing too close to the rain pouring from its overhead cumulus source would give me the ride of a lifetime—perhaps a final roller coaster ride to oblivion.

The Luscombe and I were soon around the monster but ahead lightning revealed another—and another. The airplane and I threaded our way around these sentinels of southern Georgia and north Florida until finally the runway at Tallahassee was beneath our wheels. After midnight all but the busiest airports are lonesome places. In 1957 at Tallahassee, the CAA operator was the only one manning the entire airport.

"I doubt if the airport manager will come out this time of night," the operator said as I told him my plans to continue on to Jacksonville. The little Luscombe only held fifteen gallons of fuel, and I suppose it would have been inconsiderate to insist on his coming for such a small profit.

"Tell you what. You can use my car. There's an Amoco station down the road. Lots of guys use hi-test unleaded in their planes down here," the station manager offered generously.

I knew that some auto fuels contained too much lead and might foul the spark plugs in the sixty-five horsepower continental engine.

"Unleaded hi test? Has anyone had any trouble with it?"

"Not that I know of."

Somewhat reassured and wanting to press on, I refueled the airplane, filtering the gas through a borrowed chamois. The CAA manager said he would return the gas can to the service station in the morning, so I was soon on my way. There were no more thunderstorms, but the Okefenokee Swamp lies between Tallahassee and Jacksonville. As I flew over the vast darkened landscape, I recalled stories of lost pilots and aircraft and of the hazards awaiting any hapless pilot who attempted to walk out of the swamp. I resolved to remain with my airplane if forced down in this unforgiving area.

No problem developed and soon the eastern coast and Jacksonville came into view. The lights of the city abruptly ended at the coast, giving the illusion that the edge of a flat earth was just ahead.

The remainder of the flight was without challenge except that (even at age 24) fatigue was creeping into consciousness. Landing at Daytona Beach, just as the sun broke into the morning sky, I entered a new day of people and activity that contrasted with the solitude of the evening before—just as the compilation of hours in my logbook contrasts with the remembrance of that brief time in my life.

After spending some time with Beth, the young lady I had met when Freddy and I had flown down in December, I flew over to Gainesville for the Board Examination and then back to Knoxville, confident that I had done well on the written test. I had no real intention of practicing in Florida, but had been advised that having a license would be worthwhile in case I retired there someday.

As an intern with an airplane, I found myself in a unique position with some of the staff. The pathologist, Dr. Franks, was well known for his flying adventures, and I eagerly accepted an invitation to fly with him in what at that time was a sophisticated airplane, a Piper Tri Pacer. Flying in a four seater was a real thrill and I remember hoping that someday I, too, could have a plane with the latest electronic equipment and more horsepower and room. One of the staff physicians, an ear, nose and throat doctor, asked me to fly with him to Middleboro, Kentucky. It was only after we had returned to Knoxville that I found an explanation for his rather erratic flying and slurred communication. Tom Kesterson once again tried to provide some protection for the I pilots utilizing his facility. "Dr. Smith is an alcoholic and he's been known to "tip a few" before a flight." *I wish I had known before I flew with him,*

I never had the opportunity to fly with another flying physician, Bob Lash, a pioneer cardiac surgeon. But, perhaps because I was a pilot he requested that I help in an upcoming open-heart case—the patient also was a pilot.

"This'll be the first time we've done this procedure," Dr. Lash confided as we scrubbed. In those days there was no heart-lung machine and any surgery performed was accomplished at great risk on a beating heart. "We're going to try to open a congenital constriction in the aorta," Dr. Lash explained. "This patient won't be able to fly anymore unless we fix this problem, but it's pretty risky. Come on Justis, let's do our best for this fellow pilot."

And we tried.

"Hold pressure here – that's good, now I'll open the heart here."

The warm heart exposed by large rib retractors, beat regularly at first but seemed to flutter at our touch. The lungs inflated to the anesthetist's rhythm.

"Uh oh, he's fibrillating," Dr. Lash shouted. "Hand me that epinephrine syringe." He plunged the needle deep into the heart muscle. No response. Again. No change. The heart was still. Then, with resignation, "I'm afraid we've lost him."

It was over quickly and our hopes for this pilot, this patient were gone. Once again we choked back our own emotions as we tried to explain to this man's wife why she would now be a widow. Dr. Lash had done a masterful job of preparing her for such an eventuality, but it was still hard and I found yet another aspect of medicine that I would forever be uncomfortable with.

All of us in the intern years talked about the "what ifs." What if we had to help a patient with a cardiac arrest away from the hospital.

"I'll tell you what I'd do," Don said confidently. "I always carry a surgical kit just so I could open a chest if I had to."

"Yeah, but what's wrong with just using intracardiac epinephrine?"

"If I had it I'd use it but, but I'd open anyone's chest if I could not get a pulse."

We all worried about making a mistake, but in the days before CPR, opening the chest was the only option we had to save a patient in cardiac arrest. During my rotation covering the emergency room, I often felt on edge when considering what might happen; however, the worry was often worse than what I was actually faced with.

"Dr. Justis, come quick—we've got a man struck by lightning." I was on daytime ER this time and had just come back from lunch. "He was playing golf when he was hit. It happened about ten minutes ago," the nurse said breathlessly as she led me to the treatment room. The middle-aged patient was lying face up on the stretcher. His face was blue and his clothes were dripping wet. He was wearing white shorts and his legs had purplish marks as if each blade of grass had been imprinted on his skin. He was cold and unresponsive. I could hear no heartbeat. I hesitated just a second then said, "Get me the open heart tray." The nurse responded and I grabbed the #20 scalpel and quickly made a curved incision following the ribs just below his left nipple. I cut through the intercostal muscles and heard a slight "whoosh" as I entered the chest cavity. It took both hands and considerable effort to stretch the ribs open and I was unable to get the rib retractor set properly so I plunged my hand into his chest feeling for the heart. There was some warmth still but no motion, not even fibrillation could be felt in this organ. I squeezed. I could feel blood moving in the heart but refill was slow. I squeezed some more. My hand ached. The ribs closed about my wrist cutting off the circulation to my hand. With the nurse's help and with my free left hand we managed to get a retractor between the patient's ribs and with the pressure off my wrist I was able to continue pumping on this golfer's heart. I think I knew he was dead on arrival but at that time in my training I felt I should try something.

"Good job, Justis," the attending said when he finally arrived. He had also been playing golf and was still wearing his golf shoes. "I think you can stop now—he's dead—see—pupils fixed and dilated."

This acceptance of death and dying was nothing new to him but to me it was still something I was uncomfortable with. Yet becoming a physician does not give one extraordinary powers—just ordinary human capability channeled into a specific endeavor. We are all subservient to the natural laws to which we owe our existence; circumstance and chance and perhaps even the patterns of chaos determine our success or failure as much as our self determination. But we can and must try.

It was during my daytime emergency room rotation that I would occasionally fly to Memphis at night. I thought nothing of leaving the ER at 6:00 pm on a Friday, going by the quarters for my bag, and taking off from McGee-Tyson Airport about 7:30. I'd refuel in Chattanooga and then fly past Lookout Mountain to stop again in Huntsville or Decatur. It was during these visits that Lisa and I began dating once more—a very tentative exploration of feelings. Was I ready? Was she ready? I was unsure and I felt there should be no doubt. "Besides, this ER rotation is a killer," I rationalized and occasionally I was right.

"Dr. Justis, Dr. *Justis*," the nurse banged hard on the door of the "on call" room as she shouted my name. "We've got a guy hit in the head with an ax. We need you." I was back on the night shift. It was 2:00 am. I rolled out of the cot with a tinge of anxiety at what might confront me, and quickly entered the emergency room. As I threw back the curtain I saw a large black man on the gurney, his hair matted in blood, which still oozed out of multiple scalp lacerations dripping slowly onto the stretcher and floor. In spite of blood loss, the patient's vital signs were good.

"He's drunk," the nurse said. "God must protect drunks and children."

The patient was sleeping and hardly stirred as I started my work; irrigate and sew, irrigate and sew. The smell of blood and alcohol was strong in the small space. It seemed an endless task as I began to repair each gaping wound. If the patient could only remember what infraction precipitated his wife's attack, perhaps he could avoid a repeat session in the emergency room. Scars elsewhere on his body belied the use of good judgment, however. After several hours of work, I felt I had gained a *lot* of experience in suturing. *I think I'll try a horizontal mattress suture on this one; maybe I'll use a running stitch on this cut; let's see, let's try a vertical mattress on this two inch cut.* After finishing that suturing marathon, I was glad to get off at 6:00 am and I didn't have to be back until 6:00 pm. Twelve on and twelve off for three months with a few weekends off in between was the routine.

Originally, each intern (of the first group at the University of Tennessee Hospital) was paid the princely sum of seventy-five dollars a month plus room and board. After six months of twelve hours on, twelve hours off and the stress of being awakened to some test of our abilities and judgment, many of us decided we needed more pay. After all, I had to support an airplane—even though gas was only 25 or 30 cents a gallon and my parking fee five dollars a month. One day we marched en-mass to the administrator's office. After making our request, we were informed that if we didn't like the arrangement we could leave any time. The administrator had called our bluff. We couldn't leave, of course, and we weren't sure how much we were needed; fortunately the medical staff was on our side and later our salaries were increased to $125 a month.

After a hard week, George and I were pleased to spend a Saturday at Jim Smith's lake house on Douglas Lake. Jim was a young dentist who contracted with UT Hospital for the dental care of charity patients. He knew of my dad. (Most dentists I had met had heard of my dad who had been treasurer of the American Dental Association for nearly 20 years.) We became friends. He was a bachelor also, so George and I looked forward to the afternoon. He had invited several single women that he had met previously and after a while I struck up a conversation with Norma. After my previous experiences in Murphreesboro and with Betty, I was cautious enough to ask, "Are you married?"

"No, I'm divorced; I've been divorced about six months," she replied.

I relaxed a bit. Norma was probably thirty at the time, an attractive blonde and quite mature compared to the young nursing students (bound by curfew).

We spent the afternoon drinking beer and lounging around the pool and deck at Jim's cottage overlooking the lake. His boat house floated off shore 30 feet down the embankment.

"Let's take the boat and go over to the Dock House Restaurant for dinner", Jim suggested as the sun slowly streaked the lake in gold and purple. The mahogany inboard CrisCraft rumbled to a start, and we climbed in for the thirty-minute ride across the lake. The lake was glass smooth and the running lights reflected green and red in the water as pinpoint stars began to fill the blackness overhead.

It was a romantic evening to be sure, but as we approached the pier behind which a bright neon sign signaled "Baileys" Norma grabbed my arm. "Oh, we can't go in here."

"Why not?" I asked.

"I've been here before with my ex-husband. I think he comes here a lot."

"Well, you are divorced aren't you?"

"Yes, but he's—he's still jealous."

"I don't see why he should be if you're divorced," I reasoned.

"You don't know Bill!"

Now here we were again. How had I managed to get myself into this kind of situation once more? You'd think anyone smart enough to get through medical school would be able to detect potential trouble; perhaps it's true that most physicians are as socially inept as they are inept at business.

We could not sit out dinner in the boat, and I was not about to admit that I had concerns, so I said strongly, after swallowing an inexplicable lump in my throat, "Come on, Norma, I'll protect you if he gives you any trouble."

Her hands were clammy but she relaxed a bit as we entered the dimly lit restaurant-bar.

"Thank goodness he's not here," she said as we sat down at a long table covered with a red and white-checkered oilcloth. We ordered fried chicken, slaw, and potatoes and while waiting I began to tell Jim about some of my flying adventures. I was vaguely aware of commotion behind me but didn't stop talking to Jim until I noticed that Norma had gotten up from the table. Someone had grabbed her by her arm and was shouting obscenities louder and louder. "You bitch; you know I told you not come in here!"

Bill, Norma's ex, had apparently just come in with a few of his friends.

"And I told you if I saw you with another man—I'd..."

Instinctively I stood up; I was going to explain to this unreasonable fellow that I felt Norma should be free to do as she pleased. She *was* divorced after all. I turned, ready to calmly discuss the situation when—WHAM!—my head flew back, the momentum throwing me back onto the table. I was stunned, my lip was bleeding; then I realized what had happened. The "flight or fight," adrenal reaction began and I jumped to my feet and lunged toward the source of my pain and humiliation. I never liked fighting as a child and although in grammar school I had pleaded for some boxing gloves, I was never comfortable hitting someone else. I would hold back; therefore I would usually be on the receiving end in any boxing match. This time, however, I had been struck aggressively and in an unprovoked manner. I had to defend myself; so my emotions told me. By then George and Jim had gotten up and both of them grabbed my shoulders and kept me from moving forward. Apparently, Bill's friends had seen him lash out at me and were pulling him back.

"Let me go! That son-of-a-bitch hit me," I shouted.

"No—it's not worth it Jeff." George pulled hard on my shoulder and arm.

"Bill, please leave me alone, please," Norma pleaded.

"Come on Bill—you gotta let her go—she ain't worth it," Bill's friends pleaded.

Finally, the restaurant manager talked Bill and his friends into leaving with promises of a free meal the next day.

I was shaking but slowly calming down. Norma squeezed my arm and said, "Thank you, now you see what I was worried about. That's one reason I got a divorce—he's crazy."

We finished dinner, although I had a little trouble eating chicken with a swollen lip. I was subdued on the ride back across the lake and wondered to myself what might have happened had my friends not intervened. I'm glad I was not tested on that occasion and vowed to use better judgment in the future. It may have been that event that began the process of domestication that leads a bachelor to consider the virtues of married life. Settling down! Men are not born married but at some time must consider a future beyond Saturday dates.

During my internship year I enjoyed (at least to some degree) all of my rotations. I liked the physical specialties the best, as opposed to those quiet, contemplative specialties such as internal medicine, radiology, pathology, etc. Even OB/GYN had some attraction in spite of my ineptitude in allowing a primipara to precipitate during medical school. With a competent OB nurse, even an intern can be made to look good.

"Dr. Justis, Mrs. Graves is ready in room two. She's completely dilated!" I walked into the delivery room. Mrs. Graves was already in stirrups.

"Don't push, Helen. Don't push! Take a deep breath—another—take a deep breath." The nurse, monitoring the fetus with a stethoscope, coached the young mother who was alternately panting and grunting with an occasional, "It's coooming—it's cooming."

The head was crowning, stretching the thinned perineum. *Man, she'll tear if I don't hurry.* I quickly injected some local anesthetic into the perineum overlying the black-haired object trying to exit its confines. I then took the curved "mayo" scissors and cut obliquely across the lower left aspect of her stretched out vagina.

"Now push! Push!" I shouted. The nurse pressed on her bulging uterus. Suddenly, there was a head in front of me. I suctioned the little mouth and nose with a rubber bulb syringe. Then, with a gentle tug and the able assistance of the mother, first the left, then the right shoulder delivered. With the head serving as an effective battering ram, the remainder of the baby slid into my arm. Slick and slippery, I tried to cradle the newborn on my left arm with my index and middle fingers on each side of its neck. Suddenly the baby slid off to the side.

"Damn!" I had to lower my arms nearly to the floor to keep from dropping my charge. Finally, with everything under control I was able to cut and tie the cord, deliver the placenta, and place the now crying baby boy into a bassinet. I repaired the episiotomy with the hope that the rather extensive scar would not be a source of future contention between my patient and her husband.

Later during that rotation, I was called STAT to the newborn nursery. It seems a nurse had been trying to remove a bandage from an infant's foot. The rather large bandage scissors had cleanly amputated the child's fifth toe; the nurse was in shock and had much more trouble handling the accident than did the baby's mother. There was nothing to do, of course, except to sew up the wound and accept the loss, which certainly was minimal cosmetically and functionally. Most people were much more accepting of medical accidents in those days than in the litigious times in which we now live.

With time slipping by and with yet no firm idea of specializing, I began to consider the future. I had gained in confidence, and when one of the staff suggested that I contact the mayor of Wartburg, Tennessee about practicing there, I began fantasizing about small town practice. Although I was only 24 years old, I was invited by all of the VIP's of that small community. A local dentist (he also knew my dad) was in charge of physician recruitment. After a day of showing me around and dining me and offering me a clinic building at no cost and guaranteeing a salary, my ego had appropriately enlarged and under some pressure, I said I would give it a try. They wished I could start now but were willing to wait until I had completed my internship.

I drove back to Knoxville thinking of all the people I would cure, the responsible roll I would have in the community and the babies I would deliver. *Deliver? Did they mention home delivery?*

There was no delivery room in the clinic, there was no knowledgeable delivery room nurse, I would be called at any hour to find my way to some woman's home in the country and alone help her deliver a baby. What if—my imagination ran wild and I broke out in a cold sweat at the thought of a placenta previa or other complication. A seed of doubt began to grow.

"Aubrey, tell me what you know about Wartburg," I asked my good friend who had grown up in east Tennessee.

"I know they can't keep any docs. They've built a great clinic but the longest anyone has stayed is one year."

"How come?"

"Hell, they kill'em in that time. On call all the time! They expect the doc to be at their beckon call—especially for the big-wheels in town."

"They told me they'd give me time to fly my airplane and have some weekends off."

"I wouldn't count on it", Aubra offered. "You better get out of that deal."

I was beginning to feel trapped in a situation of my own making. The more I learned about Wartburg and the medical situation there, the more concerned I became. In 1958, doctors were subject to a doctor draft, and I had duly registered with selective service after graduation from medical school. I had no way of knowing when or if I would have to serve, but the thought occurred to me that perhaps the military would be a way out. In high school I had secretly wished for the draft to help delay important decision-making. Now, wishing would not be necessary. I had not signed up on the Berry Plan, a government program which would have allowed me to complete a residency before serving, simply because I had no idea what specialty I would choose.

I contacted the Air Force medical recruitment office. There was no question about the branch of service. I was a pilot after all. The enticements to volunteer were significant. Time in the reserves for pay purposes began on graduation; one could get full credit for service time from sign up until entering active duty; I would be a 1st Lieutenant on sign up but would become a captain on entering active duty; and I would not have to go on active duty until July 1959.

This became an easy decision; the reality of solo practice in a small town had overwhelmed the idyllic dream; I could serve in the military as a physician and later decide on a specialty.

"Dr. Bowen, this is Jeff Justis in Knoxville. I-I'm afraid I'm not going to be able to come to Wartburg next year."

"Oh no—please don't tell me that. Everyone's been counting on you." Dr. Bowen, the local dentist sounded truly disappointed. "What's happened?"

"Well, the Air Force has called me."

"Oh, don't worry; this town needs you. We can get you deferred."

"Well, I'm already committed," I protested as I began to get that trapped feeling. I had taken the Oath of Office several days before and was officially in the Air Force Reserves.

"We can probably pull some strings to get you out," he persisted.

"No, I really think I should do my part. I'll talk with some of the other interns about Wartburg," I offered.

"We are terribly disappointed, you've let us down," he said just before hanging up. Of course, I knew they were disappointed, but, in a way, I felt they had been less than candid about what they expected of me or perhaps I had been blinded by misplaced enthusiasm for a dream. Joining the Air Force, however, is a decision I have never regretted. Much like my decision to learn to fly or to go into medicine as a career, my life has been fuller as a result.

GUN RUNNER

Memories are bits and pieces of an encoded past. What we may wish to recall with clarity—what we perceived as important at the time—may elude us. Yet some event or inconsequential personal thought may intrude on our consciousness and bring forth old emotions buried by day-to-day living.

1957 was an exciting year. I was in the middle of my internship and a future full of opportunity was ahead. The 1948 Luscombe 8A that I had purchased from my former airplane partner for $625 (my total investment was only $1,100), was my key to adventure, and I did not hesitate when any excuse for a flight arose. Having previously passed the first part of the Florida Medical Boards, I was eligible to be interviewed for the second and (it turned out) the most critical part. My reason for wanting a Florida license was the reason for most rejections. The local medical community did not want doctors to have a license unless they were committed to begin practicing after completing their training. I'm afraid I approached the whole process almost as a lark—and that attitude was apparent to my interviewer.

The examination was to be in Miami on June 24th. It so happened that my good friend from medical school, Marianna M., was staying with an aunt at Miami Beach and was going to go to Havana, Cuba for three days with a friend. Batista's Cuba was a favorite destination for Americans and Floridians in particular and having just obtained my commercial license and having read about the adventure of flying over water, I found the combination of enticements too much to pass up. Thus, the medical examination and interview took a back seat to the more exciting flight planning of another adventure.

June 20th saw the beginning of my venture with an hour and forty-minute flight from Knoxville to Atlanta. On to Albany, Georgia, then in the dark of the night over wood and swamp to Valdosta and Jacksonville, the Luscombe and I continued. I remained overnight in Daytona, and visited a friend from medical school, Ed Lindsey, in Orlando and arrived in Miami the evening of June 23rd.

After the interview the following morning, I was ready to enjoy the Miami area. Marianna was happy to hear my voice.

"My aunt wants you to stay with us."

I demurred, "That's not necessary."

"I know, but I want you to stay."

Marianna and I had dated in medical school. I had flown her to Mobile to see her mother while in medical school and had taken her on a few local adventures to Horseshoe Lake, Blue Lake and Maddox Bay. She was one quarter behind me and we were more than just friends, although my internship had put miles between us both physically and emotionally. But, I was still attracted to her, so when I heard "I want you to stay" it didn't take long for me to agree. Marianna and I did have fun together. However, she was more serious about our dating than was I. This was to become quite obvious soon.

"That was a wonderful dinner," I said to Marianna's aunt.

"I'm glad you enjoyed it – now why don't you two go out to the beach and enjoy yourselves?"

"Can't we help you clean up?"

"Come on Jeff; the sun will set shortly, and I want you to see the Atlantic Ocean at dusk." Marianna grabbed my hand and led me out the door onto the path to the beach. "Isn't it beautiful?"

"Sure is."

We sat under a palm tree, looking over the darkening blue sea. The buildings along the beach had an orange glow from the sunset, and sea birds swooped low over the waves.

"Jeff, I know you love me," Marianna said quietly as she reached for my hand.

"Yes I do, Marianna." I answered after a pause.

"Then why don't we get married?" I half expected that—I had sensed it building for a long time—but still...

"I—I—I do love you—but—but I'm just not ready to get married yet. Don't you see? I've got too much adventuring to do—too many places to fly."

"I can go with you—don't *you* see?"

"But being married—that's different. Besides, I'm going into the Air Force. No telling where they'll send me."

I did not want to hurt her, because I did care for her, but I wasn't ready to get married.......or was I. Lisa remained in my thoughts.

We sat in silence for a time as the boat lights began to sparkle on the horizon. I could sense that she was silently crying, and it made me sad that I was responsible for her unhappiness—yet I felt a release.

"Come help me plan my flight to Cuba. We'll have a good time together while we're there." I tried to be cheerful.

The next morning she drove me to Tamiami airport; and we made arrangements to meet at the Grand Havana Hotel in two days.

I prepared N71478 for her maiden over water flight. The first leg was a one hour, thirty-five minute flight to Key West with easy navigation along Highway 101 past Marathon Key and on to the southeastern tip of the United States. The green, sand-rimmed keys were placed like stepping stones in the blue water off southern Florida. Boat wakes patterned the sea below and the shadows of cumulus clouds sprinkled false islands in the distance. Time passed quickly and soon the airplane tires squeaked onto the pavement of Key West International Airport. I was able to rent a life vest complete with shark repellant and emergency flares, but I didn't have room for a life raft. Besides, who at age 24 doesn't feel immortality coursing in his veins? My navigational equipment was simple—compass and eyes. I did have a very high frequency (VHF) transmitter and a low frequency (LF) receiver, primarily for communication with control towers, but it was also able to receive the low frequency four-course range signals that could be used to track in one of four directions. The technique involved listening for a signal tone when tuned to the station. With the aircraft on the centerline of the course the signal was constant. If one drifted to one side of the course an increasing dot-dash-dot-dash signal was heard and if to the other side a dash-dot-dash-dot signal. I planned to take up a compass heading of roughly 180° and check the range signal as a backup. Since the airplane was equipped with a low voltage wind-driven generator, I preferred to save my battery by turning off the radio except in the terminal area.

    I filed an international flight plan for Havana, estimating arrival in approximately one hour and fifteen minutes. So with full confidence and full tanks the little Luscombe and I lifted off Key West and turned south to span the ninety miles of water between Key West and Cuba. The wind was southeasterly so I made a slight correction in my heading to 175°. I listened for a few minutes to the scratchy tone of the south limb of the four-course range and with the accompanying din of the sixty-five horsepower continental engine thought that what I heard was the steady tone indicating "on course." I turned the radio off and glanced back as the tip of Florida receded beneath puffy white clouds. The engine droned smoothly, and at 2500 feet above the sea the vastness of the space above and water below was even more apparent—a dramatic contrast to my small craft and its lone occupant.

    I estimated that at about forty-five minutes into the flight, I should see the coastline of Cuba. For thirty minutes I contemplated the ships moving through these waters. Down there, perhaps, was Hemmingway's Old Man of the Sea struggling with his destiny.

Forty minutes—forty-five—fifty. Where is the north coast of Cuba? There! No! That's just a cloud shadow; nothing but blue water and white clouds. Fifty-five minutes—one hour. Where is it? Could I have missed the whole island? Could the winds be strong enough that I'd fly past the west end of Cuba into the Caribbean? I'll run out of fuel long before reaching Yucatan. Wait! There!—There's a line of white in the distant haze— yes—I shoreline..

Hallelujah! Land—Finally—a land fall—salvation of the ancient mariner and of this young pioneer of the sky. *But where is the big city of Havana?* I scanned to the east and west. The green fields and palm-studded coast of Cuba grew larger and brighter as I approached but no gleaming white buildings announced the capital of the island. I studied the chart for any clue.

Is that dry river bed this blue line on the map? Is that a major highway or just a gravel road? Should I turn east or west to find Havana? I've been flying an hour and a half now. If I turn easterly and can't locate my position in thirty minutes, I'll have to reverse course and that will give me thirty minutes to get back and only thirty more minutes to find Havana. If I run out of fuel I'll have to make an emergency landing. Which way should I turn? The winds were easterly—maybe they were stronger than forecast. Okay, I'll turn to the east and remain inland. Here's hoping I'm right.

I wasn't concerned with my safety; after all, there were plenty of places to land. I just hated to be embarrassed by a show of poor skills in flying.

What's that large paved area 5 miles to the north? Yes, that must be this military field; I felt more confident as I placed my finger over the airport symbol on the chart. And ahead—shimmering white towers—man made beacons leading to the densely populated port of Havana, Cuba.

"Jose Marti tower, this is Luscombe N71478 approaching from the West."

"Roger Luu-Scombe, you are cleer-ed to land," the controller responded in broken English. A railroad track crossed the airport at the north end with signals to halt rail traffic. I hoped no train would ignore the signals as I rounded out my glide to gently touch down on Cuban soil.

As I taxied to the area designated for customs, I noticed several uniformed armed men exit cars parked in a semicircle.

Hmm! I wonder who they're after.

This, of course, was Batista's Cuba, and in 1957 Castro and his revolutionaries were making life uncomfortable for the reigning dictator.

Uh-Oh.

The police surrounded my airplane as soon as I shut down the engine. "Como se 'nama," one of the men said as he approached with his gun partially raised.

"Uh, uh—I—I'm an American." In those days to be an American still carried a lot of weight. "What did I do? I—I filed a flight plan in Key West."

"You are late," an English speaking policeman came up to me when I climbed out of the plane. "Where did you stop?"

"Uh—nowhere. I didn't land anywhere 'til I got here."

"Where have you been for the last hour?" the interrogator persisted.

It seems that Castro had been receiving arms and supplies through clandestine flights into country airfields, and Batista was determined to stop all such activity.

I carefully explained how I had been blown off course and ended up approaching the airport from the west instead of the north. I showed them my license and other papers and perhaps, because I looked honest or, more likely, because of the obvious limited carrying capacity of the little Luscombe, I was warned and allowed to leave for downtown Havana.

Several days later I was conversing with two shaken American pilots who had not been so lucky. It seems that they had become lost and landed at a military field by mistake. The first three days of their week in Cuba were spent in jail while the authorities sorted through their paperwork. I resolved to be quite thorough in my flight planning on departure.

Havana was the Paris of the Caribbean—a city where everything goes. Gambling and nightlife attracted Americans in droves. When I met Marianna and her friend in the lobby of the Grand Havana Hotel, we planned a little day sight seeing and later a nightclub tour.

The presidential palace was splendid in the equatorial sun but armed guards reminded us of the on going revolution. Havana harbor covered the USS Maine whose sinking started the Spanish American war, and Moro Castle, overlooking the harbor, contained Batista's political prisoners, some of whom would, in turn, imprison their oppressors after the revolution.

Everywhere there was talk of Castro. "He'll never win! American money will keep him out."

"It would ruin this country if he takes over."

"Batista's done some bad things but look at the good he's done."

Still, the taxi driver said, "Castro's very popular."

"The peasants think he's their Savior."

"If the power is with the people, Batista is doomed."

In general, the wealthy were for Batista and the poor for Castro. Hasn't it always been so: that the oppressed will overthrow the oppressor only to become trapped on the other side of the jail cell as the new oppressor?

My trip to Cuba was a maturing event. Until then, I was a consummate bachelor, a self-perceived adventurer, with great plans for a future unencumbered by anything or anybody. In Havana decadence was pervasive and the gentleness and goodness of Marianna stood in sharp contrast to a life that could have been. As we said goodbye at the Jose Marti Airport, I knew that I was leaving one opportunity for a settled life but I soon realized that the life of "freedom" I espoused was, as the sixties song says, *just another word for nothing left to do.*

I turned left after take off on runway 18 and flew parallel to the north-south runway of Jose Marti Airport, crossed over Havana Bay and entered the lonely world of the solo pilot or sailor. Only the surrounding physical presence of the vessel gives comfort to the lone occupant who views the vastness of the ocean and the sky with awe and whose life can be changed by natural forces over which he has no control. It is a humbling experience and yet we yearn for adventure; it is better to be humbled by the power of nature than by our own inadequacies.

On schedule the Florida Keys appeared out of the haze and I pulled back on the throttle control to slowly descend and land back on United States soil. This odyssey was nearly over, but as I continued the northerly trek toward Knoxville, I found myself reflecting, not on my next "lone eagle" adventure, but on the possibility of sharing what I loved with someone else; that someone was not Marianna. But Lisa stood alone and seemed to represent both the stabilizing influence I needed and the adventuresome spirit I wanted.

"I'll do it—I'll call Lisa as soon as I land," I said to myself as I flew up the west coast of Florida toward Tallahassee.

It is not unusual for arctic driven cold fronts streaming from the northwest to run out of power just about the time they reach north Florida. This evening was no exception. I had to descend lower and lower to stay beneath the overriding clouds of the now stationary front ahead. It was dark and with the cloud cover there was no visible horizon. Ground lights, at first sharp and bright against the earth, began to glow with an eerie halo and I knew that fog would soon be forming. Tallahassee was still at least one hundred miles ahead. Switching on my radio, I tried to hear the weather broadcast above the din of my engine and the crackles and pops of my low frequency receiver.

Tallahassee Weather—crackle-hiss—overcast—obscured—crackle—visibility zero—hiss-pop-hiss—rain and fog.

Visibility zero—I'd better get out of here. I turn to a heading of eighty degrees. Is that a wooded area or is it water—no lights—there! Is that a highway or—yes—runway lights—dim but they're lined up the way they're supposed to be for Cross City, Florida. Down into a black bowl with nothing but the parallel rows of runway lights to lend perspective, I guide the Luscombe.

Faith in the aviation system that had evolved since the brothers Wright, allowed me to continue toward a strip of asphalt I could not see. Feeling my way downward gently, gently, then "squee-squee" the tires announce our arrival. I slowly lower the tail. Opening the left window, I use a large flashlight to stay on the taxiway as I inch toward the CAA shack. I shut down the engine. The airport is eerily quiet in the rapidly forming fog.

"Boy, you got in just in time," the friendly solo operator at the Cross City Civil Aeronautics Administration Flight Service Facility said when I opened the wooden door and entered the white painted clapboard building.

"Yeah, I sure did. That fog was forming fast. I came up from Key West and didn't have any trouble 'til a short way back."

"Well, it looks like you'll be here 'til late morning—that's when we expect improvement."

Between his answering calls from over-flying aircraft and taking barometric and temperature readings, the lone operator of this isolated facility managed to entertain me with stories of other lucky or not-so-lucky pilots that had come this way. I was glad to be on the ground this foggy evening.

"Look, if you like, you can stay in the equipment room tonight. It'll save you cab fare and a motel bill."

I had told him how much salary an intern made and I suppose he sympathized since as a government employee, he was not overpaid himself. I appreciated the offer. It was nearly 10:00 pm.

"I'm going to use the pay phone before I turn in. Thanks for the offer." I replied.

"Lisa! This is Jeff: Guess where I am?"

We talked a long time, mostly small talk. She was interested in everything and wanted more detail. She even said she'd like to fly with me some place—maybe to Kentucky Lake to show me the cabin her dad was building. We planned on my flying to Memphis on my next free weekend.

"Lisa, I want to see you."

"I want to see you, too, Jeff."

She wants to see me—me—the non-jock—the guy who thought he had lost her forever when she became engaged to someone else?

I floated back into the briefing room. "Everything ok?"

"Couldn't be better—couldn't be better," I said as I opened the door to the equipment room, humming with an electron flow and warmed by the filament glow of hundreds of vacuum tubes, unsuccessful in their attempt to outshine the glow I felt in my heart that foggy night in Florida.

LISA

I sometimes envy the sociopath's immunity to loneliness although I have learned that true love for someone else—the kind that hurts the most when lost—is worth the pain.

Toward the end of my internship, I began making more trips to Memphis. Lisa met me at the airport, even occasionally at 4:00 in the morning, and our conversations grew more intimate. She planned to fly (commercially) to Knoxville to visit her cousin, Cotton Berrier in Pigeon Forge. So we arranged for a weekend visit together and I began to consider asking her to marry me, but was I ready to give up the life of a bachelor intern? On returning to Knoxville Sunday afternoon I wasn't sure.

"Whatcha doing this evening?" Shirley asked when she called late Sunday afternoon so I suggested that we go out for dinner.

She sensed that something was wrong. "What's the matter?"

"Oh nothing, I guess. I'm just thinking about the future. You know, the Air Force, practice, all sorts of things."

I couldn't bring myself to tell her about my plans for Lisa, not then. Later in the week I called Frank Farris' uncle, whom I had met once when I visited Frank. He was a Jeweler and helped me pick out an engagement ring when I flew to Rogersville Saturday afternoon. Lisa was scheduled to fly into Knoxville the next Saturday; I had told no one at the hospital of my plans. Lisa had been my ideal from the first time I met her, totally feminine, yet a talented craftsperson and appreciative of blue-collar skills. I knew that we would be inseparable, bound by common understanding. We could be alone together—in a room full of people—communicating without speaking. I wanted nothing more than to venture through life with this wonderful girl.

I had arranged to be off all weekend, so about noon on Saturday I drove to McGee Tyson Airport and waited as the DC6 taxied to the gate. The forward door was pulled in by the crew while stairs were rolled to the opening and secured. Lisa appeared at the top of the stairs, saw me and flashed a broad smile. I was hooked and on top of the world as we drove to Pigeon Forge. Cotton Berrier, golf pro at the country club, and his wife hosted Lisa for the weekend. I was a bit anxious when we drove up to the Riverside Inn in Gatlinburg for dinner since I had been there previously with Shirley and was concerned that someone might recognize me and say something that might cause embarrassment. My fears were unfounded, however, and we enjoyed a delightful evening. Later I was invited to sleep on the couch at the Berriers but I preferred the mountain air and rolled up in the car for the night. That bit of bravado cost me a slight crick in the neck.

To show Lisa the Appalachian Trail on which I had adventured as a teenager, we drove to New Found Gap. The canopied trail was cool and green and birds brightened the gentle breeze with song while we walked hand in hand a mile or so to the northeast along the pine needle path. Pausing under a canopy of leaves over an out cropping granite shelf, we embraced, and I muttered something about feeling like a clod and that I had a present for her. Fumbling in my pocket I finally retrieved the small black and gold box and handed it to her.

"Oh Jeff. It's beautiful," she said when she opened the box.

"Does that mean you'll marry me?" I asked tentatively.

"Yes, it most certainly does. I love you."

We kissed and, I believe, flew down the hill. I wanted to tell the world. Lisa, the unattainable, was going to marry me after all. She had chosen a mechanic over a football player.

BLUE COLLAR DOCTOR

From that moment on I was committed to her. Everything I did from that point on had her interests and desires in mind. I called Mr. Rollow asking if he had any objections to my proposal. Mrs. Rollow seemed pleased, probably having had some suspicion about the possibilities. One last hug before Lisa climbed the stairs and disappeared into the plane later Sunday night, and I felt strangely homesick for her already. Wherever she was, I should be there also.

I was struck with a feeling of loneliness that I had not had since that first summer at Maywood, a boy's camp near Olive Branch, Mississippi. I was eight years old, and now I was 24. That independent spirit I valued only protected me to a point. I was like a child who wanted to run free but would rush back from the cliff's edge for reassurance. I told myself on the drive back to the intern's quarters, "I've got lots of planning to do and I have got to research a job." I would not have to enter the Air Force until July 1959, and I didn't want to start, and then interrupt a training program.

George Barker and I had heard about the United Mine Worker's of America Welfare Fund and a chain of ten hospitals built in Appalachia by John L. Lewis, the bushy eye-browed president of that powerful union. There were also opportunities for young physicians in many small towns in east Tennessee and east Kentucky. Wartburg was out, of course, and I was glad to be relieved of that obligation; I did not want to feel owned by a community. In our search for a job, George and I spent one Sunday visiting another small town in east Tennessee. We followed the young practitioner on several of his house calls and soon realized why he was leaving after a year. He could not get away at all unless another doctor in a nearby community covered for him. Although the tradition of in home medical practice was as old as our country and often fulfilled a great need in rural communities, change was coming. No longer did the doctor's bag contain everything needed to treat most ills; patients had to be convinced that they should come to the clinic for an EKG or x-ray. When doctors began to feel that the trip to the patient's home was wasted time (after all, when Uncle Joseph complained of chest pain, the hospital was the place for him) patients misunderstood and would criticize any doctor not willing to make the effort. Resentment bred resentment and the great regard most patients had for physicians in general began to fade. Now impersonal emergency rooms staffed with "providers" have taken the place of in the home care, but in this small town Dr. Bowman was still revered. We watched as he checked the blood pressure of an 80 year old lady living deep in back country ten miles out of town. Newspaper stuffed cracks in the wood planked walls. A single light bulb illuminated the small room.

"John, you really need to bring Annie into the clinic so I can get an x-ray," Dr. Bowman said to the thin elderly man standing beside Annie's bed.

"I know doc, I just ain't got no way now. You just do what you can and I'll try to pay you somehow," he said with some resignation.

"She's in failure. See the pitting edema." Dr. Bowman pointed out her swollen legs to George and me. "She has been on digitalis and may get toxic if I increase it any. I just need to get her in the hospital"

We could sense his frustration and I tried to visualize how I would handle this situation. For someone who likes control and structure, there would be many uncomfortable days in this type of practice. We left with an appreciation for the tenacity of Dr. Bowman and with continued uncertainty about a future course.

A friend from medical school, Roy Page, had graduated several months before I and was already working in a Miner's Hospital in Middlesboro, Kentucky. He was enthusiastic about the practice, experience and income. "A thousand a month," he had said.

"A thousand dollars?" I was incredulous. After all, I had been subsisting on one hundred twenty-five dollars a month plus room and board, but now that I was to be married I had to have more income.

"You will be assigned as a general physician but you can work with a surgeon if you prefer," he explained.

Soon I filled out an application, buoyed by Lisa's enthusiasm and laughed at my new membership card: *United Mine Worker's of America*, signed by John L. Lewis.

"You're going to work where?" One of the staff at UT Hospital asked when I told him of my decision. "Don't you know that's a socialistic program. Socialized medicine, that's what it is." He implied I might even be "black balled" in the County Medical Society. It seems that practicing medicine is not just taking care of patients, it is also politics.

I had never thought of that before. Wasn't being a good doctor enough? Organized medicine was strongly opposed to health plans that hired physicians on a salaried basis. Kaiser-Permanente in California had been established and now John L. Lewis had opened his Miner's Welfare Fund Hospitals. Local physicians, having lived with fee-for-service, viewed any other system as a threat to their integrity. After all, most physicians considered charity work as an obligation. They would willingly staff a charity clinic or write off an indigent patient's bill or accept some small gift of tomatoes or squash as payment in full. Motivation may be lost when the free will behind charity cannot be exercised. When incentive is tied to a salary as in prepaid plans, there is a tendency to expend the least effort. However, on a personal level, in dealing one-on-one with a patient, there is no difference between a doctor's private office, or a Kaiser clinic or a Mine Worker's Hospital.

So, I was experiencing the conflict between organized medicine, a political entity, and personal medicine. I was training for the latter but had to live with the former.

"Well, it's a good salary for someone just out of internship," I observed.

"Yeah! Just don't be surprised if you don't get invited to the local medical meetings", the UT physician warned. He was right to some degree but later in my tour with the Miners I was less ostracized than anticipated. Medicine was beginning a change that has continued through to the present time.

I sit by the phone for a while reflecting on this turning point in my life. No longer will my future be determined by my desires and needs alone but in concert with another who is already a part of my life.

Lisa and I had agreed on a wedding date, January 4, 1958, and she remained busy making arrangements in Memphis and working at the microbiology lab at Kennedy Veteran's Hospital. My internship was winding down. I had gained in confidence and experience and was hopeful that I would never again question my own ability or feel inadequate. I was to learn however, that one's "old self"—the child within—can never be forgotten. One can only hope to add a layer of confidence through experience.

In the three months or so I was to remain in Knoxville, I flew back to Memphis on many free weekends. Logging this flight time in my logbook, plus my previous night flying, I had accumulated enough time to qualify for a commercial license. With the help of Tom Kesterson, I studied for and passed the written test. Since my near-sightedness was disqualifying for the necessary class II physical exam, even though I was corrected to 20/20, I was required to take a medical check ride for a "waiver." The FAA examiner who flew with me one fall Saturday afternoon put my glasses in his pocket after hand propping the airplane for me.

I had no difficulty flying, even with blurred vision, and impressed the examiner with my ability to pick out suitable emergency fields. Using subliminal clues, I even noted the difference between a herd of cows in one field and horses in another. I pointed out transmission lines and towers; landing was no problem.

Later when I tried to take the Commercial Flight Test, however, my skills were lacking in performing some of the maneuvers, and the examiner suggested I needed more practice. I eventually succeeded in my quest and could then brag that I was a "commercial pilot." I was hoping to use the Luscombe on the honeymoon that

Lisa and I were planning, but an annual inspection revealed problems with the engine that interfered with that plan.

The nights when I was not on call were particularly lonesome for me in the months before I was to be married.

"Jeff, how about coming to Laura's with me tonight. She's having a party with several of the nurses." Laura was George's current girlfriend. Although I had not broadcast my engagement, word was getting around.

"I don't know George. I better not," I replied.

"Aw, come one, you need to get out. Besides, you'll know some of the girls there." *That's what I'm worried about.* After all, I was committed to Lisa. "Okay, I'll come by for a little while" I said after a pause.

I found it easier than I had anticipated carrying on a conversation with some of the nurses at Laura's house that evening. Casually mentioning that I was engaged provided a shield that was a welcome aid in overcoming temptation. Later, I was sorely tested when Shirley S. called me at the intern's quarters one especially lonesome evening. I had been working on a Heath Kit radio that I was building as a surprise for Lisa.

"Jeff how *are* you? You haven't called or anything. I've been missing you," she asked in a soft voice.

"Hi Shirley. I'm sorry I haven't called, but I wasn't sure what to say."

"What do you mean Jeff, what's happened. We used to talk all the time."

"I know but I guess things are different now. I got engaged to my college sweetheart." The phone was quiet. "Shirley........Shirley.....are you still there?"

"I'm still here," she finally answered; her voice was a little broken.

"I'm sorry." And I *was* sorry for any hurt I may have caused. "We are still friends aren't we?"

"Can't you come over for a while, just for old times sake?" she asked, regaining her composure.

"I don't think I should."

"Why not? I really want to see you." And at that moment, I wanted to see her very much. Memories of our good times, Gatlinburg, lakeside picnics, flights in the Luscombe all conspired to add fire to my temptation to see her one more time. I hesitated.

"Please Jeff, I …"

God help me. Surely no one would be hurt. No one except Shirley or me would even know. "I…..I want to Shirley, I really do; but don't you see I can't. I have been in love with Lisa since I first met her. For years I was free, but she was always in the back of my mind and I promised myself that if by some miracle she and I were to be married, I would devote myself to her totally."

"But, you're not married yet."

"I'm committed, though, and if I'm not faithful to her now I may never be."

Then Shirley said something that made my resolve a little easier. "Well, it's my loss, I guess, but I'd say she's a lucky girl."

"Thank you Shirley, but I'm the lucky one—and, Shirley, I want you to know—I'll miss you."

"And I'll miss you, Jeff. We'd better say goodbye now…… before….. goodbye."

I waited a few moments and then picked up the phone to call Lisa. "Lisa, baby, I just called to tell you I love you."

Her response, "I love you too, and I'm glad you called because I was missing you tonight more than usual," buoyed my spirits and relieved my restlessness, and I was finally able to sleep with a piece of mind that helped me through the few months remaining in my year of internship.

❧

There was much to be grateful for toward the end of 1957. I had a good paying job waiting for me at Wise Memorial Hospital in Wise, Virginia, I was commissioned a first lieutenant in the Air Force with an active duty date of July 1, 1959, and most importantly, Lisa and I were to be married on January 4, 1958. In researching for a honeymoon site that would be unique and memorable, we decided to take a freighter out of New Orleans to Puerto Rico. Neither of us was interested in a "pleasure cruise." That did not fit with my blue-collar ideal. We were not interested in "show," but in substance. I would have preferred a flying honeymoon, but we would have to wait until later to start our flying because of the maintenance that was required on the Luscombe.

I remember few details of the preparations of what was to be a big wedding—not that I was uninterested but Lisa, her mother, and father did most of the planning. The reception was to be a rather dry affair in the cloister of Southwestern at Memphis in deference to the Diehl's and the many friends of the Rollows who had lived and worked on the campus since it's move to Memphis from Clarksville in 1925.

My parents planned on a post wedding party at the University Club when we returned from our honeymoon. At the time, I was much more interested in the future in which Lisa and I would make our own way and our own decisions than in any obligations that accompany a wedding.

I have to look at pictures of the event to recall bridesmaids and groomsmen. Lisa had asked four of her best friends from Southwestern to be bridesmaids: Ann Riley Bourne, Mim Heard, Mary Rodriguez and Esther Jane "Poochy" Swartzfager. The men I chose (with Lisa's advice) for groomsmen was an eclectic mix. Neal Ross was certainly a logical choice, and Lisa's sister, Ann Ross was lady in waiting. Lisa Dahne Ross was the flower girl. Bill Callicott was the only Southwestern friend to be in the wedding and certainly my friends from high school years: Hugh Humphreys, Bobby Smithwick and Walk Jones had to be included. Medical school friends, Aubra Branson, George Barker, and Frank Farris participated. Joby Walker, a dentist who had worked in my dad's office for several years, had married Mary Beth Kilpatrick, another Southwestern friend. I had been a groomsmen in their wedding in Clarksdale a year or so before, so Joby was a logical choice. I had also been in Bill Justis' wedding with Yvonne and asked him to join. I would have included my other cousin, Frank McKay, had he been able to attend. Stan Justis was a child at the time and was not a part of the wedding party. My Dad was to be my Best Man. Dr. John Millard of Evergreen Presbyterian Church officiated. I can remember the degree of seriousness with which I viewed the whole affair. I did not enjoy the public display nor, I believe, did Lisa, although she presented a most outgoing affect.

Through the haze that shields the past I recall those days in January 1958 that were to change my life forever. The reception line at the Cloister seemed to go on forever and when Walk Jones and several other groomsmen clamped police handcuffs around my wrist and to a railing, I good-naturedly accepted my fate asking Lisa to wait for me no matter how many years I remained in jail. Later, I was released when a uniformed policeman came to retrieve his handcuffs and Lisa and I could make our way under a hail of rice to my black and white 1956 Chevrolet.

Later when we arrived at the one story, white ranch style Holiday Inn in Clarksdale, Mississippi, we were both quiet and contemplative but close in our feelings as we would remain; our love for each other was palpable. All the years of doubts and uncertainty and experimentation of youth were dissolved in the reality of this new life together. We talked together, we were silent together, we were at peace with each other in a crowd; a glance from across a room could be reassurance of continued love and respect.

Leisurely we drove through the Mississippi Delta to New Orleans. There we visited Lisa's landlady (during her post graduate work at Tulane). We stayed one night at the St. Francis Hotel and boarded our freighter—a vessel belonging to Waterman Lines to begin a cruise to Puerto Rico. Twelve cabins on the upper deck of our cargo laden ship accommodated the paying passengers. We had the run of the ship, dining with the captain every night, exploring the engine room, even taking the helm on occasion.

One evening, after an especially enjoyable meal with wine, we heard a rather noisy conversation in the adjacent cabin. The discussion deteriorated into a shouting match just outside our cabin door. Then a door slammed and an angry man, locked out, banged so hard on the door that the ship vibrated with the blows. The captain eventually calmed the man down and found him other accommodations for the evening. For the rest of the journey, the couple was rather subdued and, I suspect, embarrassed. Lisa and I knew we had a special relationship and that incident was not the first time that we would be able to see the contrast between many married couples and ourselves. We were fortunate.

Docking in San Juan, after saying goodbye to the crew and new friends, we rented a car to begin a self-guided tour of the island. With Lisa in the right seat of our Volkswagen Bug, we drove east in the late afternoon toward La Cordillera Central, the highest range of mountains (at 4400 feet) on the island. With no reservations, we were disappointed to find the resort hotel on the north shore near the El Yunque National Forest full. Our only choice was a set of cabins off the road near the top of the 3500 foot peak of El Yunque. The shuttered, dark structures were surrounded by dense undergrowth and a single bulb lighted the rather austere accommodations; a lumpy bed covered with a faded, tattered, multi-colored quilt shattered our expectations of a romantic mountain top retreat.

"We'll think about it. Gracias senor." Neither of us wanted to hurt the feelings of the proprietor, but after looking in the AAA book and discussing the situation, we decided to drive to a resort hotel close to the center of the island which, after all, was only 40 miles wide. We called ahead to be sure we would have a room for a late arrival. Darkness was palpable along the winding road; houses on each side seemed deserted until a sliver of light through a shuttered window gave evidence of the life within. In low areas, our headlights illuminated hundreds of frogs migrating across the highway from one pond to the next. Finally we arrived, weary but relieved, at our Shangri La. Our room was bright and cheerful, overlooking pleasant farmland as the morning sun melted the mist and fell across our bed.

We were on our honeymoon. No one in the world could possibly be as happy as I was on that sunny morning in Puerto Rico.

The next day we drove farther south to Phosphorescent Bay where millions of plankton glowed in the wake, excited by the passage of our tour boat as we plowed through the dark waters.

I wanted to be the perfect husband and Lisa made me feel successful in that endeavor. If I suggested we take a side trip, she would say, "That's a good idea." Even when the road became increasingly rough, she would let me decide when to turn around. So, when we started our drive up the west coast of Puerto Rico, I felt I had failed my responsibility with the sudden, shattered stop of our Volkswagen.

"Look at that view," Lisa had said as she pointed to an opening in the trees and a vista of blue water and beach. I glanced to the left momentarily.

Bam! Lisa and I jerked forward. Lisa's head hit the windshield. The Volkswagen had struck a tree with its right front fender and headlight. Fortunately, we were not going very fast at the time and neither of us was hurt badly although Lisa had a goose egg on her forehead. I felt that I had let my wife down.

"I shouldn't have told you to look when I did," she apologized.

"No, it was my fault. I wasn't paying attention."

Later we laughed about the incident that nearly ruined our honeymoon.

On our way to *Luis Munoz Marin International* for our flight home, I saw several Cessna's and a few Pipers in the pattern and dreamed that someday we would fly to Puerto Rico in our own airplane. It was a dream only partly fulfilled: for in another time, I did return to the island that had seen the beginning of this life together with Lisa.

Back in Memphis, we were treated to a rather large reception in our honor at the University Club. Although we enjoyed seeing old friends, many of whom we would never see again, we were anxious to begin our new life together in Wise, Virginia.

APPALACHIA

Nearly 40 years later I am able to see the beauty in the changing color of the leaves. No longer does darkness and coal dust cover everything. Nature has reclaimed the flattened hills and stripped areas.

I was scheduled to begin work on the first of February. Hauling the trailer John Rollow and I built for the occasion, Lisa and I spent the night in Crossville on the way to Southwest Virginia. A mile or so east of Wise, the fifty-bed modern hospital dominated a wooded hill at the end of a winding tree-lined drive. A water tower penetrated the sky at the top of the hill. Tired but excited we were ushered to our furnished apartment, behind the hospital and further up the hill. The two story complex, with five upper and five lower units, had the prefab appearance of World War II housing. From the parking area we walked over a short, green, wooden bridge on the same level into our second floor, sparsely furnished four room apartment, overlooking the roof of the hospital. The newness of the facility, built with funds raised by the United Mine Workers of America Welfare Fund, contrasted with the poverty evident on our drive through Appalachia. Adding to the depressing atmosphere, stripped mountainsides, flattened hills, and mounds of black coal overwhelmed the visual sense.

DR. E. JEFF JUSTIS

We were introduced to our neighbors, Ben and "Tenny" Norfleet. Ben and I shared duties at the hospital, although he was to work more on the medical service and I was assigned to the surgical service. I was a real doctor, I mused on the way to the emergency room, although at age 25, a white coat and stethoscope hardly compensated for my youthful countenance.

"Are you sure about this doctor?" the weatherworn retired miner asked. I had just suggested an antibiotic for his wife who had come to the emergency room with a mild cough. "Don't you think that she ought to be put into the hospital to be sure she will be alright?" The old man was concerned. The patient had a low-grade fever. Her cough was bronchial and non-productive and she could certainly be followed as an outpatient the next day.

"I really don't think your wife needs to be in the hospital tonight," I protested and once more I listened to her chest to reassure the patient and myself that I was using good judgment. There were several other family members in the room during the discussion. One of the younger men in the group left for a moment, and when he returned a nurse whispered to me that I was wanted on the phone at the information desk.

"Dr. Justis, this is Frank Smithson. I am the president of Local 502 of the UMWA here in Wise County. Tell me about Joe Jacob's wife, please." I explained the situation to him. "Well, you know, doctor, these miners feel that this is their hospital. You understand, don't you? Old Joe there has worked 35 years in the mines. He probably has lungs as black as the coal he pulled out of the ground and until John L. Lewis came along and gave him hope, he had nothing to look forward to. Now, with this hospital—*his* hospital— he feels he doesn't need to worry anymore. When his wife gets sick, the hospital is there for her. You understand?"

I understood what he was saying and I understood to some degree what the old miner was feeling. *But, doesn't a physician have to use some judgment? Otherwise, the hospital could be overwhelmed by unnecessary admissions.* Well, I could have stood my ground and refused, but then one of the staff doctors would have admitted her anyway, so I acquiesced to make her husband and the union happy. After all, I couldn't be absolutely certain she would improve if I had sent her home. I swallowed my ego and as cheerfully as I could wrote out the admission papers. She remained in the hospital for several days, the anxiety faded from old Joe's face as her cough lessened, and I received at least partial credit for her improvement. I came to realize that relieving anxiety may be as important as prescribing an antibiotic even if a physician has to let the patient's wish override a scientific judgment.

Ron Shelley was a tall man, of light complexion, with piercing blue eyes and a military style haircut minimizing the gray. He had retired from the Naval Medical Service as a captain and, having a rather brusque northern manner, was not averse to ordering the nurses around as though they were ensigns. I faired little better and during the first procedure in which I assisted him, I resented his put downs and badgering.

"Justis, hold the G'damn retractor where you put it, will ya?"

"Sponge—don't pat—sponge."

"You'll tear the G'damn gut if you do that. Move—move out of the way."

Man, why do I have to put up with this. I'm a doctor now. I've finished my internship. I could walk out of here right now and hang up a shingle and practice medicine on my own. If I ever get to do surgery, I'll never treat anyone like this.

This "rite of passage" was unnecessary. I remained silent, however, and slowly, after many more cases, Ron came to appreciate my manual skills. The verbal abuse lessened and eventually, although his brusqueness remained (it was, of course, a part of his nature), he allowed me more and more freedom to operate and he even assisted me on herniorrhaphies, cholecystectomies, and appendectomies.

The use of one's hands in surgery (as the root, *chirurgiae* implies) provides the operator with a sense of direct control. Medical skills on the other hand rely on an indirect approach to a problem. A patient in cardiac failure is given an extract of the foxglove plant and we observe improvement. Often, the only physical act accomplished by the physician is in writing the order or prescription for the medication. Although I enjoy designing a piece of furniture, true fulfillment only follows the eventual construction of the piece. It was obvious that I was leaning more and more toward a surgical career.

"Dr. Justis, we need you to check Miss Joan Collier in room 206." The 17 year old had been admitted because of nausea and vomiting and diarrhea of several days duration. She was dehydrated and I had started IV fluids with D5W (dextrose 0.5% in water). The young patient seemed confused, her pulse was thready and I was concerned. The vomiting had stopped and her diarrhea was under control. Still she was getting worse. What's going on? One of the visiting staff general practitioners was on the floor, and I asked him for some advice. After checking the patient and the chart, he announced *Water Intoxication*. I could not believe my own inadequacy. Somehow, fluids and electrolytes had been a source of confusion to me in physiology and now I had damn near killed a patient. I subsequently mastered a few basics (two of water and one of salt), but I never was comfortable managing a patient's fluids and electrolytes. Fortunately, with increasing specialization later in my career, there was always expert help available in those areas in which I felt inadequate.

I shared night call with Ben and was only a few steps away from the hospital. Even so I began to realize the restrictions that being "on call" required. I became increasingly appreciative of my free time and the weekends during which Lisa and I could adventure together.

"Let's climb the tower," I suggested one Sunday afternoon. "We'll be able to see the next county."

"That would be great." Lisa always responded in the affirmative; my suggestions, it seemed, were always welcome or so she made me feel. Should I have been more perceptive? Did she really want to climb that tower with me? I know only that she wanted to please me and in that, there were, I am sure, sacrifices.

I started the climb up the ladder surrounded by a steel frame that ended in a small circular platform around the tank proper.

I was a pilot. I had never been afraid of heights but this was different. Only my grip protected me from disaster. In an airplane, structure provides security. The thin metal strips of the ladder and frame of this ladder seemed as threads in the air that surrounded us. Still, we climbed.

"Are you okay Lisa?"

"I'm fine." She would not give up. Determination framed her smile. "Kind of scary up here, isn't it?" she admitted as we climbed out onto the platform. We both leaned back against the welded steel tank away from the thin railing.

"Yeah, I'd rather be in an airplane."

"Me too," she said.

The view was breathtaking and we slowly relaxed. It was a memorable time in our young marriage. We would confront fears in the future that were not of our own choosing and those fears would be far greater than those that were the result of our many adventures.

The elderly patient had been going down hill for several days. Her husband sat quietly by her bed holding her hand. Everything had been done but she was now in the terminal stages of kidney failure. Uremic frost powdered her face and lips. The quiet resignation on the weathered face of the old miner touched me in a way that maudlin displays never do. Sometimes words detract from true feelings and the quiet touch of a hand on another carries more meaning that all the platitudes and preaching of those who profess great sincerity. Later that evening, I was trying to think of a way to tell the old miner that his wife had died. He had gone home for a short time when I had been called to the hospital to pronounce her dead. The nurses put him into a small room when he returned to the hospital. I should not have worried about what to say, but thinking that this poor old gentleman was fundamentalist in his beliefs, I asked, "Are you a Christian?" It was uncharacteristic of me to ask such a question for I have struggled all my life with what being a Christian really means. Does it mean one has to believe all of the dogma? Does one have to believe in the 'Holy Catholic Church'?

DR. E. JEFF JUSTIS

The Communion of Saints? Is belief in the Immaculate Conception essential or can one accept Christ, even as the illegitimate son of a carpenter? Can a Jew or a Muslim be a good Christian? I believe one can and therefore there may be hope for those of us who aspire to goodness but cannot accept dogma. My question to this man, intended to generate hope, did not spring from the heart.

He looked at me for a moment and then he said, his voice cracking, "Does it matter? I've lost her, haven't I? Forty-five years we've been married. I'm sure going to miss her. That's what matters."

I placed my hand on his shoulder and his sadness became mine for a moment. He would forever have to live with his loss. Later I too would learn the meaning of permanent loss, but for now I could walk away from his sadness and look forward to having my fears and doubts washed away with a simple smile of appreciation by Lisa.

Lisa wanted to join the Presbyterian Church in Wise and I willingly agreed. She knew of my questioning and concerns about the seeming hypocrisy of organized religion. The church was in the throws of reorganization and met in the basement of a building near the hospital. There was a pleasant feel to the congregation while it was making do in less than ideal circumstances. I recall a Christmas pageant performed by the children on a makeshift stage. Although we liked children in general, neither Lisa nor I related strongly to the children of others. We both felt that we would save our love and appreciation for our own children. We became a little disillusioned about the church once the building program began. We were "visited" on more than one occasion. Pressure was applied in many ways to obtain a large donation for the building project. The more pressure, however, the greater became my resolve. I could not believe in the importance of the structure. My excuse, "We will soon be leaving Wise for good," proved adequate to decrease pressure during the months remaining in our tour in Appalachia.

In March of 1958, Harry Wilson called with the good news that the engine overhaul was complete and that I could pick up the Luscombe any time. I flew commercially to Memphis and after a short visit and test flight of the Luscombe, I began the five hour flight to Norton, Virginia. Norton was another mining town about ten miles northeast of Wise and by comparison a bit darker and more depressed. The airstrip, if it could be dignified by the name, was a flattened area carved out of the side of a small mountain. The surface was a mixture of black coal and gravel and the 1,500 x 200 foot "runway" terminated in the shear cliff of the carved out strip mine that had been the origin of this desecration of nature. Some local pilots had briefed me on the technique of getting into and out of this challenging strip before I had gone to Memphis for the return flight. I made one slow circle to be sure the runway was clear before descending below the level of the mountain and turning toward the strip. Once on final, the Luscombe and I were committed to the landing since attempting a go-around would not be possible with the blackened wall looming directly ahead. After landing the Luscombe on the steep up hill grade of the runway it came to a stop in about 300 feet. Lisa was there to meet me and she climbed into the right seat for a 30-minute late afternoon ride over southwest Virginia. With increasing altitude, the man-made ugliness gave way to patterns of interest and early spring colors that for a moment let us forget the dreariness below. We learned that winds were a potential problem at the Norton strip, and although it was conveniently located, we decided to relocate our plane to a better landing area.

After some searching, we finally settled on a grass strip in Powell Valley, about 15 miles from Wise. The strip was actually a pasture; cattle kept the grass at a low level. On the north side of the east/west landing area, was a fenced off section where about four airplanes were tied down. Only once, to my knowledge, did a cow break through the protective fence. Our all-metal airplane did not entice a particularly hungry Holstein, but a fabric covered Stinson did not fair so well and several holes had to be repaired in its fuselage. A large hill, affectionately called "unnecessary mountain" by the local pilots, rose up only a mile or so beyond the west end of the pasture. Powell Valley airport occasionally presented other logistical problems. Returning from one of our weekend trips late one Sunday, we followed the usual procedure of flying at low altitude over the runway to alert the farmer who lived adjacent to the pasture. Usually, he would quickly move the cattle scattered across the runway to one side so that we could land. This day, however, the farmer-airport operator was gone and his substitute was not familiar with the requirements of aviation. We circled and circled. I "buzzed" the cows that were not the least intimated by our little Luscombe. Low on fuel and daylight, I was about to head for Tri-Cities airport when, finally, the farmer ushered the cows to the side and we touched down on the bumpy pasture. Except for the obvious hazards of cow pies and delays due to cattle on the runway, many adventures began and ended at Powell Valley during our stay in Wise.

I had joined the Flying Physicians Association in 1956 and was considered a charter member. I was anxious to take Lisa on a long trip in the Luscombe and in April of 1958, the national meeting was to be in Phoenix, Arizona. Another adventure awaited us.

By today's standards, the Luscombe was slow, averaging about 85 miles per hour on a long trip, but in the days before the interstate highway system the same trip would have been difficult by car in the time we had planned. After an overnight stop in Abilene, Texas, we flew to Carlsbad, New Mexico for a visit to the famous caverns before continuing past Guadalupe Peak on to El Paso for another overnight stay at a local hotel. The next morning we flew over the west Texas mountains north of the Rio Grande to Douglas, Arizona where Gertie and J.B. Terry lived. Gertie Mayo was Lisa's aunt. Her husband was a physician who had recently moved his practice from Helena, Arkansas to Arizona. We enjoyed a quick visit and I accompanied J.B. on a few house calls before dinner. One patient was an old alcoholic with hypertension and heart failure; in his sleazy hotel room bottles of whiskey, mostly empty, were scattered about and the dark room reeked of alcohol. The bearded derelict brightened when J.B. and I entered. "Hey doc, thanks for coming. I'm out of my medicine."

"I know John. Here, you take one of these now and one in the morning. Lie back and let me check your belly. Here Jeff, feel this." I placed my hand over the right upper quadrant as the patient inhaled.

My God, his liver's way down here. I felt the bumpy edge of the patient's liver well below its normal location. As we left John alone in his stupor, I asked J.B. if he had tried to get John to stop drinking.

"Oh, he's been in the hospital several times but checks out as soon as he gets thirsty. He's killing himself, of course, but preaching to him won't do any good."

I wondered then if a physician should be more aggressive in seeing that a patient receive the proper care. I have known many physicians who, perhaps with a bit of arrogance, suggest that the patient "do exactly as I say or get another doctor." I am somewhat uncomfortable with that approach. Physicians who insist that they always know what is best for the patient, in my opinion, lack sufficient empathy and respect for the individual. Our goal should be education so that the patient can make an informed decision, and even if we disagree with his choice, we should always be ready to offer our support.

On that short visit, J.B. had offered his perspective in the art of dealing with patients. Once more, however, I found myself leaning more toward a physical specialty than toward a non-structured general practice.

The following day we planned to fly to the Grand Canyon by way of Gila Bend. The wind was gusty and the heat generated thermals made for an uncomfortable ride. At the airport, pictures on the wall reminded us of the tragedy that had occurred over the Grand Canyon in June 1956. Two air carrier aircraft, not in a radar environment, had collided over the Grand Canyon while trying to show their passengers the majesty below. There is an emotional connection with all who fly and that accident was destined to affect everyone involved in aviation for years to come. Our feelings, combined with stronger winds and turbulence on route to Gila Bend, dictated a change in plans and we flew directly to Phoenix. Soon the arrival of the other flying physicians and the resulting camaraderie boosted our spirits. Lisa and I were the youngest members at the meeting and as such achieved celebrity status. At the banquet I was called upon to describe our 2,135-mile trip from Wise and although my old discomfort with public speaking began to creep into my consciousness as I was announced, a squeeze of my hand by Lisa instilled confidence. One of the older members was so impressed with us that he offered the use of his Cessna 172 for a planned flight to the Grand Canyon Airport, since he had other obligations in Phoenix and was unable to go. So Lisa and I were able to cruise in luxury over the high country north of the Arizona desert. In subsequent years, the Flying Physicians Association has played an important part in my aviation and medical careers. Lisa and I gained many friends who helped bridge the transition I was to someday face.

The following months were filled with new experiences in medicine and with adventures in flying. Because of the unpredictable nature of the four-legged occupants of Powell Valley Airport, we moved the plane to Coeburn, Virginia. The sod runway was in a shallow valley with an open "T" hanger shed along one side. It was a step up in that we no longer had to dodge cow pies but once, after a rather heavy rain, we had to abandon an attempted takeoff when the wet grass and mud held us back too long. I was unable to taxi out of the mire and several fellow pilots had to help push the Luscombe to higher ground.

Lisa and I had been married for about six months when we began to discuss the possibility of having a child. At one point, we both thought five children would be a nice number. Ah, the foolishness of youth. No thought was given to the logistics: college education or quality of care to each individual in such a large family. We would learn through experience. Once we abandoned birth control methods, every month was approached with anticipation. For me, it was a take it or leave it situation.

I failed to appreciate the depth of emotional investment Lisa placed in becoming pregnant. After several disappointing months, we decided to adopt—not a child, of course, but a dog. Through friends at the hospital, we learned about a kennel in Knoxville that bred German Shepherds. We flew into Island Home Airport, rented a car, found Timberlake Kennel and were introduced to a family of beautiful shepherds. We picked a fluffy brown and black ball of female puppy that we registered as Dark Shadow of Timberlake. As young as she was she was a lap full for Lisa in the right seat of the Luscombe. I began to think that perhaps we needed a larger airplane. It is claimed that, when a couple gives up on trying hard to conceive a child and adopts, more often that not, pregnancy follows shortly thereafter. Thus, the adoption of Shadow into our family may have been responsible for Cathy's conception. Humans may be more influenced by fellow creatures than we could ever dream. We were happy to realize that our family would be growing but as many young couples have found, once the code is broken, controlling that growth may be a problem. Although there was an obstetrician at Wise Memorial, Lisa, who usually liked everyone, was not comfortable with him, so we commuted to Knoxville for prenatal visits. As Lisa grew, the Luscombe seemed smaller still and I began actively to look for another airplane. On one visit to Rogersville during medical school, Frank Farris had introduced me to Rhea Armstrong who owned a 1948 Cessna 170; the four seat airplane was kept in a barn near a large field used as a runway on Rhea's farm. I was pleased that he would consider selling it and after some negotiation we settled on the price of $3,200. In the late twentieth century, the same airplane in reasonable condition would probably be worth $20,000. We left the Luscombe in Rhea's barn and, after a brief checkout flight, Lisa and I flew in our new airplane back to Coeburn. Now, we had a more comfortable and faster airplane that would accommodate our growing family and one in which we could take friends and family.

We had an interesting encounter with Frank Farris just before we closed the deal with Rhea Armstrong. Frank had completed his internship at DC General and was joining the Navy. When he learned we were buying the Cessna 170, he made a trip to Wise in an effort to talk us out of buying that particular airplane. It seems that he had been considering buying it for some time and admitted that he thought of it as his airplane. Lisa and I both thought that he acted somewhat like a spoiled child—piqued that he was not getting his way. I would see him for the last time several years later.

In January of 1959, we took Ben and Teeny Norfleet to the Greenbrier for lunch. In early March we flew to Miami for a medical meeting and later that same month, we picked Ann and Neal Ross up in Clarksville for a flight to Marathon Key in Florida. We were certainly utilizing the airplane and enjoying every minute of our new life together. It was the best of times for us, although we realized there would be big changes in our lives in the summer of 1959 when our first child would be born.

I was still undecided about a future career path in medicine when George Barker visited us one evening having driven over from a neighboring United Mine Worker's Hospital. He arrived late with the frightening story of his girlfriend having fallen out of the car on a mountainous curve. She had some superficial scrapes and was a bit shaken but otherwise, luckily, sustained no major injury. After a dinner of grilled steaks I showed George the corner TV cabinet that I was building out of some walnut John Rollow had given me.

"Hey Elvis, you ought to go into orthopaedics." George was one of my friends who consistently referred to me by my first name.

"How come?" I asked having previously given the specialty only passing consideration.

"You're a natural, that's why. Anyone who can build furniture can certainly fix bones."

"Well, I might think about it, but I'm going in the Air Force in June."

"I tell you what Elvis, Sage said everyone has to apply several years ahead to get into Campbell Clinic. You ought to apply for the heck of it."

I had met Fred Sage during my senior year at medical school through George who had worked as a "papoose": x-ray technician and gofer at the Campbell Clinic. Fred had obtained a Master of Orthopaedics degree during the December of 1956 medical school graduation ceremony and was now on the staff of the Campbell Clinic.

"You think he would remember me?" I asked.

"Sure he would. Why don't you write him?" George replied.

Although I may well have given orthopaedics consideration sometime in the future, this seemingly small incident began a thought process that led to the realization that the mechanical nature of orthopaedics fit my personality and self-image better than any other field of medicine. I wrote Fred for information and an application. I would have to complete a year of general surgery residency or equivalent before I could be accepted for a fellowship at Campbell Clinic. Ron Shelley had become increasingly friendly and helpful during the year that I had been with the Miner's Hospital. My decision not to react to his initial harassment paid off in his increasing confidence in my abilities. Since he was a Board Certified Surgeon he suggested that the time I had spent with him might suffice as a preceptorship and that, with his recommendation, I perhaps would not need a formal year of general surgery training.

As I look back on Ron's friendship and help, I wish I had expressed my gratitude more as the years passed. Many, many people are involved in the development of a physician's skills. Since study and work can be extensive, there is a tendency for the young physician to credit his success to his own efforts, but almost everything that we accomplish has its basis in the efforts of someone else. However, surgical technique was not all I learned from Ron. At first, it was difficult for me to understand the relationship between

Ron and Dr. Benko. Benko was an older general practitioner who had pioneered in this community and, as was the custom in the 30s and 40s, had never refused to do any surgical procedure that came his way. On most procedures Ron assisted him, gently coaxing and protecting him (and the patient) from disaster.

"I wish I could keep old Benko from pouring merthiolate into the abdomen," Ron confided one day. Every time Dr. Benko finished an abdominal case, he poured a cup of merthiolate into the abdominal cavity to cut down on infection. Instead, he was setting many patients up for post op adhesions.

"He is a good man but medicine has passed him by. I am going to retire before *I* get left behind," Ron said after Benko had left the hospital. I admired Ron's loyalty in trying to protect the honor and reputation of his old friend. Incompetence through lack of training is less of a problem now than is poor training. Mandated peer review organizations preclude protecting the occasional bad apple. In the later years of my practice, I was called upon to offer opinions about the work of other orthopaedists. I tried to give each doctor the benefit of the doubt, placing myself in his position, but in the end I had to be honest when commissions or omissions did not meet the standard of care.

On one weekend trip to Knoxville we stayed in a local motel for a visit with my mom and dad who were in town for a dental convention. On Sunday morning while shaving I noticed a peculiar feeling in my face as I pulled the razor over my right cheek. *What the...* I peered into the mirror and noticed that my face was asymmetrical. I could not raise my right eyebrow. When I smiled, one side of my mouth pulled unevenly. *Bell's Palsy.* I instinctively knew the diagnosis. I had seen several patients during medical school with rather grotesque deformity, but fortunately my neurological deficit was rather mild in comparison. I reassured Lisa that I had not had a stroke. Later, a visiting neurosurgeon confirmed my diagnosis and as predicted, the facial weakness gradually improved without specific treatment. However, to this day, I have slight facial asymmetry when smiling or raising my eyebrows.

Before leaving for my internship in 1957, I had built a large tool chest to accommodate many of my hand tools. I brought it to Wise and, not long after arriving, I began building a walnut corner cabinet to house our HiFi equipment. I introduced myself to the maintenance engineer of the hospital, and he was kind enough to let me use the circular saw and jointer and other power tools in the basement of Wise Memorial Hospital. Winter evenings and weekends often found Lisa and me in the basement processing the walnut so that I could do the handwork in our apartment. Although I tried to be a good neighbor, one evening I was embarrassed when the downstairs tenant banged her ceiling hard with a broom several times in response to my drilling and pounding on the floor. The cabinet slowly took shape and initially housed the Heathkit high fidelity tuner and amplifier that I had built during my internship. Later, Lisa and I designed some large chandeliers with walnut arms for use in the cabin that John Rollow was building on Kentucky Lake. We flew to a small airstrip near the cabin for several weekend visits during our time in Wise, Virginia. John Rollow's love for fishing was infectious and Lisa had grown up with no greater wish than to be invited to fish alongside her dad. I had always enjoyed still fishing, but on these excursions Johnny showed me the intricacies of fly-fishing. I remember the quiet times that Lisa, her dad and I had casting under the willows of Kentucky Lake when the "May flies were falling." I often wish that life allowed more time to experience the many skills awaiting our endeavors. It seems that the greatest pleasure lies in the quest for knowledge and skill. Certainly there is enjoyment in the continued practice of an accomplishment but nothing is as fulfilling as the challenge of mastering a new skill.

Once we bought the Cessna 170, Lisa, perhaps with a little encouragement from me, decided to take flying lessons. So on quite a few weekends during the early months of her pregnancy, we would fly over the ridges to the broad valley that was home to Tri Cities Airport. One beautiful Sunday, while Lisa was practicing with her instructor in a new Tripacer, the operator of Tri Cities Aviation asked if I would like to ride with him while he demonstrated a brand new 1959 Piper Apache to a prospective customer. I jumped at the chance, enjoying the luxury of that twin-engine plane as we flew over the verdant hills of east Tennessee. I never dreamed that some day I would own a similar Apache that would play a major role in my life.

Our time in Appalachia was coming to a close. I was scheduled to begin active duty in the Air Force in July of 1959. Ben Norfleet was to enter at the same time but, because of his having had ROTC training he could proceed directly to his assigned base. Lisa was due to deliver in June 1959 and we were to be in Memphis for that event. All young couples need to spend time away from their parents during the early years of their marriages. Lisa and I certainly gained closeness in our year and a half in Wise and our subsequent Air Force tours. This closeness and self-reliance would have been difficult to achieve had we been living in daily contact with our parents. However, we were grateful for their support, especially during Lisa's final month of pregnancy.

I had completed the corner HiFi, or TV cabinet, and had designed a special cradle to support it during our upcoming move. We said our goodbyes to all of the friends we had gained with no sense of the finality that experience and age dictate must accompany life changes. To the young there will always be another day and the oft said "we'll see you later" or "until we meet again" is said with sincerity, knowing that the wish may fade with the memory.

We had the trailer that John Rollow and I had built (I had learned to weld during its construction in the basement of the Physics Building at Southwestern). All of our possessions would fit in the trailer and our 1956 Chevrolet. Lisa was to drive with Shadow and I would fly. Sometime in early June 1959, we arrived back in Memphis. We stayed in the gatehouse at Southwestern with the Rollows. Lisa contacted Ralph Bethea for her prenatal checkup and we eagerly awaited our first child. As my date to report to Gunter Air Force Base in Montgomery, Alabama approached, I became concerned that Lisa might not deliver soon enough but on June 27, labor pains began in the early morning. In those days, even a physician-father was not expected to be present during delivery, and I waited with the other expectant fathers for word. By that afternoon we were the proud parents of a baby girl. (Interestingly, Ralph Bethea was out of town and Jack Adams, an associate, actually delivered our first-born. In 1965, he would also deliver another first born to a young lady whose life would intertwine with mine in ways unimaginable in 1959.) When I first saw that dark-haired girl, who would be named Catherine Ann, through the glass wall of the nursery, I was struck with a sense of awe and wonder at this bit of creation that was ours alone.

As the date of my departure for Montgomery approached, I felt a beginning separation anxiety accompanied by the usual fear when faced with unfamiliar situations. In my early years, I had enjoyed the Boy Scouts with its uniforms and regimentation and, on one level, I felt comfortable with my decision to join the Air Force. At the same time, the irrevocable certainty of "orders to report" and the fact that I must now leave my family, my new family of three (four including Shadow), fueled my anxiety. Lisa had wanted to breast feed but, in spite of requested isolation, footsteps in the hall or whispers distracted her and, as she said, she "dried up like a prune." This, plus a febrile episode secondary to a urinary tract infection in the early post partum days precluded this most natural way of feeding a newborn. I wanted to remain with Lisa but soon the day arrived for my departure for Montgomery. I flew the Cessna, of course, and I planned to return each weekend during the month long tour of duty at the Basic Orientation Course for medical officers. A new career within a career was about to begin.

AIR FORCE

I climb the ladder to nail up the long truss for the lean-to I have put together to protect the engine, wings and cabin of the Cessna 170. I look down at Lisa holding Jeff on her lap; Cathy is playing by her mother and Shadow is content in the shade. I am truly fortunate in this life—surely this happiness will last forever.

After parking N2634V at Montgomery Aviation, I took a cab directly to Gunter Air Force Base. I dismissed the cab at the information center only to find that I had to carry my bags nearly a mile to my assigned quarters. My room, on the second floor of a World War II era wooden barracks with a communal toilet, was not exactly what I thought Officer's quarters should be. The object of all of this was to indoctrinate new medical offices in the traditions of military life. My Boy Scout experience helped; saluting as a courtesy was not anathema to me as it was to some of the young doctors I would be associated with for the following month. The only thing that provoked some anxiety was the requirement that weekend trips be restricted to a 300-mile radius. Instead of ignoring the rules, as did some of my colleagues, my compulsive nature required that I obtain official permission. In spite of my fears, there was no problem once I explained to the commanding officer, a major, that my wife needed me because of her infection and that I would only be two hours away by plane. The class of 59C socialized at the officer's club during the week. Some of us went to movies and a few of the doctors used the freedom away from home to satisfy prurient interest. I recall one young man of doubtful character who insisted on telling us of his nightly conquests. He described how easy it was for him to claim he was unmarried and to hide the telltale indentation of his wedding ring by wearing a large class ring on his left ring finger. The majority of my classmates remained faithful during this short tour of duty. As for me, I lived for the weekends when I could fly home to Lisa. I usually left on Friday evening and returned late Sunday.

A local general practitioner who served as a medical consultant to the base asked several of us to dinner one evening and tried to persuade us to return to Montgomery to practice after leaving the Air Force. I told him that I was considering orthopaedics, and he laughingly indicated that I must not want to work as hard as he had to work. He was right. A general practitioner did work hard and had little time he could call his own. His practice *was* his life. With my multiple interests, I knew that I had to have a life outside of medicine and I was structuring decisions in that direction. Years later, after giving a lecture on office orthopaedics at a University of Tennessee sponsored seminar, I was surprised when this same doctor complimented my presentation and said that he had known I would someday be a success. I appreciated his complement.

The Basic Orientation Course was interesting in that it gave us guidelines for triage and necessary decision making when dealing with mass casualties. We learned about military traditions and protocol and even how to march. That came easy for me because of my Boy Scout experience but the most unlikely candidate was chosen as our squadron commander. Jerry Nelson hated the military and was planning to get out just as soon as his two-year obligation was satisfied. To his credit he did his job of issuing marching orders to a bunch of left-footed docs better than expected, although we could all sense his discomfort.

After a month of classroom and field work, it was time for our assignments to be published. I had applied for a slot at the School of Aviation Medicine at Brooks Air Force Base in San Antonio, as had many of my contemporaries. Most ended up with GMO (General Medical Officer) assignments but a few of us were lucky and obtained our first choices. With our silver captain's bars and our fresh uniforms, we were on our way to becoming flight surgeons. Not only would we be in a favorable position in the medical hierarchy but we would be *required* to fly; imagine that: "Please don't throw me in that briar patch." I called Lisa with the good news. She had recovered from the infection, and Cathy Ann was thriving on formula. Shadow was good with our new baby and we were ready to move on to new adventures. I had arranged for a classmate to drive our Chevy to San Antonio so that we could fly the Cessna. Cathy was nearly six weeks old when we tucked her into the aluminum framed safety bed that John Rollow had made for the purpose and fastened the top down before taking off. Shadow sat on the floor between the front and rear seats. Lisa and I could hardly keep from laughing at the three "mamas," Sissy, Mama C and Wees, crying between comments:

"I can't believe you're taking that baby in that airplane all the way to San Antonio."

"Why don't you drive?"

They were still standing on the ramp, waving as we taxied away from Dixie Air Service at Memphis Municipal Airport on our first adventure as a family of four.

In San Antonio we rented a car to search for an apartment. For one or two nights we had to stay in a rather sleazy motel with a cramped kitchenette. After much searching and with help from the Brooks AFB personnel office, we located a nice apartment complex. All of the units were four-plexes and on the ground floor but a sign at the registration desk announced: *No Dogs*. Lisa's pleading and assurance that ours was a well-behaved house dog that would never be allowed out by herself convinced the desk clerk that we would probably be okay for our six weeks tour in San Antonio. As with many assignments in the Air Force, there is some buffer time between sign-in date and duty. I was happy for a few extra days when my friend arrived with our 1956 Chevrolet. We could hear him coming, the engine rattling and backfiring into our carport. He explained that about 100 miles out of San Antonio, a valve suddenly blew, but he was able to limp along on five cylinders. I bought a few socket wrenches and went to work. I took the head to a machine shop for the valves to be replaced and for new seats. I was cleaning the block in preparation for a new gasket when, without thinking, I used gasoline as a solvent so when I turned the engine over with the starter momentarily, a flame and black smoke rose from the engine compartment.

"Lisa, get some water", I shouted, through the back screen door. I slammed the hood down to smother the flame. A large black bubble of paint swelled from the hood as the dying flame cooked the thin metal. I was mad at myself and embarrassed at my mistake. Eventually, I got the engine back together and even repainted the bubbled area. Though I could always see evidence of the incident as long as we owned that Chevy.

Over the next six weeks I was immersed in Aviation Medicine. The academic lectures were interesting and altitude chamber training, the centrifuge, parachute training, and orientation flights in T-33 trainers made for a memorable time professionally. Although I never was enamored of organized sports, I enjoyed individual challenges. When we climbed the high parachute tower for jump training, I was confident in the harness I was wearing and in the thin cable that would support me as I jumped, feeling momentary weightlessness before my fall was arrested by the harness and cable. I qualified as a marksman at the shooting range and basically enjoyed being a soldier for a short time.

Several of my classmates and I carpooled so that Lisa could have the car most of the time. I think she enjoyed playing house and would tell me of her adventures with Cathy Ann and Shadow. One day she was a bit distressed when Shadow had pushed through the door to intimidate a small white poodle that belonged to a neighbor in the adjacent unit. No harm was done but the lady was not very accepting of Lisa's apology and threatened to report our *vicious dog*. We were to leave soon, however, so we didn't let the event spoil our remaining time.

As new parents Lisa and I were both overly concerned about our baby disturbing others. In a restaurant, for example, we would thrust a bottle or pacifier into Cathy's mouth at the first sign of restlessness. In general, Cathy (and the others later, for that matter) was quite good as I recall, but meals out were often tense affairs. This expectation of quiet, unassuming behavior may have led to a tendency toward inhibition and inward reflection in some of our children.

Overall, San Antonio was good for our young family. We had established ourselves as an autonomous unit. I was excited to be a flight surgeon and learned that I was to be assigned as the commander of the 4090th USAF Dispensary at Wilmington, Ohio. There were rumors of big changes at Wilmington, and I was to be a part of it beginning in September, 1959. When I try to remember the details of arranging for a car and belongings to be moved to our new assignment, I find the fog of years blocking the view. I am grateful, however, for the assistance of many friends and family who have transported cars and trailers so that I could have the privilege of flying. After a few days in Memphis and another tearful farewell at the airport, we were on our way to South Central Ohio. The closest airport to the base at Wilmington was at Sabina, Ohio, a small grass strip operated by memorable Helen and Dick Williams. They lived in a tiny room attached to the hanger where Dick maintained a fleet of Piper Cubs and Aeronca Champions. Our 170 Cessna felt at home here and so did we.

Jerry Nelson had been in my BOC (Basic Orientation Course) class at Gunter Air Force Base and had preceded me to Wilmington. Jerry was assigned as a general medical officer and since Flight

Surgeons are a part of the "reason to be" of the Air Force, most command positions are filled by Flight Surgeons in the Medical Corp and by pilots in the line. I was assigned as dispensary commander. We soon learned that Wilmington was a boomtown because of rumors that the base was to become a Strategic Air Command Refueling Wing. There was no rental property available. The four of us, including Shadow, were invited to stay with Jerry and Ann Nelson until we could find a place to live. Ann, who had no children, adopted Lisa and Cathy as her own but in doing so assumed the position of super mom. Everywhere Lisa wanted or needed to go Ann was there too. Although we were grateful for the hospitality in the several weeks it took us to find a home, the closeness wore thin on Lisa and presented real problems later own. With FHA financing, we were able to buy a small new home in a subdivision about five miles from the base. We liked the simplicity of the one story red, wood-frame house with a large living-dining room combination, one large and two small bedrooms, one bath, kitchen, and a full basement. The basement was to be my shop and before too many months had passed, I had installed the Delta lathe I had been given at age 12. This was our first home and, as we would someday realize, the only home that would be truly ours.

At the base I soon learned that the Dispensary was only an interim facility and was to be replaced by a Strategic Air Command Hospital. I would then be assigned as hospital commander. I was only a Captain and there were few hospital commanders in the Air Force below the rank of Colonel. The boom in Wilmington was fueled by the influx of SAC personnel in anticipation of the change over to an Air Refueling Wing. In the late 50's, the B-47 bomber was the mainstay of our strategic defenses. Refueling was accomplished by the turbo-supercharged four-engine KC97 (Boeing Stratocruiser). It was somewhat of a mismatch as the B-47 had to slow down significantly, and the KC-97 had to fly as high and fast as possible to allow for fuel transfer so that the bomber would be able to fly over the arctic to Russia and return. Almost as soon as the base had been programmed for build up, there were further rumors that the KC-97 program would be phased out. The B-52 bombers were coming on line and KC-135 tankers would replace the piston engine KC-97. One hand of the government was saying build up the base to the maximum and the other hand knew that decommissioning was inevitable. What a waste.

My orders were changed, officially assigning me to the Strategic Air Command, conceived by Curtis LeMay, largely responsible for our eventual success in the Cold War.

Although I had gained in confidence in medicine, I still experienced a bit of anxiety when facing situations in which I did not have full control. In the clinic I was in charge. Sgt. Chalifour, a career medic, was my right hand man, and I relied on his experience in most military matters. So when he said that Col. By....er wanted to see me right away, I suddenly felt uneasy. Col. By....er, soon to be a general, was the SAC Wing Commander of the base and had the reputation of being tough. *What have I done?* I was nervous as I entered the colonel's office and saluted.

"Well, doc, where are you from?"

"Memphis, sir."

"Have you had any experience running a hospital?"

"No sir."

"Well, you know you're assigned as hospital commander don't you?"

"I guess so—I guess—yes sir, I do."

"Don't worry doc," he said, sensing my anxiety. "That's a long way off. You'll do just fine running the clinic. If SAC ever builds the G'damn hospital, they'll have to staff it properly and you'll have lots of help. Meantime, if you need anything, let me know. By the way, I want you to come to the staff meetings as hospital commander."

"Thank you sir," I said, with renewed confidence. As young and as inexperienced as I was, I was to be accepted as part of the team.

Months later, the colonel called me into his office and, with a slightly embarrassed tone asked, "Doc, what the hell is this?" He opened a tissue on the desk. I inspected the small black insect. "It looks like a crab lice."

"That's what I was afraid of—damn dirty toilet. What do I do, doc?"

I prescribed Quell and agreed that this visit would remain confidential.

I won't say the colonel gave me preferential treatment, but when I wanted to repaint the Cessna 170, a rather large, empty KC97 hanger was available for my exclusive use and VOC (Verbal Orders of the Commander) permission to fly into the base was easily obtained throughout my time at Wilmington. Although my officer rank was low, my status as a flight surgeon and hospital commander brought me into daily working and social contact with all the higher ranking officers. I respected them and their accomplishments and I in turn, earned their respect. I was privy to many details of Air Force life that many officers would prefer to remain hidden. Lt. Col. Smith, an operations officer was a lonely, divorced alcoholic. He befriended Lisa and me, and on more than one occasion we would drive him home after a base party.

"Always clear the sky before turning, doc," he was fond of repeating. "Clear right," he would declare, or "Clear left," at every stop until we deposited him at his house. One evening I got a call from the base commander.

"Hey doc—we need you. Col. Smith's in trouble. He's down at the jail in town. Come on down. I'll brief you when you get here."

I hurried to the courthouse. "Here's the situation", the commander said as he greeted me on the steps of the courthouse. "Smith was driving home and missed his drive, running into a ditch. He wasn't hurt but the police say he has been drinking. Now, we know he has been taking some prescription. Can you say that this drug is what caused him to lose control?"

The drug was a tranquilizer and, of course, combined with alcohol was a deadly combination. When the police asked my opinion, I said that the drug alone could have caused a loss of coordination, and since it was a prescription drug the colonel was not responsible. The base commander assured the police that Col. Smith would be referred to Wright-Patterson Air Force Base for proper evaluation and would not be allowed to drive until he was off his medication. Later Col. Smith was treated for his alcoholism but his career faltered and soon after we departed from Wilmington we learned that he had died.

One of the perks of Aviation Medicine was the requirement to fly. I even obtained flight pay for something I would have done for nothing. I flew night missions in the KC-97's and on occasion, flew helicopters with the Army Guard Unit stationed at Wilmington. The pilots all knew I had my own airplane and usually let me fly the "heavy iron" at altitude. It was a great thrill to control that four engine tanker but nothing compares to the day I flew and landed a DC3. Some of the KC-97 pilots were required to take transition training in the DC3 (the military designation was C-47) and for some it was their first time to fly a tail wheel equipped airplane.

"G-dammit Lieutenant, can't you hold this thing straight on the runway," the instructor pilot shouted to the trainee who was zigzagging down the runway. I was riding jump seat. It was obvious that the Lieutenant was over-controlling. His third attempt at landing was a near disaster as we veered off the runway. Fortunately the ground was hard and the instructor was able to regain control.

"Doc, you fly a tail dragger, don't you? Get up here and show the Lieutenant how to fly this thing." The Lieutenant, somewhat chagrined, gave up his seat and I strapped into the pilot seat. After a few familiarization turns and slow flight, I felt ready. Except for a heavier feel, the old D-3 handled as I expected. I felt confident as we approached for a wheel landing. I slowed the rate of descent feeling for the ground and was surprised when the wheels touched. I thought I was way too high in comparison to the Cessna, but with slight forward pressure on the control wheel the old bird remained planted on the runway. The Lieutenant made several more attempts that day but I am not sure if he ever qualified.

Across the street from our home in Wilmington lived Col. John and Madeline Hudson. They had grown children at the time and adopted Lisa and me as their own. We had good times together and John, who was a high time command pilot, served as a mentor, flying with me in the Cessna on occasion. Later in our tour of duty at Wilmington, John was assigned as Base Commander at Wurtsmith Air Force Base in northern Michigan. One weekend he and Madeline invited us up for a visit. It was quite a thrill for this captain and his family to land at a SAC Base with the base commander himself greeting us at Base Operations.

Jerry Nelson and I had a good relationship although I suspect he may have resented some of the times I was flying while he was running morning sick call. We shared night call in a practice that was as close to being a true family practice as I would ever experience.

"Doc, little Allison's been sick all day. I am worried about her. Do you think you could come over this evening?" The airman sounded concerned so after getting directions, I found the two-story farmhouse that he and his family rented about five miles in the country south of the base.

"Does it hurt when I do this, Allison?" I pressed gently on her abdomen, first on the left then at McBurney's point. She grimaced in pain with pressure in the right lower quadrant of her abdomen. Rebound was painful. "Appendicitis," I announced. I called the hospital in Wilmington, made arrangements for her admission and obtained transportation through our base for an ambulance. I was gratified when Allison's dad let me know that my diagnosis was correct and that she was recovering nicely following surgery.

Making house calls is not without its hazards, however.

"Captain Johnson's wife wants me to check one of their kids. I won't be long," I announced to Lisa after hanging up the phone.

Captain Johnson's house was dark as I entered the driveway, although a sliver of light could be seen through blinds in a front window. I had met Captain Johnson's wife, Gwen, at the clinic on previous occasions but was somewhat surprised when she opened the door clad in a rather thin nightgown.

"Please come in." she smiled. "I appreciate your coming. I'm worried about Johnny." She ushered me into the living room. I expected to see the child. "Would you like something to drink?"

I declined. "Where's the child and what seems to be his problem?" I asked.

"I get worried when Bill is off flying. I get lonesome, too," she added as she reached for my hand.

What's going on here. I flushed in the darkened room. "Please show me your baby and let me see what's going on. What are his symptoms?"

"He's been crying all evening. Maybe he just misses his dad."

"Does he hurt anywhere?"

"I don't think so. He just cries." The house was quiet. There was no crying baby.

"Maybe he's better now. Let me check him," I suggested.

She led me upstairs to the baby's room. The baby was quietly sleeping. Breathing was regular and pulse was strong. He hardly stirred when I gently turned him over onto his back to check his abdomen and to listen to his chest.

"He seems fine to me."

"I guess he got better. You must have a way with babies doctor." She brushed against me as she leaned over to cover the baby. "Thank you for coming. Can't you stay a while?" She seemed to be pleading as I started down the stairs. "Please, I get so lonesome," she said somewhat provocatively.

"No, I must go. I am glad your baby got better. I need to get back to my family now. Lisa is waiting up for me." My mention of Lisa provided a barrier and I was able to leave a rather uncomfortable situation. A doctor may occasionally find himself in a vulnerable position through no fault of his own, but to take advantage of his authority would violate the tenets of the Hippocratic oath and should preclude such behavior. When I told Lisa of my escape, she smiled and suggested: "Maybe I better go with you on house calls in the future."

"I would be glad to have your protection."

We laughed. Another advantage of an orthopaedic practice—no house calls.

Having obtained certification from the American Board of Orthopaedic Surgery approving my work at Wise as equivalent to the required year of general surgery, I had rather nonchalantly sent an application to the Campbell Clinic for a fellowship beginning in 1960 or 1961. I was disappointed to receive a letter from Dr. Tom Waring some months later. *We regret that we are unable to offer you a position at the Campbell Clinic in 1960 or 61. Although your application was well received, no openings are available in this time frame. You are welcome to reapply in the future if your circumstances permit.*

Lisa shared my disappointment but we tried to look on the bright side. I would investigate taking an Air Force residency and at least not have to take a pay cut since, at the time, the monthly stipend for an orthopaedic resident at a civilian facility was $125 a month.

As a part of the Strategic Air Command, our base was subject to ORI's (Operational Readiness Inspections). Our first surprise inspection was announced by the obtrusive claxon horn blaring over the whole base. Immediately Base Ops warned us of the inbound crippled bomber loaded with nuclear weapons—code word: *Broken Arrow*. Sgt. Chalifour and I had written plans for the drill and within a short period of time were setting up a decontamination area on the flight line. We were shown a scenario and were quite proud that our small medical squadron responded appropriately. We had passed.

The medical service officer from Eighth Air Force, Col. Shute, was quite complimentary. We became friends as he visited the base on several more occasions and especially when I was officially invited to attend the Eighth Air Force Hospital Commander's Conference at Barksdale Air Force Base in Shreveport, Louisiana. Again, I was somewhat out of my league as the lowest ranking officer among many colonels, lieutenant colonels, and majors but I was made to feel welcome in the group.

We invited Col. Shute to our home for dinner on one of his visits to Wilmington. He spoke highly of my work at the base and strongly urged me to consider the Air Force as a career. He said that he had connections in Washington and he would do anything he could to see that I obtained a residency. I told him that I was planning to reapply to the Campbell Clinic but would also like to look at the residency at Lackland Air Force in San Antonio. He assured me that, either way, he could guarantee me a career. Lisa and I discussed the possibilities. Other than the fact that orthopaedics had become my first choice in specialization, we had no firm idea of where we might settle down and if by some chance I was not accepted into an orthopaedic training program I would much prefer to remain as a flight surgeon in the Air Force.

Meanwhile, the impulsiveness of youth prevailed and we learned in early 1960 that Lisa was pregnant with our second child. "We want them all out of diapers at the same time," we rationalized. In the days before ultrasound, the sex of this baby was unknown so we prepared a unisex room for the new addition due in September of 1960.

I was able to obtain TDY orders (temporary duty) for a POV (privately owned vehicle) trip to San Antonio to check out the program at Wilford Hall USAF Hospital, Lackland. Of course my POV was an airplane. Lisa stayed home with Cathy and Shadow while I guided the Cessna to the southwest, landing at Ft Worth to check out Carswell AFB Hospital, which also had a training program, then flying on to Stinson Field just to the south of San Antonio International. I was impressed by the program there but made no commitment. On the way back, as the sun slid beneath the horizon behind me and I approached runway 06 at Shreveport Municipal, I was surprised when the Cessna descended into a fog bank forming on the runway. Within minutes the field was socked in. My plans to fly into Memphis that evening were scrapped, and I called Lisa in Wilmington using a pay phone in the terminal.

"I think I'll stay in the airplane tonight so I can get an early start in the morning."

"Don't get a crick in your neck," she warned.

Late into the evening, I spent time with the control tower crew. They were glad to have company on such a boring evening since the airport had gone down below minimums. There was no traffic.

"No need to get up early", they advised. "This fog won't burn off until 10 or so in the morning."

I slept somewhat fitfully on the back seat of the Cessna, unable to stretch out and was glad to the see the daylight, although the fog was as thick as ever, hiding the control tower less than 50 yards away. After a leisurely breakfast in the terminal I noticed a few light spots in the slowly lifting fog; eventually the visibility improved enough so that I could obtain a special VFR clearance. Climbing out to the west of Shreveport underneath the low hanging clouds, I saw a large patch of blue sky and aimed the Cessna toward the escape hole. Soon I was on top of a white blanket extending as far as I could see. For most of the flight into Memphis, the cloud cover broke occasionally to show the dark ground below. As I approached the Mississippi River, however, the clouds dissipated completely to allow an uneventful arrival.

I was scheduled to meet with Dr. Tom Waring at the Campbell Clinic the next morning, spend the day at the clinic, and attend the Monday Night Meeting. Dr. Spencer Speed was the Chief of Staff, and after shaking hands remarked, "You boys are getting younger all the time."

I just wish that youthful countenance, so obvious then, was still with me. I mentioned to Dr. Waring that I was considering having the Air Force sponsor me through the residency and, as an ex-military doctor he thought that would be no problem. Unfortunately, he failed to mention my connection with the Air Force to the other staff members and, I was to learn later, when papers and requirements of the Air Force Sponsorship Program began to arrive, I was nearly voted down.

While in Memphis I looked into the only other local orthopaedic training program at the Veteran's Administration Hospital but wasn't too impressed. The program closed not too many years later when the Chief of Orthopaedics, Dana Street left.

Back home in Wilmington, Lisa, small as she was, was growing rapidly with her pregnancy. Her obstetrician, Dr. Robert Olseys, was a respected family practitioner in Wilmington. I had met him at conferences in the hospital and on one occasion he had helped me in public health inspections at several of the town's eating establishments, frequented by enlisted personnel from the base. In uniform, armed with the power to declare a facility "off limits" to military personnel, I was not a welcome site at many of the places we visited. As Lisa's due date approached, Dr. Olseys told me that I could be in the delivery room if I wanted to and, since self-analgesia by Trilene inhalation was preferred in the sixties, I might be of some use. The atmosphere at the Wilmington Hospital was more relaxed and less formal than that of the large Memphis hospitals. When I was introduced as Dr. Justis, any door was opened to me.

On September 28, 1960 Lisa began having labor pains. In the labor room, my job was to see that Lisa got the Trilene mask to her face. As soon as the drug took effect her hand fell away pulling the mask strapped to her wrist with it. When another pain began in her groggy state, she was unable to find the mask. That was my job. Soon the nurse announced that she was fully dilated and we wheeled her into the delivery room. Within minutes Dr. Olseys announced, "It's a boy."

I was somewhat dazed by the event and it took me a while to appreciate the reality of another healthy baby being a part of our growing family. Lisa remained at the hospital for several days while

I prepared the house for her return. Ann Nelson volunteered to keep Cathy Ann for a few days, until Lisa could manage our new arrival, Jeff Rollow Justis, and our expanded family of five.

Meanwhile, my work continued at the base as I awaited word from Campbell Clinic. Ann was certainly a big help to Lisa but her possessiveness eventually soured their relationship. There were times when Lisa would be unable to go to the grocery store without Ann. She would come by the house daily and insist that Lisa bring the babies to her house. If Lisa declined, Ann's feelings were hurt and only Lisa's relenting placated her.

Our traveling was curtailed somewhat with two children, although we planned a visit to Memphis over Christmas. I did my share (at least for that era) as a father and I did change diapers and assist with bathing. But on weekends, holidays, and evenings, when a job needed doing at the airport or on the airplane or on a project on the lathe in the basement, Lisa made the children feel that their job was to "help daddy" by not interfering with what he was doing. Lisa and the children played with Helen Williams' cat in the small, attached bedroom, heated by a gas heater, at Sabina Airport while John and I disassembled the Continental 145 engine of the Cessna for a major overhaul. We shipped the parts to Columbus, Ohio for certification and later, in our basement, I began reassembling the engine. Final assembly took place under John's watchful eye at the airport. It was this experience that started me down the path that would eventually allow me to obtain the coveted Airframe and Powerplant rating.

We were a family of five, if we included our first "child," Shadow, who provided a mop up service for spilled food and other edible food "gifts" from the children and others. For a get together of some of the officers at the base during the holidays, I made a batch of Uncle JL.'s famous eggnog, laced generously with Kentucky Bourbon, It was quite cold that late afternoon before the party, and I was putting a large bowl of eggnog on the back step when my foot slipped and bowl tilted, spilling the creamy bourbon-laced fluid all over the steps. "Shadow will clean that up'" Lisa suggested.

"Maybe I can scrape it up," I said, half seriously. "I guess I better make some more, much as I hate to waste this."

Shadow eagerly came out of the house to do her cleanup job as I started the egg beating process all over again. A few minutes later we heard a strange wailing sound from the back porch. It was Shadow, sitting with her head back and an unmistakable toothy smile, calling to her wild cousins. Although her inebriation was short lived, she was unusually subdued for the next several days with what was probably a large canine hangover.

Sometime after that Christmas party I received a telegram from Dr. Tom Waring accepting my new application for residency training at the Campbell Clinic.

I accept with pleasure and appreciation your offer for a fellowship in orthopaedics beginning July 1, 1961, was my response by return telegram.

Once I had been accepted for orthopaedic training at the Campbell Clinic, we were elated at the prospect, having been away from Memphis just long enough to forget some of the problems associated with too much closeness with one's family. (I'm convinced that many young couples need time away from parents and in-laws to establish their own identities as primary family units.)

The one-room house that had served as Annie Lou's place during her many years with my mother was available. Johnny Rollow was always ready with advice and consultation on a house that I was eager to build. On an extended leave over Christmas of 1960 and on long weekend trips in early 1961, I began modification of the converted barn. In the forties, the 12' x 12' wood framed structure served as a home for my horse, Clark, whom I road through fields and woods that, years later, would succumb to urban sprawl. To accommodate Annie Lou, who had been rescued by my mother from a less than ideal country shack, the barn had been floored and electrified but, much to the shame of our southern heritage, there was no plumbing. I installed a septic tank and added a large living area and kitchen using lumber from demolished World War II Quonset huts that had been used as housing and classrooms at Southwestern in the early post war years. By early summer the "Little Green House," as Lisa and the children were to call it, was ready.

I had one more decision to make. Should I remain in the Air Force for sponsorship through my residency or should I separate? The salary at the Campbell Clinic was only $125 per month, so I knew I would be dependent on my dad if I were not sponsored. I had been completely independent financially since Lisa and I had married and I certainly preferred that. My primary worry was that the Air Force might change its mind about which sponsored program it would approve. I called Col. Shutt with this concern and within a day had an official letter assuring me that I was approved specifically for the Campbell Clinic Training Program.

I received orders, completed my duties at Wilmington which included closing the alert facility that we had spent so much time and money upgrading to SAC standards during the 18 months under that command, made arrangements to rent our house, and sent the moving van to 4209 Walnut Grove Road, Guesthouse Rear.

The house we had bought during the SAC build-up boom time in Wilmington now was an albatross as the Strategic Air Command vacated the base. The rental barely paid the note, and we celebrated happily several years later when the house finally sold.

Another passage of life was coming to a close. We had gained new perspectives and new friends since our marriage. I had enjoyed working with Air Force pilots, flying with them, and being a part of the Air Force family. Now I was to begin surgical specialization. I would spend as much time studying orthopaedics as I had the entire field of medicine during medical school. I wondered if I was up to the task and whether lingering doubts would fade with increasing experience.

A COLD CHRISTMAS

The whole world is white, but dark lines signal man's community through roads and his separation through fences. Towns, where lives of individuals touch, provide us with guidance on our course.

It was the first big snow of the season in Wilmington, Ohio. The flakes were large and clung tenaciously to everything they touched. I knew the tail of our Cessna 170 would be covered, but at least the wings and cabin area were protected by the lean-to hanger I had built on the back of John Williams' shop and home. The "home" part was a room about six by ten feet with a bunk bed at one end, a couch that served as a bed sometimes, and a gas grill and heater at the other end. Helen, John's wife, always had a pot of coffee on the grill and cheerfully offered every airport customer a cup insisting he sit in the office while she pumped gas into his aircraft. This was a typical "grass roots" airport of the late 50's with a single turf runway paralleling the highway between Wilmington and Washington Court House. There was no hangar, but two large doors could be swung open in the side of John's shop so that an airplane could be nosed in for work. John was an A & P mechanic with an inspection authorization, and with his help I had overhauled the Continental 145 HP engine that powered our family airplane. We spent many happy evenings in John's shop warmed by a single pot bellied stove as Lisa, Cathy (one and a half) and Jeff (three months) were entertained by Helen.

John had lost part of his right hand in a propping accident (he said a magneto was ungrounded) and had difficulty manipulating tools; but he knew engines and airplanes as well as any professor knows his subject. I, as his student, learned much during the months the airplane was down for overhaul. I remember being very careful to install the connecting rods with the bearing inserts and the stamped numbers aligned according to *my* interpretation of the overhaul manual. John immediately noticed my mistake in reversing the location of the stamped numbers in three out of six cylinders. I will never forget that lesson.

With the overhaul completed and the test flight successful we had planned to leave for Memphis after work December 21, 1960, but the cold front bringing heavy snow had moved in by midday. We could only hope that VFR weather would soon follow. Luck was with us as we awoke to a crisp blue sky and a beautiful, though snowbound Ohio. By eight we were slowly making our way down the rutted highway toward Sabina. Mounds of snow from the road scrapers lined each side of the highway.

I almost passed the airport because the landing strip looked like every other snow covered field in the area and the drifts had all but covered the west side of John's building. Only a limp, somewhat tattered wind sock on top of the weathered William's home and shop, gave evidence that this was, in fact, our airport.

Helen's pot of coffee was ready as expected, and she warmly invited Lisa and the children in out of the cold. Even Shadow, our German shepherd, was welcome and glad to lay down by the gas stove. John and I walked around to the back of the shop on the east side where the Cessna was nosed up to the shop. The lean-to shed that I had built some months before had protected the fabric covered wings of our 1948 Cessna 170. A foot of snow covered the horizontal stabilizer and drifts had blown along side the aft quarter of the fuselage.

If we were going to fly that day, I had much work to do. I had taken off on a snow-covered runway before but never in snow this deep. It must have been twelve inches on the runway itself because the drifts in the area behind my airplane and the shop were at least eighteen inches. I began shoveling a path for each wheel so that I could pull the plane back and turn it toward the runway. John, who was disabled by emphysema from heavy smoking, came outside occasionally to offer moral support, but the shoveling and pushing and inching the plane back was up to me. Winded, I finally was able to pull the plane far enough back and turned toward the runway that I could start the engine—or rather *try* to start it. With congealed oil and the 20° temperature one or two turns of the prop used all the energy left in the battery. My energy was used up in snow shoveling so hand propping was out of the question.

With some difficulty I moved our Chevrolet close to the Cessna, attaching jumper cables between batteries and finally, after much priming, the Continental coughed and rumbled and shook itself to life.

My relief was short lived, however, because with full throttle I tried to inch the empty airplane forward through the snow, and it would not budge. The drifts were too high. Discouraged, but not willing to give up, I let the engine warm up some more, shut it down and went inside to warm myself up and get a cup of coffee.

Jeff was asleep and Cathy was entertaining herself on the couch. Lisa was tired of the wait but understood. She wanted to help so Helen kept the children while Lisa and I shoveled snow in two paths toward the runway. My plan was to taxi the plane back and forth on the runway enough to pack the snow in ruts for two-thirds the length of the runway. I recalled that attempted takeoff in our 65 HP Luscombe from the very muddy strip in Coeburn where, using my best muddy field technique, the 65 horses just could not get the wheels out as we plowed through the thick goop and, as planned, when there was no further acceleration past the half way point, I aborted the takeoff. So on this snow-covered field, I was prepared to abort the takeoff if I could not develop flying speed in the first half of the runway.

With enough snow shoveled away in front of the plane, finally, with full throttle, the plane developed enough momentum to continue snow plowing onto the east-west runway. Not daring to slow down for fear of getting stuck. I coaxed the Cessna toward the west end making a wide full powered tear-drop turn in the snow coming back into the ruts that I had just created.

Back and forth—back and forth—I lost track of the number of times I plowed that runway but each time the ruts got a little wider and the Cessna struggled less in her effort. During the last run down the runway, I again advanced full throttle and this time felt the plane lift slightly. As long as I stayed in the ruts, I knew I could coax her into the air.

Taxiing back to the east end, I turned around, lining up in the twin tracks and shut down the engine. Lisa, the children, and Shadow trudged through the snow to the waiting Cessna and loaded our bags behind the rear seats. Jeff was placed in the padded traveling crib that was strapped in to the left rear seat. Cathy had her own seat on the right and Shadow was on the floor between the seats. Lisa strapped into the co-pilot's seat. The engine started promptly. After checking and double-checking everything, we were at last ready to leave on our Christmas vacation.

I expected slower acceleration with our load, but using a technique that worked well with the small flaps on this early model 170, I kept the tail glued to the ground until the airspeed slowly increased and I could sense the first lightness of lift. Reaching down to the flap control between the front seats, I quickly pulled the lever up for full flaps, and the Cessna fairly leaped into the air freeing itself from the clinging white snow.

Gingerly I played with pitch control, lowering the nose with each second's increase in speed. We accelerated in ground effect, skimming inches above the snow and as the west end of the runway passed underneath we climbed free and clear into the bright early afternoon sky.

The farther southwest we flew the winds grew stronger from 240 degrees and at 6500 feet the outside air temperature gauge read minus 5°. In spite of full cabin heat, the little 145 HP Continental was not capable of adding much energy to the frigid air passing over the exhaust tubing.

Lisa and I had numb toes. Shadow was curled into a black and tan ball; Cathy was bundled in a thick snowsuit and Jeff had been quiet in his padded "airplane box." A bottle that Lisa had propped in his mouth had apparently satisfied him for a while, but now he was crying; well insulated and packaged, he did not seem cold. The cause for his distress became apparent when shaking the bottle produced no milk—the bottle was frozen. "It really *is* cold!" Lisa and I agreed.

Our ground speed was abysmally slow in the strong southwest wind and I had to cancel our planned refueling stop at Bowling Green, Kentucky, about half way to Memphis. It was getting later in the afternoon, and daylight would soon be fading. We were all tired; it had been a long day, and my muscles were aching from the exertion of the morning and the cold of the flight. Louisville, just ahead, beckoned, although the runway at Bowman Field, recently plowed, was difficult to distinguish from the surrounding white fields. Touchdown was smooth, but as I played the rudder on rollout I felt an uncomfortable skidding sensation with each slight deviation from the center of the runway. It was impossible to turn onto the taxiway with any forward speed at all. Coming to a complete stop in the middle of the runway, I began carefully sailing, skidding, and occasionally rolling toward the F.B.O. If I had ever considered flying further toward Memphis that evening, the final exercise of skimming the ice covered runway and taxiways at Louisville made the decision to spend the night in a motel an easy one.

Another blue sky, crisp day, with lessening winds greeted us the following morning and we were in Memphis by noon to begin a family Christmas celebration.

CAMPBELL CLINIC

I gently palpate the deformed forearm, then with quick manual pressure bring the bone ends into correct alignment. The sense of accomplishment on viewing the improved appearance of the post-reduction x-ray renews my conviction that orthopaedics is the right career choice for me after all.

Lisa and I were excited about returning to Memphis to be with old friends and family again, and I was happy to begin a career in orthopaedics, although I only had a vague idea of what the field encompassed. Certainly the mechanical aspect of "fixing bones" prompted me to consider the specialty in the first place. But what else was there? On one of our trips to Memphis during which we were reconstructing the barn-house in the back of my folk's lot, I contacted an old Southwestern friend, Tommy Strong. Tommy was a resident at the Clinic, having started in January 1961.

"What would you suggest I read before I start in July?" I asked.

"Well, of course, you ought to read both volumes of Campbell's Operative Orthopaedics then Watson-Jones, Charnley, and—and I'd review Gray's Anatomy."

"Wait a minute, Tom, I couldn't possibly read all that."

"Well, *I* did. I also read..."

Obviously I had asked the wrong person. Tommy was smart. We knew that at Southwestern.

"How about something just to give me a general feel for the specialty as a whole?"

"Okay—I guess Philip Wiles' Text will give you a start. Turek is also good."

In the weeks before I was to begin the program, I attended the Monday Night Meeting, a mandatory and traditional staff and resident conference. As I listened to the discussion I suddenly felt very inadequate and wondered if I was in over my head. Would this be like organic chemistry? I had been accepted into a very prestigious residency training program. I did not see myself as an academician, yet here were residents only a few months ahead of me presenting cases in a confident matter, and discussing pathology and anatomy. Tommy's obvious erudition did not ease my anxiety.

I had taken terminal leave from Wilmington in preparation for my assignment at Memphis. We used most of June to complete what was to become our home (the "Little Green House") for the next three years. With July 1 just two weeks away, Lisa asked her sister, Ann Ross, to keep Cathy and Jeff while we flew to the Black Hills of North Dakota. As a child, traveling with my parents, I had been to Palmer Gulch Lodge and wanted to share this with Lisa. For about five days we relaxed in the clean North Dakota air, went on trail rides, and enjoyed being alone together. I read Philip Wiles' Textbook of Orthopaedics, wondering if I could remember all the names—Hibbs, Albey, Andre, Smith-Peterson, Jewitt, etc.—so common in the specialty.

There were many more facets to orthopaedics than I realized, and I was eager to get started. July 1 fell on a Saturday; I duly showed up in the office and began the process of "knocking down white flags." The clinic had plastic "flags" on hinges in front of each examining room. When a single white flag was extended, each resident knew that a patient was ready for him to obtain a history and physical. Yellow indicated that an x-ray was needed and various color combinations signified that the patient was ready for a specific staff man.

The clinic provided a unique experience in learning. The small staff (then only thirteen) worked one-on-one with the twelve residents. I considered each of the members of the staff to be a true gentleman. No longer was I subjected to the verbal abuse I had previously experienced in surgery. As junior residents our primary responsibilities included "working-up" patients, applying casts and splints, and serving as second or occasionally as first assistants in surgery.

The first three or four months at the Campbell Clinic were frustrating in that I felt I was not "doing" anything—I was not "setting bones." Then the opportunity came.

"Here, Jeff, you try reducing this supracondylar fracture," Hoyt Crenshaw suggested one evening after I had called him back to the clinic for an emergency. "Put your thumb on the olecranon and push the distal humerus over as you apply traction to the forearm."

I had a real sense of accomplishment as I felt the bones move when I applied pressure. It was a good feeling to be able to visualize the underlying deformity and correct it manually.

My contemporaries, Bob Tooms, Kent Peterson, and Mac MaCauley, had also started the program in July 1961. I did not realize at the time but I was older by a few months than any in my class. Bob Tooms was a tall, distinguished, prematurely bald man who had wanted to be a resident at the Campbell Clinic so much that he had spent a year in research at the University of Tennessee just to be close and increase his chances of being accepted. As in my case he had not been accepted on his first application but perseverance triumphed eventually.

Bob was assigned to "anatomy and pathology" his first three months and accordingly was to present cases during his very first Monday night meeting. I remember envying his presence of mind, his maturity, and his seeming lack of anxiety. Just the thought of my having to present a case caused me to experience that uncomfortable feeling of stage fright I had never been able to shake.

Kent Peterson, my good friend, was affectionately called the "acid assassin." Nothing was sacred to Kent. He would cut to the core of any situation with quick wit and sharp tongue. Mac

MaCauley was a laid back person who did not seem to hold the staff in the same degree of awe as did the rest of us.

Although the first few months involved working up patients in the office as junior residents, we also were second assistants on many operative cases. The more senior residents picked their cases and were the first assistants. Thus on a hip procedure, for example, I would be on the side opposite the operation holding large Hibbs retractors.

Can't see a thing, I would think.

"Here! Pull here—pull!"

How can I learn if I can't see? I grumbled to myself.

But gradually, as if by osmosis, I was learning and later realized that just observing the staff was a valid way to learn. Dr. Harold Boyd was a wonderful presence, a large man with strong sure hands. Deliberate and confident he placed the utmost importance on the care of the patient.

"Doctor, please help move Mrs. Smithson from her room to the OR," Dr. Boyd requested one day. Although we had orderlies that usually transported patients, Dr. Boyd was worried about this particular patient. For some reason I didn't get to the floor on time and didn't catch up with the patient until we got to the operating room.

Dr. Boyd was upset. "Doctor, I wanted you there to assist with her traction. You see how the orderly just tied the rope to the stretcher! That's not good," he lectured. I vowed not to disappoint Dr. Boyd again. Through him I learned to put the patient first.

Dr. Waring was a mentor in the operating room and in the office. A very conservative surgeon, "Uncle Tom" as we affectionately called him, would listen carefully to the patient and after explaining options for treatment would place his hand on the patient's shoulder and say, "Now you don't really need to have that operation do you? I think we can help you without surgery"—this to a patient who had been primed for surgery by many other doctors but whose problem really could be best treated conservatively.

Dr. Speed was getting ready to retire. In the 60s before malpractice insurance coverage became such an issue, a surgeon could slow down by operating one day a week if he desired or by choosing to operate only on uncomplicated cases. Such flexibility now is impossible because of the expense of malpractice coverage and the need to generate enough income to cover increasing overhead. Since Dr. Speed was doing relatively minor foot surgery, I could, even as a junior resident, be his first assistant, a job that required exanguinating the extremity and applying a restricting tourniquet. Struggling through a bunion operation with oozing blood interfering with visualization, Dr. Speed pointedly suggested "Get John, the orderly, to show you how to put on a tourniquet." Another lesson learned.

Dr. Hugh Smith was a genius, and like many extremely bright individuals, he was easily bored. He never wasted time. The quintessential history and physical attributed to Dr. Smith was not an exaggeration:

Past history: non-contributory
Chief complaint: twisted ankle
Present illness: patient twisted ankle while running yesterday.
Physical examination: swollen ankle
Diagnosis: sprained ankle
*Treatmen*t: ice and elevate. Return if not better.

Surgery was just as rapid fire. "Ten minutes, skin to skin" was not unusual for a femoral neck fracture in Dr. Smith's hands. Harold Boyd and Hugh Smith were opposites in personality, but each respected the other and occasionally they would engage in a friendly speed contest in the O. R. Dr. Smith, a chain smoker, was usually the first one out of the O. R.—if for no other reason than to have a cigarette.

I had quit smoking in medical school and felt no need to smoke during my internship or at Wise or in the Air Force. My self-imposed expectation was for this residency-training program to be a learning experience without the anxiety I had felt in medical school and in previous uncontrolled situations. That illusion was put to a test when Dr. "Cal" asked me to present a talk at the Monday night meeting on axillary neuropathy after tetanus antitoxin injection. Suddenly the thought of standing up in a meeting brought back the "cold sweat" of anxiety I thought I had left behind.

Won't I ever get over this? I was frustrated at my perceived weakness. Doing the research and writing was no problem, but I agonized over the upcoming presentation. Then it was Monday and my uneasiness grew. Lisa knew I was uncomfortable.

"You'll do fine," she said, as we finished dinner before the meeting.

On the way downtown for the 7:30 meeting, I impulsively pulled into a service station and purchased a package of Kent cigarettes. In doing so I was admitting to myself that I could not be the "perfect" physician; I was flawed (as is everyone). When I inhaled that acrid smoke and felt the nicotine induced dizziness for the first time in years, a little of my stage fright ameliorated—as much because I had lowered my self expectation as because of the pharmacological effects of the drug.

I was not alone. In those days the meeting room was smoke filled; many staff and residents were smokers; ashtrays on the back of the seats overflowed. Such a scene would be unimaginable forty years later. My first presentation was acceptable, and I did manage over the next three years to develop some confidence in my ability to get through similar ordeals. However, my career as an orthopaedic surgeon never followed an organizational or political tract because of my discomfort with public presentation. Even after taking a public speaking course at night for six weeks through the University of Tennessee, I remained uncomfortable and avoided situations that often are stepping stones to political office in any organization.

The passage of years has allowed some compensation for this disability; I learned that using visual aids (slides, charts, etc.) helped me considerably and that knowledge of the subject to be presented was essential to the development of confidence. In short —be prepared.

Although surgery often is a group effort involving anesthesiologists, nurses, and aides, the surgeon and patient are at the center. This one-on-one relationship is what appealed to me, and over the years of training I slowly developed increasing confidence in my ability to correct a problem presented by a patient whose faith in me boosted that confidence.

Allen Edmondson, a young staff member, was a giant of a man who was determined to teach the residents the correct way to do a job.

"We *always* put the cast on this way. We *never* do that." He would say as he gently corrected us.

After three months I was discouraged, however. I had done no surgery on my own and had only reduced a few fractures. I had even considered quitting and returning to the Air Force as a flight surgeon.

"I think it's important to let someone know when they're doing a good job, Jeff," Allen said to me in the fall of 1961 as we walked along Dunlap toward LeBonheur Children's Hospital. "The staff thinks you're doing a good job and should be able to handle the Gaston."

"The Gaston!" The John Gaston was the large charity hospital of Memphis. The residents did everything there: operated, reduced fractures, and treated patients in traction. It was a big responsibility.

"We think you're ready."

I had mixed emotions. However, as soon as I entered the cast room at the Gaylor clinic I knew I had made the right decision about being an orthopaedic surgeon.

"Justis, you've got x-ray fingers," was a compliment some of my fellow residents bestowed. In no other situation than in reducing fractures did I feel so competent.

The fracture clinic was a learning place and one story illustrates how our patients are our best teachers. My good friend and fellow resident, Bill Hamsa, was rushing to get to surgery when a 12-year-old boy was wheeled in with a broken forearm. The x-ray showed a slightly angulated fracture of both bones.

"We'll correct that without anesthesia," Bill announced as the young patient's eyes got bigger and bigger. Many "greenstick fractures," as long bone breaks in children are called, can and should be corrected without anesthesia, to avoid the associated risks. Most children choose the sudden, short pain of a closed reduction over a shot or shots.

Bill walked over to the youngster, grabbed his right forearm in his large, strong hands and with a deft, quick movement felt and heard the satisfying "cr—rack" of two bones giving under force.

"OH! DOCTOR! You broke my *good* arm!" The young patient hollered.

Bill paled with the fear of all surgeons. Could he have fixed the wrong arm? Could he have broken a perfectly good arm? He looked again at the x-ray and checked the boy's opposite extremity. It was okay. The cold sweat slowly evaporated.

"God, that scared me!" he said as he wrapped plaster around the child's forearm.

The young patient, who by then was comfortable, looked up at Bill with a sly smile, "Fooled ya, didn't I?"

Because of my Air Force sponsorship I had a monthly salary nearly six times the usual resident's salary of $125. However, I had to reimburse the clinic for my meals and laundry. This was a small price to pay for independence and the fact that I could afford to maintain an airplane. Concerning this, however, I wisely kept a rather low profile because of the conservative ambiance at the clinic. Dr. Speed did not approve of showiness on the part of the staff; most drove four-door sedans of subdued colors.

Fred Sage, my good friend and mentor, had been a pilot during World War II, flying secret missions in B25's behind enemy lines as part of the "carpetbagger" program. He was interested in flying again but was discouraged by Dr. Speed's attitude about small airplanes. Perhaps as a result of my coming to the clinic with an airplane and being tolerated, (as long as my orthopaedic training was not compromised) Fred Sage, Fred Strain, and Sam Hunter bought a Cessna 140 together. On more than one occasion in 1962, I took Fred Strain flying in our Cessna 170. He had completed his internal medicine residency and was a young staff member at the Sander's Clinic. He was recently divorced and had responsibility for his two children, Susan and Sam. I could not have anticipated, in the '60s, how our lives would intertwine a decade later. One flight remains memorable to Susan who nearly choked on the smoke coming from the front seat of the Cessna as Fred and I flew to Clarksville for a quick visit to see Ann Ross, my sister-in-law.

Later the two Fred's bought a Ryan Navion. By this time Fred Strain had married a young nurse, Sally VanDervort. Lisa and I had been introduced to her by Fred at the fairgrounds in May, and we met her again later at an industrial airport just south of Memphis where we had both coincidentally landed one Sunday afternoon.

We are never privileged to know how the confluence of paths today will influence our lives tomorrow. The significance of such a casual meeting was lost on me at the time, though remembered. For Sally, I was to learn later, even the memory was lost.

Fred Sage was a storyteller. So after the ice had been broken as far as his flying was concerned, lunchtime was often filled with his stories.

"Man! I had to fly to Ohio to get a prop fixed on my airplane and those guys on the radio couldn't figure out where I was going. I kept telling them I was going to Pie Kay, Ohio. *Pie Kay,* I said it again and again. Where in the hell is that? They kept asking. Pie Kay, Ohio—P-I-Q-U-A—Pie Kay. Oh you mean Piqua, they finally said. Hell! I didn't know how to pronounce it— anyway I finally got there."

Dr. Boyd was also a great storyteller and teacher. Interested in the world, his travel adventures were shared with us daily. He also became a great advocate for my flying. I loaned him one of my favorite books, *Song of the Sky*, by Guy Murchie. He was enthralled by this philosophical treatise and was interested in hearing of my flying adventures.

Unlike many other residencies in which the staff remains rather aloof from the residents, there was a family atmosphere at the Campbell Clinic through which we could learn by close association and shared responsibility. That is not to say we were equals, and there was certainly some vague fear of ever being asked to leave the program; it had happened in the past and would happen again we speculated.

DR. E. JEFF JUSTIS

A wise flight instructor once told me, "Always have an 'out' and you'll never get caught with your wings off!" Having an "out," of course, requires planning, and it requires setting minimums beyond which you will invoke your pre-planned alternative. However, merely planning an "out" is not enough unless you stick to it.

Hector Peon was a Mexican orthopedist who had just finished a training program in Mexico and was visiting the clinic for a year. We became good friends and later, when he returned to Mexico, Lisa and I decided to take a week of our vacation time (I was allowed 30 days by the Air Force but only two weeks a year by the clinic) to fly to Mexico for a visit. Although, with the assured help of Annie Lou, the wonderful maid and companion who had been with my mother for nearly 30 years, we could have left the children with my parents, we took them to Clarksville because Ann and Neil genuinely seemed to enjoy them. They were even willing to keep Shadow.

In early December 1962 we flew southwest to Brownsville, Texas under a lowering overcast, at a 1000 feet over the flat south Texas scrub. Later that evening, as if for us alone, the hotel hosted a fireworks display as we dined on barbecue under the stars.

On to Tampico and Mexico City the following day, we were met by Hector and his wife, Maria. We were treated as VIPs, and it was here that I learned how prestigious the Campbell Clinic really was. As soon as Hector introduced me to his contemporaries, and they learned that I was from the Campbell Clinic, they would ask my opinion on a case or ask what the doctors would do at the Clinic in a given situation.

Although my experience was limited, the give and take of the Monday night meeting had given me a well-rounded approach to orthopaedic surgery. In Mexico and in many other countries that I have subsequently visited, I was able to impart the Campbell Clinic philosophy that can be summarized as follows:

Treat the patient as you would like to be treated and never operate just for the sake of operating. If you contemplate surgery, be sure that the expected result of your surgery will be better than that to be expected through non-operative treatment.

Hector and Maria took us south of Mexico City past the twin volcanoes, Iztaccihuatl and Popocatepetl. At a roadside stand we were introduced to pumpkin flower pie, which was not at all the pumpkin flavored delight I had anticipated, but a rather bland exercise in chewing a raw flower, stem and all. Later my taste buds were ameliorated by tequila. The Rancho Grande was to be our hacienda for several days. A canal-like swimming pool meandered through flowered islands and Moorish arches. Lisa and Maria were deep in conversation as Hector and I swam up to the pool bar conveniently located near water level.

"Now, Yeff, I will introduce you to tequila and blood. Take this crystal of tequila and drink as I do." With that he downed an ounce of the clear liquid.

"Now for the blood." Sangria is a red wine that is gulped in one swallow.

"Now this is most important," Hector emphasized as he poured salt into his anatomical snuffbox and quickly tossed it into his mouth. 'Ahh—ahh," he said with a satisfied look.

I followed suit twice or maybe more. The resulting instability caused me to feel quite fortunate that the pool was rather shallow.

After our visit in Mexico City with Hector and Maria, Lisa and I flew past the smoky twin volcanoes for a quick visit to Acapulco, about an hour and a half southwest; our trusty 170 was becoming a well-traveled bird. The cab driver took us to a hilltop hotel overlooking Acapulco Bay. It was not luxurious but satisfied our romantic expectations. Later we watched the famed cliff divers of Acapulco as they plunged nearly a 100 feet, inches from sheer rock walls, into the churning water below. I told Lisa about an article I had read describing the early onset of cervical traumatic arthritis in the nineteen and twenty-year-olds engaged in this activity.

"Maybe you can write an article about something you're interested in some day," she offered.

"Yeah, I don't think I'd be good at writing just to be writing."

Years later I did become involved in writing and publishing medical papers; those that intrigued me the most usually were related to flying or woodworking or the hand.

Wisely, since I did not have an instrument rating, I tried to maintain a "time buffer" in my flight planning. So after discussing our options Lisa and I decided to leave early. This was a fortunate decision because our first check of the weather at the Mexico City airport provided us with a pessimistic outlook for the weather back home. Weather in Mexico in December usually is good, so, on that particular Thursday morning we drove with our friends out to Mexico City Airport with full confidence in the bright sunshine. We told our friends goodbye, and I walked up to the Weather Bureau in the Administration Building. Much to our surprise and dismay we were informed that the whole east coast of Mexico and the Gulf coast of the United States were socked in with ceilings of around 300 feet and visibilities down to a half mile. Some low clouds also extended over onto the Central Plateau in the northern region, so it seemed we couldn't fly around the bad weather.

We began our hourly vigil of the weather sequence reports. Slowly, they indicated a gradual lifting and breaking up of the stratus layer with relatively good visibility underneath. After considerable discussion among ourselves and with several Mexican pilots, we finally decided on a plan of action, which we felt would be safe and at least start us on the way home. The forecaster did not believe the stratus layer would break up any more than its present condition at Tampico: ceiling 1,300 feet, visibility 10 miles with breaks in the overcast. No one knew how far inland the overcast layer extended or whether it reached the escarpment of the Central Plateau. Our plan was simple. We would fly out from Mexico City to the edge of the Plateau. If the overcast did not extend to the mountains, then we would let down and slide into Tampico under the adequate, 1,300-foot ceiling. If the overcast was broken with large holes we could let down through a hole well clear of the mountainous area. On the other hand, if the overcast was solid and extended all the way to the edge of the

Plateau, we would execute a 180' and return to Mexico City. We estimated we could fly outbound for an hour and a half, take a look, and return to Mexico City with safe fuel reserve.

We took off at noon from the mile high airport and, although our 1948 Cessna 170 strained for altitude, shortly we were at 10,000 feet MSL, VFR direct to Tampico. An hour and 20 minutes later we were looking out on one of the most beautiful, yet discouraging, sights we had seen on our entire vacation. Extending outward from the precipitous edge of the Central Plateau was a solid sheet of white, at least 8,000 feet below our altitude. It extended north, south, and east as far as we could see. The time to make a decision was at hand, and according to our plan, we should then have returned to Mexico City. Time was passing as we scanned the horizon and the area below for any sign of a break in the white barrier. I turned to a northerly heading.

Before long we had passed our point of no return to Mexico City. I justified this change of plans to my wife and to myself by saying that we could still return to Pachuca with enough fuel reserve. (Pachuca is about fifty miles east of Mexico City.) About that time I spotted what looked like a large break in the overcast near the edge of the Plateau about fifteen to twenty miles farther north. Another ten minutes had passed by the time we reached the area, but we were elated by the fact that we could see green fields intersected by a stream through the hole. From our altitude, however, we could not be sure of the height of the overcast above the rolling hills below. We would just have to go down and see. Again, a change to our previous plan was made. If we dropped down through the hole and found conditions unsatisfactory, then climbed back to 10,000 feet, we would not have enough fuel even to make it to Pachuca.

Our only alternative then would be a landing on one of the isolated farms on top of the Central Plateau. This could certainly be inconvenient and quite possibly dangerous, but the hole in our "white barrier" was too enticing. We throttled back and started a slow tight spiral down through the hole. At about a thousand feet above the ground, we were well underneath the upper overcast but were a little worried to see a few scattered clouds drifting about 500 feet above the ground. However, visibility under the overcast was good—about eight miles—and we continued toward Tampico. We had committed ourselves irretrievably.

Our doorway to the blue-sky area above was gone; we would never be able to find it again. By now our only alternative was even less desirable. If the ceiling lowered between our present position and Tampico or if the lower scattered layer became solid, or if visibilities dropped, we would have to land on the spot. "The spot" was not too inviting, since this area of the coastal plains west of Tampico was mostly rolling hills covered with trees. We suddenly realized that we had managed to get into a situation in which the alternative or "out" was little safer than continuing into deteriorating conditions.

We need only read the accident reports to recall the danger involved in choosing the latter course of action. I believe that this is probably a basic reason why a usually cautious pilot will continue on in the face of IFR conditions. In short, the reality of a hazardous landing under tension from a low maneuvering altitude, in hilly, woody, or simply unfamiliar territory, is often more frightening than continuing into weather which "might not get any worse" or which "might get better on the other side of that hill." Fortunately for us, we were able to continue for about 40 more miles at 1,000 feet above the ground under the overcast and on top of the scattered clouds. By the time the scattered clouds began to condense into a broken layer, the ground had flattened and we could drop down safely to about 500 feet and continue on into Tampico.

This story might not be as dramatic in our country with its many navigational and radio aids, but from the time we were out of range of the Mexico City VOR until we were within 10 miles of the low-powered Tampico VOR, my wife and I felt completely alone. In fact, we were. We had no way of knowing whether conditions had improved, remained the same, or deteriorated in that two and a half hours and 350 miles. This experience taught us a simple lesson: If in the calm of the living room, Weather Bureau or Flight Service Station, a decision to fly is made with deference to the weather and with adequate and safe alternatives or "outs"—don't change your mind! From Tampico we were able to fly up the East Coast of Mexico and on to Memphis with no further weather problems.

I arrived at the Clinic in time for my Monday morning duties and was immediately brought back to reality by Kent Peterson.

"We're glad you got back. It wouldn't have been wise to be late *this* time."

"What do you mean?"

"Mac is out."

"You mean he got the boot?"

"Yeah, he's history."

I had liked Mac in the few months we had been together, so it disturbed me that he had been asked to leave. I learned that his laid-back manner had been a little too much for this group.

"Yeah, Mac got himself in trouble on several occasions," Kent related. "He was on-call when Dr. Howard, a general surgeon, asked him to come to the Baptist hospital to help with one of his patients who had a fractured hip along with other injuries. Mac asked him all sorts of questions then said, "You get the patient stabilized—*then* I'll come over."

"Boy! I know the shit hit the fan when he said that," I said.

"Then someone heard Mac tell Dr. Stewart that he had the 'gift of gab'," Kent continued.

Dr. Marcus Stewart was one of the senior members of the staff. A respected mentor in the developing sports medical sub-specialty, he was always an eager teacher. His discussions during conferences probably prompted Mac's comment which, although not meant to be disrespectful, may have been interpreted as such.

At any rate, the staff helped Mac find a residency elsewhere and, citing personality conflicts, asked him to leave. The rest of us treaded rather lightly for a long while after that.

Residency training is an apprenticeship in which one learns by observation and supervised work, but it is also a do-it-yourself buddy system in which the residents reinforce each other in achieving the common goal of becoming orthopaedic surgeons.

"Be sure to know the epiphyseal fracture types before going to LeBonheur."

"Be able to describe the differences between non-ossifying fibroma and a bone cyst."

We were constantly challenging each other to learn more; the pressure pushing us into even closer camaraderie. Potlucks were as much a part of the program as the didactics and once a month we got together with our wives for a bring-your-own-dinner and for a short time the pressures of the program were forgotten and ties were formed that would last beyond an orthopaedic career.

Louis Anderson had joined the staff less than a year before I began my residency. Only a year or so older than I, his Marie-Strumpel arthritis, also known as ankylosing spondylitis, resulted in the stooped look of a much older person. He was brilliant and an innovator, and his contributions to orthopaedics will be long remembered, but I recall the slight tremor he had during surgery. My picture of the perfect surgeon was of the steady-handed, competent operator. As long as I perceived myself to be in control of the surgical procedure I could approach that ideal, but if I became lost in the anatomy or if I felt intimidated by a staff surgeon, the resulting anxiety would show itself through my hands, much as public speaking was often accompanied by a tremulous voice.

Although Louis Anderson's tremor was more physiological than emotional in origin, I remember being comforted by the sure knowledge that even surgeons could be less than perfect. Slowly over the three-year period of learning, my self-confidence grew in no small measure because of the expression of confidence bestowed on me by a staff of gentlemen surgeons.

Orthopaedics was an expanding field in the '60s, and although one could sub specialize there were few formal fellowships. Now, nearly every anatomical corner of the body is covered by the appropriate fellowship: hip, knee, foot, back, hand, etc.

More so than in other specialties a sound knowledge of anatomy is essential in orthopaedic surgery; one must know what to expect once the integument is breached. The anatomy and pathology rotation provided ample opportunity for learning through teaching. The anatomy class that had intimidated me so as a freshman medical student now became a vehicle through which I could help students overcome their concerns. Allen Hughes, now a respected plastic surgeon, was one of the students I had the pleasure of assisting.

Although I was officially attached to the Campbell Clinic for duty, I was still very much a part of the Air Force. A colonel in charge of the sponsored residency training programs visited the Campbell Clinic on several occasions to assure compliance with the requirements.

One day an official looking packet arrived: *The following individuals are awarded the Air Force Commendation Medal—In the list I found my name: Elvis J. Justis for his work at the 97th General Hospital, Wilmington, Ohio. 1959-1961.*

I was pleased, but preferred slipping out of the clinic quietly one afternoon and donning my uniform to attend the award ceremony put on by the ROTC cadets of Memphis State University. "Elvis J. Justis," my official Air Force name, follows me to this day. Although everyone knows I prefer my middle name, not a few friends and acquaintances refer to me, tongue-in-cheek, by my more infamous appellation.

Lisa enjoyed our time in Memphis, but there were the inevitable conflicts produced by closeness with family. Lisa often remarked that her mother did not know how to hold her tongue. Since she did not want to be seen in the same way, she would often ask me to signal her if she were rambling too much or getting into areas of conversation best left unsaid. Lisa was particularly miffed by her mother's negative comments about her third pregnancy—a planned event. (We wanted our children all to be out of diapers as soon as possible.)

Lisa and my mother got along beautifully most of the time, but my mother's inability to hide her feelings about Cathy Ann's new haircut upset Lisa enough that I had to gently tell my mom to keep quiet about the way we were raising our kids. All in all, considering our physical closeness, we got along quite well during the three years we lived in the "Little Green House." Lisa gave me the freedom to continue my creative endeavors in woodworking and I completed the 18th Century Gate-Leg table that I had begun while in Wilmington, Ohio. Occasionally we spent the day as a family at the airport while I repaired or replaced something on the airplane. We took short trips to Gaston's on the White River and visited Ann and Neil in Clarksville, Tennessee.

Once, leaving Cathy and Jeff with Annie Lou and my mother, we flew to Al Gaston's for a weekend with a fellow resident, Jim Hardy and his wife Barbara. We approached the grass strip, nestled in a valley alongside the White River just below Bull Shoals dam through the river valley, turning left to the southwest onto a short final, rolling to a stop on the 3200 foot strip. Initially a bit nervous, Jim relaxed over the weekend and seemed happy about the upcoming return flight. He was riding in the right seat as we taxied to the southern end of the strip and prepared the plane for flight. I mentally rehearsed a technique I had used in the Cessna 170 for short field takeoffs. The small flaps on this model Cessna provided a modicum of extra lift without a significant increase in drag. I accelerated to nearly flying speed, quickly lowered the flaps, and jumped off the ground, skimming the grass as the little craft gained speed rapidly once freed of grassy fingers.

We began our takeoff run on the smooth turf. I raised the tail of the Cessna. Ahead the hills lining the River grew in size, the fence defining the runway end grew in sharpness and detail. Now!

I reached between the two front seats and quickly pulled the flap lever upward to deploy the flaps.

"We're going to crash!!" Jim shouted as he threw both hands forward onto the instrument panel and braced both feet against the firewall. Just then we became airborne clearing the fence by a comfortable margin.

"God! I thought you were pulling on the emergency brake—like in my Volkswagen." Jim said, as he finally began to relax. We all had quite a laugh, and still laugh today over that incident of bygone days.

Surgeons are by nature somewhat independent and enjoy being in control; thus, for some, the training period can be difficult. One must learn to keep his countenance and avoid suggesting to the staff "better ways" to solve a problem. Assisting 13 surgeons provides the resident with a broad overview and gives him the ability to choose from among the many subtleties of technique. When finally allowed to perform surgery on my own, I began to develop my own unique style. I was a careful operator, respectful of tissue, not fast but steady.

Al Ingram was a wonderful mentor, not only in surgery but also in dealing with patients. Once while working in the office he asked me to phone in a refill prescription for a patient. Working up a large number of patients that morning I felt under pressure and asked Ms. Sibley to call in the prescription for me. Dr. Ingram walked in just as she was making the call.

"Doctor! I suggest you carry out your own responsibility instead of delegating it." He was right. Ms. Sibley was not a nurse. Again I learned the importance of accepting the responsibilities conferred when granted the title of Physician.

The practice of medicine is part science, part intuition, and part luck. One can never be right all of the time. When we tell a patient to come back if no better in a certain period of time, we're hedging our bets, hoping that the patient will let us know if our first guess was valid or not. I recall a patient who made a point of calling me three months after Dr. Waring and I had seen her for back pain. At that time Dr. Waring thought that she had arthritis.

"I hope you look closely at my x-ray. Maybe you can help the next patient more than you helped me." She said ironically. "You see, I have cancer now; that's what caused my back pain." It was obvious she wanted to blame us.

Later Dr. Waring and I looked at her x-rays again and saw nothing but arthritis. "That's why I asked her to return if she didn't improve," he explained. He called her to ask if there were anything we could do to help her. He did not feel anything would be gained by trying to explain to her that many times a cancerous lesion will not be visible on initial x-ray.

Lisa and several of her friends, including Jean Peterson, took art lessons and enjoyed a time of relative freedom since Annie Lou and her daughter, Willie, could help with babysitting. Shadow helped in her own way. Our three years in the "Little Green House" passed pleasantly.

On the 7th of May 1962, I was in surgery at the John Gaston Hospital inserting a Jewett nail in an elderly patient's broken hip. Just as I was driving the nail into the femoral neck the circulating nurse told me that the Baptist delivery room had called and said that Lisa was in labor. I was excited but in some ways glad to be busy. When I finished the operation, I walked over to the delivery waiting room. Lee Adkins came out to tell me I was the proud father of Louisa, our third child.

I was molded by my father's generation, as was he by his father's generation. The '60s decade probably represents a dividing line between assured rolls for men and women and the many paths taken in today's society. This certainly has its good points, especially for women who now have much greater freedom of choice. As for me, I am grateful that Lisa encouraged me to be the primary breadwinner and to be the "adventure" provider. Working was my domain, whether at the clinic or in the workshop or at the airport. For me it was the best of times, and the children grew up with that expectation. I hope they have happy memories of a childhood centered around two people who loved each other very much and who gave something to the rearing of their children that was unique and not at all what one would see in today's society.

My residency was winding down in 1964. Lisa and I flew to Washington DC to visit the Air Force Personnel Center to discuss the possibilities for an assignment beginning in July of 1964. We preferred an assignment somewhere in Europe but were told that was unlikely. Several weeks later we received orders assigning us to Carswell Air Force Base in Texas. Converting our initial disappointment into enthusiasm we began planning the move. We purchased a new Rambler American station wagon, built a new trailer with John Rollow's help, and researched airports in the Fort Worth area to host our airplane.

I had been asked by several of the staff what my plans were when I finished; most knew of my four-year Air Force commitment. One evening as Fred Sage and I enjoyed a late evening snack after finishing an emergency procedure, Fred asked me if that commitment was final. I assured him that it was.

"Too bad! You'd be fixed for life in orthopaedics if you didn't have that to do." It was the first time I realized that I had been seriously considered for a staff position. I was flattered but felt it would be best for me to test myself away from home, so to speak. Besides, Lisa and I were ready to adventure once again.

The first part of the orthopaedic board examination was to be held in Atlanta in May, 1964; Bob Tooms and Kent Peterson flew with me in the Cessna. I bought a carton of Kent cigarettes for the trip even though I was secretly considering a life altering decision. A year or so before that trip Kent had called me into the doctor's lounge at the clinic.

"Look!" He pointed to a blood-tinged glob of sputum in the washbasin. "I just coughed that up." A short time later he underwent a pulmonary lobectomy for a benign adenoma. "If I had been a smoker that would have been a cancer, sure as the world," he would often say after his surgery.

He was right, of course, and the incident hardened my resolve that had been building during the past several months. Many late evenings

I had found myself opening my third pack of cigarettes and recently had noted an irritating cough each morning. I also realized, from what I had learned in aviation medicine, that I was starting every flight with an oxygen saturation equivalent to an altitude of over 5000 feet.

Our flight to Atlanta was beautiful in the mid-south spring sky, and I felt prepared for the upcoming examination and eight hours of intense concentration. I remember looking over my answers one last time as I puffed on a long Kent.

That's it! I crushed that last cigarette into the full ashtray. That was it—the end of my smoking habit. Taking the board examination is surely the hardest thing I will have to do; therefore, I don't need to smoke anymore. I feel guilty for having given Bob Tooms my remaining cigarettes that may have contributed to his subsequent arteriosclerosis.

Kent Peterson still recalls the flight back from Atlanta with amusement. "Justis, if you don't climb and get out of this rough air I'm going to throw up all over your airplane!" I was flying low to limit the effect of the headwind, but we were being bounced around a good bit. Bob Tooms turned to Kent and said with a grin, "Jeff's so cheap he doesn't want to burn the extra gas." Much to my passengers' relief we did climb into smoother air.

About six weeks before I was to complete my residency I was surprised by a phone call from Col. Schmidt at the Air Force Personnel Center in Washington.

"Captain Justis, how would you like to go to Wiesbaden, Germany?"

"I—uh—I..." I was speechless, then I mumbled something about the orders to Carswell AFB.

"Let me put it this way—we plan on rescinding those orders. You'll receive new orders shortly," he interrupted.

All of our carefully thought out plans had to be changed. Europe was, after all, our first choice for an assignment. Lisa was shaken by the news. We both liked to stick to a plan, and to suddenly adapt to a new situation provoked anxiety. We would have to make arrangements to have Shadow flown over. And our new car would have to be shipped. Gradually things fell into place, however, and we once again became excited about entering a new phase of our lives.

Leaving the clinic was anticlimactic. I spent my last day saying goodbye to friends and thanking the staff for their patience and immense help. I now had a background of knowledge and experience that would permit the growth of confidence and skill in the years to come. Although I was anxious to begin my new Air Force career, I knew that the next several months would be difficult since accompanied travel was not permitted for captains. I would have to precede Lisa and the children and find housing before they could fly over to Germany on orders.

When my orders to Germany were certain I considered options for our airplane. What about shipping it to Europe? The cost was prohibitive. I was not instrument rated so the possibility of ferrying the plane to Europe did not seem practical and I reluctantly advertised the Cessna for sale. The day I watched N2634V takeoff from Memphis Flying Service for the last time was bitter-sweet. I had $5200 in my pocket, more than I had paid for the Cessna 170, but the faithful airplane had been a part of our family since 1958. The sound of her engine faded and she grew smaller and smaller in the late afternoon southern sky. *Oh well, Germany is going to be an adventure for us, and, besides, there is an aero club in Wiesbaden.*

Lisa and I were to drive the car to Philadelphia for shipment to Germany and I was to fly to Frankfurt on a contract flight the next day. We drove through Gatlinburg, climbed Mount LeConte and spent several leisurely days on the skyline drive overlooking the Shenandoah Valley. These were bittersweet days and reminded me how much in love I was and how much I was going to miss Lisa in the coming months. I walked away from her in the terminal at Philadelphia International Airport, choking back my emotions, rationalizing that this was, after all, only a temporary separation.

GERMANY

Parting from Lisa after six years of togetherness is hard. Compounding my foreboding sense of separation is the uncertainty of when the Air Force will allow my family to follow me to Germany. I am beginning another adventure and am excited, but lone adventure no longer appeals to me. I miss having Lisa beside me as I board the military contract aircraft, a DC 6-B.

Although I had been in the active service since 1959, three years of that time had been at the Campbell Clinic, and I did not know or remember the many tricks used in dealing with the military bureaucracy, important information usually learned from a good First Sergeant. Thus I did not question the mandate against unaccompanied travel. Only later did I find that most officers paid for their family's travel rather than waiting for funds to be appropriated by Congress.

The flight was long—nearly 12 hours with a refueling stop in Iceland. We arrived in Frankfurt around noon the following day. My uniform was wrinkled from the hours of sitting and I was fatigued from lack of sleep. My sponsor, John Hinchey, an obstetrician, who had been in Germany for a year was to pick me up at the airport. I had never seen him before so I stood around the terminal waiting for some captain to come over and introduce himself. Gradually the crowd of uniformed personnel and dependents thinned as I stood self-consciously guarding my baggage. I must have waited an hour before I finally realized no one was going to pick me up.

"The bus to Wiesbaden will be here in 15 minutes. I'd take that if I were you," the airman manning the information desk offered when I inquired.

Because of my previous experience in the Air Force, I had anticipated that things would go smoothly for a captain arriving at a foreign airbase. I would learn later that my experience would have been better had I been a full colonel. That privilege, however, would have to wait many years to be experienced.

Piling my three large bags beside me, I finally sat down on the military bus, dejected by the lack of a proper welcome. As the bus rumbled out of Rhine-Main Airbase and onto the Autobahn, the visual impact of the cultural differences between the United States and Germany hit home. Not only did I feel quite alone without Lisa but that sense of isolation was greater for the lack of familiarity with the neat villages and tile roofed houses we were passing. A yellow sign announced *Wiesbaden* and soon we drove through the main gate into Wiesbaden Airbase.

"Is this where the hospital is located?" I asked the driver.

"Only a clinic is here," he said. "The hospital is in town."

The bus made several more stops and finally turned into a large complex, an iron archway over the drive announced HEADQUARTERS USAFE (Headquarters United States Air Force in Europe).

The bus emptied.

"Where is the hospital?" I asked the driver who had been looking at me with a quizzical look on his face.

"Oh, it was back two stops ago."

I had seen no sign and certainly no building that looked like a hospital.

"Where are you going now?" I asked rather helplessly.

"Back to Frankfurt." The driver made no further offer so I offloaded my bags and stood alone in the middle of Headquarters

United States Air Force in Europe, contemplating my next move as the bus rumbled off. After a while I began to formulate a plan to hide my bags behind some bushes while I tried to obtain some transportation. Just as I was reaching to pick up my bags, a blue motor pool car pulled up in front of me.

"Captain, you look lost."

"I am! I'm looking for the hospital."

The friendly captain smiled as he opened the trunk and helped me load my bags.

"I'm Chaplain Schmidt." He offered his hand.

"You are a lifesaver—thanks." I shook his hand.

"Well, I'm supposed to be a soul saver." We laughed as we drove out of the headquarters complex, down tree lined avenues, past the Amelia Erhardt enlisted hotel, and into the former Luftwaffe Hospital compound. The USAF Hospital Wiesbaden, a curved building, with a large white cross permanently tiled into the red roof, stood as a monument to the German penchant to build for the future. I was sure that the monolithic concrete structure would stand for hundreds of years, outlasting many political regimes.

"The hospital commander's office is in here." The chaplain helped me put my bags in the foyer. I thanked him and offered to set any bones he might break. He, of course, hoped he would not have to take advantage of my offer.

Captain John Compton looked up from his desk in the room adjacent to the hospital commander's office.

"I'm Captain Justis, and I have orders to report to Colonel John Hennessen, Chief of Orthopaedics."

"How did you get here?"

When I explained my ordeal he seemed embarrassed. He thought that my sponsor had arranged for someone to pick me up. Hinchey had gone on leave a few days before my arrival.

"I think I'm supposed to sign in with Dr. Hennessen." I repeated, wanting to make a good first impression with my new boss.

"No! You don't want to do that. Don't worry. I'll sign you in now."

John was an MSC officer (Medical Service Corps)—an administrator—and in that capacity, along with his first sergeant, in essence, ran the hospital. The Hospital Commander, Colonel Joe Henry, was a fine gentleman with whom I eventually developed a close working relationship. After a brief introduction, he suggested that John take the rest of the day to help me get settled in.

"Let's get out of here!" John said. "I don't want you to run into Cactus Jack."

I was puzzled. I had received a letter from Colonel Hennessen, welcoming me to the orthopaedic department. "Why?" I asked.

"Oh, the Colonel has been on call every night since Sullivant went on leave and Anzel rotated back to CONUS (Continental U.S.). The rumor is that he wanted you to be on call tonight."

"Tonight!" The long night and day of travel was taking its toll so I agreed with John that I was in no condition to be on call.

I will never forget the helping hand that John extended to me in the three months I was destined to be without my family, although at the time of our first meeting I was sure Lisa and the children would be able to travel to Germany within weeks.

He arranged for me to get a room at the Von Steuben Officer's Hotel and then suggested that we have dinner with Hank Meiger and his wife. Hank was an internist and a major who lived on the economy (private housing rented to military personnel by local German landlords). I would not be eligible for base housing for a year so I would have to obtain local housing before Lisa's travel would be approved. John, of course, promised to help me find suitable housing and with this reassurance I began to relax a bit.

Hank introduced me to Bier and Sect (beer mixed half and half with German champagne) and I can attest to its potency. Soon, camaraderie and libation eased my transition from the comfort of home and family to these new surroundings, and I would someday regard my three years in Germany as some of the best years of my life.

"Cactus Jack," as Colonel Hennessen was affectionately known, albeit behind his back, was a red-haired Scandinavian with a temperament to match. I was to learn that before I arrived he had been at odds with John Sullivant, a major and second in command in the orthopaedic department. Capt. Farrell, a young man who only had a year of general surgery training, was attached to orthopaedics. Orhan Alemdroglu, a Turkish national who had lived in Germany for many years, was a civilian employee of the U.S.A.F. Orhan was a well-trained orthopedist who had become a fixture at the hospital. Many military orthopedists had come and gone, but Orhan remained a stable influence.

The day after my arrival I was in the saddle with a full load of patients. True to form, Jack had placed me on the call schedule the night before. Muttering that he had been unable to find me he had revised the schedule so that I was standing by for emergencies my second night in Germany. A hand injury required my services just before my head hit the pillow at the Von Steuben. Base transportation picked me up at the hotel for the short ride to the hospital. I was still fatigued by the time change and, as I had previously experienced in new situations, a vague sense of uneasiness came over me. I was well trained and had demonstrated competence while at the Campbell Clinic, but I was on my own now and was about to operate on my first private patient, courtesy of the Air Force. I not only wanted to do a good job but wanted to project confidence. In public speaking, a shaky voice betrays stage fright. In surgery that betrayal may be a shaky hand. The anticipation of what I might find in the emergency room evaporated in the reality of a routine case, and I walked out of the operating room with renewed confidence that increased with experience over the next three years.

Apparently my style and operating ability impressed my boss, Jack Hennessen, and he began to send many VIP's to me for consultation, bypassing John Sullivant. John was an aggressive surgeon who liked to operate even if conservative treatment would have been better. "I'm a surgeon and surgeons operate," he would say. Jack and I agreed on one thing: surgeons *can* perform many operations but, quite often, *not* operating is the procedure of choice.

I had obtained an apartment at 8 Willimenen Strasse within a week of my arrival and had immediately requested travel orders for Lisa and our three children. Every week I would check with the travel office about the status of our orders and would be told to expect them shortly.

Although my work helped the time pass, Colonel Hennesen realized that my morale was suffering because of separation from my family. Weeks turned into months—still no date for family travel was forthcoming. Queries to headquarters finally revealed an explanation: Congress, in its wisdom, had failed to pass an appropriations bill, was in a recess, and would take up the matter again "soon."

I called Lisa occasionally, wrote often, and lived a quiet, celibate life at 8 Willimenen Strasse, a 1st floor apartment in a four-floor walkup. There was no television but I managed to keep busy in the evenings, putting together some model kits for the children, reading, and visiting friends. I bought a new Volkswagen for $1200 so that I would not have to rely on base transportation and could explore on my own. In the rather insular Air Force community I received many dinner invitations. John Compton and I became good friends and on weekends he would show me many of the local attractions that I would later be able to show my family with the authority of a native.

Before John rotated from Wiesbaden to a new assignment, he told me that he had decided to get married. He was approaching forty. Having observed many couples and seen many isolated Air Force men use separation from their spouses as an excuse to philander, he had decided against marriage until he saw how happy Lisa and I were and how separation had brought us closer together in spirit.

Finally in late September word came that the travel orders for Lisa and the children were being issued. They would arrive on Jeff's fourth birthday, September 28, 1964. I baked a cake for the occasion and waited eagerly at Rhine-Main Air Force Base. I spotted them through the glass as they cleared customs but had to wait much too long before I could hug them all. We were a complete family once again except for Shadow who was scheduled to arrive in about a week. Everyone was travel weary and my touring narrative fell on dull ears on the way to Wiesbaden. Lisa related how Louisa had become lost in the Pan American terminal while Jeff and Cathy were supposedly watching her. This incident and the long flight added to Lisa's fatigue, and she gladly plopped on our bed as soon as we reached our apartment.

After a few days of rest we settled into a routine of work for me, alternated with family picnics in the woods, exploring villages, going to movies at the base theater and generally enjoying our surroundings.

Chris and Bill Herndon lived in the apartment above us. Bill was a pilot and a major. We all became good friends. Their children were the same ages as our children and after we moved into base housing a year or so later, the children became even closer. Thirty-six years later we still maintained contact.

One of the advantages of Air Force or military life is the availability of thirty days paid leave each year. I arranged a schedule so that every three months we adventured for a week. We would alternate a vacation for us with one that included the children. Good live-in babysitters were a wonderful benefit of living in Germany; Frau Stelder and Helen Bock were favorites of the children.

My practice was interesting and although I was on call about every 4th night and weekend, I rarely had to operate past ten in the evening. About once every four to six weeks, however, I had to stay in the hospital as medical officer of the day. In those years majors and above did not have to take MOD duty so when I received word that I was on the promotion list to major, I was elated. Col. Joe Henry, the hospital commander called me and another captain to his office, congratulated us, then informed us that because of another failure of our esteemed Congress to appropriate the necessary funds, we would be unable to wear the gold leaves or receive the increased pay until Congress acted. What a disappointment!

There were two of us who had graduated from medical school in 1956. All other medical officers of that graduation year were already majors but our residencies had deferred our promotions. We pleaded for relief from the MOD roster on the basis of seniority, and when Col. Henry finally approved this, we were grateful. On my last MOD call I was called to the ER to see our neighbor's child who had fallen from a slide. I interpreted his skull X-ray as negative. When the neurosurgeon pointed out a depressed skull fracture to me the next day, I realized once again my limitations. Gratefully surgery was successful and no harm was done. Often the fund of knowledge required of a generalist may exceed the capacity of most physicians—that's why specialization arose in the first place—a fact often lost in today's managed care environment.

After my promotion was official, Jack Hennessen called me into his office. "I'm making you Chief of Orthopaedics since I've been asked to take over as deputy hospital commander," he said rather briskly.

"What about John?" I questioned, since Sullivant outranked me.

"Don't worry about him....if he gives you any trouble, let me know."

This move was unusual but the antipathy between Col. Hennessen and Sullivant was deep. About a year later Sullivant rotated back to the States and a fine orthopedist, Ken Tomberlin, replaced him.

The quality of our orthopaedic practice was excellent, in my opinion, and USAF Hospital Wiesbaden was a referral center for all of Europe. We received patients via Air Evac from North Africa, Greece, Iceland, France, and even Turkey. One of my patients, a diplomat's wife from Izmir, was Julide Yumlu. She sustained a fractured femur in an automobile accident in Turkey and was transferred to Wiesbaden for care. She remained in our hospital for many months. Later we visited her in her home in Izmir; she has remained a friend to this day.

If one has the opportunity to live in the foreign country, shouldn't there be a constant awareness of the cultural differences? I found that the routine day-by-day work and recreation was much the same as it would have been had I been practicing in the States because of the ready availability of U.S. goods in the base exchange, first-run movies, and several officers clubs in the area. The only time we really appreciated living in Germany was on free weekends or during our vacation time.

Wanting to get back into woodworking as soon as possible, I investigated the base hobby shop, which included a well-stocked woodworking area. The German superintendent of the shop was a great help to me, pointing out the value of a traditional Hobelbank (planing bench). I had grown up with workbenches equipped with metal vises, but once I tried holding my work piece in a sturdy Ulmia bench with wooden end and a front vises, I was hooked. Before going to Germany I relied too much on power tools in most of my woodworking, but on advice of the German Shop-Meister, I realized how much more I could accomplish by hand were I to have a better bench.

Lisa surprised me with a wonderful workbench on my birthday and on its steady surface I began several small projects in our apartment on Willimenen Strasse. Before leaving Germany we drove to Ulm in our Rambler station wagon and, with the end of the long crate protruding two feet out the rear, brought my second eight foot Ulmia bench home to be shipped with our household goods. During our three years in Germany I purchased some fine German carving tools, clamps, gauges, marking tools, wooden bodied planes, and other quality tools that fill my workshop to this day.

After about a year we were approved for base housing and moved into a third floor walk up in Aukamm, substantial concrete housing built after the war for Americans under the status of forces agreement.

We had many good times there, enjoying our neighbors, and becoming much more self-sufficient. The workbench, in front of the picture window facing west in our living/dining room, served as a buffet table when we entertained. I spent many happy evenings at that bench, cutting dovetails while the children played and Lisa worked at her easel.

Cathy, and later Jeff, were enrolled in German Kindergarten and learned many German songs but not much else. For first and second grades they attended the Air Force sponsored school for military dependents and, of course, were appropriately Americanized.

Shadow was a wonderful companion for our family in a country that loves dogs. Lisa told of an incident that was rather strange in its aftermath. At a stoplight, adjacent to a park, Shadow spotted a small Dachshund and, before Lisa could respond, jumped out of the window of our Rambler to sniff the strange creature. Shadow meant no harm, but the little dog yelped and cringed in fear. Later we received a bill from a German veterinarian for psychological services for the little dog. For the sake of good international relationships we paid the bill.

In 1965 my folks traveled to see us and accompanied us on a memorable trip through Austria, Yugoslavia, Bulgaria, Turkey, and Greece. In his later years my dad always remembered this European vacation as the best trip he had ever taken. Dad and my mother picked up their new Volkswagen at the factory in Wolfsburg and drove it to Salzburg, Austria where we met to begin our tour. We all piled into the 1964 Rambler American station wagon, my dad and I in the front, Lisa and my mom in the back seat, and Cathy, Jeff, and Louisa on a mattress in the back. (In those days the kids were unbelted and free to bounce around behind the rear seats.) I built a large plywood box and bolted it to the luggage rack on the top of the station wagon, providing protection for luggage and food supplies. Shortly after leaving Salzburg we stopped along the side of the road for a picnic. A friendly Austrian lady, working outside her half-timbered home, saw us with the children and brought us some freshly picked strawberries, the innocence of our children providing manna from Austrian fields.

Zagreb was our first overnight stop in Yugoslavia. The hotel, in a wooded area outside the central city, at the end of a winding drive, was neat and clean with a red tiled roof, although the indoor plumbing left something to be desired. The light was out in the bathroom so I stepped up on to the commode to see if the bulb was burned out. Suddenly the flimsy plastic top of the commode gave way and my foot splashed into the waiting water.

"Damn it!" I shouted. The children laughed, Lisa laughed, and after extricating my soaked foot, I had to laugh. At least I didn't get stuck in the plumbing.

After driving through Yugoslavia we entered the communist country of Bulgaria. Although I had been issued a military passport, we were advised to use a civilian passport when traveling through eastern block countries. There was a risk, albeit small, that a military person wearing civilian clothes might be considered a spy in some countries so we did not want to advertise the fact that we were in the Air Force. After clearing customs uneventfully we relaxed and began looking for a picturesque spot for our lunch picnic. We pulled off the road under a large shade tree and began to eat our sandwiches, cheese and crackers, and fresh fruit when a young boy, riding bareback on a small horse with his mother holding the reins, came up to us from an adjacent field. They smiled, waved and gestured, taking each of the children for a bareback ride on the black and tan horse. In return for the favor they accepted some fruit but seemed as pleased as we were to see the happy smiles of our three children, as each was led on the Bulgarian horse around the field.

Driving through the agrarian countryside we noticed that most of the fieldwork was done by women of all ages. Where were all the men we wondered? In Sophia we found that at least some of the men were busy watching us!

In the capital city of Sophia late in the evening, we were told by Intourist personnel that the hotels were booked. However, they found accommodations for Lisa and me and Jeff and Lou in a fifth floor walk up apartment. My folks and Cathy stayed in another apartment. Two "translators" were with us when we sat down for wine and cheese with our hosts, a nice Bulgarian couple trying to supplement their income, when we went to bed, when we awoke. The Bulgarian government probably took a significant cut out of what we paid for our Bed and Breakfast. There was a monolithic dreariness to the Lenin complex in which we spent the evening. We were given the only bedroom, Jeff and Lou sharing a mattress on the floor, and our hosts sleeping on a couch in the adjoining, and only, other room. We enjoyed our stay but did not feel free to explore the city because our "translator" wanted to be with us at all times.

We left Sophia later than we anticipated and it was late afternoon as we crossed the border into Turkey. The roads seemed to be a rougher on the Turkish side, and after an hour of driving I noticed a significant vibration that I hoped was just a reflection of the roughness of the road surface. A pull to the right dashed my hope. We were stranded in the darkness in the middle of western Turkey. After changing the tire we felt somewhat insecure without a spare so we stopped at a roadside service station where we were able to get the tire patched. The tire had sustained significant damage and I knew we would have to find a replacement, hopefully at an Air Force facility. By this time it was quite late, and we were exhausted when we arrived in Istanbul. Even with maps of the city we became disoriented and had a difficult time locating the hotel. Never did an American-style hotel look so good to the travel weary as the Istanbul Hilton did to us that night as we drove under the marquee at one in the morning.

Throughout our travels Cathy, Jeff, and Louisa were troopers—often forced to bunk up together, to share meals, and to endure tours and museums and hours in the Rambler—all without complaint.

Occasionally they were rewarded in unusual ways. A visit to Istanbul is incomplete without a boat tour of the Bosphorus, so the seven of us ventured on board a vessel that would take us as far as the Bosphorus Strait leading to the Black Sea. As we embarked, the Turkish crewmembers took delight in pinching the cheeks of our children, much to their disgust. A smiling, snagle-toothed seaman was especially interested in Louisa who had been watching him eat corn on the cob. Before we knew what was happening he had Louisa in his arms and was allowing her to nibble away at the scattered succulent kernels bypassed by his missing teeth. This disturbed my mother more than it bothered Lisa and me. We had seen Louisa eat many things less appetizing than that!

Throughout our travels Lisa was faithful in sending news-filled letters to her parents. Having been written contemporaneously, those letters contain many more details than I am able to recall nearly 40 years later. Nevertheless, I remember the sense of excitement we experienced as a family traveling through the "Gateway to Asia." Toilet facilities with their "squat pots" were a source of amusement and occasional consternation. In spite of our eating in restaurants of questionable sanitation we remained healthy until we arrived in Izmir where we met with my former patient, Mrs. Yumlu, who took us to a Diplomatic Club for lunch where I managed to surprise Lisa with a birthday cake on July 11th. However, she became sick for a couple of days after that; I hoped it wasn't the cake.

Several days later Cathy, following her mother's example, decorated the stones of Ephesus when we toured that ancient ruin. As we walked the well-worn streets of the subject of Paul's Epistle and passed through archways into rooms open to the sky, it was humbling to consider that a human hand shaped these stones and placed them purposely one on top of the other to create a structure for daily use. When I create a piece of furniture, I am thinking only of its use in the short span of my life and, by extension, the lives of my family. However, perhaps someday someone will, in passing, contemplate the work of my hand just as I contemplate the work of another human hand some two thousand years ago.

We surveyed Helen of Troy's legacy and the Dardanelles and slowly found our way out of Asia, back into Europe and the land of Socrates and Aristotle. There is no love lost between the Greeks and the Turks, and while in Turkey we learned of Greek atrocities. As we crossed the border into the cradle of civilization, we learned of Turkish atrocities. I am sure there is truth to both sides just as there is when we consider our ancestors, the American Indians, the Jews, and the Arabs, the Catholics, and the Protestants. Perhaps the nature of man is one of conflict. Perhaps the nature of life itself is born of the conflict with death.

The Athens Hilton was our Grecian headquarters. A photographer, having received a request from a Memphis newspaper, arranged for us to meet him on the roof of the hotel. Louisa kept asking when we were going to get the ladder; after reassuring her that we would not have to climb after all, our Memphis friends would soon be able to see pictures of the seven of us on the roof of the Hilton. Later that day, my dad, Jeff, and I drove to the American base on the outskirts of Athens where, with dad's financial help, we purchased some new tires and replaced the irreparable spare.

We toured the Acropolis and the Parthenon, and marveled at the artistic and engineering skill of the ancient Greeks. The simmering summer heat, reflecting from the white stone, and the uncertainties of the local cuisine combined in an unpleasant way to cause Lisa to leave her mark in this historic place. The children, my parents, and I fared somewhat better.

Lisa recovered after a nights rest, and we all climbed aboard a Hydrofoil vessel at Pyreas for the quick trip to the island of Corfu. Lisa, the children, and I donned bathing suits for a swim in the Adriatic. A hill, stepped with white houses and red-tiled roofs, glistened in the sun and provided a fitting backdrop to the beach and blue waters. What a fun time we had at that fleeting but precious time of our lives. Life was good. Would it not always be so? We savored the moment, but we had to move on.

Out of Greece, through Macedonia and Yugoslavia, we worked our way back to Salzburg where we said goodbye to the grandparents and traced north on the autobahn to our Wiesbaden home.

Once again I settled into the routine of patient care and, for the most part, was gratified by the appreciation of many happy patients—with a few notable exceptions. The patient had chronic back pain with no significant physical or radiographic findings. She was in her early thirties, obese, and obviously unhappy with her life situation. Muscle relaxers did not help. Physical therapy did not help. She demanded stronger medication and brought her husband, a staff sergeant, to the office for reinforcement. As I attempted to explain my rationale for management and to discuss her x-rays, the Sgt. constantly interrupted, becoming increasingly belligerent, and ended by saying he thought I was incompetent. Trying to maintain some composure, I told him that I could no longer deal with his abuse.

"I will ask one of the other orthopedists to take over care of your wife, and I will also recommend that both of you see a psychiatrist. Hopefully he will be able to help both of you handle this situation. Addictive medication is not the answer."

Later I learned that the patient's husband remained a thorn in the side of everyone in the department until about three months later. It was a quiet evening on call. I was working on a project at the workbench in the dining room of our Aukamm apartment when I heard a screeching noise followed by a loud crash coming from the direction of the highway a mile behind the housing complex.

"Did you hear that, Lisa?"

"I hope that doesn't mean you'll have to go into the hospital," she responded, knowing how I dreaded major trauma in the middle of the night. I was unable to continue my work with any sense of peace and, as expected, the phone rang sometime later.

"Some guy, a Staff Sgt., tried to kill himself running into a tree." The corpsman continued, "Major Plugge, the general surgeon, is working on his spleen and liver now. He's got a broken femur so I guess you had better come on in."

At two in the morning I found myself staring into the swollen and unconscious face of the abusive staff sergeant as I applied skeletal traction for his fractured femur. My assessment of his and his wife's need for psychiatric care had been correct but too late. He died of his injuries several days later, and his wife returned to the States, hopefully, to a better life.

Then there was the sad case of a 50-year-old warrant officer with a firm mass overlying his left hip and fixed to the underlying bone. The biopsy report indicated a highly malignant fibrosarcoma; the lesion could not be locally resected and he would have to return to CONUS (Continental United States) for definitive treatment. As I explained his diagnosis to him, I found it difficult to maintain my composure.

"Doc, my wife and I just arrived in Germany. We have been looking forward to this tour for years—now this."

There was sadness in his voice but also resignation. Military people tend to accept orders from above with magnanimity—and my warrant officer was a good soldier. He listened quietly as I explained the probable course of his treatment. I was saddened in the face of this unfolding human tragedy. Some months later I learned that he had died while at Wilford Hall (USAF Hospital in San Antonio).

"Dr. Justis, report to the emergency room STAT. Dr. Justis..." The pager was insistent so I left the orthopaedic department and rushed down one flight of stairs to the ground floor emergency room. I could hear loud screams as I pushed open the swinging door.

"Get it out! Get it out! Oh God, Get it out!"

A young airman was lying on a gurney holding his right wrist tightly with his left hand. A two-foot long coiled steel spring, an inch in diameter, waved painfully from the palm of his right hand. With each involuntary spasmodic motion the spring would move, precipitating further screams of pain.

The airman second class had been cleaning a sink trap with a motorized rotor- rooter when the spring steel broke twisting the coil into his palm.

"Get it out! Get it OUT!"

"Get me some 1% xylocaine without epinephrine – NOW!" I shouted to the corpsman standing by the patient. Quickly I injected the anesthetic around the median and radial nerves at the wrist level and within minutes the young airman was quiet.

"Thanks Doc."

"Now let's get that thing out." We wheeled him into the operating room where the lighting was better and I could explore the wound through a larger incision to be sure there was no nerve or tendon damage. Subsequently the young airman recovered fully and kept his coil as a souvenir.

Politics and medicine don't mix well. The status of forces agreement with Germany required that injured or sick US civilian citizens traveling in Germany be treated in local hospitals and not in US military facilities. However, when the CEO of Bethlehem Steel and his wife were injured in an automobile accident, they were soon transferred to USAF Hospital Wiesbaden under orders from "higher up." Jack Hennessen, now deputy hospital commander, greeted the VIP's telling them that I would be managing their orthopaedic care. He later took me aside: "I want you to get them out of here as soon as you can."

X-rays of Mrs. Bethlehem Steel were initially negative so my goal was to get her mobilized quickly. She had multiple bruises and complained of hip pain. Jack agreed with me that she did not have a hip fracture. Still, I could not get her up without groans of discomfort. I insisted. I prodded. I arrogantly implied that only I knew what was best for her.

"But I hurt and I can't—I won't!"

I thought she was a rather spoiled rich lady. Finally, after four or five days we managed to get her on her feet.

"That's not so bad now, is it?"

"Yes it is," she insisted. "I know I have something broken."

"Well, let me get another x-ray." I suggested more to appease her than out of a sense of urgency.

Repayment for arrogance comes to the physician in many ways. The x-ray of my patient showed quite clearly a displaced fracture of the ischial and pubic rami.

"Uh—Mrs. Steel—uh—you were right—you *do* have a fracture."

She did not say, "I told you so." In fact she was relieved. She had a reason to hurt. Even though I had erred in diagnosis, her management—that is early mobilization—had been correct, although it would have been much more effective with more empathy and humility on my part. I was not the first, nor will I be the last physician to fall prey to the infallibility fantasy.

Major Cloudus was an internist of rather poor reputation. Not only was he mean to patients, especially those of lower rank, but also he would refer patients too late for effective management of a problem he should never have tried to manage in the first place. Few physicians on the staff at Wiesbaden had not been "Cloudused."

"Hey, I have this crock of a patient that keeps complaining of back pain. You don't see anything on this x-ray do you?"

Cloudus held the KUB up to the window of the cast room.

"I can't see any details here, let's take it to the x-ray department," I suggested.

"Naw. If you don't see anything that's good enough for me," he said as he waived the film in the air and left. About a week later I was talking with another internist who asked if I had heard about the metastatic spine lesion Cloudus had missed. I realized that I too had been "Cloudused."

Our tour of duty was three years and, with thirty days leave per year available, we planned travel so that the children would be included as much as possible and alternately that Lisa and I would also have our own time together.

I don't know how Cathy, Jeff, or Lou remember the time in Germany, but my recollection is one of pleasure: picnics on weekends, camping trips in the Rambler station wagon, Amsterdam, Vienna, Salzburg, Bertchesgarten, Garmish, Denmark, Italy, Rhine cruises—a travel log of memories.

The year was 1965 in Madrid near the beginning of a ten-day driving tour of Spain Lisa and I had been enjoying. We called home to check on the children; I could tell by the expression on Lisa's face that something was wrong.

"Frau Stelder's brother died—she had to leave!" Lisa said with obvious concern. "The substitute baby sitter can stay only four days."

"Ask her if she can get someone else," I suggested and Lisa spoke with the baby sitter a few more minutes then, after hanging up, "I'm worried, Jeff,"

I grumbled, "We shouldn't have called," but Lisa's concern and my understanding that she would probably not relax until we started home prompted a change of plans, one that satisfied both of us. We would continue the trip but eliminate part of Portugal and Gibraltar and arrive home in time for the baby sitter to leave.

Popular wisdom confers a "laissez-faire" attitude on fathers. My dad was the one who allowed more adventurism. My mother was the cautious security base. This push-pull is healthy in my opinion but may be modified by circumstances. "Mothers worry too much," I've said and thought many times; but I have also worried. Men just don't verbalize their concerns as much. We sometimes act, however.

Vienna 1965: Lipenzaner horses at the Spanish Riding School, the Boys Choir, ice skating at the Continental Hotel. Lisa and I had left the three children in our hotel room with a young baby sitter and were happily experimenting on wobbly ankles with ice-skating in the outdoor Continental rink. We tried to imitate other couples skating arm in arm but succeeded only in pulling each other to the ice. The rink was filled with better skaters accentuating our awkwardness. We rested against the railing.

"Where's our room, Lisa?" I asked looking up at the high-rise hotel overlooking the skating rink.

"Let's count up—let's see—seven floors—and we're on this side," Lisa said pointing up.

"Hey! There's Jeff, isn't it?" I exclaimed.

A small figure was standing behind the window glass in a room seven stories high. Before we could think, the small figure slowly began sliding the framed window to the side. It *was* Jeff and he was standing in a now open window high above the ice skating rink.

"JEFF! JEFF!" I shouted.

Ice skaters stopped. There was a gasp as others looked upward. Lisa grasped my arm. I do not remember ever being as frightened as I was that day.

"I'm going up!" With my ankles turning from side to side, I ran on those thin blades across the ice into the lobby and into the elevator for the longest ride of my life. Into the room I bolted, ready to grab Jeff down from his precarious perch. Jeff and Cathy were sitting innocently on the floor. The baby sitter was putting Louisa to bed. It was as if nothing had happened. My heart was racing and fear turned to rage. I was mostly upset with the baby sitter, but Jeff's teeth rattled as I grabbed his shoulders.

"Don't ever—ever do that again!" Then I turned to Cathy, "You're the oldest—you are responsible!" Poor Cathy paled as she always did at my anger. I over-reacted, of course, prompted by fear, later realizing that Jeff was exhibiting natural curiosity, and Cathy shared no blame for a baby sitter's or a father's negligence.

As I think back over those early days of parenthood, I see that I was too concerned with control. I was afraid to let the children be spontaneous. I believe that with their mother they were more content and perhaps less stressed than when I was around. I provided the adventure factor, organizing hikes up mountains or into the woods but the price extracted was uncomplaining acceptance of the inevitable fatigue, hunger, or pain. Cathy and Jeff plodded along, putting up with my drive; Louisa resisted and I often lost patience with her obstinacy. Now, of course, I appreciate her independence.

We learned that Lee and Betty Milford would be traveling along the Rhine during their European tour. We were happy to see them as they stepped off of the Rhine cruiser and as we discussed our plans for a day of touring, Betty suddenly exclaimed "Our bags! Where are our bags?" Apparently the crew of the cruiser had failed to off load their bags in the short layover near Rudesheim, and it was already steaming down the Rhine River toward Bingen. We raced down the winding road along the north side of the Rhine to get to Bingen before the ship arrived. We made it just in time and later had a good laugh about the chase. We knew that the Milford's were going to continue their tour throughout Europe and we wished them well. A week or so later we began our own weeklong camping adventure through Bavaria, Austria, and into Italy.

Camping in a green field beside the Tauber River and sheltered by a hill overlooking the walled city of Rudesheim ob der Tauber, we enjoyed our first evening on the road. While Lisa started preparing our dinner, I took the kids for a short hike up the hill. Cathy and Jeff kept up a good pace, but I soon lost patience with Louisa. Much to my shame, in looking back, I shouted at her to keep up, quit whining, and quit being a baby (which of course she was). I am sure that my voice reverberated against the hill, shocking fellow campers in the valley with the shouts of another angry American.

Our tour continued into Italy and while we were admiring the statute of David in the Plaza of Florence, we were surprised once again to see the Milfords. We found out that they were also going to Rome where, later, they visited us at our campsite on the outskirts of the eternal city. As I look back on our traveling in Europe with children, camping in our homemade tent and Rambler, experiencing the usual tourist sites, I do not remember large crowds or long lines. By way of contrast, years later, crowds seemed oppressive and every activity seemed more difficult; or was it just the difference in my age, then and now?

In many ways Jack Hennessen reminded me of Ron Shelly. Both men were somewhat volatile but both were excellent surgeons and, for some reason, both seemed to appreciate my talents. Jack had been complaining about calcific tendinitis in his right shoulder for sometime. One morning around seven Jack called me at home.

"Jeff, I want you to operate on my shoulder."

"Uh—when?"

"Right now! I made all the arrangements. I'll meet you in the OR."

I had two cases scheduled that morning but Jack put himself on the schedule before them. Even while being operated on he wanted to be in charge. Most surgeons want to be in charge and military rank certainly adds another layer to that personality tendency. The surgery was uneventful and even though I might have initially injected most patients, I surgically removed the calcium from Jack shoulder at his insistence. It proved to be a permanent cure as far as he was concerned, and when I visited him some thirty six years later he was still bragging about his pain-free shoulder.

For many years I kept track of the operations I performed while in the military service. Such records were necessary for membership in the American College of Surgeons and the American Academy of Orthopaedic Surgeons. Now the numbers have faded and only occasionally will a word or image trigger a lost memory of a specific day or incident.

I must have been in a particularly confident mood one fine day as I performed a Keller bunionectomy on one of my dependent patients. The corpsman assisting me enjoyed slapping the instruments into my palm as I requested:

"Hemostat!"

"Kelly clamp!"

"Scalpel!"

My hand was out but the corpsman and I both misjudged and the scalpel hit the edge of the surgical tray, did a flip in midair and, straight as an arrow, speared my foot through sterile shoe cover, leather shoe, and skin. I looked down to see the handle vibrating vertically out of my right foot.

"Well I'll be damned," I said. It felt as if a large rock had just hit my foot for I did not sense a cut or sharp pain—that is until I asked the nurse to pull the knife out "please."

"I guess you'd better get me another scalpel so I can finish the case."

"Are you all right, doctor?"

"Yeah I'm fine."

When she disengaged the blade from my first metatarsal into which the knife had penetrated, I felt a sharp pain but subsequently, just soreness.

I finished the case in about forty-five more minutes then inspected my foot. There was very little bleeding and tendon function was unaffected. That metatarsal remained sore for six months.

After all the years of medical school, internship, and residency, I had finally developed a sense of self-confidence that apparently projected to those around me. Never mind the nagging anxiety that accompanied a call from the operating room one evening. I was not on call so being called at home concerned me. My fears, however, were always greater than the reality.

"Dr. Farrell needs you, Dr. Justis! He's been working on this suicide attempt for two hours and he hasn't gotten anywhere."

Sam had been on call and a young, depressed airman had presented with a self-inflicted laceration of the wrist. When I arrived in the operating room Sam was sweating. The open wrist looked like a bowl of spaghetti with eleven tendons and the median nerve tagged with sutures.

"I can't figure out what goes where," Sam said, obviously exasperated.

"Let's see..."

I began systematically identifying the proximal and distal ends of the tendons. The median nerve was easy for me to identify, although several doctors had previously referred me cases in which the median nerve was mistakenly sutured to a tendon. I knew the anatomy and was proud of my ability to create order out of chaos.

Soon we had everything back together and it was gratifying to see the normal posture of the fingers and later to watch the patient gain in strength and mobility.

Since the orthopaedists in the facilities I am visiting are my contemporaries with good training, I don't feel comfortable in an inspector's role. I will offer a second opinion when asked and I will help in getting patients transferred by AirEvacuation.

Because of my position as Chief of Orthopaedics and with the recommendation of Col. Hennessen, I was appointed Consultant in Orthopaedics to the Surgeon General of the USAF in Europe and was required to visit other orthopaedic facilities throughout the European theater. Although some of these TDY trips (temporary duty) were without Lisa, I was able to meet her in Spain on a consultant visit to Torrehon Air Base and later we were able to drive to England for a consultant visit at Lakenheath AFB Hospital.

One of my first consultant visits was to Athens where I met Custas Passios, one of the few American Board Certified orthopedists in Greece at that time. He introduced me to Uzo and octopus, neither of which is high on my culinary delights list. Uzo tastes a bit like turpentine and octopus a bit like—well—octopus. My travel was by military air and after a day or two in Athens I flew to the island of Crete to visit the small USAF hospital at Iraklion. I can't remember the name of the lone orthopedist there but I appreciated the time he took to show me the beauty and sophistication of the vanished Minoan civilization.

These consultant visits were usually short, less than a week, and did not interfere with our family weekends. However, when Col. Henry asked if I would like to become the team physician for the Wiesbaden area football team, I realized that this would require travel on weekends to many bases in Europe. I agonized over my initial positive response to his request since I felt somewhat duty bound to accommodate him. The next day I told him of my concerns.

"Col. Henry, you need to know that I am not a football fan (never have been and never will be) and that being with my family in my spare time is my first priority. If you could find someone else, someone who loves football, for this assignment I would really appreciate it."

Apparently Col. Henry was not that fond of football either and soon asked Sammy Farrell, the young general surgeon assigned to orthopaedics; he was quite willing, if not eager, to take the job. That meant, however, a few more days on call for the rest of us during football season. That was a small price for me to pay.

Another memorable consultant visit was to Wheelus Air Force Base in Tripoli, Libya, North Africa. An interesting orthopedist named Jean Paul met me at Base Ops. He lived on the economy in this Muslim stronghold and as we drove through dusty streets past Arabs and camels he warned me not to point my camera directly at the people as this was not accepted in Muslim tradition.

He and his wife entertained me at dinner that evening in their unscreened, concrete and stucco home. Later we visited the Souk in downtown Tripoli. There is something exotic about a Muslim country market or bazaar; the cacophony of the sellers and buyers as they bargain with each other, the smell, the light filtering through high windows, the stalls overflowing with blankets, brasswork, live chickens and barbecued camel, all combined to heighten the contrast of life in Tripoli with that of the West.

The next morning Jean Paul picked me up at the BOQ (bachelor officers quarters) and gave me a quick tour of the hospital. One wing had been set aside for the care of the King of Libya and his family. This, of course, was before Khadafy overthrew the monarchy and kicked the U.S. Air Force out of Libya. We conducted rounds on the orthopaedic patients then, driving through the base, near the entrance I noticed a large four-blade propeller mounted high on a stone monument. The inscription read: *Dedicated to the Memory of the Airmen of the Lady-Be-Good.* This B-17 crew on the way back from a bombing raid over Germany, flying on top of an overcast, had not seen the north coast of Africa and continued south over the Sahara desert until their fuel was exhausted. They all survived the crash landing 300 miles south of their destination. Many years later the empty wreck was found, remarkably preserved in the dry desert air. Almost all the bodies of the crewmembers were located many miles north of the crash site; they had all perished in the harsh desert in a vain attempt to walk back toward Wheelus Air Base.

The purpose of consultant visits was to report to the Surgeon General on the quality of orthopaedic services in outlying USAF hospitals. I developed good rapport with Air Force orthopedists in the European theater. Since we were a major referral center, I even earned the respect of army and navy physicians during my three-year tour in Germany.

In the spring of 1966, I was asked to report to the commander's office. *What now!*

"Major Justis, how would you like to go to Africa?"

Before I could answer, Colonel Henry continued, "We've just received an urgent request from the Pentagon to retrieve a young man injured in Malawi and get him back to Frankfurt, ASAP."

"When do you think I should leave?" I asked, realizing that I had already "volunteered."

We've arranged a C97 flight leaving at 0600. You need to be at Wiesbaden Air Base at 0400 tomorrow."

After finding out that the 19-year-old son of an army Colonel had sustained a closed fracture of his left femur in a mountain climbing accident, I requested that our cast tech go along to help. We spent the rest of the afternoon getting our supplies together—plaster rolls, traction bows, local anesthesia, cast cutters, I.V. fluids. We did not know what to expect at the hospital in Blantyre, Malawi, but the impression we got in the various messages concerning this young man's situation was that he was in a native hospital and that surgery was planned in a few days.

In those years (circa 1966) open reduction of femoral fractures was rarely indicated especially in marginal situations. The nineteen year old had been in Malawi as part of a Peace Corps team and had fallen while mountain climbing a week before. Getting him to a U.S. military medical facility before questionable surgery or complications developed was our mission.

Early the next morning the flight crew helped load our equipment, and we launched into gray German skies on schedule. Our initial destination was Addis Ababa in Ethiopia, a refueling stop. Because of problems with our diplomatic clearance, we all had to remain in the plane during refueling, and we were on our way to Kenya within thirty minutes.

Flying from Wiesbaden to Kenya by C97 over the vastness of the African continent required the whole day; fatigued, we finally entered the teeming city of Nairobi where we were scheduled to remain over night. Our hotel, a white colonial structure, showed some signs of the neglect that seems to follow independence of former colonial governments. Dirt streets paralleled broad avenues and open crate shacks leaned against flat-roofed stucco buildings. Shops in the market area exhibited the results of poaching with racks of lion skins, elephant hoof tables, and other "souvenirs", indicting man's dominance over other members of the animal kingdom, a sad commentary on our insensitivity to the natural world to which we owe so much.

Bureaucracy, it seems, is that part of all governments whose sole reason to exist is to obstruct progress. Even with the power of the U.S. government behind us we found obstacles to a prompt departure at Nairobi International Airport the following morning. Minor officials took delight in requesting one more form or one more fee before we could be on our way. We were under a time constraint because Malawi somewhat resented our coming to "save" an American from their medical service and had given a limited diplomatic clearance that expired at 1700 the day of departure from Nairobi.

Finally we were able to fly out over the plains of east Africa toward the south. I would have enjoyed observing the wildlife in the savannas below but that was impossible at our altitude. Thinking of the other animals on our small planet, maintaining a tenuous hold on life in this ever more crowded world, I wondered about the role of the medical profession in increasing mankind's pressure of numbers on this planet. If man does not improve the world for *all* life—what *is* our imperative?

The engines continued their steady drone as Kilimanjaro loomed high and snow-capped to the east of our position. Headwinds hindered our journey and by the time we landed in Blantyre my cast tech and I had only forty-five minutes to retrieve our patient and return to the airport. Fortunately, the hospital was nearby. As we approached the flat, tin roofed, one-story complex, we were amazed at the number of brightly colored tents and lean-to's scattered around the hospital where native women, leaning over open fires and glowing charcoal cookers, prepared food for their own family members, filling the air with pungent smells. The double entrance doors were propped open; a nurse directed us to a four-bed ward. Open windows allowed free circulation of air and smoke and insects. A relieved young man greeted us from his bed.

"Am I glad to see you guys!"

"How are you feeling?" I asked as I checked the crude traction and sling arrangement supporting his left lower extremity.

I explained what we were going to do as we prepared to insert a Kirchner wire under local anesthesia. This wire, placed through his upper tibia just below the knee, would be used to apply fixed traction in his cast. We improvised a body support using cast boxes, as no cast table was available. The doctor in charge of the hospital never came around to see or help us. Apparently he resented this medical kidnapping. First we put a cast on the lower extremity, incorporating the traction pin, then crudely wrapped plaster around our young American's chest, waist, and opposite thigh. Finally we could free him from his bed "prison" and move him over to a stretcher for transfer to the ambulance. Mummified in plaster, he had very little pain in the move and was joking as we jarred out of the hospital grounds and sped toward the Airport. Two engines had already been started, and we began taxiing as soon as we boarded the C-97. We all breathed a sigh of relief as we lifted off. If we had not departed before the diplomatic deadline, many days might have been spent while governments large and small played the power game at the expense of common sense and human life.

My patient was comfortable, considering the crude cast we had so hastily applied. We should have had a flight nurse to keep up with his vital signs, because at a little over a week after injury, this young man was a prime candidate for fat embolism or a pulmonary embolus. We had obtained approval for our patient's overnight stay in the British hospital in Nairobi for that evening, and I was happy to turn over responsibility for his care for the next twelve hours. The next day was again to be a long one—and more worrisome to me when I learned that our encased young man had an elevated temperature.

Flying up the east coast of the Dark Continent past Lake Victoria, the Nile Valley, and across the Mediterranean we finally arrived at Rhine-Main airport. I accompanied my patient to Frankfurt General Army Hospital and delivered him to my contemporaries, the Army orthopaedists. I found out much later that the colonel's son had made the trip back to the United States successfully and eventually recovered fully. Of all my consultant trips this one was the most memorable, providing a richness of experience through the mystery of the Dark Continent, the political uncertainty, and the unknowns in our rescue mission.

I miss flying. With less than six months to go before rotation back to the States I am already daydreaming about getting another plane.

Louise and Johnny Rollow and Ann Ross all came to visit and tour with us on a driving trip to the Netherlands in 1966. Madurodam, a representative miniature city, intrigued the children, and a visit to the beautiful Kuykenhof gardens thrilled all of us with the most wonderful colors and smells of tulips. Of course, a working windmill fascinated Jeff and me with its engineering efficiency.

In January of 1967, I was to take the oral and written exam for the American Board of Orthopaedic Surgery. In order to study effectively I found that a reward system prompted my best efforts. Thus in December of 1966, we scheduled a trip to Berchtesgaden in Bavaria. Beginning our adventure, on the way south, we encountered a snowstorm, and it was dark as we climbed the winding mountain road to the Air Force hotel that in WW II was used by Hitler's officers. We didn't get very far when our tires skidded on the fresh snow, so we reversed course and installed tire chains at a service station in town. With the improved traction were able to slowly wind our way up the mountain and arrived at our hotel about eight o'clock in the evening.

I planned to divide the day into morning and afternoon sessions so I could study in the morning and have fun with my family the rest of the day. Lisa entertained the children while I studied, then skiing, touring the Eagles Nest, or visiting the Salt Mine, was a good stimulus for academic persistence.

Upon returning to Wiesbaden I was given temporary duty orders to return to the United States for the Orthopaedic Board Examinations in San Francisco in January 1967. I was to fly military air to the States and then transfer to a commercial air carrier for the flight to San Francisco. There I met with my contemporaries from residency, Kent Peterson, Bob Tooms, and Jim Hardy. Kent, Bob, and I were not too up-tight about the upcoming boards, because we figured we had studied enough and there was nothing we could do to alter the outcome at this late date; so we partied and had a pretty good time the night before the exam. Jim Hardy, as I remember, was so tense that he couldn't sleep. However, he did pass the examination, as did the rest of us.

I had been granted permission to take a few days of leave before returning to Germany so I arranged for a flight to Memphis. While home I used the band saw in the shop to cut the serpentine fronts of the two small mahogany chests I had started while in Germany. I had used the shop at Wiesbaden Airbase for some of the heavier work but the base band saw was not as precise as the one Dad and I shared, and I was happy to spend a few hours in the workshop that I had missed for the past three years.

I had missed something else during my tour in Germany: flying. So Dad and I rented a Cessna 172 at Dixie Air Service on the southwest corner of Memphis Municipal Airport and flew for about an hour in the Memphis area. My dad was always a willing partner in my flying, much to my mother's chagrin.

Not long after our arrival in Germany, however, it soon became apparent that my flying was going to be curtailed. The Wiesbaden area aero club had been closed the month before when a student pilot strayed over the East German border creating a diplomatic incident. The plane had been confiscated and the base commander embarrassed. A year later I learned of an Army club that was an hour's drive south. I checked out in a Piper Colt and managed to take each of our children flying locally. Lisa and I even planned a few trips, but when the club president and three passengers were killed in a stall/spin accident, that club, too, closed. Getting back in the air was proving to be difficult. A year later I managed to check out in a Piper Cub at another Army club, but trying to maintain proficiency was a logistical nightmare.

Our three year tour in Germany was coming to an end. What a wonderful experience the Air Force had provided for us in Europe! Lisa and I discussed the possibility of extending for another year in Wiesbaden, but we were beginning to consider the possibilities for future practice and felt that it would be easier to investigate opportunities if we were stateside. I had my choice of assignments and Keesler Air Force Base in Biloxi became our first choice since we were considering Clarksville, Tennessee as a possible practice site. We would easily be able to fly there by light plane.

So an experience that began with what was interminable waiting for my family to arrive ended all too soon, and our familiarity and comfort with European customs gave way to the culture shock of returning home. Frenetic living, fast food, self-service, neon and billboards shocked our sensibilities as we drove home from McGuire Air Force Base in New Jersey.

CONUS

Being stuck in a small motel room for three days with three children and being oppressed by fog and drizzle were enough to try the patience of a saint. Lisa's patience with the children and with me certainly qualified her for sainthood. I know now that her patience was external. I learned later that the price she paid for repressing anger or resentment or anxiety was greater than I could possibly imagine at that time.

We were assigned to Keesler Air Force Base in Biloxi, Mississippi, but we had close to three weeks before having to report. The money I had obtained when we sold our Cessna 170 (N2634V) had been invested wisely (interestingly in Cessna common stock) and within two weeks we had another family airplane—a Cessna 172 (N4051F). Lisa and I flew to Biloxi to sign up for on-base housing and to enroll the children in school. Shadow remained a constant companion and on more than one occasion startled a lineman when she was the first to exit the airplane.

Upon assuming my duties at Keesler Air Force Base hospital I was happy to find that Col. Joe Henry, my old boss at Wiesbaden was hospital commander. I was assigned as Chief of Orthopaedics and Col. Henry said that if I were interested I could initiate an Air Force residency-training program. At the time the primary orthopaedic program was at the Wilford Hall hospital at Lackland Air Force Base in San Antonio. I thought about the opportunity and certainly if I were to continue with my Air Force career, being chief of a second training program would have many advantages. However, I did not consider myself an academician and my long-standing fear of public display contributed to my reluctance to undertake the program. I confided in Col. Henry that I would probably separate from the service at the end of my obligation. I had certainly enjoyed the Air Force and with increasing rank and stature I had a good bit of control over my time off, but always, the needs of the service outweigh the desires of the individual. Vietnam was "our war" and we received a number of wounded that were usually transferred through Travis Air Force Base in California. Most of us in the military accepted the war as a part of the job and had I remained on active-duty I would eventually have been assigned to Southeast Asia. I remember a young airman with a badly infected knee. He had fallen into a booby-trapped hole filled with bamboo spears one of which had penetrated his knee joint. I also remember a recently transferred dermatologist who discussed many of the parasitic and venereal diseases endemic in our military. The romance of war was often lost on those of us in the Medical Corps.

Soon I settled into work at Keesler aided by my first sergeant, Mel Gara. Our workday began at seven-thirty with most surgery completed by around one. The goal of the hospital staff was to be finished with all non-emergency work by four-thirty. As a major and as chief of orthopaedics I did not have to serve as MOD (Medical Officer of the Day) but, of course, I shared orthopaedic call with Ken Tomberlin, Maury Schultz, John Evans and, Tom Evans. I have subsequently heard from Ken Tomberlin and later, as a reservist, I spent some time with Maury Schultz. Even as late as the 90s I renewed my acquaintance with John Evans. John is a Seventh-Day Adventist who tried his best to convince me of the logic of his beliefs. Needless to say he was unsuccessful, but I enjoyed our arguments and good-natured ribbing. In fact I admired him and his wife for their vegetarianism; she was and is a most attractive lady who does not use makeup.

Not long after we arrived at Kessler, I was quite surprised when Col. Henry called me to the podium at "Commanders Call" to present me with my second Air Force commendation metal for my work in Wiesbaden. My commanders appreciated me, and if I had been promoted ahead of schedule I probably would have considered remaining on active-duty. When I completed my residency in 1964, there was considerable delay before I was promoted to major. Now, men who were just coming out of their training programs were promoted to major immediately and would be considered for lieutenant colonel at the same time that I would be eligible. Many of us felt that this was unfair to those of us who had served more time as fully trained orthopaedic surgeons.

We lived in a little three-bedroom cottage on St. Alban's Fairway in the officers' section of base housing. Soon after we moved in I fenced the backyard with chain-link for Shadow and installed a wall in the open front of the garage so that I could set up my workbench.

Most mornings I could easily walk to work through a gate in the fence that separated the hospital compound from base housing. With long days in the summer and with the clinic closing at 4:30 in the afternoon we were able to enjoy being together as a family on the Gulf coast. The Cessna 172 allowed us to fly back to Memphis in two to three hours on weekends, and we visited Ann and Neil in Clarksville several times. One weekend we loaded everyone in the plane for a flight to Sweetwater, Tennessee and the "Lost Sea," an underground lake that we all enjoyed exploring. I needed little excuse to fly; three years in Europe certainly had its compensations, but I had missed the freedom only pilots can experience in a small plane.

The engine had low compression in several cylinders when we bought the airplane, and I was not too surprised when the mechanic at Robbins Aero at Gulfport airport said that it needed a major overhaul. So, for the next six weeks or so we were grounded. We used the time to install some new equipment in the plane preparing it for instrument training.

In January 1968 desire for the coveted Instrument Rating became an obsession. We had flown to Sanibel Island in Florida for a New Years holiday. Our destination was a resort adjacent to the grass strip airport—an idyllic location. We enjoyed exploring with the children and investigating the large "alligator" pond behind our cabin; as long as we were doing something unique I could expect them to remain close-by. As with all children, however, familiarity resulted in less caution, especially on the beachfront.

I was absorbed in reading while "watching" the three children romp in the gentle gulf surf late one afternoon. Cathy, Jeff, and Lou were jumping and shouting with glee as waves broke cold over them. I looked up from momentary distraction and was chilled by the sight of two, not three, bouncing bodies.

"Where's Louisa?" I shouted. "Where's Louisa?"

Jeff and Cathy shrugged as if to say "why should we know or care."

"When did you see her? Where was she?" I was filled with a sense of guilt. Why hadn't I been watching closer? I envisioned her floating face down in the water and panicked.

"LOUISA! LOUISA!" I ran down the beach in the direction of the off shore current. Then I saw her small figure intently engaged in sand castle creativity about 100 yards down the beach. She did not see me coming but was jerked into reality by my powerful, angry grip around her arm. "Don't you *ever* do that again!" Of course it was never clear exactly what she or Jeff or Cathy had done wrong. Again my anger was triggered by guilt. In spite of that afternoon's excitement, the trip was a success and enjoyed by all. New Year's day was clear and sunny with a warm southerly wind providing a nice tailwind for our flight back home. This Caribbean air mass brought with it a surprise as it collided with the colder air bulging from the north; clouds and precipitation formed a wall across north Florida. We had to land at Perry Foley airport, because flying through that stationery front was impossible without an instrument rating and trying to fly under it would be unsafe.

As instrument-rated pilots departed through the relatively thin overcast and I felt increasing pressure to return to work, I resolved to further my flying skills. After three days waiting for a break in the weather we finally vacated our motel prison and drove home in a rented car; I flew back later in a friend's airplane to pick up the Cessna.

Frank Fleming was a young flight instructor who loved the challenge of instrument flying. He was about my age and aspired to fly for an air carrier; the more he flew the better. I am forever grateful for his encouragement and persistence in helping me learn the intricacies of flying without outside reference.

"Hey, Jeff! Come on to the airport—the fog's rolling in." Frank called me on a winter's afternoon. We spent hours practicing approaches into Gulfport airport on such days.

As we cranked up the 172, the ceiling was five hundred or so and the visibility less than a mile. With Frank guiding my performance we flew circuit after circuit seeing the runway only in the last few minutes of each approach. "Good job," Frank would say.

"Cleared for takeoff and you'd better make this the last one, Frank," the tower controller warned. "It's going below minimums!"

Actually it was already below minimums as I nursed the Cessna through the murk to intercept the localizer. The glide slope indicator came alive – 400 ft – 300 ft – 200 ft – where's the runway? Then strobe lights glowed through the haze leading us finally toward the halo-ringed runway lights and home. My instrument rating was certainly a "wet rating" with plenty of clouds, rain, and even a little ice time filling my logbook. Because of this, though, I was confident in my ability to pile Lisa, children, and dog into the Cessna and launch into weather that used to keep us ground bound.

I don't remember encouraging Lisa to learn to fly, but she began taking lessons while we were in Wise, Virginia. We would fly over to Tri-Cities airport in the Luscombe so that Lisa could fly in a Piper Tri Pacer for an hour or two on weekends. However, she had only accumulated four or five hours of instruction by the time we began our Air Force tour. Now, in Gulfport, Frank began giving her instruction in our Cessna 172, preparing her to solo. Before she could be turned loose in the airplane she had to get a physical examination for a student permit. It was during her flight physical that we learned she had mild hypertension probably secondary to internal stress. This was the first time that I recognized Lisa's fragility. In all the years of our marriage Lisa had always exhibited such strength and determination that I had never had even a passing thought that I might outlive her. Jim Key, the flight surgeon, had her rest for 30 minutes on several occasions and was finally able to get her blood pressure down to minimum standards for a class III physical. Lisa was so outwardly calm that it was hard to realize how much she internalized worry about the children, her parents, and, of course, her husband. Whether true or not, my perception was that we were totally compatible—meaning that Lisa was a willing partner in any endeavor that I suggested. Probably because of a desire to please me, even though I had not knowingly applied any pressure, she eventually soloed to the delight of the children and me as we waited for her to taxi to the ramp. A picture of the six of us by the airplane fades in color just as memory of that time and place softens and seems part of another life.

Lisa developed a cough that I thought was a simple bronchitis. Her coughing was so severe, however, that she developed several rib fractures that were quite painful. In an ill-advised attempt to relieve her pain I taped her chest. This gave her relief but the decreased airflow to her lungs resulted in viral pneumonia and she was hospitalized briefly. John Evans and his wife were kind enough to help me with the children, feeding us many good vegetarian meals during this period of time. Lisa recovered and, although she quickly regained her energy, I would hence forth be more concerned about her vulnerability. She was a plodder and would keep up a steady uncomplaining pace on any task and in this way gave the impression of strength, but again I think she repressed her own desires. It was up to me to recognize her fatigue and say, "Let's rest."

We had not discussed having a fourth child while in Germany and whether we would have reconsidered our original thoughts on family size became moot as we learned, six weeks after an evening's lapse of caution ("Do you think we need to use the diaphragm? What time of month is it? Oh I think it'll be O.K."), that Lisa was pregnant. John Alexander was a good friend and an excellent OB/GYN physician. Lisa was progressing quite well in her pregnancy until one day she called me in the office.

Her voice was shaking. "Jeff please come home. Something's happened."

I rushed out of the office, through the fence and to our house as quickly as I could.

Lisa was crying. "I think I lost the baby. Look!" She pointed to a bloody clot in the commode. Previously she had been spotting a little.

"I don't think so, baby," I tried to be reassuring. "I'll call John."

After an examination John again reassured her that he thought everything was going well, but he wanted her to spend more time resting. Over the next several weeks the spotting decreased. Soon she was able to feel the baby move and before long the fact of her pregnancy became obvious for all to see. Although we had not planned for this pregnancy, once it was a fact we were both enthusiastic and looking forward to the new arrival. In the days before ultrasound we had no idea whether our gift would be a boy or girl.

Weeks passed quickly in this, our last year on active-duty. My practice was gratifying, but the people and events that tend to be remembered are those that give us the most concern.

A rather foul smell emanated from the examining room as I shook hands with a retired Army sergeant.

"Hey Doc," he said with bravado, "this damned osteo is flaring up on me again."

He had been wounded thirty-five years earlier during World War II by shrapnel in the left femur, just above the knee. Since that time he had had numerous flare-ups of recurrent infection with drainage. This latest episode had not responded to antibiotics and the drainage was especially foul. I was planning a debridement of the wound and curettage of the bone, hoping to find a sequestrum, a dead fragment of bone acting as a foreign body potentiating the infection.

It happened that "Red" Aldredge, a well-known orthopaedic surgeon from New Orleans was a civilian consultant to the Air Force and was visiting us at the time.

"What do you think, Dr. Aldredge?" I asked as he examined the patient with me. Wisely he didn't discuss his opinion with me until we were in my office.

"Jeff, I think he's got a fistula carcinoma!" Red explained. "I've seen several cases like that and the smell is characteristic. Be sure to get a biopsy."

I had not even considered that possibility and several days later during surgery I was grateful for Red's insight. Not only was the biopsy positive for cancer but also the patient had evidence of pulmonary metastases. He and his wife were accepting of the diagnosis and over a period of weeks I got to know and appreciate the patient's resolve not to let this get him down. After all, he had been through combat. What could be worse than that? However, over the next several months I watched him deteriorate as his breathing became more labored. His terminal week was spent on the medical ward. Each day I would stop by to say hello to his wife with whom I had developed a good relationship. On Friday I told her I was off on the weekend but would check on her husband Monday.

Lisa was planning to shop with the children so I went to the airport to work on the airplane Saturday morning.

"Hey Doc, there's a phone call for you from the hospital." The linemen had come from the office with the message. I was under the instrument panel of the Cessna installing a new instrument and, as a goal-oriented person, I resented any interruption.

"Okay, tell them I'll be there in a minute."

"What's the problem?" I grumbled as the hospital operator connected me with a nurse on the medical ward.

"Sergeant Elhart just died and we need someone to pronounce him," the nurse told me rather matter-of-factly.

"You know I'm not on call don't you? Did you call the medical staff? He's on their service."

My first thought was selfishly to preserve my time. I did not like having my planned day changed.

"Well Doctor, I wouldn't have called except that Mrs. Elhart wanted to see you."

As I thought of this nice lady sitting with her dead husband and how she and I had been able to communicate as her husband became less responsive, I had increasing pangs of guilt tempered by sympathy.

"Tell her I'll be there as soon as I can, but it may take me forty to forty-five minutes."

Always in my medical career my first reaction on getting an emergency call was one of resentment, but once I knew I was needed resentment was replaced by resolve. Inevitably, as soon as I entered the room with a patient, negative thoughts disappeared and a sense of fulfillment would come over me.

"I'm sorry, Mrs. Elhart," I said quietly as I hugged her.

"Thank you for coming. I just wanted you to tend to him."

I did a brief death-certifying exam and even though I could do nothing for the patient I felt better for having come for his wife's sake.

DR. E. JEFF JUSTIS

Dan Riordan, whom I had met in Germany, was another of our Air Force consultants in practice in New Orleans. He readily accepted my offer to pick him up in my airplane at Lakefront airport and fly him back to Keesler for his day's visit. During the year Dan would visit every three months or so and seemed to enjoy the short flight each time. He asked me if I thought he was too old to learn to fly (he was 55 at the time). I reassured him that he certainly was not and pointed out that he seemed to have a natural talent for controlling the plane when I let him fly from the right seat. Later Dan would begin flying, buy an airplane, and enjoy fifteen or so good years flying to meetings, clinics, and on hunting expeditions. In years to come I was to spend a good bit of time with this fine gentleman.

Jack Wickstrom, another consultant from New Orleans, was just the opposite. A fiery, redheaded orthopaedist, Jack told how he had flown many times and could get his license any time he wanted. When I turned the plane over to him momentarily he was all over the sky, very uncoordinated. He was an excellent orthopaedist but a poor pilot. I had introduced him at commander's call as he was about to begin a lecture for the medical staff when a slide jammed in the carousel. The airman running the projector, in trying to correct the problem, turned the carousel upside-down without the locking ring. Seventy-two slides fell out on the floor. I thought Jack would have apoplexy then and there, but he calmed down enough to re-sort most of the slides and gave a somewhat abbreviated lecture. Since the airman worked for me, I was also rather embarrassed by the incident.

The Society of Military Orthopaedic Surgeons was meeting in Denver. Always eager for a flight, I convinced Lisa to ask Ann and Neil to keep the children and we were soon on our way in the Cessna by way of Clarksville.

Dr. Marcus Stewart, a colonel in the Army reserves at that time, was a guest speaker at the meeting. He had been one of my mentors at the Campbell Clinic during my residency, and I was flattered that he remembered me and quite unexpectedly surprised when he called me aside and said, "We've been discussing getting someone else on the staff and although I'm not supposed to be soliciting anyone, would you be at all interested in coming back if the group were to ask you?"

We had been considering practicing in Clarksville or some other small town, but we had also been talking about the possibility of Memphis. I had been hoping that a small East Memphis hospital might be constructed, because I just didn't relish the idea of a multi-hospital big city practice.

"Jeff, I don't want you to count on this or say anything to anyone until the staff has had a chance to consider its options. As you know the vote must be unanimous," Marcus warned.

"I am honored that you thought of me, Dr. Stewart. Lisa and I will have a lot to talk about."

It was exciting for Lisa and me to consider the possibility of a group practice, especially at the Campbell Clinic, which had an international reputation in the field of orthopaedics. Lisa really liked the idea of Memphis and closeness to family after our four-year absence.

My daydream of a small town practice was based on perceptions gained more from fiction (*Arrowsmith* and *The Citadel*) than from any real experience with small town living or practice. The qualms I had were based on my own sense of inadequacy in an academic world. Although I had done well intellectually in medical school and residency, I always experienced anxiety whenever I had to display that knowledge—that is give a talk or produce a paper that would be subject to scrutiny or criticism. Perhaps I was too severe a critic of others, albeit silently, and therefore feared similar criticism of my own work. Still, it was an honor to be considered and I didn't have to make a decision anytime soon.

Back in Biloxi we settled into the routine of my orthopaedic practice, Lisa's pregnancy, and rearing our children.

"You need to fuss at Jeff!" Lisa prompted as I opened the back door after work on a spring day in 1968.

"What happened?"

"I found all three of the children down at Back Bay, playing in the water." Jeff had learned about Back Bay from one of the Evan's boys. The Bay, adjacent to the housing area, was accessible through an empty lot with bushes and trees that made it seem like a secret place. We had told the children not go near Back Bay so this was quite a transgression. I think my demeanor was enough discipline for the three little ones although not being able to watch Star Trek added further punishment.

On one of our trips to Memphis I attended the Monday night meeting at the Campbell Clinic for the first time since my residency. I surprised myself when I was asked to tell the group about my experiences in the Air Force and did so without my usual stage fright. Not long after that meeting Dr. Harold Boyd called and invited me officially to join the staff of the Campbell Clinic. He suggested that I take a week before making a final decision. I had previously discussed practicing with Dr. B. G. Mitchell and Henry Stratton among others, but the emphasis in most groups was on productivity. I had been an employed physician since my graduation from medical school in 1956 and had no experience with the "business" of medical practice. I had come to feel that my job was to treat patients and that compensation was remote in time and relationship to that patient. I would have been satisfied with a perpetual allowance and with the freedom to practice good medicine, build good furniture, and fly airplanes. Lisa helped me make the decision that would lead far into a future that could not be known, but that seemed as bright and endless as the dreams of all young people.

"Dr. Boyd, I would be honored to join the staff of the Campbell Clinic. I just hope you don't expect me to write a lot of papers," I said in a half joking matter.

"Doctor, the Campbell Clinic is a very unique group. We have doctors interested in research, in organized medicine, and in clinical work. If you get interested in something you may want to write about it. But if you just want to practice good orthopaedics you'll be welcome."

I was reassured. Now we could plan in earnest for our return to Memphis. Of course, Mama "C" and Granddad were delighted with our decision, as were Wees and Gran John.

Air Force life had been good and we had gained many new friends in my years of service. Just as in any large group practice there are difficulties and there were some irritations. When we signed out of base housing we were required to have the house inspected. We were told that it would be best to have the house professionally cleaned; it was implied that the civilian inspectors sometimes received a kick-back from the cleaning services. Not wanting to give in to graft, Lisa and I cleaned the house. I became quite angry when the inspector failed our work and as much as accused him of the under-the-table arrangement that had been rumored. When he returned to inspect the house and passed us, I felt somewhat better and apologized for my outburst. In retrospect I believe I responded to Lisa's distress with a protective concern that often manifested itself in anger.

Once while I was at work, Shadow broke through the screen door, ran across the street to a neighbor's house, and intimidated their small dog. No harm was done and Shadow immediately returned when Lisa called. Lisa thought little of the incident until later in the evening after I had returned home when she answered the door to a very irate lady who proceeded to verbally abuse her. I became livid and jumped up from my seat and said some things that I would not normally say to a lady. I felt bad about it later, but I always felt that I should be the defender in chief, especially when I could see that it really bothered Lisa.

There was some discussion about staying in the reserves as I was signing out of Keesler Air Force Base, but I was starting out on a new and exciting road and holding on to my Air Force life did not seem important at that time.

So to Memphis we came: Lisa, Cathy, Jeff, Louisa, Sunshine (Cathy's collie puppy), Shadow, and I. Lisa drove the Rambler American station wagon and I flew the Cessna 172.

MEMPHIS (ALPHA AND OMEGA)

An unlimited future lies ahead. I feel secure in my practice and we are not planning to move again. Finally Lisa and I can begin thinking of a new home. The "Little Green House" is getting smaller and smaller, now with four children and two dogs.

I separated from the Air Force July 1968. I delayed my start at the clinic until near the end of July so we would have enough time to settle into the "Little Green House." During our absence my folks had rented the house to several clinic residents (Dave Hankin had been the last) while we served our four-year Air Force tour. Now we moved back into the modest house that I had remodeled in 1960-61. There were three children and two dogs in this two-bedroom cottage so I added a partition in the back bedroom. Louisa and Cathy slept in one side and Jeff in the other. The small room to the south of our bedroom would be converted into a nursery for the new baby. In those days we had no way of knowing the sex of this baby, but at this time in our lives we really didn't care; we just wanted another healthy child.

I was especially glad to be back close to the workshop that had always been such a big part of my life. It was fun for all of us to be close to the grandparents. Mama "C" was in seventh heaven with Cathy, Jeff, and Lou running through the yard.

It did not take long to build a practice at the Campbell Clinic. New patients were funneled to each of us routinely. Seven of the thirteen staff members took call, so compared to the Air Force, I was better off since I had covered emergencies every three to four days then. Now I was on call once a week and one weekend a month. Financially I broke about even. As a major my pay had been about $15,000 a year, but I did not have to pay for health insurance or malpractice insurance. My initial salary at the Campbell Clinic was about the same but each year I could look forward to a greater increase than I would have received in the Air Force. Full partnership in the clinic required an astounding fifteen years, but change was in the air and eventually incorporation brought increased pay and only a couple of years to full partnership. I didn't join the clinic for the pay, however. I felt that the practice structure would allow me the freedom to continue my woodworking and flying. Of course I would be involved with teaching the residents but that became a great pleasure over the years with the one-on-one association in surgery and in the office. My friend, Fred Sage, and I began a personal arrangement in which he would see my hospital patients on my day off and I would reciprocate on his day off. In the late '60s we had office hours for half a day on Saturday and a whole day off during the week. My day off was Tuesday, and I was determined to use that time for my many avocations. On one occasion Dr. Boyd reinforced my resolve.

"Doctor, are you doing any surgery tomorrow? I have a bilateral bunionectomy and wondered if you could do one side."

"Uh—yes sir, tomorrow's my day off so I'm not doing any surgery."

"It's your day off? No. I don't want you to come in on your day off. I'll find someone else."

"Are you sure, Dr. Boyd?"

I did not persist. I'm sure some of my colleagues would have insisted on helping the "Chief," but if a physician ever gives up his day off or afternoon off to "catch up" or do "one more" case, he will never get that time back.

Dave Sisk who had been two years behind me during residency training had also been asked to join the staff. Dave would be involved with sports medicine covering various games nights and weekends. I would take over Crippled Children's clinics in Tupelo and Clarksdale and would staff clinics at LeBonheur, LePasse, and Crippled Children's Hospital. Finally I would have the opportunity to begin using my airplane, not only to attend meetings, but also to fly to these out-lying clinics every month or so. It was, for me, a very happy arrangement.

As early as July 31, I began flying to Tupelo in the 172 for a Crippled Children's Clinic. In November, when Lisa was eight months pregnant, we flew to Cleveland, Ohio for a biomechanics seminar. It was on this trip that we experienced a problem with icing that was the subject of an article that I published in the AOPA Pilot magazine.

The directional gyro slowly rotated toward the East. The electric turn needle remained straight up, but the artificial horizon was tilted ominously, indicating a left bank. In the red-tinged panel light, the suction gauge pointer was slowly passing one inch of mercury toward the zero mark.

Notwithstanding these obviously unreliable instruments, the remote compass still reassuringly indicated 20 degrees and the altimeter read 7000 feet. Lisa and I gained little reassurance, though, when glancing outside. Swirling gray clouds engulfed us, undoubtedly planting white crystals of ice on the leading edges of the prop, in the two ventures, and on the inconspicuous, but important, pitot tube. The airspeed indicator showed a steady 115 mph, and I knew this wouldn't change – not with a quarter inch of ice built up in front of that 1/8-inch pitot tube.

"Cleveland Center, this is Cessna 4051 Foxtrot at 7000, picking up moderate rim ice; request lower altitude."

"Cessna 4051 Foxtrot, Cleveland Center; standby, please."

About 30 minutes earlier, we had been skimming through the tops of puffy white clouds at dusk, picking up very light crystals of ice through each puff of cloud. We had requested and received a higher altitude, hoping to remain on top. It was apparent, however, that the clouds had the same idea. They followed us up to and beyond 7000 feet where we found ourselves confronted with a much more serious icing problem. Although the en route weather from Dayton, Ohio, to Cleveland was forecast to be above VFR minimums, my wife and I wanted to file IFR, primarily to wear the "new" off my instrument ticket. Always eager to a add more "wet" time, we filed for 5000 feet to place us in the clouds, since the freezing level was forecast to be above this altitude. Our problem began when icing was encountered at 5000 feet and we weren't clear of clouds above the freezing level.

Let's see—needle, ball, and airspeed. But I don't have airspeed; that leaves needle, ball, and altimeter. I still have the altimeter. Thank goodness for that! The remote indicating compass is a little more help than the standard compass. Let the airplane basically fly itself, once it is trimmed out. Keep the wings level with the needle and ball. Maintain altitude with the throttle.

With emergency instruments only, *and* solid instrument weather, it feels like walking a tightrope—with the slightest wobble, control of the situation might be lost.

"Cleveland Center, Cessna 51 Foxtrot," I said again. "Request lower altitude."

"Cessna 51 Foxtrot, Cleveland Center; standby."

"Cleveland Center, this is 51 Foxtrot, I am picking up pretty good ice, and I am going to declare an emergency unless I get a lower altitude."

"Cessna 51 Foxtrot, Cleveland, Roger; descend and maintain 5000."

I suppose they didn't want to go through the paperwork required if I had exercised my emergency authority. Regardless, I was happy to be able to pull back on the throttle and begin a gentle descent. At 5000 we were still in the clouds still picking up ice, and I again requested a lower altitude and was given 3000. At 3000, although in and out of clouds, we were below the freezing level, and the ice gradually began to melt; the suction gauge gradually indicated increasing suction pressure, and the air speed needle flickered back to life.

Several thoughts crossed my mind during the fifteen or so minutes that we were faced with icing in a minimally-equipped aircraft and in IFR conditions. Suppose with a little added turbulence or a little less cockpit attention the remote compass had begun turning and the sound of the wind passing the cockpit had indicated an obviously increasing speed, even though the air speed needle changed only with a change in static pressure. And suppose the altimeter had begun unwinding quite rapidly? Sure—center the needle and stop the unwinding of the altimeter. What then?

I remembered a technique from years ago, which was an integral part of the AOPA 180 degree-rating course. Even today, with the minimal instrument capability required of all pilots and the instrumentation found in most of our aircraft, this technique can be a lifesaver in a situation such as I found myself. Throttle back, trim the nose high to retain a slower but adequate air speed, and adjust the throttle to maintain altitude—keeping hands off the wheel, maintaining directional control with rudders alone. This, I feel, would have been my "out" had I not been able to maintain control with emergency instrumentation only.

Since I knew the cloud base was above 1000 feet, my second "out" was a formal declaration of an emergency then a controlled descent to below the clouds. But what if the conditions had been IFR in the Cleveland area? An instrument approach with no artificial horizon, directional gyro, or airspeed indicator would certainly be an interesting experience, to say the least. Fortunately we were spared this experience, which is best reserved for a simulator.

Never again will I think that just because I am instrument rated, I can take any airplane into almost any kind of weather, especially into icing conditions. I feel a safe instrument flight depends on three main factors: (1) a qualified instrument pilot with current instrument time, (2) a well-equipped aircraft, and (3) weather that does not exceed the capabilities of either the pilot or the airplane.

I do think that some instrument flights can be made in perfect safety, say, for example, in a Cessna 150, with a single nav/com transceiver. However, regardless of the qualifications of the pilot flying such an aircraft, there obviously are limits on the type of weather and the minimums required for an IFR flight in such an aircraft. On the other hand, I feel there is some weather beyond the capabilities of even the most qualified instrument pilot flying the most sophisticated, dually-instrumented and de-icing equipped aircraft.

Minimums should vary for the same pilot flying different aircraft and in differing weather conditions. The trick, then, is not just deciding, "go or no go," but "how go and when go."

On our many trips back to Memphis while we were living in Biloxi we had used Hi Air as our fixed base operation at Memphis Municipal Airport. The folks at the front desk were always helpful and friendly and glad to have our Cessna 172, N4051F. Maxine Bailey got to know our kids quite well and Paul Stillions, the manager, helped us in many ways. So it was natural that we chose to base our plane at Hi Air (a subsidiary of Holiday Inns) when we moved permanently to Memphis.

As we settled into a routine of practice, I realized that many weekends would be available for short trips and that if we were to depart after work on Friday for Florida, for example, we could enjoy two days of relaxation. So my mouth began to water for a more capable airplane, especially one with redundancy. I was eligible for VA benefits and could be reimbursed for multiengine instruction and for obtaining an instructor's rating if I so desired. There just happened to be an Apache, a 1956 blue and white twin-engine airplane, for sale at Hi Air. Ten thousand was a lot of money in 1968 so I contacted Jerry McCandless, the man from whom I had purchased the Cessna in 1967. Jerry was an interesting man, a businessman who owned several barbeque restaurants in this area. He and I had flown together in the 172 to an auction in Cape Girardeau looking for a bargain airplane. He was interested in a partnership, but Jerry was a fundamentalist in his religious beliefs so much so that he tried to proselytize me—to no avail, I might add. I was turned off by his fundamentalism and his anti-Semitic views; however, he was interested in a partnership and had given me a deposit for the Apache, but by the time we were ready to sign for the airplane he had changed his mind. I never regretted the loss of that partner even if borrowing the money did give me some anxiety considering my level of income. I rationalized that my income would increase each year and that my job was as secure as anyone could hope.

So it was that we became proud owners of Piper Apache N3130P. I obtained my multiengine rating in that aircraft and with our growing family we were destined to fill every seat and fly many places. For a while I had both the Apache and the Cessna, but by February of 1969 I had finally sold the Cessna.

Dr. Speed had retired after 1964 when I left the Campbell Clinic for the Air Force. I always admired Dr. Speed because of his determination to maintain a balance between the practice of medicine and the need for personal relaxation and gratification. He was a hunter and it was often said that when Dr. Campbell couldn't find Dr. Speed he would growl: "My God! Thpeed must have gone hunting again." But Dr Speed was in frail health in 1968 and died in the fall of that year. Dr. Boyd had been Chief of Staff when I returned to Memphis and would remain so for several more years.

I was in surgery on December 13, 1968 when the circulating nurse pushed open the operating room door with a message, "Dr Justis, your wife is in the labor room at the Baptist."

"Great! Tell her I'll be there soon as I finish this case."

Back in 1962, when Louisa was born, I was also in surgery at the old John Gaston Hospital so this scenario was familiar. By the time I had finished the case and made my way to delivery, Lee Adkins greeted me with the news of Kim's birth. It was a happy day.

For several years I had been drawing sketches of a future home. I had even made a small model while we were in Germany. Mom and dad had offered us a one-acre lot just off White Station road. We walked the lot and planned and talked—then we visited my friend, Walk Jones, who had been my high school roommate and had been in our wedding. Walk was in charge of the architectural firm founded by his father and had designed the Baptist Memorial Hospital in midtown Memphis.

"Jeff, this house will cost you at least $75,000!"

"$75,000? I'm not sure we can handle that at this time. I guess will have to think about it a little while."

And that's what we did. Mama "C" had an idea. "Why don't we build a small house for dad and me. Then we will sell you the big house."

Lisa liked the idea, and although I had always wanted to build a house, I realized there would be several advantages to moving into 4209 Walnut Grove. There would, of course, be more room for our large family and I would be able to continue using the shop that dad and I had built up over the years. I was already beginning to formulate plans for expansion of the shop. It seems that my two German workbenches would not fit in the original 12 X 30 ft. concrete block structure.

We obtained a loan through Leader Federal for the property at 4209 Walnut Grove and with that money my parents began construction on their new home at 4285 Longleaf in the spring of 1969.

Having a full day off every week was a luxury even if I did have to see patients in the office for two hours every Saturday morning. Soon I had drawn up plans for an 18 X 24 ft. extension on the shop. Johnny Rollow offered his advice and helped me get the footing and slab poured. I was then, and am now, happiest when fully engaged in some construction project. Lisa brought Kim up from the "Little Green House" frequently, offering encouragement and, as always, making me feel as if I were the best construction worker in the world.

"It looks great," she would say.

Cathy, Jeff, and Louisa were busy playing and dividing their time between Mama "C", Granddad, Wees, Grand John, Sissy, and Kim.

ANYTHING BUT A BROKEN HEART

My philosophy of life is quite optimistic. There are always concerns about what might lie ahead, but having four healthy children, having achieved goals that we had set in the Air Force, and having the job security of being associated with the Campbell Clinic, the future holds the promise of continued good fortune. Lisa too is optimistic. Act as if everything will work for the best and it usually will. Beneath the outward expression of hope, however, we hide the dark threat of reality—of tragedy.

Lisa did well after Kim's delivery except that she again had trouble nursing and had to resort to formula. She really wanted to nurse but had trouble relaxing. She would laugh and say, "I dried up like a prune." At six weeks post partum, Lisa was hospitalized for a tubal ligation (wisdom and experience finally dictating a limit to family size) and a repair of a defect in the abdominal wall. No abnormalities were noted internally and recovery was uneventful.

Shadow developed what I thought was an inner ear problem with a consequent tilt of her head, but at eleven years she was an old dog and with arterial disease had had a stroke. Lisa nursed her and we tried to keep her comfortable at home. When she became unstable and unable to walk one weekend we put her in the hospital. We visited her one evening and we left reassuring each other that she seemed more alert. She died that evening. We had lost our first "child." Lisa's stoic acceptance belied the depth of her feeling. We never discussed Shadow's death again.

Grand John, as the children called Lisa's dad, had been a stable base in Lisa's life and there was little doubt that she was his favorite. She had grown up in the "gate house" at Southwestern and would follow him on his rounds as college engineer. He was her mentor, and when we married I knew that it would be difficult to be the one Lisa would rely on, but she never made me feel that she would prefer her dad's opinion to mine. If she did seek his ideas, I was never made to feel less than the most important person in her life. Mr. Johnny, as every one at Southwestern had affectionately called him, was my mentor also. I had learned much from him during my years in college and always respected his opinion. When Grand John had a heart attack while repairing his house in late 1968, Lisa and I hoped that he would eventually be back to his energetic level of activity. It was hard to imagine him not working or fishing or figuring something out. But damage to his heart was extensive and in those pre-bypass surgery days, supportive care was all that was available. In spite of his shortness of breath, Mr. Johnny couldn't be still for long.

"I can fix anything but a broken heart," Grand John would often say, and he could not fix his own great heart. One evening in March of 1969 after changing the oil in his car, he developed acute cardiac failure.

"He's wheezing and can't breathe," Wees anxiously called late in the evening. "Should I call an ambulance?" She was frightened.

"Yes. Do you want us to come?" I shouldn't even have asked, but if we act as if everything will be okay.....then...

But this time everything was not okay, and Grand John finally got the rest he had been looking forward to someday. When the hospital called to tell us that Grand John had died, Lisa did not cry; she said very little as she dressed. I hugged her briefly as we got into the car for the sad drive to the Methodist. I'm sure her heart was broken, and as hard as I tried, I could not mend that loss. If there is a relationship between grief and stress to a weakening of the immune system, Lisa's experience may well be a prime example.

Later in March, thinking that getting away from home for a while might help her spirits, we flew to Lehigh acres in Florida on a promotional trip during which we had to listen to a salesman for about an hour. Otherwise the trip was at no expense and relaxing. In May we flew with all the children to Huntsville, Alabama for a weekend Flying Physicians Association meeting. Most of the time we imposed on, seemingly willing, grandparents (usually Mama "C" and Grand dad to keep Kim during her infancy). In recalling this period of time, I must have been responsible for planning these weekend trips. I was determined not to let the children interfere with traveling—a selfish attitude I'm sure because, although she never said so, Lisa felt the stress of arranging for Kim, getting the children ready, and seeing to it that the children with us did not interfere with the planned "good time." Cathy, Jeff and Louisa accepted the restrictions that Lisa and I expected in public places. Spontaneity was discouraged and they were gracious in conforming to our unobtrusive, quiet adventurism.

In June we flew to Lake Placid, New York for the FPA national meeting. Again Mama "C" kept Kim and Aunt Ann, as always, was wonderful to us in wanting to keep Cathy, Jeff, and Lou during our many trips without them. On this trip in the Apache, Lisa and I took Frank Yates and Roy Page with us (chaperoning them if you will) to this fun meeting. Weather was a problem as we missed the approach into Lake Placid and had to divert to Plattsburgh, New York. This was the first FPA meeting that Lisa and I attended since we returned to the U.S., but we quickly renewed our friendship with the members we had known from years before. Everyone loved Lisa. It was to be her last meeting although we had no way of knowing it at the time. Frank, who had an unhappy relationship with his wife, always seemed envious of the relationship that Lisa and I had.

He wanted to be with us, almost to a bother, especially when he had a bit too much to drink.

I remember thinking, as we got ready to leave the Lake Placid area how great it was to be able to use our airplane for such travel; there would certainly be many more trips ahead for us.

Professionally, I was enjoying my practice, which included working closely with the residents. I would usually see five or six new patients during my office hours and maybe ten or fifteen return patients. Compared to other practices this was relatively small number, but we were not concerned with productivity. It was more important that we spend quality time with our patients. I operated about three half days a week usually doing two to three procedures a day. I always looked forward to my Crippled Children's clinics since I got to fly to Tupelo, Clarksdale, and later to Greenwood and Oxford. Not only did I get to fly, taking one or two residents and our Crippled Children's Service administrator, Dorothy Tatum but I could usually get home in the afternoon in time to go to the workshop. It was a good break in the routine of patient care.

Lisa had learned of Camp Monterey and Camp Country Lad near Cookeville, Tennessee, and we both felt we should give our children the opportunity to experience camp life. So we left Kim with the grandparents again and the rest of us all flew to Cookeville over the weekend of July 5 and 6. The Holiday Inn pool was inviting on this warm summer day.

"Hey, Jeff—watch Mama dive," I called to Jeff who was engaged in pushing a toy log truck through the sand in the play area near the pool. He looked up in time to see his mother step up onto the diving board at the end of the pool. Cathy and Lou were dangling their feet in the pool.

"Go ahead Mama, **jump! Jump!**" they shouted.

I watched with pride as Lisa stepped to the end of the board. I was in love with that girl and had been since we first met our freshman year at Southwestern. She seemed unattainable then because of her popularity. Lisa was just too wonderful for me. Although we dated, my love was kindled from afar. I remember being so excited when she was selected as Miss Southwestern that I shouted out loud in the auditorium and ran backstage to congratulate her. I could barely speak. I wanted to hug her and tell her that how much I loved her, but every other male admirer had the same idea and I was just one of the crowd. I had a memorable time with Lisa when I was invited to go to Maddox Bay with her and with "Mr. Johnny" and Louise Rollow. I worked for "Mr. Johnny." I respected him and wanted to gain his approval for the mechanical skills that I had. Besides, everyone knew how much Lisa loved her dad—she followed him all over the campus and helped him in his many jobs as engineer. I tried to emulate "Mr. Johnny" as much for Lisa as for my own desire to be able to "fix anything except a broken heart." At Maddox Bay, Lisa and I adventured on our own away from the Houseboat that was our home with Johnny and Louise. We could return to some of the best biscuits and gravy and fried chicken or roast beef in the world. The country air, quiet, and closeness with Lisa added to the great sense of peace that marks those few days in my memory forever. I dreamed of an idyllic place and time and of my "desert island," alone with the love of my life; but the reality of that time in love—in life—surpassed even a dream.

And there she was, my wife, getting ready to show our children a smooth dive—an inspiration for their performance. She bounced once then stopped and leaned over as if in pain.

"What's the matter, baby?" I asked.

"I—I don't know—just had a sharp pain here," she said pointing to her abdomen. She lay down in the lounge chair beside me. "Probably that lunch meat I had," she said cheerfully—always cheerfully.

Later I talked with Leigh Adkins, Lisa's gynecologist who felt that the large mass we felt in Lisa's abdomen was an ovarian cyst and should represent little problem in removal. "There is, of course, a slight chance of malignancy." The words didn't register—after all, for us, everything always turns out O.K.

"We'll fly to Gaston's when you get over your soreness," I suggested.

"Great." Lisa responded, once again making me feel that my planning was perfect.

I leaned over the gurney and kissed her lightly on the cheek as she was wheeled groggily toward surgery. If you behave as if everything will be okay—it will— an optimistic philosophy. So I went to the office to see patients while waiting for Lisa's return.

"Dr. Graves wants to see you," Mrs. Sibley, our office nurse, said as I came from a patient's room an hour and a half after leaving Lisa.

It was about 10:30 and I had been expecting a call. Surgery had taken a little longer than expected. "Hi, Lester." I shook hands with Leigh's partner.

"Where can we talk?" There was concern in Lester's voice.

We went into a vacant room and closed the door.

"Lisa has a malignancy, Jeff." There is no way to soften the words, although I have tried with my own patients: "your child has a growth—a tumor," or "your mother may have a spread of tumor to her bones."

Whatever the word used, the meaning is the same. A disease, whose potential development lies dormant within each of us, has begun its relentless destruction of its own source of life. Some trigger or some immune response failure has allowed cells to grow uninhibited—an unthinking binge of reproduction —of overpopulation—leading to self destruction and with it, the loss of the whole organism. My medical experience provided no sense of hope. Instead, the opposite—I knew the ultimate hopelessness. It was not *if* death would follow, it was *when*.

Many years later, I have a different perspective. The advances in chemotherapy and in the management of previously incurable cancers have been dramatic and there is much more reason for hope. Thus a physician's demeanor and the patient's or family's response can be truly hopeful.

But at that time—1969—I knew that the words spoken by my friend were tantamount to a death sentence for my wife of a little over eleven years.

"The undifferentiated carcinoma was caked onto the omentum and there were metastases all over the peritoneum. We asked Bobby Hughes, an excellent gynecologic oncologist, to come over, and he's in the process of stripping away as much of the carcinoma as possible."

"It sounds bad, Les," I choked out finally.

"It is, but we're going to do everything possible."

The years with Lisa seemed to fold into a single fleeting moment—a fragile firefly's light in a dark sky.

"God help me through this," I muttered to myself as I rapidly left the clinic to wait in Lisa's hospital room. I did not pray for a miracle. We cannot alter the laws of nature. To do so would be to tamper with God's integrity and the integrity of all that is: from the unity and the "Big Bang" to our universe and world.

How long I waited in that hospital room is a blur. My oft expressed optimism was shattered by the hammer blow of reality. I could feel the loss of my life, the loss of *our* life, smothering me in a future I now dreaded.

Bob Hughes, a talented oncologist, was by nature hard spoken, yet he offered a sense of hope in explaining his technique for removing the bulk of the tumor followed by radiation and chemotherapy. The facts, however, were undeniably indicative of a poor prognosis. He knew it and I knew it, but I never discussed this with Lisa or anyone else for that matter. *If you act or speak as if everything will be okay then certainly it will.*

Lisa returned to the room and although sedated, told the orderly, "I can help me move over."

Later she said to me, "I hate putting you through all this, sweetheart."

I choked out, "I—I hate for *you* to have to go through this, baby."

Bob told her the facts but placed the emphasis on the more immediate problem of overcoming the inevitable ileus (sluggish intestinal function).

Over the next several days I remained by Lisa's side. I read. I contemplated the future as I held her hand. We celebrated and laughed when she finally "passed gas" and looked forward to her return to the "Little Green House."

Life would never be the same but I began to be grateful for each day. Ever the planner, I could plan for the evening. "We'll watch Star Trek with the kids at seven."

"That would be fun," she would say.

"Lisa, I'd like to take the Apache up and circle the Baptist so you can see us. I'll wiggle the wings for you."

"Oh please, Jeff, do that. I'll be watching for you.

"You're sure you want me to go flying? I shouldn't be gone too long."

"Oh yes, that will be fun for you."

Again she made me feel that my plans were the best.

It was a clear afternoon and the Apache climbed eagerly to the west. I flew to the south of the largest private hospital in the country and moved the wings slowly up-and-down in a salute to my wife.

This was my first flight since I was faced with the terrible reality of Lisa's malignancy, and I relished the freedom of flight, the escape, however brief. Three dimensions of freedom: I climbed, banked, and spiraled down then sought the clouds again and willed to stay up in the blue forever—but gravity's pull, like hard reality, brought me back to face once more what was to be.

Later in the week I returned home to prepare the "Little Green House" for Lisa's return. It was late in the evening; I was alone and as the shower flowed over me I suddenly felt the overwhelming power of grief and shouted to God, "Oh God! God—God Damn—God Damn!" In my heart Lisa had died and I would never, ever be the same. Yet I knew that I had to go on and that I had to be strong.

I see myself at that time as self-centered—*my* suffering, *my* sacrifice. Too little did I consider Lisa's fears and anxiety and I didn't consider those who loved Lisa—her mother, her sister, my parents, and, most of all, our children. It was my duty to be with Lisa, and for the months of her illness until her death I cannot recall comforting or even discussing what was happening with our children. I truly regret this. Again, I felt that continuing our plans as if nothing had changed would forestall the inevitable. So it was that we completed the move from the "Little Green House" to the big house at 4209 Walnut Grove in the fall of 1969. Every picture must be hung, every shelf neatly filled, and every closet arranged. It was as if by this frenzy I could create a sense of permanence in a very insecure world. Lisa sat quietly in her long green housecoat giving encouragement and much needed approval. In many ways, we were happy during those months—we were closer than ever before. She knew that I would be with her as she spiraled toward the inevitable "black hole" we know as death.

It's hard for the human animal to acknowledge an end to consciousness, and we try to find in religion (life everlasting) or in science (the immortality of genetic information or alternate universes) some reason to hope that all will not end with the last mortal breath. Whether or not we verbalize "true belief" or "agnostic doubt" or "atheistic certainty," each of us feels there is *something* eternal within us. Our atoms—our "star stuff" bodies surely will be transmuted—the "gold" of another day. And whether in an open, ever expanding universe, or in a closed and eventually collapsing system the "stuff" of which we are made is there to be reused as energy, mass, or perhaps the immeasurable spirit.

Each day was a gift and each minute was sufficient province for hope. Rarely did the reality of Lisa's cancer intrude on this "one day at a time" philosophy.

For the children I was determined to make everything seem as normal as possible. I continued to work in the workshop. In fact I had begun constructing a set of kitchen cabinets for the house at 4285 Longleaf that my folks were building. I returned to work with determination and even attended the journal club that I had co-founded with several of the younger doctors at the Baptist. In those days the clinic held office hours on Saturday morning, but I arranged to see my patients from eight to ten in the morning so that we could have a little longer weekend.

One Saturday we were planning to fly to Gaston's on the White River. Before noon Lisa called the office in obvious pain from a partial bowel obstruction. "I don't think I can.....I'm sorry." She obviously didn't want to disappoint me but I was brought back to the reality of the situation—don't plan too much ahead—one day at a time. This was after she had had some of her radiation therapy. Antispasmodics helped and later we did manage a short trip to the White River Resort when her symptoms abated.

Christmas of 1969 was bittersweet. The children were excited as usual and Mama C and Granddad had moved into their new house. Annie Lou and Hickman were there to help with dinner and Lisa was her usual cheerful self. Wees had been a great help with Kim and the other children, but her loss of Johnny in March of 1969 left her with a bitterness and sadness that colored every relationship for the rest of her life. Sissy and Kim, her husband, were always welcome and added brightness to the occasion. Below the surface of cheerfulness, however, was the specter of darker days ahead.

In February, a little over a month before Lisa's death, we flew with the three oldest children to Key West, Florida. We stayed for four days and enjoyed this last time together, although Lisa's illness was taking its toll; her eyes were sunken and her abdomen was swollen with ascites.

"Are you pregnant?" a waitress at the motel asked innocently, prompted by concern at Lisa's appearance.

We laughed. "No, I've got fluid in here—not a baby."

There was a tinge of bitterness in Lisa's response. When the metastasis induced ascites first appeared, she had pleaded to Bobby

Hughes, "I've got a new baby and I've got a lot to live for. Please do what you can."

With each day she sensed an inner loss of strength, as did I. I would only speak positively—even though we both knew what we were facing. In retrospect, I wish we could have talked of death and of what she wanted for the children and me, but it was easier and perhaps less emotionally traumatic to live and act as if we had forever.

Lisa seemed weaker by the time we started back home, but she maintained her usual cheerfulness. The children rode in the three forward seats of the Apache and Lisa was in the fifth seat in the rear. Once, when encountering some turbulence, I looked around to see Lisa's face, gaunt in the shadows and filled with anguish. As soon as she saw me, she smiled and flashed an okay sign.

Some days later with increasing pain and evidence of intestinal obstruction, surgery was suggested offering some hope of palliation, but we both knew there was little hope of longevity. It was thus with a sense of foreboding tempered by resignation that Lisa and I entered the Baptist Hospital late in March of 1970; an ileostomy was performed for palliation. Lisa returned from the recovery room groggy but still determined to help move herself over onto her bed.

"How are you doing, baby?" I asked as I leaned over to brush her forehead.

"Sore," she replied.

We had private duty nurses and Ann, Lisa's sister, had driven down from Clarksville so I felt free to go to the office for the rest of the day. "Act as if everything will be okay…"

I did not have any unrealistic expectations but the call from Ann a little later that day brought me back to the harshness of reality.

"Jeff, you'd better come back over. Something's happened to Lisa."

I ran across the parking lot and up the stairway to the fourth floor of Union East. As I approached Lisa's room, several scrub-suited personnel were standing with Ann.

"What happened?" I asked breathlessly.

"Your wife arrested—probably had a pulmonary embolus. She's breathing on her own now, however. Everyone knew I was a physician, and as I stood quietly by Lisa's bed watching the Harvey Team efficiently tidy up their resuscitation effort, secure the I.V.'s, and reinforce the abdominal dressing, I sensed their respectful silence. I knew the end was near. I choked back the emotions rising within as I slowly moved my head back and forth in quiet despair.

The few days remaining were spent with Lisa. The nurses respected my wishes and did not try to engage me in senseless conversation. They were there to help and were appreciative of my willingness to assist with dressing and bed changes. Often I was alone with Lisa for long periods. Initially, I detected some response as I spoke quietly with her. "It's okay, baby; don't worry about anything. I love you." I could feel a slight squeeze as I held her tiny hand. "Do you hear me, Lisa? Do you know I'm here with you? Are you pressing my hand or is that your heart beat I feel—or mine?"

"Everybody loves you, Lisa, but no one loves you like I love you," I whispered. "It's okay—you can let go; we'll be all right and we'll always love you—somehow—someway you'll live in me—in us."

I felt that she was fighting, but I knew it was futile. "Let go, baby, let go."

For several days she struggled on with a weakening life force as I remained by her side. I eased my ache by sketching her hand as it rested quietly on the bed. Even the small I.V. puncture wound was a part of my art. I wrote a short story that was surely a poorly disguised projection of hope. I put together a few model German houses that Lisa and I had brought back from Germany in anticipation of building a model railroad for the children.

Lisa had been heavily sedated since her cardiac arrest and, of course, there was to be no further effort at resuscitation. In fact, Bobby Hughes apologized for having neglected to write "No Harvey Team" on the post op orders.

As I sat beside her in the early evening of the 28th of March, I had no thought for the future—for our life together was near an end.

I was thoughtlessly piecing together a model castle. Occasionally I would gently cradle her motionless hand in mine trying to feel the little life within.

Her breathing became noticeably labored; she took two deep breaths in succession, made a slight gurgling sound, half lifted her head off the pillow, opened her eyes glassily and fell back as a thin trickle of blood altered the corner of her mouth.

The life that had become part of mine was no more, and I was left half the person I had been. The loving nurse gently laid her hand over Lisa's eyes to close them and wiped the blood from the corner of her mouth.

I stood quietly by her bed for a minute. "Lisa, my Lisa, you are beautiful to me even when you're dead." I leaned over and kissed her forehead.

THE BACK ROOM

Hopefully, through understanding, will come acceptance of the darkness and anticipation of the brightness of a new day.

When I left the hospital room a little later, I knew I would never see Lisa's form again. We had always agreed that the body viewing perpetuated by funeral homes was paganistic. The sooner the body could be returned to nature, the better. Our star stuff needs to be recycled.

Bob Tooms came by the room shortly after Lisa's death; I appreciated his support. We had been through three years of residency together and our families were close. Friendships between families, however, are often altered irrevocably, by the loss of one person, and I can think of no relationship that was unaffected by Lisa's death.

I signed for an autopsy, gathered our possessions, paid the nurse, and with my Dad's help left the hospital. My dad, who was seventy-two years old at the time, with broken voice said, "It's just one of those things we can't help."

"I'm glad it's over, dad." At that point there was a great sense of release. My grief began the day of Lisa's initial surgery, and I was awash with pent up emotion; in fact I may not yet have resolved all of my feelings. But I was determined to live and be in control of my life.

Picking out a casket and arranging the funeral was more an aggravation than a duty. I did not believe in the funeral process, but I conformed only to the extent that I would not offend other members of the family or friends.

"Of course, you want a concrete casket holder, and we have this beautiful walnut casket . . ." the funeral director was appropriately solemn.

"What do we need that concrete holder for?" I asked.

The funeral director was embarrassed. "Well—it's to protect the casket," and when pressed, "you see as the casket collapses the ground will cave in above it."

"Good! I don't see any need in preventing that. Now show me the simplest wooden casket you have."

"Well this is all we have," he said waving his hand toward the silk lined, brass and wood vessels lining the selection room, "unless you want one of the caskets we keep for Jewish funerals." There was a little disdain in his tone of voice.

"Show me."

We were ushered into a back room. There, very simple stained wooden caskets with no adornment other than a wooden Star of David were resting on sawhorses.

"That's what I want—Lisa would like that."

"We—we can remove the star," the director said.

"No! Leave it there—put a cross beside it." It was a statement no one would see because of the flowers that covered the casket at the funeral. I was thinking of Ed Kaplan, one of Lisa's dear old friends from Central High, when I told the director to leave that Star alone, and I think Lisa would have been happy with that choice.

I wish I could have been better support for Cathy, Jeff, and Louisa. My expectations after Lisa's death were unrealistic. It was as if I thought they could go on about their lives after the funeral with acceptance and adjustment. How they could have done that when I have yet to accept and adjust to that momentous change in my life is beyond reason.

Yet, with my left hand resting on Louisa's tiny shoulder, feeling her quiet sobs, and my right arm over Cathy and Jeff, and choking back my own tears, the funeral service seemed to offer a completion—an end to this suffering. I had written a poetic eulogy, but John Millard and Paul Tudor Jones felt it was too filled with emotion and did not read it; I would have been unable to maintain my composure had they done so.

Following the graveside service we returned home to a different life than the one begun by Lisa and me eleven years before. Nothing would be the same for me again. Yet I expected my little children to be more mature than I was—to be better than I was—to continue living as if Lisa had not even been a part of their lives—to forget the pain of loss when I could not expect that of myself. But I could act as if that were so.

The day after Lisa's funeral I took the three older children and Ann to Memphis International Airport for a tour of the control tower, and for several months I tried to take the children to special places on my day off. Even Kim was able to come along with Jeannie Anderson's help.

Kim had been neglected by me during the last week of Lisa's illness, but Jeannie Anderson was faithful and loving in helping to maintain a sense of family, and Wees and Mama "C" and Granddad provided stability and love in caring for Kim during those difficult days.

Because of my schedule (I returned to work two days after Lisa's funeral) I found it difficult to be considerate of those helping me. I was determined to keep Kim with her siblings as much as possible and would leave Kim with Wees odd hours. Wees would have liked for me to let her keep Kim all the time—this I could not tolerate.

At best, in the first months after Lisa's death, I was able to maintain the family unity; at worse, I was unsupportive of the needs of my children who had just lost their mother. Because my own sense of loss was so great, I thought no one else could feel as I did and that acting as if life were normal (we didn't talk about Lisa and I didn't encourage the children to express any emotion about the past) would lead to a happy, normal family.

From the perspective of increasing age, I see that repression of the pain of loss was not good for me or for my children. Nothing can change the facts of days past but perhaps through these words I can finally understand the depth of feeling that remains within me, the children, and everyone touched by Lisa.

PART II

INTRODUCTION

Beginning Again

Learning to accept the finality of my loss and the darkness that ensued in 1970 was difficult. Returning to my orthopaedic practice, working on and flying the Apache, and returning to the workshop helped. I took the children to special places on my days off, and I was determined to maintain our family unity. I was fortunate to have help from my parents, my aunt, Lisa's mother, Louise, my sister-in-law, Ann Ross, Jeannie Chenier, Jeannie Anderson, and many, many others in the months that followed Lisa's death.

In trying to act as if everything were normal, I repressed my own grief, however, and therefore did not provide my children with sufficient emotional support to help them deal with their loss. But, in spite of everything, I did maintain a sense of hope—hope that after the darkness I would see the brightness of a new day.

SALLY

As I slowly gain awareness of this new day, I feel her warmth against my side and rejoice in her presence. I lay my arm across her and pull her closer. This partner in living fills empty places in my heart and for that I am forever grateful.

For about three months, I immersed myself in work. Although I had begun work on a grandmother clock (small case pendulum clock) before Lisa's illness, I was slow in regaining my enthusiasm for that project. The Apache remained a source of pleasure, however, and I began planning a revision of the instrument panel. Talking about my flying experiences opened many conversations with the nurses with whom I came in contact on a daily basis. Before long I had worked up the courage to approach a pediatric nurse with whom I had sensed a mutual attraction.

Hesitantly, I asked, "Uh, how would you like to fly with me over to Jonesboro Sunday? They've got some interesting aircraft in the hangar."

Evangeline had shown some interest in my flying so I was hopeful she would answer in the affirmative. Flying had always been a good ice breaker when I was a bachelor. But this was different; I was a widower with four children. How was I to act?

"I'd love to," she responded. I was elated. Companionship is its own reward for the lonely.

I dated Evangeline off and on for several months, but once I had taken that first step it was easier for me to ask other young ladies out. Norma, Mary Margaret, and Lola are some of the names that I recall through the haze of time. I knew that there would never be another Lisa in my life, but I hoped that someday there might be someone who could fill some of the emptiness I was feeling.

My mother instinctively knew how vulnerable a widower could be, but I tended to belittle her concern, until Lola. It was a another routine day of seeing patients in the office, when a divorced mother in her early thirties brought her five-year-old son in for a checkup of his feet. She mentioned something about his footwear. The youngster seemed unconcerned, and I could find no abnormality; the mother was oddly inattentive.

"I was so sorry to learn of your wife's death," she suddenly interrupted my discourse on the advantages of good support shoes.

I don't know this gal. How does she know about me? I wondered. Apparently, the word was out that there was an eligible widower at the Campbell Clinic. Before I knew what was happening she had invited me to dinner, and, amazingly, I had accepted. Only later did I realize the trouble I was in when after a few drinks she began singing, "Whatever Lola wants—Lola gets—whatever Lo-la wants—Lola gets……." Needless to say, that old trapped feeling came creeping back. I never dated Lola again, but Jeannie Anderson said she called me many times during the next month.

Fred and Anita Sage were good to me after Lisa died. Our children often played together. One day Jeff and I had flown Fred and his son, Payne, to Missouri, landing on a hilltop grass strip near a trout farm for a weekend of fishing. Later, he invited Jeff and me to their home for dinner. Anita asked who I was seeing and casually mentioned Sally Strain. Lisa and I had met Sally years earlier at the Mid-South Fair in 1962. Her husband, Fred Strain, and I had been friends. Although Fred was about five years older than I, we had developed a friendship during my residency primarily because of our common interest in flying. I received notification of his death while I was stationed in Germany. "It's been a bad year for the flying physicians in Memphis." Fred Sage had written. "Frank Yates had to have brain surgery for a subdural hemorrhage. We think he'll be okay, but our friend, Fred Strain Jr., just died of a neuroblastoma." Sally doesn't even remember our meeting in 1962. She demures saying that Fred had introduced her to so many young couples. There was no way I could have known then the impact Sally's loss would have on my life.

Somehow I had previously gained the impression that Sally was really into sports and that opinion was being reinforced by Anita's comments about her tennis playing.

"She's engaged isn't she?" I asked, vaguely interested.

"I don't think so—but she's been dating a guy named Gary," Fred answered.

"Sounds too complicated for me. How old is her little boy now, anyway?" Steve, Sally's son, had been born two days before his father died.

I didn't think much more about our conversation. Besides, I was beginning to enjoy dating a number of young ladies. Then on a busy day in the clinic Mrs. Sibley, our staff nurse interrupted, "Dr. Sage wants to see you." *What now* I thought somewhat irritated but met him in the hall anyway.

"Hey Jeff! How about taking a look at Sally Strain's elbow and tell me what you think. She's got some sort of a lump I can hardly feel."

I opened the door to the examining room and walked in—to my future—although I didn't realize it then. Sally's blue-green eyes, blond hair, and bright smile warmed my heart as I tried to maintain a professional attitude, telling her that the lump was most likely a subcutaneous fibroma. Small talk followed, then.................

LIFE'S LOG BOOK

Flying has been such a large part of my life that my several flight logbooks, accumulated over the years, serve as a diary of sorts, bringing into sharp focus the emotions chronicled by the entries. After the darkest day in March, 1970 the first entry on the 31st for 30 min said, simply, To Begin. These brief notations were an acknowledgment that the gift of life would continue for me and that I could still revel in the exhilaration of flight, especially in the still morning air with the sun creeping above the horizon, giving my world a new day.

I worked up the courage to ask Sally if she would like to bring Steve to the airport for a local flight. She seemed enthusiastic, and I was excited about the prospect and anticipated the beginning of a new relationship. Arrangements were made for the three of us to go to the airport the following weekend. But, it wasn't to be.

"Dr. Justis, you've got a phone call in the surgery lounge," the circulating nurse informed me as I was leaving the operating room.

It was Paul Stillions, the manager of HI Air (owned by Holiday Inns of Memphis) at Memphis International Airport where the Piper Apache was based. "I hate to give you this news, but your Apache has been damaged."

"Damaged? How? How bad? What happened?" I demanded.

I was to learn that Roy Leggett, an aircraft salesman, had hand started a Cessna 172 across the ramp from my Apache and that the inexperienced lineman sitting at the controls of the 172 had panicked and pushed full throttle. The plane had jumped over the wheel chocks, barely missing Roy, and had sped across the ramp and into the left side of the nose and left engine of my twin-engine airplane. I felt as if a close friend had been hurt—it was, after all, the Apache that had helped restore a feeling of hope in me. I was also disappointed that the promised flight with Sally and Steve would have to be postponed. To make it up to them, the following weekend I let Steve sit in the cockpit of the damaged Apache in HI Air's hangar and pretend he was flying. Steve, a blond, cherubic faced five-year-old was all over the controls in his enthusiasm. I kept one hand on the control wheel to limit the stop-to-stop extremes.

Later, after HI Air's liability insurance company accepted responsibility and began repair work, I started renting airplanes to get back into the sky. On July 4, 1970, Sally and Steve finally got their first ride with me in a rented Cessna 182.

From then on I was a regular visitor at 3282 Central Avenue, Sally's home. I remember wishing that I didn't have to compete with all the people in Sally's life. I would have enjoyed her undivided attention, but she was a widow with two stepchildren and Steve and I was a widower with four children. There could never be the same freedom in the relationship between Sally and me as there is between two people unencumbered by a previous family.

Nevertheless, from the day of our first date when she opened her door on Central with a welcoming smile, my affection for her grew quickly with each date. We flew to Nashville and later to Athens, Georgia to visit her sister, Sue. Sally had continued dating Gary and I had also continued dating other women. One weekend, we ran into each other with our respective dates at a movie. I couldn't help being distressed to see Sally with Gary. Then, one day in August she mentioned that she was going to visit Gary and his family in Kansas. I didn't quite know what to think about their relationship, but on August 12, 1970, a Tuesday, and my day off, the shop phone rang.

"Hi Jeff, it's Sally."

"Where are you?"

"In Wichita with Jean Peak." Jean was one of Sally's nursing school classmates.

She explained that she had visited Gary and his family but had left early. She wanted me to come get her in Wichita. This was certainly going to be a rescue mission, and the fact that she expressed a need for me prompted a promise that I would soon be there. I made arrangements for a rental aircraft and was on my way late in the afternoon. No matter that it would soon be dark, no matter that we wouldn't get home before two or three in the morning, no matter that I would have to work the next day—I was in love and my prayer that Sally might love me in return showed promise of being answered.

The annual Flying Physicians Association meeting of 1970 was being held in Vancouver BC. Since the insurance adjuster had led me to believe that I would be reimbursed for flying while my plane was being repaired, I checked out in a Twin Comanche and took off on the 29th of July with Cathy, Jeff, and Louisa, leaving Kim with my parents. I wanted to ask Sally, of course, but I was afraid of what such a trip might do to our blossoming relationship.

Eph and Lucy Wilkinson flew in rough formation with us in their Aztec to Yellowstone Park and then to Vancouver. Unfortunately, Jeff suffered some airsickness and probably had a gastrointestinal virus that manifested itself in Yellowstone. Cathy, Louisa, and I left him in the motel room while we went horseback riding, but I felt guilty for doing so and was anxious until we returned to find him watching TV from the bed. He recovered and was ready to fly over the Cascades to British Columbia.

I called Sally on several occasions, missing her more each day. But seeing old friends and hanger flying made the time pass quickly. One evening the kids and I were eating at the hotel restaurant when our waitress began a conversation. There must be something about a man with three kids that tugs at the feminine heartstrings, for it was not long before she knew my life history and I was asking what time she got off work. After putting the kids to bed, I met her for coffee. She was a student at Vancouver University and working to earn extra money. After a while I called the room to check on my three but got no answer. I was pretty sure they were asleep, but I felt I should check on them. My waitress friend said she had to study anyway! Thus ended my last fling. Later, I mailed a letter to Sally with a poem that attempted to tell her what I was feeling. She was surprised and pleased.

While the three children and I were in Vancouver, Sally and Steve had flown to Columbus, Ohio to visit her mother, and during a phone call she hinted that she might like to be rescued once more. Plans were made and after the meeting the Comanche took up a steady heading to Columbus. It was there that I met Mame, Sally's mother, for the first time. She seemed to accept me as a potential part of the family. But, was *I* ready? Dating at that time in my life was always accompanied by a feeling of concern for my children. Often, however, the frenetic pace I seemed to be living served to dull my guilt in failing to provide emotional support for my children and the inward ache I was repressing about Lisa. Sally was different in that she had come to terms with her own loss and accepted me as I was, in spite of, or perhaps because of, my children. However, my expectations for Sally were unrealistic; she was not Lisa. I was very pleased, however, that she took an interest in my workshop and would occasionally sit for an hour or more watching me work. Although at the time Sally seemed somewhat laid back (she later said it was because she had chronic tonsillitis with a low-grade fever), I was eventually to learn that for all of us the pressures of living often interfere with the luxury of relaxation.

We loaded the Comanche with two more than when we started out on our trip, and four hours later we were in Memphis once again.

In my youth, whenever I was faced with a challenge or uncertainty, I would sit on the patio, look up at the stars in the night sky, reflecting on life, trying to connect with the Mystery through which and in which we have our existence. I never considered myself a religious person in that I gained no emotional gratification from the *words*, including those in the Bible, which others have used to provide answers to the great questions that have always confounded mankind. I often felt self-conscious, uncomfortable, and even a bit hypocritical when participating in communion while attending mandatory "chapel" at Woodberry Forest (an Episcopal affiliated school).

During such meditative moments, I began contemplating a future that would include Sally. But what about Steve? There were differences in Sally's style of dealing with children and mine. My way, in my previous life, however, had always been modified by Lisa's influence. Initially, Sally didn't quite know how to deal with my more controlling approach. One day Sally, Steve, and I stopped at a McDonalds for lunch. Sally let Steve order anything he wanted and, as I expected, he left half the food on his plate. I grumbled to myself since I would have ordered what I thought he could eat so as not to waste food. My folks would have told me: "Your mouth is bigger than your stomach." My role, I presumed, was to be the disciplinarian, and my wife's roll was to mollify, but not countermand. So it was with some concern about how we would deal with these differences that I contemplated the evening sky. I loved Sally but should I take on the responsibility of another child? On the other hand, I reasoned, Steve needed a father. "It is a far-far better thing that I do......." Ironic, isn't it, that the words of Dickens should come to mind as I decided to ask Sally to marry me, for I had no realization just how much of an influence that decision would have on Steve. My wish was for that influence to be positive; I now have reason to question that influence. At that time in my life I was incapable of providing emotional support for any of the children.

My hope that Sally loved me as much as I loved her was realized when she accepted my proposal of marriage. Together we dutifully visited and informed Fred's parents, Dr. and Mrs. Strain, Louise "Wees" Rollow, my folks, and many friends and acquaintances. My mom and dad were gracious in accepting our decision, but just as the Strains and Wees had expressed, our getting married involved being responsible for many lives. Although I acknowledged that responsibility intellectually, for me the most important thing was the relationship between Sally and me. Everything else would naturally follow. I was wrong, of course, because the powerful influence we would have on the children would be altered by my own repressed emotions and by our respective responses to each other.

Cathy, my oldest at eleven years, had taken on more responsibility as a surrogate caregiver and probably resented the perception that she would no longer be needed when I remarried. Jeff, who was ten years old, had already been thoroughly castigated by Lisa's mother when he commented, "at least I still have a father." I felt that Sally would be able to give him the emotional support that only a mother can provide for a son. In reality none of the children had a choice in my decision to remarry, and, in retrospect, I should have involved them more. It was after all a decision that would influence them the rest of their lives. Louisa, eight, was closest in age to Steve and thought it might be fun to have a younger brother but was a little intimidated by the inevitable change. Steve, during his five years of life, had been brought up without a father, he was the center of attention, and he was anxious about being brought into a houseful of strangers and accepting a father with whom he was unable to connect. In many ways, I believe he felt abandoned in this life-altering transition. Kim, at a little over two years, had no recollection of

Lisa. She now wishes that I had shared more memories of a life she never knew.

The regret I have in the days before remarrying was my failure to reassure my children that they would continue to be loved by me. I assumed that if we didn't talk about their mother and how much we missed her our sense of loss would improve. Our old "normal" life would never return, and I thought that if I only talked about the future, this would reassure them that life could be good again. Sally had already developed a natural relationship with my four, and she was much more attuned to their emotional needs than I. My failure with all of them, including Steve, was by assuming that all they needed from me was my presence, my authority, and my mentorship. What they needed more than anything and what, because of my personal pain, I was unable to give, was an expression of love and understanding.

Sally and I began planning for the wedding and honeymoon. Sally who had received a master's degree in psychology at the University of Memphis had started a longitudinal development evaluation program sponsored by the Federal Government and was required to travel to other medical centers for coordination. Since her expenses would be paid, it made sense for us to plan a honeymoon accordingly. Meanwhile, repair work on the Apache was progressing, but it was unlikely the plane would be repainted by September 21st, the date we had chosen for our marriage. In 1958, when Lisa and I had married, the little Luscombe's engine was being overhauled, and there was no way we could have used the airplane to fly somewhere on a honeymoon. So I was excited that finally my dream of having a flying honeymoon was soon to be realized, even if the airplane did have a green, primer-coated nose.

Our wedding was on a Monday night, giving me a good excuse to miss the Monday night meeting at the clinic, a tradition that in the 70s was considered mandatory. The chapel at St. Mary's Episcopal Church was filled with in-laws and children, including

Sam, Sally's stepson. Her stepdaughter, Susan, was away at college and unfortunately could not attend.

This was to be a serious step as far as I was concerned, so much so that when someone asked if I wanted a beer before the wedding I replied, "There are some things one should approach with a clear mind—getting married is one of those things."

After the brief ceremony and obligatory photographs, Sally and I met Doris and Jerry Boone at the Rivermont Hotel for a celebratory drink. There we were to spend our wedding night and begin a new life for both of us. Our mutual friends, Anita and Fred Sage, kindly offered to keep the older children. Kim would stay with my dad and mother, Mama C, during our honeymoon.

It was around 2:00 a.m. on our wedding night at the Rivermont that I was awakened by Sally rummaging for something to eat, finally settling on some Snappy Tong mix. I learned then that I should never interfere with her eating to satisfy low blood sugar.

HONEYMOON

When one has had a special relationship, a soul mate, with whom needs and desires are mutually fulfilled, the loss of that companion leaves a void that, though it can never be completely filled, is misted over with love.

Tuesday morning we met the photographer at Hi Air for more wedding pictures in front of the Apache. I had written "JUST MARRIED" on the zinc chromated nose of our airplane. Every time we landed, smiles were generated as the linemen signaled us to a parking spot.

It was a beautiful fall morning, winds were favorable and soon we crossed the Pennsylvania state line ahead of schedule. Sally was looking through the AOPA (Aircraft Owners and Pilots Association) airport directory and found a description of the Indianhead Resort located near Somerset County Airport.

"Why don't we land and see if it suits us," I suggested. This proved to be a wonderful find—a beautiful resort perfect for a honeymoon.

The next morning dawned bright and clear, with smooth air at 9000 feet as we flew into Massachusetts and directly to Logan International, which in those days was more friendly to general aviation than it is in the 21st century. Our destination, Boston, was special because Sally had spent time as a nurse at Boston Children's Hospital shortly after graduating from nursing school. John and

Bunny Shillito treated us to a hotel stay at the Ritz-Carlton—a fun wedding gift. The Shillito's had befriended Sally when she was in nursing school and later when she worked at Boston Children's in the early 60s. They had known Fred Strain; now they accepted me as well; we have remained friends for many years.

Although I was obviously in love with Sally and happy for the many things we did have in common, there were differences in our personalities that occasionally led to conflict or withdrawal to avoid conflict. With Lisa, life had seemed to flow rather easily. We would discuss plans, express our desires, but the end result always seemed to fit with my wishes. Undoubtedly, that was either the result of a remarkable compatibility or perhaps, more likely, due to her sensing my desires and enthusiastically adopting them. Regardless, I was a unprepared for Sally's directness.

"How about going to a German restaurant tonight," I might suggest.

"Oh, I don't want German food tonight. Let's go to a little place I went to when I was here in Boston."

"You want to ride the subway?"

"No, I'll drive. I know the way."

I wanted to be the one to make suggestions that would please her. I wanted to be the hero, the instigator of all good adventures. So it was difficult for me to allow her to have her own desires and to express her will. However, as of this writing, I have learned that the world was not created just for first born sons or only children and that there are others with whom we must share this special life.

Sally spent several days at the medical center evaluating and comparing investigative data while I enjoyed the time at the Museum of Fine Arts and the Gardner Museum. We visited "Old Ironsides" and, of course, Thaniel Hall and Market Square. We enjoyed prime rib at Durgan Park and seafood at the Old Union Oyster House. Sally took me to see her old apartment on Park Drive where, in the 60s, she believes, the Boston Strangler visited and attacked her roommate, leaving her injured but alive.

The Shillito's invited us to visit them at their vacation home in Duxbury, so on the weekend we returned to Logan where the old Apache had been parked for a reasonable fee. (On a more recent trip I found that there would be a $75 charge just to off load a passenger at the General Aviation Terminal, plus a very large overnight charge). We taxied out, sandwiched between several heavy jets, and took off for the short flight down the east coast to Marshfield Airport, which was within a few miles of Duxbury. For several days we enjoyed boating and sightseeing in this classic resort area with John, Bunny, and their children.

Our adventure continued with an afternoon flight to Nantucket. As we prepared for our approach, we could see a fog bank creeping across the island. I concentrated on the instruments and began descending on the localizer.

"Keep looking for the runway. If we don't see it at 400 feet, we'll have to do a missed approach and probably return to the mainland," I told Sally.

Just as I was preparing to push full throttles for another go around, Sally exclaimed, "There it is—the runway!"

The landing was uneventful, but taxiing was a problem because of the fog, which was thickening by the minute. We had landed just in time.

Through an airport employee, we located a bed and breakfast. Had we not had a recommendation from someone who knew the owners of the B&B I'm not at all sure we would have been able to stay, since the owners were rather strange and seemed a little reluctant until they learned we were honeymooners. We rented bikes and enjoyed exploring Melville's island. Of course, I had to do a little racing, perhaps showing off a bit, and in spite of Sally's warning, I lost control and crashed, gratefully without personal injury.

The next leg of our trip was to Halifax. On another wonderful fall morning we climbed out over the Atlantic, passing Boston to the west, for the relatively short trip to the tip of Nova Scotia, then on to Halifax where we rented a car for further exploration of the Provence. Peggy's Cove, with its iconic lighthouse and wave-splashed rocky shore, remains a romantic highlight of our honeymoon. We sat for a while on a granite outcropping while I sketched the light house for a watercolor I would complete later.

Unfortunately, all good times must end and the realities of life intrude. Five children awaited our return along with the challenges of dealing with a blended family. We were soon to begin a learning process that continues to this day. Regretfully, most of what we have learned since that time was of no help in the early days, when that knowledge would have provided the greatest benefit.

BACK TO WORK

One does not have to travel to another country to experience culture shock; one only has to return to a home of memories now filled with new expectations.

The honeymoon was over. After a wonderful escape from responsibility for others, culture shock greeted us on our return from New England. Our five children were glad to see us, and soon we were in a routine, with Sally cooking meals that were so good it was hard for us to leave when we had other social obligations. Most evenings all of us were seated around the white pine harvest table I had built several years before. I was at the head of the table and Sally was seated to my left near the kitchen doorway. This "breakfast room" was large enough to accommodate the seven of us, and a large picture window overlooking a birdbath and Dogwood tree added to a feeling of spaciousness. Nevertheless, after several meals during which everyone seemed to be engaged in back-and-forth conversation and occasional bickering, I installed soundproofing to the ceiling of the reverberating rectangular room.

That certainly helped, but on occasion I would have to insist, "Y'all just hush and listen to me!"

Then in a whisper, "Aw! Dad's going to give us lecture number 535 now."

I would expound on some pertinent subject, requiring, but not always getting the attention of the crowd, and on occasion I was interrupted by Sally who was more concerned with serving a hot meal and seeing to it that the kids drink their milk than listening to me.

In October 1970, the Campbell Club was meeting in Memphis, and the staff wives "welcomed" Sally by asking for her help in taking some of the spouses to the many planned activities. I added to her burden by suggesting that Kent and Jean Peterson stay with us during that meeting. I was accustomed to Kent's confrontational approach (we called him the acid assassin), but he and Sally got in an argument over raising kids and how permissive a parent should be. Sally, of course, was on the side of more freedom of choice. I should have kept a low profile or left the room because Sally sensed that I was not taking her side. Thus, the inevitable newlywed's first argument materialized. I'm not sure what I expected, but out of the pain of my loss I wanted to be consoled. In an argument, Lisa usually relented, letting me believe that we were of the same mind, but Sally was direct in giving her opinion whether or not it agreed with mine. Any disagreement with Sally precipitated in me a period of depression that varied in length from a few hours to a few days. This was stressful for Sally, no doubt, but as time passed, such periods became less frequent and shorter in duration. In spite of my longing for the comfort of Lisa's voice, I knew that was an unrealistic expectation, and eventually I was grateful to have Sally by my side.

It was during this Campbell Club meeting that Al Ingram, our Chief of Staff, asked me to introduce one of our guest speakers. Once again I experienced disproportionate anxiety over such a simple request. Although I managed the task satisfactorily, the mere fact that I remember this after forty plus years bears testimony to the discomfort I felt.

In spite of the fact that public speaking and display were anathema to me, the Campbell Clinic provided the ideal environment for my personality. For me, being able to relate to patients as individuals without consideration of productivity was very important. Believing in the surgery I was to perform often limited the procedures that I would recommend. In other words, unless I could foresee a good result, I was reluctant to undertake something that might have been recommended by others. So, like my mentor, Tom Waring, I was rather conservative in my approach to surgery, many times discouraging patients who seemed too eager for a "quick fix" of a problem.

As it had been since early childhood, my workshop was my salvation. The grandmother clock that I had set aside after Lisa's death now became Sally's clock. I reveled in the creative process even though the clock was not my original design but based on plans that I had purchased. Lisa and I had traveled to the Black Forest while in Germany (1964 to 1967) and had obtained the mechanism from one of the many clock manufacturers in that area. Sally seemed pleased with the Black Walnut clock case, thus encouraging me to produce even more. Perhaps if she had known how hard I would work for her praise, I might have started construction of her personal Taj Mahal.

That desire for Sally's approval led to a painful incident with Sam Strain early in our marriage. Sam, Sally's stepson, did not live with us. Doctor and Mrs. Strain had taken him into their home in his rebellious high school days when Sally was having difficulty controlling his behavior during the mid to late 60s. I always felt that Dr. Strain was a bit too permissive in not insisting that he return to Columbia Military Academy and in not demanding more responsibility from him. However, on a day when I should have been more in charge, I too ignored my better judgment.

Sam had approached Sally asking if he could borrow the Volkswagen, my favorite car. I had paid $1200 for that new German car shortly after arriving in Wiesbaden and I had developed an emotional attachment with the "People's Car."

I was caught by surprise when Sam burst into my workshop late one afternoon. "Mother told me to ask you if I could use the Volkswagen for a little while tonight."

My first impulse was to say, "Hell no!" However, I was under the impression that Sally had okayed the use of the car, so to please her, I reluctantly agreed. Later I learned that Sally was hoping that I would say no. That may be one of the mistakes we make with teenagers - allowing the teenager to work one parent against the other. There should be one consensus by both parents.

At around 12:30 a.m., ringing of the front doorbell awakened me. Sally responded, and I could hear muffled conversation from downstairs. I heard the door shut just as I started down the stairs.

"Jeff, Sam said he ran over a curb with the Volkswagen... thank goodness no one is hurt," Sally said.

"Did he bring the car home?"

"He says it won't run."

"Won't run! What the hell does that mean? Where in the G-damn hell is it?"

I was getting increasingly angry. That German car was my connection with the past. By the time I got downstairs, Sam had disappeared, apparently rescued by one of his friends who had driven him to our home. I was fuming as Sally and I drove to Perkins Extended and Perkins where an island separates a division in the road. My Volkswagen rested forlornly in the middle of the island having been stripped of her undercarriage.

I drove Sally home afraid to utter a word. I was mad at Sam. I was mad at Sally. I was mad at myself for having been unable to maintain control. With our children (my four and Steve) I felt that I was able to maintain a sense of order — of control. But with Sam I had no clout. Sally, therefore, took the brunt of my anger — my frustration. I couldn't sleep. I left, still angry, and, for the first and last time in my life, drove to a local bar. Sitting there, with a busy, unsympathetic bartender (no Cheers in Memphis) I finally calmed down, common sense prevailing, and returned home after a single drink. Subsequently, from that low point everything improved. We found a similar later model Volkswagen. Sally liked VWs as much as I, and we both enjoyed that sun-roofed car for many more years.

During Lisa's illness, my partners at the clinic had been understanding and helpful. I was grateful, but I was not going to lose myself in my work, as would many men under similar circumstances. Although I enjoyed my relationship with patients and the sense of accomplishment that followed successful surgery, I valued my time off. Tuesday was the one day that I could spend all day in the shop, and soon I was starting a new project. At the time I wanted to reproduce 17th and 18th-century furniture and was inspired by measured drawings of furniture masterpieces published by Lester Morgan, Gottshall, and others. I was looking for a buffet or side board that Sally wanted. Nothing I showed her would suit. Then she handed me a picture.

"I've been saving this for years. It's what I want." She told me.

So, armed with a magazine picture of a Southern Huntboard, I began designing and constructing the first of many pieces I was to build using Sally's inspiration.

In December 1970, to celebrate Sally's birthday, we flew to Gaston's White River Resort in Arkansas. Kim stayed with Mama C for the weekend. For a pilot, Gaston's is an idyllic destination, nestled in a valley below Bull Shoals Dam in northwest Arkansas. Comfortable cabins overlook the White River, and a swimming pool overlooks the grass runway.

We were not concerned while the four kids were exploring the area until only three of them returned to the cabin.

Three! "Where's Steve?"

"Uh... I dunno. He was with us a minute ago," one of them replied.

I went ballistic. "You are supposed to be responsible for each other!" I shouted, recalling my own guilt years before in Florida when I thought that Louisa was lost in the ocean.

I was hard on Cathy, Jeff, and Lou, but when we finally found Steve, obliviously eating breakfast in the restaurant, I was hard on him too. Such independence! I perceived this as a threat to my authority, but I'm sure he felt put down by my assault, and Sally was caught in the middle of an unpleasant situation. At the time I thought little of long-term consequences. I have since learned that there is an emotional memory that far outlives day-to-day interactions. The lesson for parents is to moderate ones response so that the child's emotional reaction is also moderated.

Gaston's White River Resort is a wonderful place that I had flown to several times in the past. The grass landing strip is a challenge because the approach to the southwest requires flying in a river valley just before turning final. Take-off is usually in the opposite direction regardless of wind because of high-tension wires crossing a short distance to the southwest of the runway. The Piper Apache (essentially a twin-engine Cub), however, had no problem getting in or out. After that first visit of our new family in 1970, we enjoyed several subsequent visits.

During internship and residency everything was new and exciting, and even during my active-duty Air Force years, each patient presented a new challenge with a feeling of satisfaction following a successful outcome.

In the beginning of my association with the Campbell Clinic, my practice was that of a general orthopaedic surgeon, much as it had been in the Air Force. I did a little of everything including back surgery. At that time our indications for back fusion were much less stringent than those that evolved with further experience. In the 60s and early 70s, if a patient had previous failed disc surgery or x-ray evidence of disc degeneration or spondyolisthesis, a one- or two- level fusion was recommended. At that time, in the Memphis medical community, the neurosurgeons did the disc surgery and orthopaedists did the fusion in cooperation with each other. Now, unfortunately, the pendulum is swinging again and there is, in my opinion, way too much surgery performed than necessary, and because of economics and competition, both specialties perform both procedures.

In addition, I even did tumor surgery and can remember how hard it was for me to tell the parents of a child with Ewing's sarcoma, for example, that their child had a tumor that could be fatal. This was before St. Jude's revolutionary and dramatic childhood cancer research, followed by miraculous cures.

So when Al Ingram, who had just taken over as Chief of Staff of the clinic when Harold Boyd stepped down, asked me to choose a subspecialty field of expertise (he mentioned the need for a tumor expert) I immediately suggested hand surgery. Lee Milford was the only hand surgeon on the staff, and it was generally agreed there was need for another. The intricate work involved in that type of surgery appealed to me. At that time a formal fellowship in hand surgery was not required for membership in the prestigious American Society for Surgery of the Hand, so in lieu of a formal fellowship, I set out to arrange an observership at Dan Riordan's clinic in New Orleans. Dan and I knew each other from Keesler AFB when he worked as a consultant for the Air Force. The observership wasn't to begin until August of 1971, so before embarking on the trip to New Orleans, Sally and I headed for Santa Domingo in May to do some work for a charitable organization.

CARE MEDICO

Although I had always felt that missionaries, in wanting to convert indigenous people to their particular brand of religion, practiced the arrogance of certainty, I admired the likes of Albert Schweitzer and Tom Dooley who dedicated their lives to helping those in need.

As a youngster, just after World War II, I sent several Care packages to European children, so I was intrigued by Care Medico, started by Tom Dooley, especially since it was a secular organization. I had read about the Orthopaedics Overseas (a division of Care Medico) program in the Dominican Republic in one of the orthopaedic journals, and the idea of contributing to those in need by using my medical and piloting skills appealed to me. I was hoping that the clinic would support such a plan by approving time off in the same way the partners allowed time for political endeavors and presenting scientific papers. However, the group would only agree to let me take some meeting time as well as vacation time for the proposed trip.

On the seventh of May 1971, Sally and I loaded the Apache with donated crutches, braces, and other medical equipment for our first over-water adventure together. Sally was a good partner. She fretted over the children and worried with all the necessary arrangements (Mame, Sally's mother, was often willing to come to Memphis to baby-sit). I was occasionally irritated by her initial and quick negative reactions to some suggestions of mine, but her subsequent willingness should have made me forgive such a minor surprise in our relationship.

The first day we flew to Eleuthera in the Bahamas Sally discovered that she had neglected to pack a bathing suit. We walked into the little village where she found a rather revealing bikini. It served her well for that trip but regretfully has been misplaced in the years since. We waded out into the glass-clear water of a cove near the Peace and Plenty Club, a place Lisa and I had visited years before, for a bit of snorkeling. We were having fun when all of a sudden Sally began jumping and hollering, climbing out of the water onto my back. Evidently, some seaweed had wrapped around her ankles causing her to panic. As long as she can float or swim, she's okay; she says just doesn't like things crawling around her feet.

The following morning we flew farther southeast over the blue-green, shimmering Caribbean Sea, along the Bahama chain of islands to South Caicos. The Turks and Caicos Islands are the last in the chain, which geographically is a continuation of the Bahamas but politically remains a British Protectorate following the independence of the Bahamas in 1973. We refueled, had lunch, and launched for the relatively short flight southward to the large island of Hispaniola, discovered in 1493 by Columbus. Ahead, cumulus cloud buildups over sun-baked land provided assurance that waves would eventually give way to Hispaniola and the Dominican Republic, sharing the island with Haiti on the western third. Soon the mountains along the north coast came into view, and we began zigzagging to avoid the bumpy clouds until finally we could begin our decent toward the south coast and Santo Domingo.

The assistance of our Care Medico contact and Dr. Mois Hache facilitated customs clearance in spite of our load of crutches and braces. It did not take long before we were on our way to downtown Santo Domingo. As we passed Diego Columbus' Palace and drove along the palm-lined coastal avenue, armed soldiers stood ominously at every corner with rifles at the alert. Later, at the hotel we observed that all of the bar patrons were absorbed in a news program on the television. We learned that the president (Balaguer) had discovered a coup attempt against his regime and that the man on TV was being exiled. (Gratefully he was not being executed.)

"I hope this doesn't mean we'll get stuck here," Sally said with some concern. "All these armed troops make me nervous."

We met with the administrator of Care Medico in the Dominican Republic. For our volunteer work we were given a car and a small apartment, and we had the use of the swimming pool at a nearby luxury hotel. The physician with whom I had the most contact was Mois Hache who had trained in traumatology in South America. He was a fine gentleman, and I was privileged to work with him. He was paid for his work at the Dario Contreres Charity Orthopaedic Hospital, owned and operated by the Dominican government. I had volunteered for a three-week tour with the Orthopaedics Overseas program which was to bring fresh ideas to local physicians so they could continue caring for the large number of orthopaedic patients in this small country.

Previous volunteers had often alienated the local doctors by a too-aggressive approach. Although three or four patients might be scheduled for surgery beginning at 7:30 in the morning, it was rare for the anesthetist to show up much before 8:00 or 8:30, thus delaying each case to follow. Then, at about 11:30 or 12 the anesthetist might well announce that he had to leave to go to another hospital. Thus, two or three patients would be put off until the next day. Emergencies would, of course, preempt elective cases. I remember seeing a child who had been waiting several months for definitive surgery on a rather large osteosarcoma of the distal femur. But, as Mois would tell me, "We are on Dominican time!"

To rush in, American-style, and push everyone to "get going" certainly was not going to win friends. Realistically, in three to four weeks, a volunteer, under the best of circumstances, would hardly make a dent in the backload of orthopaedic cases. So the best we could do was to teach a commonsense approach to orthopaedic problems and to impart a conservative philosophy. Many of the doctors were interested in the newest techniques that were emerging in the United States, but with the limited equipment and facilities available, especially in this charity hospital, emphasizing the older but proven techniques for solving problems seemed to me to be a better approach.

Most of the Dominican physicians had private practices through which they earned most of their income. Their routine usually required that they leave Dario Contreres hospital at 12:30 or 1:00 for lunch and a siesta lasting until mid afternoon. Their waiting rooms would be full at 4 p.m., and they would work until 9:00 or 10:00 p.m. Dinners were always late. Adapting to these hours meant that I had many afternoons free so Sally and I had a great time exploring the capital and the surrounding countryside. In the evenings we were often treated to the warm hospitality of the Dominicans, enjoying Sancocho and other Dominican dishes and, of course, drinking our share of Dominican rum and Coca-Cola.

Mois and his wife Marta treated us to several excursions, including one to the compound of the former dictator, Trujillo. This was a classic revival structure located in the mountains of the western third of the island that separated the Dominican Republic from Haiti. The view from the Villa was spectacular, and we were impressed by stories of the apparent decadence of that regime.

Sand beaches to the east of Santo Domingo were pristine, with palm trees providing needed shade. We were enjoying a lazy afternoon when Sally saw a beautiful black lady in the surf and assumed she was a native. Asking if she could take her picture, Sally was surprised to find out of that she was an American airline flight attendant. So much for local color!

Medically, the great number of complicated cases at Dario Contreres Hospital impressed me, and I began to realize that much of what we do in the United States is practicing "luxury medicine."

In the Dominican Republic, many patients from outlying areas had severe deformities after simple fractures. These deformities could have been prevented if physicians had been properly trained. However, trying to educate without intimidating can be a difficult task.

"Doctor 'Juicetas', please to look at this X-ray." A local doctor was eager to show me pictures of a young patient with a lateral condylar fracture of the elbow. He was convinced that he could treat the fracture satisfactorily by closed reduction. I suggested that this fracture should be treated by percutaneous pinning or by open reduction.

"I can fix it," he said confidently and proceeded with manipulation. When he saw the postreduction x-rays and the significant displacement that remained, he shrugged, smiled, and said in broken English, "Is okay." He then left to return to his private practice. Thus, another deformity would be seen months later at the hospital.

We had been assigned a translator whose name was "Sony." One evening at a party, when he learned that we had flown our own airplane to the island, he began discussing the possibility of riding back to the States with us.

Naively, I said, "Sure. Why not?"

He became very excited, telling his wife and family of his plans. Our tour was drawing to a close so I discussed the plan to take Sony back to the States with the director of the Orthopaedics Overseas program. His immediate response was to discourage me. It seems that unless Sony had a specific work visa or family that would take responsibility for him, I would have to become his sponsor financially and guarantee that he would return to the Dominican Republic when his tourist visa expired. Sony had been so excited about the possibility of his flying with us to the States that I felt guilty having to tell him that we could not take him with us. Even in those pre-9/11 days the legal implications would have been daunting.

There was a medical school in Santo Domingo, and the students were given lectures on occasion at the Dario Contreres Hospital.

DR. E. JEFF JUSTIS

Just before our departure from the island, Camasta, one of the professors at the school, asked me to give a presentation to the students. I was happy to do so, having brought some slides in anticipation of such a request. After all, I would be in control. Camasta was an interesting character—hard drinking and politically active. In fact, on one of our later tours to Santo Domingo he was actively running for president of the Dominican Republic. Several years later he and Mois visited the Campbell Clinic in Memphis. Although we had heard many stories about the legendary Camasta, we can add a few details of our own through experiences with this interesting gentleman.

For three weeks we had been immersed in the Dominican culture, and as we flew north over Hispaniola and along the Bahama chain of islands to Florida and home, we were increasingly grateful to live in a country that allows such freedom of travel and adventure that we had just enjoyed.

DAY TO DAY

As with many husbands of the 60s and 70s, I had insufficient appreciation of the sometimes thankless task of rearing children.

Back at the clinic it was work as usual for me, while Sally jumped back into the job of mothering our five; carpooling, attending mandatory school functions, counseling, and trying to keep peace in a blended family were just a few of the requisites —not to mention the needs of a husband who had been reared as an only child, a personality burden accentuated by events of the previous year.

Private practice at the Campbell Clinic evolved into a day-to-day routine with occasional spikes of great anxiety or excitement. While practicing orthopaedics with the Air Force, I felt my training had prepared me well to tackle most anything that walked or was carried through the door. In fact, the conservative way of thinking I had learned at the Campbell Clinic often contrasted with the "cut first" attitude of some of my contemporaries. On first returning to the Campbell Clinic as a staff member in 1968, I continued the Air Force tradition of trying to solve all orthopaedic problems, and I benefited greatly from the Monday night conference during which problems could be presented to the whole group. However, I found

I was feeling less confident about managing injuries that I had not seen for several months or even a year or so.

The culmination of that reticence came when I was performing a cervical fusion ("Rogers wiring") on a young man who had a potentially unstable cervical 2-3 fracture. He had no neurological deficit, and as I worked with a lone medical assistant (the residents I usually worked with for some reason were unavailable that morning) I remembered a horror story another orthopaedist told of a similar case in which the wire was inserted too deeply and penetrated the spinal cord with disastrous results - a quadriplegic patient.

Carefully, I worked with a towel clip to create a hole in the spinous processes of C-2 and C-3. I was under such tension as I did so that I vowed to never do another cervical fusion. I was certainly grateful when the patient responded by moving his arms and legs vigorously in the recovery room.

A break in the routine was needed, so what could be better than a family trip on the weekend to Holly Grove, Arkansas where my dad was restoring an old fishing cabin perched on a wooded bluff overlooking Maddox Bay, a tributary of the White River. We would fish, let the children shoot a shotgun, experiencing bruised shoulders in the process, and explore the bay in an outboard flat-bottom boat, but mostly we worked on some project such as repairing the roof or porch. Sleeping arrangements were primitive, and Sally was bothered by the mold in the damp cabin. Overall, however, I think most everyone enjoyed the outings. On some weekends we loaded the Apache for a quick flight, landing on a duster strip not far from the cabin. This certainly was more fun for me but when we did drive, I liked to entertain the children with ghost stories, reminiscent of those from my Boy Scouting days.

I remember one time telling a story on the drive. Cathy, Jeff, and Louisa were listening in rapt attention, hanging on each word, and waiting for the next sentence, which I was slowly formulating in my mind, when:

"Did he get killed when he went in the house? What was that noise he heard? I think I know why the ghost came."

"Steve! Shush! He hasn't finished," Cathy, Jeff, and Louisa shouted in unison.

Frustrated that my story had been interrupted, I said, "Now I've lost my train of thought. You all be quiet!"

Steve, ever eager and quizzical, had figured out what he thought I was going to say and wanted answers that I had yet to figure out. He was too quick for me, or I was too slow for him.

෴

In the meantime, I was becoming comfortable with my work and enjoyed talking with and learning from patients. In today's managed care environment, time is money, and physicians no longer have the luxury of sitting down and truly communicating with their patients. It has been said in the past that doctors should make friends of their patients but not necessarily make patients of friends.

The Monday Night Meeting, a tradition started by Willis Campbell himself, provided expert opinion on any orthopaedic problem. I was quite proud to be a part of such a dedicated group of doctors. My shyness, however, kept me from participating fully, and I was still intimidated by requirements that were not of my choosing. There was considerable pressure to write scientific papers and give talks at various meetings and to get involved politically in medical organizations. My dad had certainly been an outstanding member of the dental profession and is remembered years after his death for his many contributions. One of the underlying reasons for my choosing medicine over dentistry was my reluctance to follow a similar and expected path. Association with the Campbell Clinic provided opportunity for significant advancement in orthopaedic organizations.

DR. E. JEFF JUSTIS

At one point, on first joining the staff of the clinic, I felt confident enough to tentatively consider more political participation, but Lisa's illness and subsequent death changed me in ways that I have yet to fully understand. Subsequently, I chose, as much as possible, to avoid uncomfortable situations.

HAND SURGERY

For over three months, Dan Riordan, one of the original founding members of the American Society for Surgery of the Hand, was my mentor in the art of improving the function of injured, deformed, or disabled hands.

Finally, my planned tour with Dan Riordan was to begin in August 1971. The Campbell Clinic was quite generous to new staff members, and in order for me to gain experience in hand surgery, I was to be paid my regular salary plus expenses during my stay in New Orleans.

Sally and I discussed her staying with me, but with the kids soon starting school and with their needs being foremost in her mind (as they should have been in mine) we agreed that I would fly home when I could on weekends. She drove the Volkswagen down to NOLA, and I flew her back to Memphis so that I would have wheels and wings. "Sarg," Dan Riordan's secretary, had arranged for me to have an apartment near Dan's office, and during my three months in New Orleans, Sally did manage to come down to the "Big Easy" for a few days.

With Dan as a mentor, I learned by observation and listening. His expertise in hand surgery was practical, based on common sense, and his results reflected this approach, as patients understood what he was trying to accomplish and what should and should not be expected.

Long before outpatient surgery was generally accepted Dan was doing most of his surgery under axillary nerve block, and patients were sent home the same day or the next day, at the latest, after surgery.

"I hate making rounds," he often said.

My relationship with Dan was unique in that he had hand fellows already signed up for his year long program. I was to be an observing visitor. For that reason his fellow, Dave T., did most of the so-called scut work. My job was easy, especially since Dan did not hide his frustration with Dave's tendency to talk, perhaps a bit too much.

On surgery days Dan began operating at seven-thirty in the morning and we'd work straight through until two or three in the afternoon. Dan was trying to maintain his weight so we usually skipped lunch. Fortunately, Dave shared his peanut butter sandwiches with me.

Although most of Dan's hand practice was elective, occasionally he would be called to the hospital for emergencies. One afternoon a power company lineman had sustained a high-voltage injury to his left upper extremity. As a result, his skin, nerves, muscles, and vessels were essentially cooked with significant necrosis of these structures. Massive debridement was necessary, and I wondered what function might be salvaged. We were raising an abdominal flap of skin and vessels to cover a large defect. I was straining to hold the patient's body in a semi-upright position when I felt suddenly weak. I forced myself to overcome that sensation and once again realized that being in control of any situation, whether it be flying, public speaking, or surgery for that matter, provided protection from a feeling of being trapped.

Once a week we would meet at Dan's hangar at Lakefront Airport, pull out his Cessna 206, preflight it and take off for a flight to Shreveport where Dan conducted a hand clinic at the Shriner's

Hospital. I had introduced Dan Riordan to flying when I was at Keesler AFB, and he had subsequently become a pilot. It was tacitly understood that, on our time off, Dan would practice instrument flying while I flew as a safety pilot-in-command. He was working on his instrument rating, and as a flight instructor I flew right seat and filed instrument flight plans in my name so that Dan could gain experience in actual instrument conditions. He was as precise in his flying as he was in surgery, but he was intimidated by the instrument written examination and, to my knowledge, never became certified for instrument flying.

Since I was not an official hand fellow, I was not required to be available for emergencies on weekends, so for the three months of my stay I flew home to Memphis, usually leaving after work on Friday and returning on Sunday evening. I gained a lot of night-instrument time during that period. Late one Friday we learned that a hurricane would make landfall near New Orleans within the next few hours. I hurriedly preflighted the Apache, taxied out to runway 36 at Lakefront, climbed out over Lake Pontchartrain into the blackness with rain showers and thunderstorms developing over Southern Mississippi. This was before the days of stormscopes, onboard weather radar, and at least 34 years before cockpit displays of Nexrad weather. Alone in a dark sky, occasionally illuminated by sharp lightning flashes, I was totally dependent on the goodwill and expertise of air traffic controllers. With their help I was able to circumnavigate significant weather and three hours later land at Memphis International Airport.

One of Dan's former patients had invited him to West Texas for a deer hunting expedition, and Dan asked me to fly with him. I felt rather sorry for Dave since Dan had not asked him to accompany us. However, I think Dave was probably happy just to have a little free time. I enjoyed the flight and the accommodations at the wealthy Texan's ranch that was situated in rolling hill country and peppered with scrubby trees with little undergrowth.

Early morning, waiting quietly in the woods for a deer to pass, equipped with a rifle and telescopic sight, in my heart, I preferred to see a deer, not kill one. However, when Dan whispered, "There's one!" pointing to a buck, half hidden behind some bushes, it became apparent to me that he wanted me to have a good hunting experience. I took careful aim, torn between the desire to confirm my marksmanship, as I had previously demonstrated in the Air Force, and my reluctance to kill the creature, and slowly squeezed the trigger.

"Good shot!" Dan shouted. At least, I thought, as we walked over to the fallen deer, the animal never knew what hit him, since my aim had been good and the head shot final; but whatever previous fascination I may have had with guns and hunting was dispelled by my guilt at having killed for sport and not for survival.

PRACTICE

In early December I returned to Memphis with a renewed sense of confidence in my abilities and with knowledge of many new techniques and procedures to use in caring for patients with hand injuries and deformities.

Although at that time in our practice at the Campbell Clinic, all orthopaedists were proficient in some aspects of hand surgery, most of the partners were quite willing to turn over complicated hand cases to Lee Milford and me.

Dan had taught me the technique of using fine 5-0 stainless steel wire for wound closure, and I became quite proficient in its use. It produced little skin reaction in patients so scarring was minimal. The residents struggled with its tendency to kink, and to my knowledge I am the only one who ever used stainless steel for this purpose at the Campbell Clinic. Since I doubt that anyone else has attempted to use this wire, many boxes of Ethicon 602 stainless steel wire probably remain in central supply to this day.

For the most part, I was able to concentrate on hand problems in my practice, but because all of the staff, that is those under age 50, had to be on call for emergencies I was responsible for the trauma cases that arrived when I was in the "pit." Being awakened at two-thirty in the morning was never pleasant, and it was always with a vague sense of dread that I answered the phone.

"Dr. J., I've got a man in his twenties injured in a motorcycle accident near Wynne, Arkansas about nine last night." A resident's voice said through the earpiece. We may have known the patient was coming as early as nine-thirty but getting him to the emergency room always took longer than we thought it should.

"He has a terrible looking open fracture of the femur with some degloving; also an open olecranon fracture," the resident continued. "Anesthesia says they can't get to him before three-thirty."

"Okay I'll be in shortly; get everything ready; see you then." I replaced the receiver back on its hook.

Having the residents was a great comfort. Most of them were knowledgeable, competent, and pleasant. I irrigated and debrided one wound while the resident worked on the other.

In the early days of my practice, we did not use internal fixation (rods or plates at the fracture site) as initial treatment of open fractures, therefore fractures of the femur were usually treated in traction. A small pin placed through the bone at the upper tibia was attached to a caliper with ropes and pulleys through which traction was applied with 10 to 15 pounds of weight. The wound was allowed to heal as the fracture alignment was maintained for six to eight weeks of continuous bed rest.

"Doc, when are you getting me out of this thing?" was the patient's plea during daily rounds. And after every follow-up x-ray: "Has it healed yet?"

"Two weeks," I would respond.

After sufficient healing with early callous or new bone formation, we moved the patient to the cast room, placed him on a small sacral plate with a perineal bar (vaguely resembling a medieval torture device), suspended the tibial pin and caliper to an overhead frame and pulled on his foot through an ankle wrap. Then we wrapped wet plaster rolls over cotton padding from his nipple line to his ankle incorporating the pin and caliper. After the plaster hardened, we removed the ankle traction and incorporated the foot in the cast. There was minimal room for hygiene in the perineal and anal areas, and many a marriage was sorely tested during the six weeks or so required for further healing of the fracture.

I remember well one patient with whom I had more than a passing connection. Mr. T. had gone to a small airport in Kentucky to pick up a friend who was due to land after dark in a Cessna 172. As the airplane taxied to the ramp, Mr. T. walked toward the plane when he heard the pitch of the engine noise change; he had assumed the engine had been completely shut down. It had not, and he walked directly into the spinning propeller. The blade sliced into his left thigh, severing the quadriceps muscle and fracturing the femur much as one would cleave a large hambone. We placed Mr. T. in traction after treating his open wounds and after six weeks, succumbing to his pleas, I put him in a spica cast even though the callous formation was minimal. When he returned for a checkup X-ray in two weeks we were both disheartened to see that the fracture had angulated about 30°. This was unacceptable so he was placed back in traction for an additional month. He finally did heal satisfactorily; I later visited him for a follow-up, landing at the same airport at which his accident had occurred two years earlier. This time he was careful to stay in the terminal building until he saw me leaving the airplane.

In dealing with most patients, I always felt that presenting a positive outlook or being optimistic was paramount. And, for the most part in orthopaedics, predicting a good outcome is reliable. However, I remember seeing a newborn in the nursery with a fractured clavicle sustained during delivery, ordinarily a simple problem. The beautiful little girl appeared otherwise normal, but I noticed that her sclera were lightly blue-tinged. This finding may be associated with osteogenesis imperfecta (brittle bones). I rather pointedly downplayed this possibility to the anxious parents wanting to calm their fears. But, a month or so later I was called to the emergency room where the child presented with a forearm fracture after insignificant trauma. Again, I soft-pedaled the possibility. In retrospect the parents should have been given full details of what to expect. Instead, I was responding to their need for reassurance. Over the next several years we dealt together with multiple fractures. The fractures healed in the usual time, but as the child became more active and ambulatory, deformities in the lower extremities developed, and at age five or six surgery was necessary.

One such surgery required the insertion of a pin into the neck of the femur (hip bone). Although the pin had been incorporated in a plaster cast, four weeks later on a follow-up x-ray the pin had migrated and was then in the lower abdomen near the bladder. Fortunately, the general surgeon who was called to remove the pin found no internal damage, but the incident made the parents realize the truly serious and lifelong problems that beautiful child was to face. I continued to treat her for several more years always with good rapport, although I regretted not having prepared them more realistically for the problems they were facing. Subsequently, they moved to Birmingham under the care of another orthopaedic surgeon, although I continued to hear from them for several years after that.

Another anxious patient was referred by a physician from Stuttgart, Arkansas for treatment of a tumor in the fifth metacarpal of her hand. She was wide-eyed with fear as I reviewed her x-ray and reassured her that malignancies of the bones of the hand were extremely rare. Fortunately, the pathology report following excisional biopsy confirmed the presence of a benign enchrondroma (cartilage tumor). So the patient and I were reassured until, on a one-year follow-up x-ray, there was evidence of a recurrence. Still, this should not have been too alarming since the pathologist had said the lesion was benign. A second biopsy and curettage (removal of the lesion) again was read as benign by the pathologist. Actually, this tumor may have had some microscopic characteristics of a malignancy, but the prime reason a pathologist may call the lesion benign is because of its location.

Once again I reassured the patient! Another year later a third recurrence was evident. This was an extremely rare situation. The literature offered no explanation, but by this time the possibility of malignant degeneration was raised after the third biopsy; however, the pathologist was still reluctant to call this a malignancy. After discussing our options with the patient, we agreed that removal of the entire fifth metacarpal was required to eliminate the recurrence of this apparently aggressive tumor. This procedure would involve amputation of the entire little finger since, without the metacarpal the little finger would have neither functional nor cosmetic value. With the complete specimen to examine, there was obvious breakthrough of the tumor through the cortex and periosteum of the metacarpal, and the pathologist finally admitted that this was in fact a chondrosarcoma.

All my reassurance was for naught. Perhaps those doctors who always present the most pessimistic view can claim extraordinary skill when (as is true in 85% of orthopaedic cases) the outcome is positive. Many years later this patient developed a lesion in her lung, which when removed was clearly a metastatic chondrosarcoma. Subsequently, we published a paper about this case warning that any "benign lesion" that does not *act* like a benign lesion should be presumed malignant in spite of a "benign" pathology report.

One of the great joys in orthopaedics and hand surgery in particular is in putting something back together and making it work again. This is the same pleasure I get in working wood or overhauling an engine. I would often comment to the resident while debriding a mangled hand that I was "neatening up the wound" or "tidying up this mess." After thorough irrigation and débridement (that is, removal of all devitalized and contaminated tissue) the job was to repair the nerves, vessels, tendons, and muscles and stabilize the bony structure. The skin closure was the lowest priority and could often be deferred for several days (secondary closure) or covered by a skin graft later.

The psychology of being "on call" is interesting in physicians and probably similar in policemen, firemen, emergency medical technicians, and the like. Even though in a group practice "call" is not excessive, a day or two before the scheduled night or weekend call, I always experienced a vague sense of dread. When the day arrived, I was resigned to my fate and would try to relax watching TV or even working in the shop between emergencies.

On one of these on-call days, the phone rang. "Dr. J. we've got a dislocated shoulder here that I've tried to reduce, but I'm not having any luck," the resident sounded concerned.

After a few minutes of further discussion it became obvious that I was dealing with a junior resident. A little miffed, the twenty-minute drive to the hospital served to calm me down. After all, it was my job to teach the residents what I had learned from my mentors: Drs. Boyd, Speed, Ingram, Smith, Crenshaw, Waring, Stewart, Calandruccio, Milford, Anderson, Sage, Edmondson, Hamilton, and Crawford.

Once in the emergency room, seeing the relief on the resident's face, the concerned look on the hurting patient's face, I was no longer irritated; in fact, I was glad to be there. After explaining to the patient what I was about to do, I removed my right shoe, placed the heel of my foot in the patient's axilla and began gently pulling through the patient's wrist in line with the deformed position of his arm. Traction actually relieved some of the patient's pain.

With my gentle urging to, "relax—re—lax—let go of your muscles," suddenly, with a thunk, the shoulder relocated with immediate relief.

"Oh thank you, Doc. Thank you!" The patient was grateful.

So, we were all happy. Since then, in my thirty-seven or so years of taking night and weekend call, it was a rare situation in which I did not feel gratified in having helped an appreciative patient and resident.

However, such gratification did little to ameliorate my disappointment, years later, when there was a change in rules just before I turned fifty. Prior to that particular staff meeting we all assumed that there would be no night call after age fifty. The change required that night call continue to age sixty; albeit at half the rate as for those under fifty.

Life and the day-to-day practice of medicine continued with its many challenges and occasional disappointments, in my case made tolerable by my blue collar "vocations" of flying and woodworking.

One patient, a lady from Mississippi, presented with a recurrent giant cell tumor of the distal femur that required removal of the entire knee complex. In the days before total knee replacement, our options were limited: either above knee amputation or resection, leaving a floppy and useless lower extremity. We decided to insert a long Kuntscher Rod, extending from the hip area down the femur across the resected knee area into the tibia. The patella was used to partially bridge the gap producing what amounted to a knee fusion. In spite of the inconvenience of a stiff knee, the patient was happy, and I was proud to show her x-rays at our Monday night conference.

Dealing with potentially life-threatening problems was never comfortable for me, especially if the patient was a child. In the 60s and early 70s a diagnosis of Ewing's Sarcoma was a death sentence and when, after an excisional biopsy, I had to explain to the anxious parents what we had found, I would almost choke on my own words.

Hand surgery became my "out," my way to avoid, for the most part, dealing with such issues. Crippled children presented their own problems, however, especially in dealing with parents. Congenital anomalies were a challenge but treating syndactyly could be quite gratifying. In the embryo the hand is formed as a pad or paddle-shaped appendage on the limb bud; then four indentations begin to form and eventually a complete cleft between each of the five digits delineates what will become the fingers and thumb. When there is a failure of separation, usually between the middle and ring fingers, then the fingers remain joined by skin alone (simple syndactyly) or skin and bone in varying combinations (complex syndactyly). Because of the redness and swelling that accompanies the corrective surgery, parents were occasionally disheartened on the first postoperative visit, but usually after four to six weeks with more normal appearing fingers and good function, parents and child were smiling, and my primary reason for entering this profession in the first place was justified.

However, you can't please everyone, I was to learn from the parents of a child with a condition called floating thumb (pousse fluton). In this anomaly the thumb fails to develop and can present as a "nubbin" of nonfunctioning tissue or as a partially formed thumb with a fingernail. The latter can occasionally be treated by inserting a bone graft to replace the missing metacarpal, but for the true floating thumb with little potential for function amputation followed by pollicization of the index finger is preferred. This procedure involves rotating the normal index finger into a position of opposition with the remaining fingers. The cosmetic and functional result is usually excellent, so much so that most people never notice that a patient has only three fingers and a thumb. However, if the parents become "attached" emotionally to the vestigial thumb it is very difficult to convince them that the floating thumb will be a useless appendage. Many times they will wander from doctor to doctor looking for a miracle. Having been convinced by a plastic surgeon that their child's thumb could be normal, the parents of one small patient never accepted my recommendation and were somewhat resentful on each visit to the Crippled Children's Clinic. Later, they proceeded with the surgery as recommended by the plastic surgeon, then returned to our clinic, hoping we could improve the function of the stiff "post." We again suggested that function would be improved through pollicization, but they remained adamant in wanting to keep the stiff and unnatural looking "thumb." The parents remained disappointed and so did I. In retrospect, however, it is far better to have refrained from surgery even with an unhappy patient, than to have operated and be blamed for the poor result.

No matter how much you explain what to expect or what not to expect with a given procedure patients and parents can be shocked at a given outcome. A tragic example is a young man of 20 who sustained severe head trauma in an automobile accident on his way to college. As a result he was wheelchair bound and disabled by spasticity and flexion contractures in both upper extremities, so much so that hygiene was impossible with fingers digging firmly into his palms and his wrist flexed more than 90 degrees. The recommended surgery was to better position his hands and wrists so that his palms could be cleansed and the maceration due to constant skin to skin contact could be managed. No function was expected, and the young man's possessive and doting mother was told exactly what to expect. Subsequently, I dreaded each postoperative visit during which she expressed her disappointment and dissatisfaction. This is not what a surgeon likes to hear, since many of us go into medicine out of a need for approval.

One Saturday evening another young man involved in a motorcycle accident was admitted with a fractured femur and a facial injury. The plastic surgeon treated his facial injury initially, planning definitive surgery later in the week. As was our routine, we placed the patient in skeletal traction to stabilize the fracture. The following day, a Sunday, I did not come in to see the patient since Wiley, one of my partners, was on-call and was scheduled to see all of the patients in the Baptist Hospital. Later, Wiley told me that the patient was apparently doing well that morning, but sometime in the late afternoon his temperature spiked and shortly thereafter he arrested. In spite of resuscitative efforts, he died. I did not find out about this until Monday morning. Although Wiley had been on call and had the onerous task of notifying the boy's mother, I had never developed any rapport with the mother who, I learned later, was divorced from the boy's father and blamed him for providing the motorcycle in the first place. So when the mother called me a week later, I tried my best to give her some explanation of what had happened. Unfortunately, she had refused an autopsy and I could only speculate.

"Fat embolism" was a possibility but is not that acute in onset, usually developing symptoms three to six days after injury. "Pulmonary embolism" from deep vein thrombosis could cause sudden-death, especially when muscle function is decreased as is the case when a patient is placed in traction, but this too usually develops later. Acute bacterial encephalitis from a facial and nasal injury was also a possibility, but as I explained to this young man's mother, we can never know for certain. Although I encouraged her to come to the office so we could discuss the tragedy further, she refused, probably retaining guilt for herself and blame toward her husband, her son, the hospital and, of course, me.

THE PROJECT

When well meaning plans are unrealized, what develops subsequently may prove to be a better result after all.

In 1973, when Jeff was 12 years old, I began hinting by reminiscing about the adventures I had as a Boy Scout, that he would surely enjoy scouting as much as I. Perhaps he picked up, as well, subtle clues that I had on occasion been intimidated in some of the group activities of my scouting days. I remember the fear of failure I felt as I waited my turn in the knot tying contest. Our patrol lined up 50 feet or so from the knot tying bar, a 3-foot long, 2-inch diameter rod containing an array of ropes placed at intervals along its length. In turn, each of us ran as fast as he could to the bar where a Scout leader stood to call out the type of knot to be tied: "sheep shank," "half hitch," "bowline," and so on. Quickly we had to choose the proper ropes, complete the knot, and run back to the starting point. If I messed up my knot, I would let the whole patrol down, and I was always in fear of doing just that. So it was, also with rescue rope throwing, relays, or any activity that involved the whole group. Our Scoutmaster, Mr. Alvin Tate, wanted us to learn concentration through "Grady says" exercises, which required that we respond to a parade command only if the command were preceded by the words "Grady says." Thus, from the rapid staccato voice, "Right face"—"About face"—"Grady says Left face"—"About face"—"Grady says at ease," we learned to pay attention, since a mistake required leaving the line. The last scout standing received accolades; though I occasionally remained in line with one or two others, I never was the last Scout standing.

To this day I can remember the embarrassment I felt while participating in a group program presented before an auditorium filled with parents and family members. I was to recite one of the scout pledges such as: *A Scout is Brave* or *A Scout is Honest*. I stammered: "A- A- A—Scout is......" I forgot the word I was to say. I tried again: "A Sc...." I was mortified. Then I heard a whisper from back stage: "loyal - loyal." I finally got out the words and left the stage with my confidence in public expression permanently altered. I excelled, however, in individual activities and earned many merit badges — Electricity, Pathfinding, Bird Watching, Forestry, Carpentry, to name a few — enough to qualify for Eagle Scout.

So it was years later that I took my son, Jeff, to a Boy Scout recruitment meeting at Holy Communion Church, buying him a Scout manual. He didn't even flip through the pages, and I could tell he was not enthusiastic during the somewhat boring meeting. Although I'm sure he would have joined had I insisted, I suspect he would not have enjoyed the group activities as much as he subsequently enjoyed working with me in the workshop at our home.

In the summer of 73, Sally, Jeff, Louisa, Steve, and I loaded the Apache with camping equipment, for a family adventure to the Experimental Aircraft Association fly-in at Whitman Field in Oshkosh, Wisconsin. Cathy, now fourteen, had her own agenda and Kim, five, was happy to stay with her maternal grandmother. In those early years of the EAA, we camped by the airplane, rode horse-drawn wagons around the airport, and watched movies under the stars.

Jeff and I were intrigued by the builder's forums and the many designs for experimental aircraft; we talked excitedly about building an airplane together. We liked the Volmer amphibian, a boxy, all wood experimental aircraft, built from plans, so after returning home we made arrangements to see a flying example in Talladega, Alabama. We each took a ride with the builder and promptly lost our enthusiasm. Underpowered and slow, the 85-hp machine lumbered around the pattern with barely sustained lift. Coincidentally, I had previously discussed with a patient (the nurses always knew when I had a patient with an aviation interest because I stayed in the examining room much too long) the possibility of buying a set of Aeronca Champ wings for the Volmer project. Later, when I told him I was having second thoughts, he said he would sell me the whole airplane, sans engine, for $600. On a Tuesday, my day off, Jeff and I flew to Columbus, Mississippi to look it over. Stored in a barn, the wings were void of fabric covering, and cow pies were interspersed between the exposed ribs. The fuselage, with rips in the faded blue and white fabric, sat forlornly in the corner of the barn on a distorted left main landing gear, having suffered damage in a ground loop type of accident. *What are we getting ourselves into?* I wondered. Jeff was enthusiastic, however, and John Land, my patient, agreed to deliver the plane to us.

So it was in 1974 when Jeff was fourteen that we began the restoration project, a substitute for the Boy Scouts and one that positively affected our relationship. Over the ensuing six years, Jeff and I learned welding, metal working, and fabric covering techniques; we learned by doing. Jeff became a better welder in spite of an incident in which my hair and eyebrows were singed as he inadvertently passed the flame of the torch he was holding over my face; we both laughed. I had found a used 85-hp Continental engine that we overhauled with help from an engine expert at Hi Air where we based the Apache. Over the years of reconstructing the Aeronca, overhauling the engine, installing a turbo charger on the Apache, all under the watchful eye of Vic Froemel (A&P, IA, DAR), a friend and mentor, I gained the experience to take the written examination for the Airframe and Powerplant Rating, and after completing the practical test I became a certified A&P mechanic in 1979.

Most of the work on the wings, the control surfaces, and the engine was accomplished in the workshop. Work on the fuselage required more space, so I put fiberglass siding on our open carport and built some sliding fiberglass doors for the front. Finally, we pulled the fuselage out of the carport with the freshly overhauled engine and for the first time engaged the starter for which we had to obtain an FAA field approval, since the airplane had not been initially certified with a starter. The engine started but would run only for a few seconds; each time it would start then quit as if it were starved for fuel. Frustration ensued, but eventually we found the fault to be in the newly overhauled carburetor, which was replaced with no subsequent problems.

Jeff and I learned many things together, but at times I became impatient—expecting too much. Once when we had purchased a new Plexiglas windscreen Jeff attempted to trim the piece with a saber saw. Unfortunately, the saw caught and opened a large crack in the Plexiglas. I came down too hard on Jeff for a problem I might have as easily caused myself. A saber saw was just not the right tool; an abrasive cutter would have been much better. We live and learn.

Eventually, we hauled everything to a T-hangar at West Memphis airport, and with the help of several of Jeff's friends, we installed the wings and prepared for the first flight. The day before the maiden flight was blue sky perfect. I did a few taxi runs but was determined to wait to fly until the next day when we had invited friends for a hangar barbecue party.

The big day dawned to a gray, rain-sodden sky; friends began arriving at noon enjoying barbecue and an airplane-shaped cake brought by our daughter, Cathy. The ceiling was below VFR minimums and the visibility about 3 miles. West Memphis airport had an operating control tower (this was before the controller strike), and I was able to arrange a special VFR clearance to fly and remain in the pattern. I was a little nervous about making this first post-restoration flight with Jeff as a passenger but he looked so disappointed at my reticence that I relented. With Jeff in the rear seat, we fired up the Aeronca and taxied out to a cheering crowd of onlookers. Landing after two or three circuits, we were elated by the plane's performance and our success; the date was March 16, 1980. By this time Jeff had soloed in another Champ at Olive Branch Airport, earning his private license later in 1982 at the age of twenty-two. He subsequently obtained an Air Transport Pilot Certificate as well as an Airframe and Powerplant Rating, and is an excellent pilot.

Jeff and I became close during this shared time together, but it unintentionally shut us off from the other children, especially Steve. I was negligent in not making a conscious effort to bring Steve into the shop more often in spite of his seeming disinterest in what I was doing. In many ways he seemed uncomfortable being around me and probably felt that the other children had an unfair advantage. Unfortunately, opportunities were lost forever during those formative years of nine to fifteen. Louisa until she was eighteen enjoyed working in the shop on small projects of her own design and Kim who was in grade school worked on the scale model railroad we had bought while in Germany. Cathy was already in her teens during those years and went to college, eventually earning a masters degree in biology.

POLITICS

When I first joined the staff of the Campbell Clinic I was to some extent intimidated by the stellar reputation (worldwide) of the organization and many of the staff members.

I suppose I inherited my mother's reticence, since I, too, never enjoyed being in the limelight, so much so that to this day I do not like public recognition, a rather silly quirk, certainly, but I have learned that as long as I can control the situation by showing slides, for example, or by discussing something that is uniquely mine in knowledge or research, I can manage the feeling of anxiety that accompanies such presentations. This explains why, in my medical career, I often opted out of opportunities that most orthopaedists would have cherished. On the other hand, I was proud to become a member of the American Society for Surgery of the Hand when I was accepted in 1975, mostly because of the support of my mentors, Lee Milford and Dan Riordan. Uncharacteristically, some years later I even organized the Tennessee Hand Society in which all those doing hand surgery in Tennessee, whether or not members of the American Society for Surgery of the Hand, could participate. My most likely motive in organizing such a group was to give me an excuse to fly to state parks, Gatlinburg, and other fun places.

I also joined a "travel club," the Hibbs Society, primarily because of my friend and partner, Fred Sage. Though somewhat informal there were a number of prestigious members, former and future presidents of the American Academy of Orthopaedic Surgeons, the American Orthopaedic Association, and so forth. I enjoyed the camaraderie of friends and will cherish the memory of many meetings that Sally and I attended.

One such meeting was in Heber Springs, Arkansas. While on a luncheon boat cruise on the lake, I was feeling a rather urgent call of nature, intensified by the beer I had consumed, before realizing there was no head. It was at this moment in time that the club president asked me to become the secretary-treasurer of the organization. Immediately I became anxious, adding to my urgency. I didn't want to give up time I could better spend in my workshop or at the airport. I declined the offer, quickly jumping into the water with several others to relieve myself and cool off. I let the job fall to the next member in line. Also, at the time I had been considering other practice opportunities and used that as an official excuse.

For a while, perhaps related to a midlife crisis of sorts, I began to fantasize about practicing on my own. Like all fantasies this scenario was selective. I blocked negatives such as being on call all the time, having to manage the business of a medical practice, the continuing cost of overhead when on vacation. I imagined an ideal personal relationship with patients and practicing only as I desired with time off of my choosing. I discussed renting office space at the new Baptist East Hospital, but there was always a gnawing anxiety that I couldn't shake. I called Sally who at the time was in Huntsville visiting her close friend, Laura Binger.

"Just be sure, Jeff; you know I'll support you either way." She knew I wouldn't like the business aspect of a solo practice or the persistent demands on my time. Her support was invaluable in allowing me the freedom to choose.

After a weekend of reflection, I made a firm decision. As the future has proven, I am satisfied that remaining with the clinic was the best possible decision I could have made.

Why had I been considering a change in practice? I was sensing a change in the basic philosophy of practice at the clinic. Initially, most members of the staff joined so that they could practice medicine to the full benefit of the patient without the pressure of productivity. Each could take his time with every patient as required and was not obligated to perform more surgical procedures than he was comfortable with. We could attend charity clinics without feeling pressure to make up the time for financial reasons, and I happily served the out-of-town crippled children's clinics for years during my time on the staff. In addition, we each had a day off during the week. Fred Sage and I had a very nice working agreement through which I would see his patients on his day off and he would see mine when I was scheduled to be off. For me that meant a full day in the workshop, time that I treasured, for it freed me from the emotional strain of dealing with people in a most personal way. No one comes to see a physician because he or she is happy. Patients come because they have a need. It was my job to in some way satisfy that need so that the patient might leave happier than when he or she arrived. That process, which not only required physically touching the patient but also emotionally connecting with the patient, was draining for me, albeit rewarding. Weekends and my day off rejuvenated me and were very important for my peace of mind. Thus, during a staff meeting when, because of a desire to bring in more patients, changing the day off was discussed, I became quite concerned. Were we beginning to put productivity, making money, ahead of quality of practice and life? We had been used to working the equivalent of four and a quarter days a week in that we each had a two-hour clinic on Saturday morning as well as a full day off every week. The suggestion was to eliminate that Saturday clinic and only take half a day off. Fortunately, I prevailed with the suggestion that we have a whole day off every other week, alternating with a half day off, thus continuing the four and a quarter days work schedule.

There was also more pressure to get involved politically. Doing research on one's day off was common practice, and publishing results with the help of the residents became a stepping stone to political office in the orthopaedic community. During my tenure at the Campbell Clinic, I did manage to publish a number of papers mostly concerning subjects in which I had an interest: "Patterns of Injury in Aviation Accidents," "Woodworking Injuries," "Fractures of the Scaphoid," among others.

The Campbell Clinic was also generous with paid meeting time, and because I had persuaded the group to allow travel by private aircraft to be reimbursed on a per flight hourly basis, I was able to deduct some of the expenses of operating the Apache and subsequent airplanes.

A Flying Physicians Association meeting in San Diego provided a good excuse for a flight with all five of the children. Because the family had grown significantly, I had modified the Apache (nominally a five-seat twin) with a fifth and sixth seat in the rear and a fabricated jump seat with seatbelt for Kim who was now five. Taking off from Albuquerque, our first stop, in the heat of the afternoon in July, especially after a lunch that included Mexican food, proved not to be a good idea and soon everyone in the plane, except for the pilot, was a little green from bouncing and slewing over the deserts of New Mexico and Arizona, so much so that when I pointed out the spectacular view of the Grand Canyon, Sally said, "Look! There's the airport! Land now!!"

Back in those days we tended to travel on the cheap, paper bags sufficing for baggage, and rooms with double beds providing accommodation for all seven of us, often requiring Kim to sleep on two chairs placed front to front. How Sally managed all this I will never know but will always appreciate.

After the meeting and a sailing course in San Diego Bay, we departed Montgomery Field, climbing slowly out over the Pacific because of our load to 10,000 feet before we could turn east for our return home. With the exuberance and stamina of youth (I was 40 at the time) I had thought we might get home in one day, but in Dallas thunderstorms, darkness, and fatigue, reluctantly admitted, blocked our way, and we called it a day, arriving home the next morning in time for me to return to the office.

A trip to Aspen, Colorado in 1974 confirmed the limitations of our non-turbocharged airplane, when a friend, Rod Elliott, and a rather strange friend of his, Buck, flew with Sally and me, with an overnight in Denver, to Aspen. The morning sky was clear but as we climbed toward the Continental divide, 10,000, 11,000, 12,000 feet, the wind was stronger than expected out of the west, the invisible air flowing over the crest of the imposing mountains, bubbling down chaotically on the lee side. In this downward flow, we began inexorably to descend. I reversed course toward lower land, then as suddenly as we lost altitude, we began to climb in an up-turning wave, 12,000, 13,000, eventually 18,000 feet and out of the turbulent air, reversing course again, we could finally cruise easily over the mountains and into Aspen.

The night before this flight I had felt prodromal symptoms suggestive of the flu, so after landing and checking into our condo I was feeling a bit worse. Against Sally's advice I rented skis, should have listened, of course, because for five days I remained in bed with little memory of a ski vacation. Everyone else seemed to have a good time, and on the last day I managed one run down the slope.

After this flight I decided to install an aftermarket turbocharger on the Apache. Such an exhaust-powered air pump provided sea-level power up to 18,000 feet and improved takeoff performance at high altitude airports. With the help of Ray Ladd and others at Hi Air, I installed the unit myself — a blue collar triumph.

RETURN TO THE DOMINICAN REPUBLIC

May 1976

Although Sally and I had certainly had our problems adjusting to each other and to a blended family in the short time we had been married, once again she proved her mettle by returning with me to the Dominican Republic.

This time, however, we brought three of our children, Steve, Kim, and Jeff. Louisa was enjoying Camp Monterey near Cookville, Tennessee and Cathy elected to stay home with her friends. Our friend Mois Hache met us at the airport and after taking us to the Care office where we were furnished a car helped us get settled into a motel, far less attractive accommodations than we had on our previous trip to the D.R. For a week, while I worked at the Dario Contreras hospital in the mornings, Sally and the three children enjoyed the motel pool, that is, until Sally noticed that the pool lifeguard was paying inappropriate attention to Kim who was only eight at the time. The situation was uncomfortable to say the least so Sally was relieved to learn that we were to drive north to consult with a traumatologist, Dr. Mercedes.

There in Puerto Plata we stayed in a villa in the hills several miles west of town, complete with lizards, spiders and……..."Bena Chi! Bena Chi" the short, thin caretaker called to the children with a snaggle-toothed grin, holding a large rat by the tail. Memorable, but not necessarily pleasant, is the way Sally characterizes our stay in Puerto Plata

Although I assisted Dr. Mercedes with several procedures, including a triple arthrodesis in a child with a club foot deformity, it became clear that the most a visiting consultant can accomplish in such a short time is to impart some overall philosophy of managing orthopaedic problems, starting with the adage, "First, do no harm."

With a long weekend free, we decided to fly 300 miles from the D.R. and over Puerto Rico to the American Virgin Island of St. Thomas. After renting a car at the airport we started looking for a place to stay, not having made any reservations. When I walked out of a rather large attractive hotel situated on a point overlooking the rocky shore of this Caribbean island, informing everyone that it was way too expensive, Steve told us that he was really disappointed and that his "heart sank." It need not have, because after driving around the island, stopping at several places that were also expensive, with fewer amenities, we ended up staying at that very hotel. The kids were able to explore freely; there was a great beach for snorkeling, room service for the kids to eat in the room while watching TV, and a great restaurant for Sally and me.

Jeff and I wanted to take a "tourist" scuba diving course, so while Sally stayed with Kim and Steve, we donned scuba tanks, masks, and snorkels for a quick and, as it proved, inadequate course of instruction. Five or six potential divers were taken by outboard boat to a reef about a hundred yards offshore where everyone was instructed to remain together for an underwater excursion around the reef. I followed Jeff into the water; not wanting to get left behind, I started paddling down toward the others but couldn't seem to make any headway, struggling to catch up. The more I struggled, the more I began to hyperventilate as I saw the last of the group disappearing in the murky water. Fighting panic, I went to the surface. I was to learn much later that the surface is where most divers drown, weighted down by their gear, gasping for air. After what seemed like a very long time, the dive master came up beside me and when I explained that I couldn't keep up, he told me to let some of the air out of my buoyancy vest. After doing so I was finally able to descend properly and finish the dive, although the experience dampened any enjoyment of the reef itself. I was determined that if I ever went scuba diving again, it would only be with proper instruction.

Another week of work at the hospital passed quickly and soon it was time to return home; delayed in our departure by prolonged goodbyes, wheels up was late afternoon, but with favorable winds and clear skies we were able to fly from a refueling stop at South Caicos directly to Miami. Night overtook us as the blackness below blended into the horizon and myriad stars ignited into existence, giving life to our galaxy in the bright swath of the Milky Way.

Steve, having read of the Bermuda Triangle through which we were flying alone over a dark sea, was concerned, as was Sally who kept her eyes on Polaris for assurance that our compass was true. For me, this was but another adventure; that might seem incongruous in someone so intimidated by standing in front of an audience. You might think that some of that adventuresome spirit would transfer, but no. Flying a small airplane over an open ocean at night was far less intimidating. So what's next? I began to think about the ultimate adventure, following in Lindbergh's wake, the North Atlantic.

BICENTENNIAL - 1976

Having visited Williamsburg several times in the past, Sally and I felt that a Christmas in Williamsburg would be a once-in-a-lifetime opportunity for the whole family, especially during the bicentennial of the Declaration of Independence.

At first the children seemed reluctant, not wanting to give up the familiar traditional Christmas morning ritual, but Williamsburg at Christmas time was delightful, and the freedom the children felt in wandering along the Duke of Gloucestershire Street with candle lights in every window, soon supplanted any wistful longing. My parents, who had driven from Memphis, and the children stayed at the Brickhouse Tavern, a restored colonial structure with a Christmas tree in the common room. Sally and I slept in the Brickhouse Kitchen, a separate structure with a fireplace to warm us on a cold and snowy morning. Christmas morning we all gathered in the common room to exchange gifts with excited children who found their presents mysteriously arranged around the Christmas Tree decorated with fruits, candies and wooden carvings.

We had Christmas dinner at the iconic Groaning Board, so named because after eating turkey, ham, and beef with fruit and vegetables and four or five desserts, one can do little more than groan. Williamsburg felt so safe that Kim and Steve were free to roam and enjoy meals on their own at the local "drug store." We also enjoyed authentic colonial food at Chowning's Tavern and Christiana Campbell's in the restored area. I was able to photograph for future reference colonial era furniture and accessories at the The Craft House that was full of Kittinger Reproductions.

Ever since my first visit to Williamsburg as a teen-ager, I have been inspired by the cabinetmakers at the Hay Shop, where they use hand tools exclusively in crafting fine furniture. When the crowd of onlookers dissipated late one afternoon, I pulled out a photograph of the drawers I had made for a walnut washstand constructed for Sally. I was proud of my hand cut dovetails and showed the picture to the master of The Hay Shop. Expecting praise, I was somewhat disappointed by his comments: "Humph! Yes! Nicely cut, but the tails are much too wide for the size of the pins." Somewhat chastened, I resolved to improve on my next project and to try harder to emulate the old masters, not just in technique, but in design.

We planned an early departure after the Christmas festivities and arrived at the Williamsburg Jamestown airport just before dawn. No one was in the fixed base operation, but when we tried the door, we found that it was open.

"The manager must have left this open for us," Sally suggested, and we entered.

Steve made his way to the men's room but couldn't find the light switch, and a minute later we heard "tap tap tap tap tap" reverberating from the toilet. When we opened the restroom door and found the light switch, we saw a rather wet "out of order" sign covering the urinal. At the same time, we became aware of a flashing red light racing toward the airport on the access road. It wasn't long before the police came busting through the door expecting to arrest the felons who had obviously broken into the airport office. Luckily, we were exonerated by the airport operator who finally arrived, admitting that he had forgotten to lock the door.

By then the East was a-light with a new day, and the Apache climbed smoothly over the tide water marshes of Virginia toward the Appalachians and home.

THE VOYAGE

I was born under Lindbergh's star, or so it seems, six years after his epochal flight to Paris. Thus it evolved, having been imbued with the Spirit, that I should consider flying the Atlantic in my own airplane.

No political borders can be seen when we fly, only geographic and demographic features provide navigational certainty as we sail the ether of our blue planet. Perhaps it is naïve, but in our free country we have grown accustomed to crossing state borders without the problems usually encountered on international flights. Suppose our states were independent countries. Suppose we had to land every hour or two or had to file a flight plan every time we planned an interstate flight. Flying around Europe, so comparatively small in area, necessitated landing at an airport of entry in each new country to clear customs.

Having spent three years working and traveling around Germany and other European countries (courtesy of the United States Air Force) in the 60s, I began dreaming of flying my own airplane throughout Europe, to know that part of the world just as I know my own country. I envisioned the freedom I experienced in flying in the United States and, perhaps, I would be able to capture on film the contrast in the European countryside. Flying our 21-year-old Apache to and around Europe was a true adventure for me, Sally, and Jeff, but I realize now that my expectations were unrealistic. I returned with a new patriotism, with a new enthusiasm for the freedoms we're privileged to have in our country and with a new determination to do everything in my power to see that freedom of individual thought and action is never restricted.

Planning such an extensive trip begins when the feasibility of the adventure is first considered. By this reckoning, since 1968 when I purchased the 1957 Apache, I had been obtaining equipment and reading articles with the ultimate trip always in mind. Several extended over water trips to the Bahamas and to the Dominican Republic and to St. Thomas provided confidence in the feasibility of such an adventure

Thus, in mid-June 1978, when my son, Jeff, and I departed Memphis on the first leg of our adventure, our airplane was well-equipped, and we could concentrate on the safe completion of the flight. I had flown to Florida several weeks before for the installation of a 55-gallon drum plumbed into the fuel system of the Apache, giving us well over ten hours of usable fuel. The first test of the system was a nonstop flight from Memphis to Québec city, an eight hour marathon. The next day we flew nonstop to Goose Bay, Labrador. There, Jeff and I befriended the Airport Fire Chief, Dennis Conway, who invited us to his home for a dinner prepared by his wife, Stella. The next morning we taxied across the broad, quiet ramp of the Goose Bay airport, lined up on the 10000 foot concrete runway, pushed the throttles forward, and lifted off runway 31, with a 163-gallon load of gas, survival equipment, and crew of two.

For a brief moment I questioned: was it possible, or rather, was it sensible, that our 21-year-old turbocharged Apache was climbing into gray skies over a harsh and unforgiving sea? In spite of the helpfulness of the Canadian meteorologists, we were facing many unknowns. Most important, was the forecast for Bluie West One (Narsarsuaq, Greenland) accurate for the estimated six hours of our flight? Would the winds for our flight level be stronger or weaker than predicted? Would icing be a problem? And, perhaps, the ultimate question, was the island of Greenland truly where it was supposed to be? We were accepting on faith the work and the vision of many before us, but on this day we were the explorers, alone and in a hostile environment; we sensed our inadequacy in the universe, but the experience of humanity, whether through genetic memory or transferred knowledge, sustained us. This realization of the continuity of consciousness could be called a religious experience as we sat suspended in the ether. In the clouds there was no sense of motion, only the rumble, only the drone of our engines and the slow change in our instruments. Then... whosh...out of a cloud into another...we were moving...ice crystals on the windscreen and leading edge of our wings...not bad... very light; at 13,000 feet with an outside air temperature of 15°F we did not anticipate picking up a significant amount, but if we did, the freezing level was supposed to be 3000 feet — at least that is what the meteorologists thought it would be, halfway between Labrador and Greenland.

We could neither daydream nor philosophize very long, for we had work to do, keeping an accurate heading, changing course at 5° longitude crossings. Was there really a meridian stretching north and south across the ocean? We saw no such line, but we assumed there was one and duly reported same. Our reports were broadcast in the blind, but the pilots of bigger and better aircraft than ours provided assistance in relaying our messages to oceanic control. The clouds parted 100 or so miles off the coast of Greenland and soon, far on the horizon a change in color—a darkening under a white brush mark at the bottom of the sky—and—it was there—an island in the universe. As time and space travelers we found our planet in the void. The vision grew more real as mountains materialized, rising sharply from the dark blue water, competing with floating white mountains of ice, dotted with shimmering blue–green facets like emeralds set in a white stone on blue velvet. All the trouble of preparation, all the expense, all the risk were the cost of admission to this privileged seat, priceless; we descended lower and could almost touch these floating islands of ice as dark mountains loomed closer and higher.

Then—a change—the ADF needle swung slowly forward and, yes, we listened to the code, Simultac Island is near the entrance to the infamous Narsarsuaq Fiord. Fingers of ice-laden water penetrate into numerous deep fiords. We tried to sort out the differences in the contours that we saw and compared them to our map—here, that prominence must be here, on the map—or was it *this* one—no, if it were that prominence there should be an island, about a half-mile away—so this must be it—yes, the ADF agrees!

The blue sky gave way to gray as we slipped under the cloud cover that hides the higher mountains and the icecap further inland. Thus we entered a tunnel, with clouds at the top, icy blue-black water for a floor, and gray-black mountains for sides. Stalactite clouds hanging from the ragged ceiling, dripped on us intermittently during our cavern journey. Down to 800 feet, hugging the right-hand wall, we were reassured by Narsarsuaq radio that the ceiling and visibility were adequate at the end of the tunnel. We continued past a rocky peak on our left, past a long-ago wrecked fishing boat, then turned gently to the left and there, just ahead and to the right, we saw the single runway of the Narsarsuaq Airport, sloping up from the edge of the water toward the base of Greenland's icecap blanket. Main tanks on, gear down and locked, mixtures rich, props set, a downwind slide on final approach to the uphill runway, and we had earth contact, touchdown on a planet, different from the one we left, light years ago.

We were elated at our success, and our "high" blunted our fatigue, so we decided to press on to Iceland. The icecap stretched northward as far as the horizon as we crossed the southern tip of Greenland which holds the wreckage of many ill-fated aircraft still giving testimony to the harshness of this part of our planet.

Over the Straits of Greenland the Tactair directional gyro which controlled our autopilot failed, so it was hand flying from then on; I was glad Jeff was along to assist with flying duties. I would later have a new unit shipped to Scotland, so we would at least have autopilot help on our return flight. A good night's sleep at the Loftleider Hotel at Reykjavik refreshed us for the final overwater leg to Scotland. The weather wasn't a problem on this final transoceanic leg. We originally filed for Stornoway, but with favoring winds we extended the flight to Aberdeen, flying over the lochs of northern Scotland. Was that Nessie we spotted from our vantage as we over flew Loch Ness?

My friend, Terry Neale, a professional pilot, lived in Aberdeen and had agreed to store our ferry tank during our stay in England and the continent. Sally was scheduled to fly into Gatwick the next day on Laker Airlines, and we planned to meet her there. I had assumed that I would be able to file instruments and go, but Terry said that I had to also have a ground handler's approval at Gatwick before I could file. In effect, the FBO had to affirm that they could accept my little Apache for fueling and parking. I also learned that the first hour would be free but after that there would be a charge of 10 British pounds per hour. Interestingly, as we made our approach into Gatwick in the rain, but with good visibility (for England), I heard the approach controller talking to Laker Airlines, inbound from New York. What a confluence of human activity that represented!

I was in a hurry to avoid parking fees, so as soon as we could load up my tired wife into the Apache (she was miffed because I hadn't picked her up at the terminal, and I was upset that she didn't sufficiently appreciate our transatlantic accomplishment – oh well) we flew the short distance to Coventry and a very nice general aviation airport. After a few days of rest for Sally to adjust to the time change, we flew across the Irish Sea to Shannon, Ireland and enjoyed touring the Dingle Peninsula, Lindbergh's first landfall in 1927.

Back over the Irish Sea, past Arthur's Seat on final approach, we landed at Edinburg, Scotland, spending time with Douglas and

Joan Lamb. Douglas was a hand surgeon I met when he visited Lee Milford at the Campbell Clinic.

Departing Edinburgh under clear skies with Jeff in the copilot seat and Sally in the back seat, we flew about 400 miles across the English Channel to Rotterdam where we rented a car for touring the Netherlands. Because we had been using very high lead-content fuel, we experienced some plug fouling, so while we were in Rotterdam, Jeff and I changed the plugs on the Apache. We visited the miniature city of Madurodam, Anne Frank's house, and many other sites in Holland.

We flew over the canals and windmills of the low country on our way to Odense in Denmark; there I was to attend an international meeting sponsored by the Danish Orthopaedic Society, one of the excuses I used in planning this trip. Later, we flew the short distance from Odense to Copenhagen, and I learned firsthand one of the problems pilots experience when faced with user fees. In Europe, even at that time, fees were charged for filing instrument flight plans but not if one were flying by visual flight rules. We took off from Odense flying visually until we encountered clouds halfway to Copenhagen, and I had to quickly air-file an instrument flight plan by radio; the trip was completed uneventfully, but just the fact that one knows that a fee may be charged alters one's planning of a flight, and this can certainly be a safety issue.

After Copenhagen where we visited Mrs. Stubbe, my mother's friend from a European trip in the 50s, and toured china factories with Sally, we flew south, past the East German border, over Hamburg to Heidelberg, landing at the Army base with prior permission arranged by Steve Barnes who had been a resident at the Campbell clinic and was serving in the Army. Steve and his wife, Susan, entertained us for several days.

After another short flight, we landed in Würzburg where Ulrich Lanz met us at the airport. Uli and I had been brought into the Hand Society at the same time and since he was also a pilot we had become good friends; under his tutelage we toured his home town and later Nuremberg.

Our odyssey continued by flying to Salzburg, Austria and then to Switzerland before finally crossing the channel again, landing at Luton airport north of London. Local pilots suggested that we fly the short distance to a small airport at Elstree, which was much more general-aviation friendly and closer to London. When I think back on this trip in the 70s, and how free we felt in our ability to fly around Europe as we did, I am discouraged by the changes that have occurred since that time, especially following the tragedy of 9/11. We also found it relatively easy to drive around London in those days.

We found an inexpensive bed and breakfast that was close to the airline facility where Sally tried to get standby tickets to return to the States. This required lining up in an alley outside the facility the night before in order to be near the front of the line. Sally, characteristically, became engaged in conversation with the other folks in line and was determined to stay the course. Guiltily, Jeff and I went back to the bed and breakfast to rest, with a promise to relieve her in the line. We overslept and by the time we returned she had already obtained tickets. Soon she was on her way back to the States by commercial air carrier.

Jeff and I stayed as I had arranged a wood turning course with Peter Child who had published a book on wood turning and had developed quite a reputation in England and in the States. He met us at Andrews Field, which had been used during World War II as an auxiliary field for fighter aircraft. After three enjoyable days of British hospitality, instruction, and having purchased a large number of wood turning tools, we loaded up the Apache, flew back to Aberdeen, Scotland where we reinstalled our fuel tank and where the directional Gyro we had ordered from the States had been shipped. Jeff and I installed the instrument, said farewell to Terry, and departed Aberdeen for Stornoway where we filed a flight plan for Reykjavík. The controller insisted on checking our airplane and noted we did not have a high-frequency radio. This required that we alter our flight plan to fly over the Danish Faroe Islands, 200 miles north of Scotland before proceeding direct to Reykjavik.

For nearly 6 weeks, we had crisscrossed Europe logging 97 hours for a total of 11,290 nautical miles, with an average ground speed of 116 knots (134 MPH). My one disappointment in the adventure was my inability to obtain National Geographic quality aerial pictures of England and Europe; thirty-eight hours of the total flight was in instrument conditions. On the return flight, as we reached Goose Bay in late July 1978, we were elated, having successfully completed our first transatlantic adventure. This added confidence may, under certain circumstances, have set me up for misadventure later, as you will see.

FRIENDSHIPS

Friendships come and go it seems to me, but enrich us through memories of unique times in the continuum of life. To visit the past through friends is far better than living in the past.

In 1961 Lisa and I had flown to Orange, Virginia for my 10th high-school reunion at Woodberry Forest. Twenty years and a lifetime later I introduced Sally to many of my classmates from the school that helped shape my attitudes and philosophy. Three years of living with Frank, Wallace, Charlie, Al, John, Walk and forty-five others generated memories, some fleeting, some indelible, some adulterated by time and experience, but all affecting me, and through extension, my wife, children, and friends. The fabric of life is weaved in many colors. "Who is this guy? He remembers me!—Ah! Richard! Yes, he lived in a single room down the hall in the Walker building. Funny guy. A little weird. Now? Likable? Yes, but still a little weird. Maybe he thinks the same of me."

In looking back I appreciate all that I learned at Woodberry, but for some reason I never wanted to admit later to friends in college that I was a "preppy;" secretly I envied those, including Lisa, who had gone to Central High or Humes or any of the other public schools in Memphis. Many people maintain friendships for a lifetime, and they are to be admired for their perseverance in keeping up, especially if separated by geography. So it was good to see once more the friends of my youth, to recall adventures, to laugh about being called "Shylock" while counting pennies from my vending machines, to know, of course, that each reunion brings fewer of us together as each of us, in turn, reaches his physiological limits.

In November 1978, I was invited to Santo Domingo as a guest lecturer at a meeting of the Dominican Orthopaedic Society by my friend Mois Hache. Another friend, Ken J., an orthopaedist from Little Rock, Arkansas had been invited also and suggested that we fly in his airplane, a Cessna 340A. This plane, faster and more capable than our Apache, was pressurized and equipped with radar, so I was more than happy to fly co-pilot. Sally enjoyed the roomy cabin (with facilities), and I obtained certification in this cabin-class plane since Ken, at that time, was a flight instructor. The trip was enjoyable, and we were to see Ken and his wife, Beryl, at meetings several times in the future, especially at hand meetings and meetings of the Flying Physicians Association.

I think back on my best friends, Hugh and Bobby, and how we adventured together as teens, exploring the Great Smoky Mountains and camping on the shores of Norfork Lake, and I remember how we slowly drifted apart in the parade of life in which we march. Often, as with Hugh and Bobby, the separation of lives is slow and circumstantial. At other times the separation can be sudden and turn on a word. Acquaintances often become friends through some common interest as was the case with Ken. Several of us, with our wives, were enjoying a drink in the lounge of the Hilton Hotel in San Francisco during an AAOS meeting. Bill Clinton had been elected president in 1992 to the dismay of most physicians who tended to vote for Republicans. I had voted for Eisenhower when I reached voting age and had been attracted to the philosophy of individual responsibility that at that time seemed to be a hallmark of Republicanism. What I didn't appreciate at the time was that the republican philosophy, if carried to the extreme, is a selfish, self absorbed way of thinking that implies that others, less fortunate, are in that situation because of their lack of self responsibility. Their circumstance of birth, of upbringing, of health, of education, of all life's vicissitudes are ignored or shrugged off in such an evaluation.

"If I had wanted to be a truck driver, I would have been one, and if that truck driver, complaining about low pay and long hours, had wanted to be a doctor he could've gone to medical school," Ken arrogantly announced as the conversation shifted to politics. Several in the crowd nodded their heads in approval.

"Clinton's going to ruin the country!" Someone interjected.

Sally, who had voted for Clinton, although I didn't know it at the time (she treasures her right to a secret ballot), muttered something about not everyone being able to fulfill his or her dreams. But she could contain herself no longer when Ken in a loud voice said, "Oh Lee Harvey Oswald, where are you when we need you?"

"That's the worst thing I've ever heard anyone say. You ought to be ashamed of yourself!" Sally proclaimed with determination as she got up to leave. I followed her, and although at the time, I admit, I was a little embarrassed, I was proud of her. Years before, when JFK had been assassinated, I remember the strong emotion I felt at that loss, enhanced by the guilt of having even listened to the virulent anti-Kennedy rhetoric so prevalent in the South at that time. Thus ended any close connection with Ken and Beryl.

FLYING ADVENTURES

1979-1981

As I write this, I refer to my several logbooks, jogging my memory of past adventures, each flight a unique event in a busy life.

After having obtained my Airframe and Powerplant mechanics rating in September of 1979, I exchanged both the engines on the Apache for two new engines of slightly greater horse power (from 150 to 160) and was able to sign off the installation myself—a proud moment for any blue-collar worker.

Later that year we picked up Laura and Dick Binger in Huntsville and flew to Charleston, South Carolina for a mini vacation. We enjoyed relaxing in a bed and breakfast, exploring the city and getting ideas for future reproduction furniture projects. But when Sally suggested that we leave earlier than planned because of some perceived crisis involving one of the children, I remember my disappointment. After nine years of marriage I had yet to adjust to Sally's determination. In times of disagreement, my sense of loss for Lisa, which I evidently had not yet come to terms with, seemed to surface. However, despite our differences, Sally and I soldiered on — because we both cared.

In March 1980, the same year the Aeronca Champ was celebrated on her maiden voyage, my dad, who was 82, was told that the Exchange

Building where he had practiced dentistry for over 50 years would be renovated as an apartment building. As of this writing, nearing my dad's age, I have difficulty relating to his determination to continue practicing dentistry. He truly enjoyed his solo practice, his connection with his many loyal patients, and his association with dental colleagues, most of whom were quite a bit younger than he.

Since I had harbored the idea of perhaps practicing on my own someday, I used my dad's need for a new office as an excuse to purchase a building on Brookhaven Circle in East Memphis. Sally was supportive, even though the real estate person we were using misled us on the monthly cost of the purchase. We were concerned, since the rent my dad would pay was to be used to offset that cost. The building was actually a home that we would have to convert to a dental office, a process that required special plumbing, handicap access, and so forth. A local contractor helped with the construction, although I ended up doing a lot of the interior work and constructing the handicap ramp.

The office was nearly finished except for asphalt work for the drive and parking area when an FPA tour of Alaska was announced. I wanted Sally to fly to Alaska with Jeff and me, but she felt more pressure to finish the project than I and insisted on staying in Memphis to obtain permits and to supervise the process. She did agree to meet us in Monterey later for the annual Flying Physicians Association meeting, which was to follow the Alaskan tour, so, with a modicum of guilt, I prepared the Apache for the flight with Jeff who was out of school for the summer of 1980.

The first day we flew to a small field in Fairbury, Nebraska, pitched a tent, and camped near our plane watching the orange glow of the setting sun on a calm summer's eve. The following day we met other members of the Flying Physicians at Edmonson, Alberta for a flight briefing for the remainder of the trip. From Edmonton, Alberta we flew north 500 miles to Fort Nelson, originally a trading post in British Columbia established in 1805. In 1935 an airport linked this remote outpost to the rest of Canada, and in 1942, the Alcan highway was constructed by the US Army to counter the threat that Japan might invade Alaska.

The sky domed high above the distant mountains as we inched toward Whitehorse in the Yukon Territories following the Alcan highway through tundra and valley, and over Watson Lake. As the Apache droned north by northwest, rarely did we see traffic on the lone highway below, and there were no towns for several hundred miles. *What a lonesome place to make a forced landing*, a fleeting thought that receded as we admired the stark beauty of the Northwest Territories as seen from our privileged seats.

Whitehorse still had the atmosphere of a frontier town. It had been a rest stop for weary prospectors on their hopeful journey from Skagway over the White Pass to the Yukon in 1896 at the beginning of the Gold Rush. A railroad was finally built in 1898 to ease the journey. We spent the night in Whitehorse and enjoyed frontier entertainment in one of the many local nightspots reminiscent of frontier days.

The next day was relatively easy, with a flight of only 250 miles to our entry point back into the United States at Northway. From there we continued northwest in the broad area between the Alaska Range in the South and the Brooks Range to the north, landing in Fairbanks on the 10th of July. This time of year the sun was bright until midnight, fading little before sunrise at 3 a.m., making sleep difficult even with shades down on the windows of our motel in this far north city of about 30,000 hardy souls. Nevertheless, Jeff and I were eager for further adventure, so with several other airplanes we guided the Apache north, crossing the man-made scar of the Alaskan pipeline to the gravel airstrip at Fort Yukon, a village of 600 on the north bank of the Yukon River just above the Arctic Circle. There, houses are built on wooden pilings buried in the permafrost, which, with the increasing warming of our planet, is becoming more of a problem as the permafrost recedes.

Our tour was to fly to Mount McKinley National Park where good weather would be required for landing on the gravel airstrip near Mount McKinley Lodge. Out of Fairbanks the big sky of the Alaskan interior beckoned us towards the Alaska Range in the south. There we followed the highway through narrow passes, forming a granite tunnel topped with gray craggy clouds, and finally exited into a broader valley where we found the airport atop a mesa near McKinley Lodge. We knew Denali (Mt. McKinley) was near and hidden in the clouds, and we hoped like so many before us that we would be able to see the magnificent mountain, the highest in North America. Since this was part tour and part medical meeting, after morning lectures we were usually free in the afternoon, so Jeff and I decided to climb the rock strewn hill behind the lodge, thus facing the biggest danger of our trip, running across a grizzly bear or, perhaps worse, a moose. We were told that with the grizzly we should stand our ground making ourselves seem as big as possible, but with a moose we should very quickly back away. Gratefully, we didn't have an encounter with either danger.

On departure for Anchorage several days later we had to climb into the clouds on instruments, and I requested that air traffic control vector us as close to Denali as possible, hoping to see the elusive mountain. White ephemeral clouds floated past our plane as we strained to see. "What's that, Jeff? There! That sharp edge, that's granite, that's not a cloud, that's Denali." A fleeting glance, the highest peak in North America, but we had found our mountain after all.

Our last meeting was to be held in Anchorage and while there I was asked by one of the members of the group to repair a defect in the propeller of his airplane since such repair requires a mechanic with an A&P rating. He had apparently sustained the damage as he took off from the gravel airstrip at the McKinley Lodge.

Not unexpectedly, I have retained very little memory of the medical aspect of this meeting but the flying adventurous part stands out quite sharply. The long days allowed us to venture away from Anchorage on a day excursion to Kodiak Island; the city of Kodiak was once the capital of Russian Alaska and during that time was significant in the fur trade. Unfortunately, sea otters were nearly brought to extinction by the Russians, but the Alaska purchase intervened and now the primary economic impact is through the fishing industry. Kodiak is the home of Kodiak bears, a subspecies related to grizzly bears, which have been genetically separated from the mainland grizzlies for ten thousands of years. Jeff and I took a local tour to see some of these magnificent animals that are protected in a national wildlife reserve established by President Franklin Roosevelt. Leaving Kodiak we landed at Homer to refuel before flying back to Anchorage where our meeting was to end the following day.

From Anchorage we flew over four hours along the rugged southwestern coastline to Sitka, landing under a 500 foot overcast to refuel. Being young and vigorous (at least Jeff was), we continued to Ketchikan, which is only 190 miles farther south to refuel since there would be no further stops between Ketchikan and Seattle, over 600 miles farther south. So after another four and a half hours in the air we were both tired enough to spend the night at an airport hotel in Seattle.

Rested, the following day we flew past the still smoking and distorted Mount Saint Helens, which had disastrously erupted on May 18, 1980, only two months before our flight. We landed at Concord, California to refuel; then, with the Golden Gate off our right wing we made our way down the West Coast to Monterey, the site of the Flying Physicians Association national meeting. There, I was truly surprised to receive the Airman of the Year Award. Sally had flown commercially from Memphis to San Francisco, rented a car and driven to Monterey where she picked us up at the airport. Sally, who had known about the award, had managed to keep it a secret from me. I was embarrassed but was able to say a few words giving Jeff credit for being a good copilot on the trip and praising Sally for her encouragement and support not only in our flying but in all other aspects of our life together.

Later, Sally told me of her travails in dealing with a misogynistic asphalt contractor at my dad's new office; I once again felt guilty for having abandoned her for Alaska. These were the days of marathon flights, and I reveled in a challenge, so after the meeting we flew all the way home in two stops (Prescott, Arizona and Amarillo, Texas) in 12 hours, the last four being at night.

Looking back, it's hard to believe that I was able to fly as much is I did in the 80s, but about two weeks after returning from Alaska and California, Jeff and I flew the newly rebuilt Aeronca Champ to Oshkosh, Wisconsin for the Experimental Aircraft Association fly in and air show. We set up a small tent by the plane in the classic campground area hoping that our project would be noticed by the judges. We received many compliments from fellow enthusiasts but no award. One night a downpour flooded the campground, and I woke up in a soggy sleeping bag. Jeff had managed to stay a bit dryer but was willing to leave early the next day; enough fun and way too much discomfort provided adequate motivation.

With all this flying it would be easy for a reader to wonder what else I was doing. Of course my practice continued with its routine highs and lows, successes, and, gratefully, not too many failures. With the benefit of partners, time off allowed me the freedom to fly and to build furniture in my workshop; for this I will be forever grateful to the Campbell Clinic and for my decision to continue with a group practice. As with any medical practice, one must be willing to compromise, to cover for others on their days off, and to stand by for emergencies. This was certainly a small price to pay, and with meeting time (about three weeks) and vacation time (about three weeks) we could plan many trips around medical meetings. For instance, Diving Medicine in Depth was a legitimate meeting located at a scuba diving resort.

After my near panic during that dive in St. Thomas, I was determined to learn more and become certified as a scuba diver. With Laura and Dick Binger, we flew the Apache to San Salvador in the Bahamas in August 1981. Sally initially was uninterested in becoming certified as a scuba diver but when she realized the freedom she would feel underwater and that she didn't have to touch the bottom or entangle in seaweed, she enrolled in the diving course. On our first open water dive, however, the dangers inherent in the sport became apparent when Laura, at about 50 feet below the surface, found herself unable to inhale because the valve in her regulator failed; she started for the surface and was just about to give up when the dive master caught up with her and shared his air and mouthpiece with her.

On another dive, Dick, who was a very strong swimmer, was swimming ahead of me just as I realized that I was running out of air and had to go to the surface. Unfortunately, I had given my snorkel to Sally so I had no way to put my head down and breathe while trying to swim toward the boat, which seemed an awfully long way away to me. I had inflated my buoyancy vest but I was basically helpless just floating and hoping someone would see me. Dick finally realized that I was not with him, came back with a snorkel so that I could finally put my head down and swim toward the boat. Sally and I did succeed in becoming certified scuba divers, but subsequent adventures would cause us more anxiety in the water than we had ever experienced in the air.

AIR FORCE RESERVES

Medical Officers are considered non-combatants, and I am grateful that I would never be asked to purposely fire a weapon at another human being.

I had enjoyed my tour with the United States Air Force, but after I was released from active duty in July of 1968 I was not especially interested in joining a reserve unit, mostly because that would require taking one of my precious weekends for unit training. Not until 1982 did I learn of the Individual Mobilization Augmentee (IMA) program. When Reagan became president he initiated the first build up of the military since the Vietnam War, and medical recruiters became prominent at each orthopaedic meeting I attended. I had nine years of active duty and with credit granted for medical school, internship, and reserve time following internship until I entered active service, I already had points toward retirement. After leaving active-duty in 1968, I had remained on an inactive reserve list as a Major until I resigned my commission when the time requirements had been fulfilled. So after signing up for a return to reserve service as an IMA, I was recommissioned as a Lieutenant Colonel by act of Congress.

Immediately after the Vietnam War our military was decimated. In order to entice needed physicians, the Air Force was offering commissions to full Colonel for experienced physicians, even those with no prior military service. This program was abandoned when it was found that these docs did not conform in an appropriate way to military tradition. So if I were to be promoted to full Colonel (0-6), I would have to work for it, and I did. The good thing about the IMA program was that I had to give up only one day a month during the week to serve with the active duty personnel at Blytheville (Eaker) Air Force Base in northeast Arkansas. Not only would I be serving as an orthopaedic consultant, but, as a rated flight surgeon, I would be "required" (don't throw me into that briar patch) to fly with the flight crews four hours a month. Most of the flying was in KC 135s on refueling missions, but I did fly on B-52 training missions and in the Cessna T-37 jet trainer on occasion. On long missions I was invited to the copilot's seat. It was second nature for me to hold heading and altitude. Turns took a little concentration since the response rate for a given control movement was a bit slower than in the Apache or Twin Comanche.

Every year I had to spend two weeks on active duty at some location, usually of my choosing, and although I used my vacation time, I thoroughly enjoyed this time away from the clinic. Not only was I able to fly the Apache directly to the base, but I was treated somewhat as a VIP. A return to Keesler AFB in Biloxi, Mississippi was my first two-week active duty tour and brought back many memories of my time there in 1967 and 1968. Sally stayed home, but time passed quickly since I was on call for emergencies and was busy during the day with clinics and surgery. Interestingly, the chief of orthopaedics, a Lieut. Colonel, as was I at the time, was being considered for membership in the AAOS. Because he knew that I was on the committee that had control over admissions to the Academy, he was especially nice in limiting my on-call time.

Later I was invited on a "movers and shakers" VIP tour of Barksdale Air Force Base in Shreveport where we viewed our stockpile of nuclear weapons and learned of our strategic philosophy during the Cold War. After Barksdale we flew northward in a KC 135, and I was impressed by the Minuteman missiles hiding in silos near Whiteman Air Force Base in Missouri.

DR. E. JEFF JUSTIS

At Eaker Air Force Base hospital, I helped the assigned general surgeons with elective orthopaedic and hand cases. I also ran an orthopaedic consulting clinic and occasionally gave talks to the staff on some general orthopaedic topic. These talks did not produce anxiety as I was the perceived expert. I signed up for an Air War College program and submitted the necessary paperwork to the Colonel promotion board for consideration. With this effort and having received very good officer effectiveness reports from the hospital commander, I was gratified when I was eventually selected for promotion to full Colonel. I wore the eagles proudly and when wearing the uniform at official meetings, Sally noticed, with amusement, when a group of female Air Force nurses passed, saluted and chanted "Good morning, Colonel — Good morning, Colonel." Who would not like that!

"Colonel, we've got a two-hour round robin flight tonight if you're interested", the young captain was calling from Base Ops, and knew that I needed some night time to maintain currency for flight pay so I jumped at the chance. We briefed for a refueling run with a return to BYH at 2200. About 2130 I was resting in a sling seat behind the cockpit as we headed home, the white noise of the engines lulling me to sleep.

Suddenly alert, I heard on the headset, "Doc's not going to like this!"

"What's going on?" I asked.

"Blytheville's below minimums with ground fog."

After communicating with SAC headquarters, operation officers determined our destination. Pilots had no choice in this decision. Little Rock Air Force Base would be too close and too simple. Instead we had to fly all the way to Altus, Oklahoma and by the time we landed after midnight, crew rest requirements meant that we couldn't leave until the following night. After we returned to Blytheville late the next evening, I hopped in the Apache for the short flight back to West Memphis and after very little sleep I was back in the saddle at the Campbell Clinic, a civilian once more.

Another two-week tour in February 1987 was a mandatory Combat Casualty Care Course for Medical and Medical Service Corps Officers. When I read Tolstoy's *War and Peace* I had been a member of the active reserve for several years and, although I did not and do not consider myself a militaristic individual, I empathized with Prince Andrew's embracing of many aspects of military life. In particular, the fact that following orders is, in many ways, liberating since one's dress and one's actions are proscribed and require no forethought, no decision.

Gratefully, in my life thus far, I have never had to wield a weapon against anyone; but during this two-week course I experienced the camaraderie that leads a soldier to do anything, to risk anything, to protect his buddies. My squad was ordered to take a hill at Camp Bullis near San Antonio. This was planned so that we could experience first-hand the chaos and unpredictability of combat. As we started running up the hill, concussive explosions rocked us and we dropped to a belly crawl on orders from our leader because of simulated machine-gun fire. Smoke bombs were ignited up-wind of our position. Urged on by our leader I was breathing heavily, and my lungs were burning from the acrid smoke. I was just behind a younger man who was panting as painfully as I. Later he said he had looked back at me continuing the hard climb and thought to himself, "If that old man can do it so can I." After all, I was a freshly promoted Colonel and the oldest officer in the group.

We learned never to roll a casualty face up from an overhead position but to use his body to shield us from a booby-trapped explosive that might have been planted by the enemy beneath his body. We learned that crawling uphill with an M1 rifle is a real burden and that playing "King of the Hill" as a youngster belies the reality of war.

During the same course we used map and compass to find our way to a specific location and to evade the enemy as we approached the enemy lines. Since I had told my squad the story of our crash in

DR. E. JEFF JUSTIS

1986 (see Chapter 21), the group assumption was that I would not be lost again. Wrong! I miscounted paces and misread the map so that we ended up in enemy hands. At least a search party was not dispatched for us as it had been for another group that had become lost after dark.

A FULL LIFE

While living in the present, each day flows easily into the next, but when reflecting on the past, some days stand out in sharp relief.

How fortunate am I to have been able to practice my specialty in a group that allowed such freedom, with generous vacation time, and paid attendance at meetings of my choice. During one such meeting (Flying Physicians Association) in Orlando, I took advantage of an opportunity to obtain a seaplane rating. Each afternoon for three days I flew the Apache south to Lakeland, Florida for instruction in a float equipped Piper Cub. Great fun, but of little use since renting a float plane in the Memphis area is impossible. Although for several years Jeff and I investigated the possibility of putting floats on the Acronca, it became an unfulfilled dream.

I was logging a lot of time in the air, so, with more than enough hours to qualify, I signed up for an Airline Transport Pilot (ATP) course in Columbus, Ohio, and after several days of intensive study passed the written examination. I learned how much we could load in a 727, how many fire extinguishers were required, the takeoff distance for a given load, temperature and density altitude, and many other facts, long since forgotten and no longer of any use. In July 1982 I passed the check ride in the Apache with an FAA examiner, Harris Weise. One might daydream about flying "heavy iron," as commercial jets are called, but the routine, the sameness, the reality, might soon grow old, especially to one so used to setting his own schedule; thus I was satisfied just to dream and continue to fly the Apache, ever mindful it was never without some risk.

One of my partners, Peter Carnesale, had taken flying lessons in the past and was eager to go with me on several flights arranged by the Baptist Hospital as part of an outreach program at smaller town hospitals, part of the Baptist system. Although I still could not be enthusiastic about giving talks, I found that with slides, and with the realization that I was, after all, an expert in the subject I was discussing, I could even volunteer for such assignments with little apprehension, since it gave me another excuse to fly. One night (the meetings were usually dinner meetings with the local physicians) Peter and I waited for a passing storm to subside, and after filing an instrument flight plan, we took off into the black sky, contacted Memphis Air Traffic Control Center only to be told, when we needed it most to avoid flying into a storm, that their radar was out of service. Although threatening, the lightning flashes, by illuminating the turbulence producing clouds, helped us tiptoe around the larger buildups and arrive safely back in Memphis. Now, years later, I wouldn't think of flying without the aid of onboard radar, lightning detection, and Nexrad radar imaging.

Through the American Society for Surgery of the Hand, we had met many foreign members, Françoise and Isabel Iselon from France and Douglas and Joan Lamb from Scotland to name a few. So we were excited that an International Hand Society was meeting in Martinique in April 1983. Unfortunately a strike of air traffic controllers in France caused cancellation of the meeting. Undeterred, Sally and I decided to fly to the West Indies anyway. So, once again, flying the islands of the Bahama chain, pearls in a blue setting, to St. Thomas, we reveled in the freedom that flying one's own airplane can give, though not without some unexpected problems.

We arrived in St. Thomas under a cloud studded blue sky, that turned gray toward evening and darker still as we enjoyed dinner a block away from our small hotel, high on a hill overlooking the city. By the time we walked back to the hotel, it had begun raining, soft at first, then a downpour. We retired early, listening to the drumbeat of rain on the tin roof and on the air conditioner above the head of our bed. Soon the rain came to bed with us, drip, dripping on our heads. We moved the bed, of course, but the night passed slowly. The power was out, breakfast was cold, and from the porch of our hotel we could see down the hill that the streets of the town and shopping area had flooded up to 2 feet into most of the shops. Then we heard that the airport had also flooded and there was no way for us to get there. A very strong low-pressure system (almost a hurricane) had moved into the southern Caribbean dumping an unprecedented amount of water onto St. Thomas. We had come hoping to scuba dive in the usually clear water of the Caribbean but with the muddy runoff from the rain this was looking problematic.

Finally, after two days, the water subsided, and we could check on our airplane. Water still covered part of the ramp, but the manager had moved our Apache to higher ground. Even so we were told that the water had risen to the belly of the plane. Since St. Thomas had been decimated by the flood and since the airport had finally reopened, we decided to fly further east to St. Maarten where we hoped the water would be clearer. As we climbed out over this American Virgin Isle, I discovered that our automatic direction finder (ADF) was not working. The antenna for that unit was on the belly of the plane and had apparently been damaged by the water. So we navigated by compass and map without difficulty in those days long before Loran or GPS.

In St. Maarten, trusting a local diving instructor, something we would never do again, we were taken in a rather trashy boat to an off-shore dive site where we back flipped into the water wearing questionable dive gear. There Sally felt her lungs would explode when a faulty regulator forced too much air, too quickly through her mouthpiece. Again we were learning that diving can be a hazard to one's well being.

Because there would be significant over-water flying between the Virgin Islands and the Bahamas, we stopped in Puerto Rico to have the ADF antenna repaired, after which we flew the short distance to Mayaguez in the northwest corner of Puerto Rico for one night in a resort hotel before returning home by way of the Turks, the Bahamas, and Ft. Pierce, Florida.

Sally, often torn between attending to the needs of our children and going with me, still managed to fly with me to most of the meetings I was paid to attend. There were exceptions, however, so Fred Sage and I flew without Sally and Anita to a Hibbs meeting in Indianapolis during the weekend of the Indianapolis 500. Years before, Lisa and I had flown our Cessna 170 to a grass strip in Indianapolis where we met my parents; Dad was attending a meeting and had arranged for us to attend the time trials of the 500. This time Fred and I sat through the whole race, which was rather boring for the most part, but the excitement began after the race when we felt trapped and helpless as the huge crowd of spectators tunneled toward a narrow gate. This was as close as I had ever come to experiencing acute agoraphobia while being shoved and moved unwillingly by the mass of humanity surrounding me, a very uncomfortable feeling, accentuated as a "wedge" of young men forced their way through the throng in the opposite direction.

In early March 1984, Sally and I flew the now turbocharged Apache to Aspen for an orthopaedic seminar and had no difficulty maintaining altitude, unlike the situation we had experienced in the years before I had installed the turbocharger. This old airplane, built by Piper in 1957, had served us well for 16 years, during which time I had replaced the engines twice; now I was considering another airplane. Bill Hamsa who during our residency together in the 60s' kidded me mercilessly about flying around on bed sheets (the Cessna 170 I owned at the time had fabric covered wings), had finally started flying himself and had even built a Christen Eagle aerobatic airplane (also covered in bed sheets) and co-owned a Twin Comanche. Although our Apache was reliable and had great range (six and a half hours of fuel) it was slow, 135 knots (150 mph); and I had lusted (a part of that midlife crisis syndrome) for a Twin Comanche, also built by Piper, using the same engines (Lycoming 160 hp) injected and turbocharged, but cruising at 160 knots with about the same endurance. So when Bill and his partner, Bruce Rhode, announced they were willing to sell N6922T, leather seats and all, and especially when they worked a deal I have yet to understand that involved oil wells in Texas and delayed full payment until I could sell the Apache, I readily accepted their offer. A fine machine, the Twin Comanche, well-equipped, with six seats (the rear two suitable only for small people) became ours in March 1984. Since the Apache had some equipment I couldn't part with, I spent the next couple of months swapping equipment between the two airplanes. The Apache was finally sold to a doctor in Corinth, Mississippi in September 1984 and, since I had an instructor's certificate, I checked him out in the airplane as part of the purchase agreement.

In May 1984 we flew into Boston Logan Airport in our new airplane for another Hibbs Society meeting, during which time it rained mightily for three days. After the meeting, we departed Logan, where our small Comanche was sandwiched between 747s, 727s and DC 10s as we inched toward the active runway for a short flight to Martha's Vineyard, east of Nantucket, where we had stayed during our honeymoon.

After an enjoyable stay, we took off from Martha's Vineyard, climbing out over the blue waters of Long Island Sound on our way home. I switched to the plane's tip tanks, anticipating an expected long-distance flight; suddenly I felt a yaw to the right as the right engine coughed and sputtered. I quickly switched back to the inboard tanks and the engine roared back to life. No problem, except that we had to land in Atlantic City, a short distance away. As suspected there was water in the outboard tank; although I had drained the sump during preflight, I had not drained enough to get all the water that had settled to the bottom of the tank and had been ingested by the engine. Lesson learned: drain the sump into a cup, not just onto the ground, so that any remaining water can be easily seen.

Having entertained Mois Hache and Raphael Camasta, my Dominican orthopaedic friends, on our trip to Boston back in October 1977 for a Hand Society meeting, I was pleased when they reciprocated by asking Peter Carnesale and me to give presentations at the Dominican Orthopaedic Society meeting in Santo Domingo. So on July 4, 1984, with Kim (16 years old) and Lauren, Peter's daughter, we took off in the twin Comanche, over-nighting in Bimini in the Bahamas. With tip tanks and faster cruise speed, this would be the first long-distance flight in this new (to me) airplane. Since purchasing the plane I had noticed a barely audible "pop" when advancing full throttle on takeoff. All engine parameters were normal and there was certainly no problem at cruise. Later, I was to find a tiny restriction in one of the fuel injectors, enough to produce a too lean mixture in that cylinder, an easy fix. In spite of slight concern (only in my mind, since no one else was aware of the anomaly) we climbed out from Bimini to 3000 feet, following the gems of the Exumas, in a blue-green setting, southeast to Stella Maris on Long Island for refueling. From there we continued island hopping past the Turks and Caicos islands, British protectorates, not politically a part of the independent Bahamas, where we turned farther South toward Hispaniola, colonized by Columbus in 1492. Peter and our two girls were duly impressed by the beauty of the green mountains which rose steeply on the North coast of the island from the ocean depths of the Puerto Rican and Hispaniola trenches. Landing on the Las Americas, coral laced airport just east of Santo Domingo, we were greeted by Hache.

He drove us along the Avenue of the Americas that was lined with palm trees, and treated like us as VIPs, a factor which ameliorated any concern I might have over my upcoming presentation. The girls enjoyed swimming in the luxurious Occidental El

Embajador's pool while Peter and I enjoyed a rum drink in the shade. The meeting was a typical orthopaedic conference, with papers presenting experiences of the presenter in treating a particular problem, usually reinforcing what most of us already knew (this included my paper as well). Evenings under the stars, socializing with the conference attendees, provided a pleasant ending to this short Caribbean adventure.

On the flight back from the Dominican Republic, a five-hour marathon nonstop from Santo Domingo to Fort Pierce, Florida, I again considered the possibility of returning to Europe, this time in a plane better equipped (range and speed) for such a journey. The seed was planted. As I look back on those long flights, I wonder at my stamina at a younger age, and at my bladder capacity; now..........

Later in July, the annual FPA meeting was to be in Montréal, Canada. Sally couldn't go, so I asked my dad who was 86 at the time and still practicing dentistry. Dad had always been a supporter of my flying from those early days in 1954 when he and I had not told my mother that I had started taking flying lessons, a fact that got us both in trouble when she finally did learn of my flying activities. I found out later that he had even taken one or two lessons himself, but gave it up because he felt uncomfortable trying to keep that a secret from her. Since he had a young man practicing with him in the office on Brookhaven circle, it was easy for him to take the time off for the trip to Canada. We enjoyed being together, and he attended some of the conferences especially those with an aviation theme. One day he decided to walk around town only to discover that he was developing intermittent claudication in his legs secondary to peripheral vascular disease. He told me later he had been worried that he would be unable to get back to the hotel because he had to stop so many times to rest. I often wonder, if he had been on a Statin from his early 70s, as have I, would the peripheral vascular disease have manifested itself at age 86? We shall see.

When I look at my flight logbook from the vantage of 30 years, I almost experience a twinge of guilt in that there was such a short time between trips for me to be productive in my job as orthopaedic and hand surgeon. I suppose I was good at organizing my time and utilizing my days off and weekends for travel and for my blue-collar avocations. It certainly helped that the type of surgery I was doing necessitated little or no hospitalization, not to mention that my many partners covered the few patients remaining in the hospital and for emergencies.

Barely a month after returning from Montréal, Sally and I were off again for San Francisco and an American Society for Surgery of the Hand meeting. We landed at San Francisco International Airport, which, although it is a large air carrier airport, still welcomed our twin Comanche. After the meeting, taking off to the north, banking past the Golden Gate Bridge, I recalled the flight I had made in 1956 from Half Moon Bay airport in a rented Cessna 140. Back then the protected airspace around San Francisco airport was only five miles, and I was free to fly along the coast and circle the iconic Golden Gate Bridge with a sense of perfect freedom. In the 80s there were more restrictions, but I could still enjoy the view from our high perch as we turned to the southwest to land at Farmington, New Mexico. The final leg home was another marathon flight of almost six hours. Ah, the stamina of youth and the tolerance of Sally!

In September, Steve was to begin college at Columbia in New York City, so he and I loaded the Comanche with books, clothes, and paraphernalia and flew nonstop to Teterboro Airport in New Jersey (five hours). I rented a car, loaded it with what seemed like more than what we had stuffed into the airplane, drove across the George Washington Bridge, north of Central Park near Harlem, to Columbia University. I was happy to help Steve get to New York and get him settled in his dorm room, but I felt a little put upon carrying several loads of stuff up six flights of stairs. Surely some classmates could have helped!

The mid-1980s were busy years both in medicine and in aviation. In the early part of the 20th century, orthopaedics was a new specialty, and Willis Campbell was a pioneer in its establishment, developing the American Academy of Orthopaedic Surgeons, serving as its first president. In Memphis he was instrumental in opening the Crippled Children's Hospital to care for children with orthopaedic problems such as scoliosis, cerebral palsy, and congenital abnormalities. (After all, the root meaning of Ortho-Paedia is Straight Child). It was a residential facility and a school so that children who had to remain for weekly cast changes, physical therapy, and surgery would not have to be transported great distances from rural communities in Mississippi and Tennessee. With the advent of Medicaid and Social Security, hospitals such as this gradually became superfluous. However, the Campbell Clinic continued to support crippled children's programs in Mississippi and Tennessee. There were clinics in Clarksdale, Tupelo, Greenwood, and Oxford, and I was more than willing to fly to these clinics taking one or two residents and one or two assistants including Ms. Dorothy Tatum, who helped administer the Mississippi Crippled Children's Services and who seemed to enjoy the flights. A few of my passengers became interested enough to later become pilots themselves. Dr. Rhea Seddon, a resident at LeBonheur, not only became a pilot but a Space Shuttle astronaut. Although many of the flights were conducted under instrument flight rules, I didn't have to cancel more than a handful of trips because of weather or some maintenance problem.

During those years, I was also involved in flight instruction including that of Dr. Carl Welch who had purchased the Apache and required about 25 hours of instruction for insurance purposes. My logbook shows a total of 278.5 hours of flight time for 1984. The next year was nearly as busy, with flights to Las Vegas, Pensacola, where Jeff was to begin his Navy career as a Naval Flight Officer (NFO), Piqua, Ohio, for Hartzell propeller repair work, Aspen, Colorado for an (tax deductible) investment seminar, and St. Thomas in the Virgin Islands for a Southern Orthopaedic Association meeting. Of course, all the while I was fulfilling my obligation with the Air Force reserves by flying to Blytheville Air Force Base (Eaker) once a month. While there I learned that an orthopaedic Individual Mobilization Augmentee (IMA) was needed in July of 1985 at Elmendorf Air Force Base in Anchorage, Alaska, so I quickly signed up for that assignment, which would satisfy the requirement for my two weeks of active duty per year.

With Sally flying copilot and Cathy and Kim in the middle seats, we departed West Memphis under blue skies, crossed our nation's midsection to Broken Bow, Nebraska then farther northwest to Billings, Montana and into Canada to Edmonton, Alberta where we rested after covering nearly 2000 miles in one day. I was in familiar territory having come this way before and that familiarity engenders positive and negative feelings: positive because one knows the geography but negative because of a tendency to be overconfident. I was eager to show everyone in the plane the beautiful isolation of the Northwest Territories as we flew into Fort Nelson and on to Whitehorse where we took a cruise along the Yukon River. I had arranged this trip so that we had an extra week before my assignment at Elmendorf during which time we could tour southeast Alaska; from Whitehorse we flew over the Skagway pass that had witnessed the struggles of those intrepid souls seeking their fortune during the gold rush of the late 1800s, to Sitka where the onion topped chapels gave evidence of its Russian heritage. The next day we flew north along the inland waterway, where the steeply rising mountains seemed close enough to touch on each side as we threaded toward Skagway. There we found a pilot's dream: a motel by the runway.

The next morning dawned gray and drizzly, nothing new in this part of the world. I spoke with several local bush pilots who said they were used to flying in this kind of weather and that if we just hugged the right side of the fjord we should be able to get to Gustavus where we would begin our tour of Glacier Bay. At 500 feet we were under the overcast with granite close by our right-wing and the mist limiting the view forward. The view straight down, however, clearly defined the forbidding and cold water below. We were down to 200 feet as we rounded a bend in the passage; knowing from the chart than an island was somewhere close off our left wing, I was just about to begin a climb into the overcast for an escape route, when Sally shouted, "There it is!" The airport, just visible through the mist, was off our right wing; I pushed the gear lever down, full flaps down, turned, flared, and we were down—a sphincter tight, but greaser of an arrival.

Nestled in the primeval forest of Southeast Alaska, Glacier Bay National Park is the entry point into Glacier Bay by tour boat; from that platform we had close up views of breaching whales, grizzlies searching for salmon along the shore, and the dramatic calving of the McBride glacier, which is unfortunately disappearing at an alarming rate as a result of the recent, humanity induced, global climate change. We hiked nature trails with a Park Naturalist. Cathy, already a biologist, could have done the same job with more knowledge. She had attended college at Colorado State at Fort Collins and the University of Memphis, receiving a bachelor of science in biology from Tennessee Tech and a masters degree in biology from the University of Tennessee.

After relaxing for two days I was ready to begin my tour at Elmendorf Air Force Base. On another gray, overcast morning we urged the Comanche into the ragged bases of overhanging clouds, finally breaking out on top at 10,000 feet; we hugged the steep uninviting coastline continuing northwest, past Prince William Sound and landed at Anchorage International Airport. We would stay at a rather second-rate hotel, the Musk Inn; Sally remembers that as a low point of the trip, since during much of the time that I was working at the hospital, she would be stuck in the hotel with Cathy and Kim, although they did manage a few local excursions on their own.

The well-qualified orthopaedist, Marvin VanHall, who I was helping during my two-week tour, arranged the schedule so that I had weekends off and very few nights on call. For the most part, my orthopaedic practice at Elmendorf hospital was routine. I remember one case, however, in which I had to open a child's hip through a posterior approach in order to drain an infected hip. The child did well as far as the infection was concerned, although I learned later that he had dislocated that hip, a complication of the posterior approach.

Sally and I enjoyed our brief acquaintance with Marv and his wife, who was also a physician. For some years we kept up with them but after I retired from the reserves and quit going to the Society of Military Orthopaedic Surgeons meetings, we lost touch.

On one free weekend we took the Vista Dome train to Denali, where I could introduce the family to Mt. McKinley National Park and glimpse an edge of the big mountain through a fleeting opening in the obscuring clouds. Later we flew to Homer where Sally learned that she could eat Alaska King Crab without getting sick. On a quick tour to Seward, Alaska, we threaded mountain passes at low level with Sally doing most of the flying—another bush piloting adventure.

We departed Anchorage on July 26, flying back to Whitehorse and then to Fort St. John where we spent the night. The following day we returned to West Memphis in twelve and a half hours of flying. Looking back, I can't believe I did that, especially since the last three and a half hours was at night. It has been said, and I believe it is a truism, that there is no substitute for youth; I was only 52 years old at the time. Not only that, but two days later I took two residents to crippled children's clinics in Clarksdale, Tupelo, and Greenwood.

The rest of the year was filled with routine practice, more trips to crippled children's clinics, two small meetings in Minneapolis and the Homestead and in November a trip to the Cayman Islands, overflying Cuba and the Bay of Pigs to land at Georgetown on Grand Cayman. Although a legitimate CME course, Hyperbaric Medicine was oriented toward scuba diving, and it was on an impromptu night diving excursion that Sally and I were frightened as we came up to the black, lonesome surface and could find no boat. Several members of the group had talked the resort owner into arranging a night dive and, although there was some discussion about the increasing wind, the owner decided that we could go to the lee side of the island where we should have a calmer dive. Apparently, the boat operator was not as experienced as he should have been because when the first divers jumped off the rear of the boat they quickly came back up to tell the pilot that the anchor was not set while the boat wallowed in the choppy sea. He reassured everyone that he would set the anchor and that we should all get off the boat; everyone complied, and he dropped a rope with a rather dim flashlight tied to it over the side of the boat. Usually, a strobe is attached to the rope to help orient divers at night.

We were comfortable for the first 30 or 40 minutes of the dive because we were with the other divers who were congregating over the shallow reef off the coast on the west side of Grand Cayman, near the turtle farm. Sally has always been a good dive partner keeping track of how much air I used as well as her own. When I was down to about 40 minutes out of an hour of air, she signaled for us to go to the surface. We briefly looked around for the rope with the hanging flashlight, and, seeing nothing, we headed upward. As we broke the surface into the blackest of nights, we could see a few blinking lights on the shore but there was no boat. Another couple, who was even less experienced than we were, was several yards away and nearing panic. I had just obtained corrective lenses for my underwater mask and with reasonable acuity started scanning the horizon for any sign of a boat.

Meanwhile Sally seemed to be struggling and announced in her rather determined way, "I want out of here—now!!"

I told her to inflate her BC a little more, which helped calm her so that we could use our snorkels instead of using up all the air in our tanks, just in case we needed it later. We thought about trying to swim to the shore but about that time I noticed a blinking green, then a red light, far off in the distance. That must be a boat, but was it our boat? Whatever it was, it was our best hope, so we started kicking toward the floating lights taking us even farther from the shore. I didn't say anything to Sally but I was worried that we would really be in trouble if, all of a sudden, we could hear the motor starting and see the red and green lights receding in the distance.

DR. E. JEFF JUSTIS

It took forever, actually about thirty minutes, to get to the boat; we were the first to return and nearly two hours passed before the rest of the divers struggled back on board, having run out of air and using their snorkels on the surface. Several had tried to get up on shore but found that the waves were too high and the rocks too steep. Needless to say, many of the experienced divers were quite irate and felt that the free drink offered at the resort that evening was poor compensation for an excursion that could have ended in tragedy.

Later in the year Sally and I flew to Pensacola where we were privileged to watch Jeff get his wings as a Naval Flight Officer. He spent the next four years flying naval aircraft in California, returning to Pensacola in 1989 where he met his future wife, Liz Mulaney.

I returned to Pensacola in January 1986 for a mandatory Reserve Components National Security Course. It was during this course that we learned of the Challenger disaster that was to cast a pall over our meeting and the rest of the country. Events such as this, as well as other aviation accidents, cause most pilots to pause and reflect on their own flying activities. Was I considering every possibility in planning for a new adventure?

THE SECOND BIG ADVENTURE

It has been said that "A man's reach should exceed his grasp." But in this adventure, I reached too far.

In 1978 when Jeff and I flew the Apache east across the Atlantic and, after six weeks touring Europe with Sally, returned back across the "Big Pond," our elation was palpable; the flight had not been without problems, however, but in spite of equipment failures and our rather primitive equipment for navigation (actually an Automatic Direction Finding radio was our prime means of navigation) the flight was completed successfully; this added to my sense of confidence following our landing at Memphis International Airport in July 1978.

It was reasonable, eight years later, with a newer airplane, having better equipment and better range than that of the Apache, that I should consider a repeat of this flight to be a "piece of cake." Loran, a long-range navigational system, had become available to general aviation, and a friend agreed to lend me a portable high-frequency radio that he had used on a transatlantic flight, so two major sources of anxiety for such a flight were eliminated. Weeks before the flight, after having installed a wing-to-tail antenna, I made several calls on the high-frequency radio and considered the tests satisfactory. In the nose compartment of the Comanche, I carried an extra vacuum pump as well as other spare parts that might come in handy on such a long flight. In short, I did everything I could think of to ensure the successful completion of this second grand adventure. Using an abundance of caution, especially since Sally and Kim were passengers, I planned for overnight stays in Bangor, Maine, Goose Bay, Labrador, Narsarsuaq, Greenland, and Reykjavik, Iceland; so fatigue should not be a problem for a 53-year-old pilot. Unlike on the first transatlantic crossing, each leg was to be four hours so Sally felt she could tolerate sitting that long. Kim developed type I diabetes when she was thirteen, but it was well controlled and at eighteen she didn't let the disease interfere with her ambition or activities. She was looking forward to spending several weeks with her high school friend, Kate Hunt, in Ipswich, England.

As we flew over the ice cap of Greenland, starkly white and lonely, on our way to Iceland, I recalled the vague, uneasy feeling I had experienced in the Apache. Now, however, with blue skies overhead, the visibility unlimited, and both engines running smoothly, with Kim and Sally asleep, I had a sense of peace that comes when everything is proceeding as it should. Then I noticed it. Down in the lower part of the instrument panel, the vacuum gauge, a 2¼-inch diameter instrument, indicated failure of the vacuum pump on the right engine. Although vacuum is required to operate several of the flight instruments, the failure of one is not, in itself, a big problem because the other vacuum pump continues to provide sufficient flow of air for the air-driven instruments. Nevertheless, we had lost a backup system, and I looked into the possibility of having the spare vacuum pump installed while we spent the night at the Loftleider Hotel in Reykjavik. This didn't work out, however, and since the weather from Iceland to Scotland was good the following morning, we decided to press on, landing at Edinburgh after a smooth four and a half hour flight.

The airport at Edinburgh was not particularly general aviation friendly so, after a day of rest and touring we decided to continue on to Biggin Hill south of London. Biggin Hill, during World War

II, was RAF headquarters during the Battle of Britain but now is a very good general aviation airport. I was able to have the vacuum pump replaced before continuing our flight to Spain. While flying over the Bay of Biscay on the way to Madrid, another problem surfaced; at the time this seemed to be rather minor. The Omni/DME navigational system uses ground-based transmitters to provide navigational information, and it is usually not effective beyond about 100 miles, so it is used primarily for in-country navigation; the problem was intermittent and seemed to be related to flying in visible moisture such as rain or heavy cloud.

Louisa was living in Madrid at the time, working on her Masters degree in Spanish Civilization. She had graduated from Emory University in 1984 with a bachelors degree in Psychology and Spanish and, as part of her curriculum, had visited Spain. She loved the country, returned for her post graduate work and, as it turned out, also fell in love with her future husband, Miguel Garrido, originally from Uruguay. To earn extra money she performed locally and on cruise ships as a latin jazz singer along with Miguel who is a talented bass player. Louisa was our guide during a delightful driving tour of Spain, although the Seat car we rented had rather uncomfortable sling seats.

After we said goodbye to Louisa, we flew back over the Bay of Biscay to Biggin Hill where I had the equipment checked. The bench check was satisfactory, and the technician agreed that we had probably ingested some moisture into the unit. Since everything checked out, I no longer considered this a problem.

Our adventure was winding down. Kim stayed behind with her friend, Kate, in Ipswich as planned. I had satisfied my reserve obligation as an orthopaedic consultant at Torrejón Air Force Base in Madrid and at Lakenheath Air Force Base in England, and Sally had enjoyed shopping at the potteries at Stoke-on-Trent, so after a return visit to Castle Combe in the Cotswolds we were ready for the trek home.

There is no way to deny the inherent risk in flying across the Atlantic in a light general aviation aircraft, but as the pilot-in-command, it was

DR. E. JEFF JUSTIS

my job to mitigate the risk as much as possible. Decisions must be made during every phase of flight from takeoff to landing. The flight from Scotland to Iceland is relatively easy because one can overfly the Faroe Islands and radar is available in Iceland, but it had been a long day and the lady at our bed and breakfast kept us in conversation longer than I wished, since I had wanted a little more time to go over my flight plan to Greenland. Nevertheless, the morning of our final flight dawned gray and overcast, not unusual in this part of the world. At the airport, in the flight planning area, I perused the expected enroute winds and the expected weather in Narsarsuaq. All in all it shouldn't be a bad flight; another pilot was planning his flight in what at the time seemed a rather slipshod manner. One should be careful about casting stones, however. His was, after all, a successful flight.

During the flight planning process, I considered all possibilities and made decisions based on the information obtained from the weather briefer. Although a flight plan can and should change if subsequent circumstances demand it, once the decision to proceed is made, any lingering concern decreases.

During our climb through the overcast, I was once again thrilled as the last wisp of cloud gave way to the vast blue sky above. I relaxed, perhaps a bit too much. I was tracking outbound on a VOR radial to a DME fix using the equipment that had been checked at Biggin Hill. Just 25 nautical miles out of Reykjavik I noticed an intermittent "inoperative flag" on the VOR indicator. Damn! The same recurrent problem! Was this a link in an accident chain? I dismissed the thought and kept tracking the same course. The automatic direction finder was already picking up the beacon at Kulusuk, Greenland to the north of a direct track to Narsarsuaq, our destination, so at this point I wasn't too worried about the VOR/DME; after all, there were no VOR ground navigational facilities on Greenland anyway. A short time later, I reported the first fix to Icelandic control, estimating my position by dead reckoning. When the controller, who was referring to his radar, responded, I was somewhat surprised when he said, or at least I think he said, "Advise you are eight miles south of track."

I put an X mark on the chart in my lap at the position indicated by his statement and considered my options. If I were to continue with that much error at only 100 miles I could be off course by as much as 80 to 100 miles in the next 500. That much error to the south might put us dangerously close to the southern tip of Greenland. If we missed Greenland, we would run out of fuel in the north Atlantic somewhere between Greenland and Labrador. While I was mulling over my options, the Baron, which had preceded me out of Iceland, reported to Center that he was experiencing stronger cross winds from the north than expected. In retrospect I wish I had questioned the controller a bit more to get additional information before making a decision. However, based on the information I had at this point in the flight I made the decision to alter my course about 10° to the north. That decision, it turned out, was the second to last link in the accident chain.

Soon Greenland appeared ahead, beautiful in its stark and icy loneliness. I was receiving a strong signal on the Automatic Direction Finder from two stations, one to my right and one to my left, but I was unable to receive the station at my destination. Loran, which I had found so helpful while flying in Europe was unreliable in the northern latitudes, something I had not fully appreciated before this flight. So after climbing to 12,000 feet into clouds that covered the central part of Greenland, I expected momentarily to begin picking up the beacon at Narsarsuaq. While switching frequencies to and from the stations I had been receiving, suddenly the unit went blank, the indicator needle parked to the side, and I heard no coded signal. Now what? By dead reckoning, I estimated my position and continued flying for another 30 or 45 minutes at which point I made the decision to descend based on the elevation of the mountains and my estimated position. I reassured Sally and began a slow descent out of 12,000 feet. I had just forged the last link in the accident chain. The rest is history. The details of the flight and subsequent crash are documented in the book *Halfway Home*, Jeff Justis, *2001*, Wind Canyon Books.

DR. E. JEFF JUSTIS

After our crash, I wondered if the event would foreshadow a real change in my life, specifically as it relates to flying. Having been a pilot for 32 years, I had developed a confidence in my ability to handle most in-flight situations. Having been put to the test, however, I had failed, as evidenced by the forlorn bent twin Comanche resting in the middle of the Greenland Icecap.

In the hours I have flown since June 30, 1986, I find that relaxation is more difficult and that I am more attuned to details, thinking ahead, considering alternatives. In other words, the confidence of youth has been replaced by the caution of age. Nevertheless, by July 6, I was back in the air in the Aeronca champ and actively looking for another twin. Howard Entman, a friend who had owned the fixed-base operation at HI Air in Memphis, offered me the use of his airplane, a Beechcraft Duchess, so that I could resume flights to crippled children's clinics.

While I had been traveling, the board of directors of the Campbell Clinic had approved a bonus for the partners, certainly a welcome surprise considering the financial loss of the Comanche, which was uninsured for hull damage during the transatlantic flight.

My friend, Tom Garrott, who for several years had been a partner in the Aeronca agreed that he would partner with me in a twin-engine airplane; so with that encouragement and financial capability, I flew commercially to Visalia California to pick up our Piper Aztec, N6944A. I had had my fling with a fast, sexy airplane, now I was back to a more stable, should I say staid, comfortable machine that would continue to serve our traveling needs for many years

In the mid-80s I was fully involved with the Air Force reserves and each month fulfilled my obligation for active duty at Blytheville Air Force Base in northeastern Arkansas. Shortly after our Greenland misadventure I was surprised and honored at lunch in the Officers Club by a traditional standing ovation given to a pilot who had survived a crash; better that recognition than a memorial service.

THE EXPERIMENTAL EXPERIENCE

My fondest memories of childhood are the occasions I was given a model airplane kit and working with my hands to put something together.

Although retirement was still fourteen years away, I thought I would not be needing a traveling machine as much then, with fewer required (and paid) meetings to attend; so rationalizing the need for a smaller airplane that was less expensive to operate was easy. Jeff and I both had an interest in building an airplane. He was in the Navy, stationed in California and had been to Vans Aircraft in Oregon, flying in one of Van's first RV 6 kit built airplanes. An amateur built aircraft can be licensed in the experimental category as long as the builder fabricates at least fifty-one percent of the structure for educational purposes. I had investigated the Falco all wood airplane design, and when we flew to San Francisco in January 1987 for the combined Orthopaedic and Hand Society meetings, we checked out an award-winning Falco at Oxnard, California. Sally liked the plane and would have graciously accepted my decision to build one. However, with Jeff's recommendation and after discussing the many possible alternatives with other builders in Oshkosh, I finally decided on the all-metal RV 6 and ordered the first of many materials kits. I began constructing the empennage (horizontal and vertical stabilizers with elevators and rudder) in October of 1987.

Since high school, scanning Mechanics Illustrated or Popular Mechanics magazines for articles about building an airplane, I had dreamed of building one from scratch. The Aeronca champ project had been a learning experience for Jeff and me. Now I was on my own and enjoying every minute. My workshop in Memphis, having evolved over the years from a wooden crate shack, home to a gasoline powered jigsaw, my first power tool, to a 12 x 12 concrete block structure built in the 40s, and added to in the 50s, was completed, with an 18 x 24' section I constructed in 1968. Thus, I was able to do the necessary metal working, cutting, and riveting in the old section and continue my woodworking in the larger part. I don't remember a conflict between these two blue-collar occupations, since often, after gluing up a woodworking project, I could resume de-burring holes in an aluminum sheet and riveting parts of the stabilizer while the glue dried.

There is no question that I have had a full and fulfilling life, but I still have much to learn and much to do. However, referring to my logbook again, I become almost breathless at the pace of activity it reflects.

Sally and I began the first of many flights to Chicago, landing at Palwaukee airport, north of O'Hare, convenient to Northwestern University, where Kim was majoring in the theatrical arts. Kim had begun her acting career in high school at St. Marys and while performing at Memphis University School met her future husband, Philip Eikner, a professor, who was directing "A Sound of Music." She has continued her career with amateur and professional theater in Memphis and has received movie credits and best actress awards.

By 1988 the Aztec had accumulated so many flight hours that the engines were due for a major overhaul. Richard Starnes, an experienced engine mechanic, agreed to let me use his shop at the West Memphis airport for the work, which I was able to accomplish on my days off and on weekends. Several friends let me use their airplanes for necessary flights during the downtime of the Aztec. Overhauling an aircraft engine involves sending specific parts such as crankshaft, crankcase, rods, and so forth to specialty aircraft facilities for nondestructive testing and recertification. The mechanic's job is basically reassembly using the overhaul manual as a guide. However, in the late 80s cylinders were routinely re-honed to service specifications, new valve guides, seats, and valves installed and returned to service. Since then, the trend has changed and almost all shops now install new cylinders—and for good reason.

It was another proud day for me as I fired up my two freshly overhauled engines for the first test flight. Everything checked out as expected, and several days later I flew the plane with Kim to Destin where Sally had driven for a few weeks of vacation. Kim had been dating Phillip "Flip" Eikner since high school, so when I flew Flip to Destin a week later I was facilitating this continuing romance. "Flip's" mother was Margaret Ann Eikner who was one of Lisa's best friends at Southwestern and his Dad, Jim, was a director with National Public Radio. I left Kim with Sally and returned to work in Memphis. With Jeff, who was on leave from the navy and had flown commercially to Pensacola, in the pilot seat we climbed out of Destin to our cruise altitude of 8000 feet when suddenly we felt a vibration and a yaw to the right. The right engine surged several times but continued to run roughly. We reduced power on the engine, declared an emergency, and landed in Tuscaloosa, Alabama. The emergency was handled admirably by Jeff, and I was proud of him. It didn't take us long to find the trouble after removing the cowling from the right engine; the number six cylinder rocker cover was split open, and the rocker arms were swinging in the breeze.

To make a long story short, we rented an airplane to return to West Memphis after ordering an overhauled cylinder assembly to be delivered to Tuscaloosa. Several days later Jeff and I returned with the proper tools and replaced the cylinder, thinking that the problem was probably a fluke. However, on our return flight, within 50 miles of West Memphis, slight roughness, this time in the opposite engine, belied that thought as a streak of oil crept aft on the cowling. Richard and I began troubleshooting the problem, which we thought we had isolated to inadequate clearance at the valve-rocker interface; adjusting this, changing some pushrods and again test flying the airplane left us confident that we should have no further problem.

The Odyssey continued, however, when the next weekend I again flew to Destin with Flip who was riding right seat. As we began an instrument approach after one and a half hours, again, without warning a slight vibration called my attention to the right engine where I could see a telltale oil streak once again. Nothing to do but continue the approach and landing, knowing that after three in-flight semi-emergencies, something was obviously wrong. What could it be and, worse, what could I have done wrong? Subsequently, with help from Granite City Aviation in Illinois, the company that had furnished the replacement cylinder, we learned that we had installed the incorrect exhaust valve guides that had been obtained through our parts supplier (probably due to misreading the part number). After replacing the guides in all 12 cylinders, a job I had to hire a mechanic in Destin to complete, both the engines performed well for many years and nearly 1600 operating hours.

ROUTINE ADVENTURES

*Wikipedia: "An **adventure** is an exciting or unusual experience; it may also be a bold, usually risky undertaking, with an uncertain outcome."*

At the end of September 1988 we flew to San Francisco, having been invited to attend a NOAA conference and to watch a satellite launch at Vandenberg Air Force Base. After our crash, I had written the administrator of NOAA to express my appreciation for the US/USSR cooperative effort in utilizing the Sar-Sat system on weather satellites to locate and rescue downed airmen or seamen through their emergency locator beacons. One of the principals in the administration had arranged for a few people, including Sally and me, who had been rescued by virtue of the new system, to tell their stories at the meeting. He even started a "Sat-Cat" club, hoping to get a lot of publicity out of the drama of such rescues. However, probably because of privacy issues, the club faded away after one or two years.

A memorable true flying vacation in October 1989 brought Sally, Dick, and Laura Binger and me together for a bed and breakfast blitz of New England. Except for staying two nights on two occasions, we flew to a different location every day for 10 days, enjoying the beautiful New England fall weather and relaxing in luxury.

On a quieter note, Sally and I flew to Gatlinburg and hiked the six-mile trail to Mount LeConte Lodge where I found the notations in the guest registry for 1964, when Lisa and I had first climbed the mountain and then again in 1968 when we had taken Cathy, Jeff, and Louisa up the mountain with us. Sally was a great sport to come with me on my third climb, catching my arm as I slipped on a narrow trail dropping off precipitously. Toward the end of that trek, however, she was like a horse heading home, not stopping for anything until she could prop her feet up at the lodge.

By the 90s my flirting with a midlife crisis was winding down, and I had decided that leaving the clinic was not something I should consider. Still, with retirement looming, we began to think about where we might want to live. I thought briefly about remodeling 4209 Walnut Grove or building another house on the site, but the lot was narrow, the house old, and it would've been difficult to come up with a design to satisfy both of us, especially since Sally and I had such differing ways of thinking when it came to visualization and construction.

Around the same time, a patient of mine, in conversation in the office, mentioned that she raised German shepherds. Ever since Shadow's death in 1968 I had not had a personal relationship with a dog, although many had passed through our household. One, in particular, Princess, a poodle mix, had stolen Sally's heart and was really her dog. She was broken hearted when Princess was killed by a car. Sally and I visited the kennel, and Sally helped me decide which one of the litter of brown and black puppies would suit us. Days later I drove home with Ebony's head resting in my lap and realized what I had been missing. The love of a dog may fill the few empty spaces that may remain in one's heart. Even when, a few weeks later, I discovered by accident that Ebony had a subluxing left hip, I did not consider returning her to the kennel. I had found an "Ortolani's clunk" which, in children, is diagnostic of congenital dislocation of the hip. The veterinarian was interested in this as an aid to early diagnosis for a problem that is endemic in the shepherd breed.

For years, when we traveled, Sally might see an old house in San Francisco or Monterey or Santa Fe, even as far north as Maine or Vermont and say, "That old house needs me—We could fix that up—You could have a shop in the back." We might dream for a while, before reality and life intruded. One such place was in Springfield, Vermont, a salt box home on a lot adjacent to the Springfield airport. An idyllic town, Grafton, in southern Vermont also piqued our interest with a colonial-era, two-story home, attached carriage house, and history of protecting runaway slaves before the Civil War. We made several short trips to the area, but because of the obvious impracticality of moving so far away (my parents were still alive at 92 and 85) we knew we would have to look closer to home.

After a marathon flight to Napa Valley, Orcas Island, and Seattle to visit Louisa and, her husband, Miguel, we set out looking for land on which to build in Tennessee. We made an offer on a small farm near Franklin that, had it been accepted, would have required full-time work. Instead, we ended up buying 50 acres that was part of a foreclosure on Donna Fargo's holdings. With Ebony I walked the perimeter of the property, dreaming of where I might build a workshop. Sally realized that, were we to build a house, we would have to rent or buy a place nearby so that we could supervise the project. Again, the distance from Memphis, where many responsibilities remained, was a factor in decreasing enthusiasm for that project. Besides, we had invested with Tom Garrott in a villa at Mountain Air, a fly-in community near Burnsville and Asheville in North Carolina, a wonderful retrcat for long weekends but not so practical for long stays especially in the winter. Nevertheless, dreaming was fun, and life remained full of adventures. Later we sold that property at a profit and used that money to build our Oxford home.

RETURN TO GERMANY

One can never return home again, because home is never the same as it seems in our memories.

Having lived three years in Wiesbaden, Germany, I considered it my hometown, with the intimate familiarity one gains in day-to-day living. In 1978, on that first return visit, the changes in the town and streets caused much confusion, but by April 1990 when Sally and I flew commercially into Frankfurt I felt more like a tourist than a "native." I had been invited to an Air Force conference in Wiesbaden by a fellow Air Force orthopedist, Craig Hatton, who I met through the Society of Military Orthopaedic Surgeons. We rented a car in Frankfurt and spent a few days in Ausmanhausen and Rotenberg, Germany before returning to Wiesbaden for the conference.

Later in the year, during Desert Shield, I was on orders for a two-week active duty tour at my old USAF Hospital in Wiesbaden at which Craig was the Chief of Orthopaedics.

The hospital at Wiesbaden in which I had spent three busy years, 1964 to 1967, was changing. Remodeling plans had begun but were abruptly canceled when asbestos was found in locations that would make further rehabilitation uneconomical. Radiology services were housed in a trailer adjacent to the hospital, and it was thought that the hospital would soon be returned to the Germans. The hospital had been built primarily to treat members of the Luftwaffe; there was even an underground tunnel, now walled off, that led to the Bahnhof. Craig was quite generous to me as a visiting reserve orthopedist. Although I did take call at night on several occasions, I had the weekends free and was able to show Sally many of the places that Lisa and I had enjoyed twenty-six years earlier. While I was working, Sally was able to explore Wiesbaden on her own. She fell in love with the many small restaurants and developed quite a taste for Wiener Schnitzel.

On our first weekend off, Sally and I flew into Berlin shortly after the wall had been torn down, Nov 9, 1989; Sally crawled over the rubble to hand pick several graffiti adorned pieces from a portion that was still standing. What a change I saw in this city since my first visit in the 60s during which, although I had a civilian passport (as opposed to an official military passport) and Lisa and I were on a tour bus, we experienced a twinge of fear as an East German guard waved us through Checkpoint Charlie. There had been stories of military people in civilian clothes having been accused of spying by the East Germans. Now, after reunification, Checkpoint Charlie and part of the wall were memorials to those who had died in an attempt to gain freedom. The drab facade of the buildings had been ameliorated by the smiles of people who could freely walk through the Brandenburg gate and once again enjoy life in West Berlin.

Later, at the beginning of Desert Storm, the first Gulf War, I was primed to be called for active duty in the desert. I remember being in a hotel in Florida on January 17, 1991 watching the bombing of Baghdad on television. I had given the hotel phone numbers to contacts who would call if I were to receive orders. None came, but I later learned that I was highly desired by the then Tactical Air Command that was deployed to Kuwait and Saudi Arabia; SAC (Strategic Air Command) to which I was attached at Blytheville would not release me, however, so my war experience was limited to the previous two-week active duty tour in Wiesbaden, Germany (someone had to do it).

ONE MORE FLIGHT IN EUROPE

Flying has given us a grand view of the world and, when given the chance, we yearn for that perspective once more.

In the spring of 1992, the International Society for Surgery of the Hand was meeting in Paris, France. Our daughter, Kim, who lived nearby, agreed to check on our house and care for Ebony, so reservations and plans were made. I had asked my friend, Ulrich Lanz, who practiced hand surgery in Würzburg, Germany, to help me obtain a European pilot's license so that I could rent an airplane to fly around France before the meeting. Obtaining the license by reciprocity was no problem but renting would be problematic and quite expensive. Instead, Uli generously offered us the use of his airplane (a Piper Cherokee 180). We flew commercially to Geneva, rented a car for the drive up to Neustadt where Uli kept his plane. After a check out and brief flight to Würzburg, Sally and I took off in D-EJSB, followed the Rhine south, crossed into Switzerland and landed at Geneva to clear customs. This was long before the Eurozone was established and eliminated the need to clear customs flying within the European Union.

What a grand tour we had, flying between peaks of the Swiss and French Alps to Aix-les-Bains down to the Mediterranean and Aix en Provence where we drove through the majestic southern

French countryside to Le Beau, St. Remi, and other iconic villages. Then back in the plane we flew to Limoges to refuel and on to Dinard in Britanny. We drove to the island monastery of Mont St. Michel where Sally enjoyed a solitary stroll up to the cathedral as the sun added its gold to the impressive spire. Leaving Britanny we flew low, past Mont St. Michel, over the Normandy beachheads, Pointe du Hoc, site of the brave Ranger assault and, without a single shot being fired at us in anger, to Caen. Each stop found us relaxing in a villa, castle, or mansion bed and breakfast; a nice way to visit France.

Monet's Giverny was to be our final tour. The old US Air Force Base at Evreux was the closest airport now operated by the French government. We circled several times trying to communicate with the tower. We finally learned that the larger paved airport was closed, but the Aero club grass runway located on the south end of the paved area was open. After landing we were welcomed by several local French pilots who helped us with transportation and reservations. We were even taken to the front of the line for our tour of Monet's Gardens.

We ended our tour at a nice general aviation airport to the southwest of Paris, Tussus-le-Noble, where we refueled and readied the plane for Uli who was to fly the plane back to Würzburg after the meeting. In Paris we spent a delightful evening with Francois and Isabel Iselon at their home and after the meeting flew commercially to Budapest for our first visit to Hungary since the country became free of Russian control.

FAMILY AFFAIRS

The problem with a memoir is that what seems important to the writer may seem trivial to others---and vice versa.

Back home, after traveling, I was always ready to get back in the workshop. I am fortunate that I have the ability to pick back up on a project left unfinished as if it were just the next day even though weeks or months may have passed. That helps explain why most of my major period furniture projects usually require nine months to a year to complete. During this time I had begun doing most of my surgery at the Baptist Rehabilitation Hospital on Exeter in Germantown where we had a satellite office next door. Except for the fact that I was still taking call for emergencies, this was the most gratifying time in my practice of medicine. I was concentrating on hand surgery, I could walk to surgery, and the office was somewhat informal. On occasion, I even took Ebony where she remained content in my private office, except for the time when she slipped out to nose into a startled patient's room.

In 1990 Louisa and I flew to Florida to pick up Miguel who had flown from Uruguay commercially. After graduate school, Lou had returned to Memphis, and spent many days filling out forms to facilitate Miguel's entrance into the States. They were married in our living room on May 13, 1990, the second marriage to be held at

4209 Walnut Grove Road, the first having been for Doris and Jerry Boone in 1971.

A little more than a year later, on July 26, 1991, Kim and Flip Eikner had a traditional wedding at Holy Communion Episcopal Church with a standard reception at the church and a more informal get-together at our home for family and close friends. Then, five months later, on December 28, 1991, Jeff and Liz Mulaney were married in our living room, the last such union to be held in that room in a house that can now be seen only in our memories.

For years, as a staff member of the Campbell Clinic, I had been pushing for a modified incentive program. My goal was to be able to structure the on-call schedule so that those who desired to earn more by extra work could do so, and those who (like me) preferred more time off, would earn less. However, the practice was rapidly growing, and it became obvious that less time would have to be spent with patients in order to maintain the same level of income. For me, some of the enjoyment of practicing medicine involved establishing rapport with patients, having a conversation with them, and finding common interests. No one else was interested in such an incentive program, and since I was approaching sixty, I pushed for an early retirement that would allow a staff member to quit doing surgery but continue to work in the office at a reduced salary. I was grateful that the group accepted my idea, and in 1993 I voluntarily quit doing surgery and returned to the old clinic building at 869 Madison Avenue for an office practice that would begin with two full days a week. I couldn't have asked for a better arrangement because of the free time this allowed me (five days a week). In addition to this time, I continued to have vacation and meeting time; in spite of all this freedom, I'm happy to say that I more than earned my keep in bringing new patients to the clinic.

I had been an Anglophile since my first visit in 1951, and Sally rapidly joined with me in admiring the English countryside and quaint villages after her first tour in 1978, so in February 1993, we flew commercially to Gatwick, rented a car and began another bed and breakfast blitz of England. We visited a woodworker who had a teaching shop in Southwest England. The apprentice workmen welcomed us and invited us to share tea, that is until the master of the shop returned, quickly *suggesting* that they return to work, and gave us a rather perfunctory tour. He was all business.

On September 2, 1993, Lisa Ann Justis, Jeff and Liz's daughter, the first grandchild on the Justis side of the family was born. The day of her birth we did not have to admire her through glass as had I with my first born. Rather we walked right into Liz's room and could each hold the dark haired infant new to this world. Jeff, the proud father, was then working in Memphis so we got to enjoy having her with us and on occasion overnight until they moved to Florida for a few years.

Later that year, Cathy, who was living in Seattle at the time, convinced me that I should accompany her on a father-daughter adventure tour to the Galapagos Islands. Since I had always been enamored of Charles Darwin and his voyage of discovery in the 19th century, I did not require much convincing and met Cathy in Ecuador for a two-day tour of Quito. After a short flight into the Galapagos, we spent a week of cruising island to island in a small boat, snorkeling with seals, and observing the wildlife adapted to their unique island habitat. Cathy and I had always been like minded when it came to protecting the environment and endangered species, and this trip reinforced our common interests.

How lucky can you get? In late 1993, Sally and I were at a St. Jude's fundraising event when we heard our name called. We had won a paid vacation to Palm Island in the eastern Caribbean. We were even reimbursed for our fuel. So in January 1994, we flew to Puerto Plata in the Dominican Republic, to St. Croix, St. Vincent, and on to Union Island where we were ferried by boat to the laid-back Palm Island resort.

We met an interesting couple there, Jeoffrey and Trish Wragg from Newmarket, England. He was a horse trainer and stabled racehorses worth several million-dollars. Several years later we had the opportunity to visit them when we flew into Lakenheath on an Air Force space-available flight.

I was back in the office in February 1994 when I received a call from my airplane partner, Tom Garrott.

"Jeff, our airplane has been stolen!"

"Stolen!!" I thought he had to be kidding.

He went on to explain that someone had apparently taken the plane in broad daylight, taxiing, receiving take-off clearance, and disappearing to the east from Venice, Florida where Tom had been vacationing. Was this to be another total loss? Duly reporting the event to the Stolen Aircraft Registry, we waited. I began to seriously look for a replacement; then, about two weeks later, I received a call from a customs agent in New Jersey. They had found a plane parked between two hangars at a small airport in Allaire, New Jersey. The tan stripe on our plane had been painted red, and the identification number had been changed. Apparently, the felon painter had made a mistake, however, by changing the number on the right side from N6944A to N8944A and on the left side to N6844A. The Drug Enforcement Agency (DEA) and Customs Border Protection (CBP) finally traced the plane to us through the serial number data plate.

After flying commercially to Newark and driving a one-way rental to Allaire, a small community near the Atlantic Coast, I met with the insurance adjuster, representatives of the DEA and CBP. While mechanics at the local fixed-base operation cleaned the added lacquer paint from the Aztec, I was escorted to the local police station for an interview, having brought my logbook at the request of the DEA. Apparently, my responses satisfied the seemingly friendly group of investigators sitting across from me in the interview room for not only did they release the airplane to me but they also bought my lunch.

Reconstructing a probable scenario for this incident, the DEA assumed that after flying to a small airport in Florida for the added paint, the pilots (probably well qualified, if not morally lax) flew to Columbia for their contraband, thence up the East

Coast at low level, turning inland to land at Allaire before daylight, where they rendezvoused with their accomplices hidden between two rows of hangers. All the seats had been removed except for the pilot and copilot seats; the oxygen bottle and radar also had been removed to make room for extra fuel tanks, but navigational equipment remained intact. My insurance covered most of the loss, which amounted to over $30,000. On the way home I discovered that, although the felons had disconnected the hour meter, I was able to retrieve flight time from another timer: 16 hours—enough to go to Columbia and back.

Because it was late in the day, I landed in Columbus, Ohio where Sally's brother, JD Blackfoot (Ben VanDervort), lived. JD often talked about the importance of family but, unfortunately, as later events would testify that commitment was somewhat shallow.

By mid-1994, Jeff had taken another job near Pensacola, and it was obvious that the Aeronca Champion was not being utilized enough by either Jeff or me to justify keeping it. Gratefully, the airplane found a good home with a retired airline captain who lived in a fly-in community near Atlanta. Although the champ had not been a practical traveling machine for Jeff to fly to or from Pensacola, a single Comanche, for sale at West Memphis airport, would certainly fill this requirement. Jeff and I bought the 260 HP retractable gear, low wing airplane, N6538P, which we both were able to fly for several years until Jeff and Liz moved back to Memphis permanently. In fact, Sally and I flew it to Delaware, when the Aztec was being flown by Tom, in order to connect with a space available flight to Europe, courtesy of the USAF, another postretirement perk.

Cathy was living in Seattle where much of her time was spent as an official fisheries observer for our State Department. She was on board Russian fishing trawlers in the Bering Sea for as long as three months since they were fishing within the 200 mile limit. She has many interesting stories to tell of her adventures.

Louisa and Miguel also were in Seattle where Miguel performed Latin jazz on the bass and Louisa operated her own travel agency.

Kim and Flip lived in Memphis where Flip continued teaching at Memphis University School and Kim continue to perform in local amateur and professional theater.

Steve had always been a high achiever academically and graduated with a bachelor in science in Physics from Columbia University in New York in 1995 and was awarded a five-year fellowship in Theoretical Physics. After one semester, he realized he would not be happy in that field and worked at various jobs in New York before returning to Memphis. Steve then decided on pursuing a medical career, was accepted at East Tennessee State University Medical School and, as expected, he excelled academically, graduating with honors in 1999. He and his professor invited me as guest lecturer for his anatomy class, with emphasis on clinical correlation of anatomy with hand problems.

Steve and I had a rather rocky relationship in his teens, if truth be known, because we were competitors for his mother's affection. At any rate, I could not gain his trust. In many ways it was difficult for him to be patient with me and my methodical ways and, similarly, it was difficult for me to be patient with him and his quick ways; before I would even have a chance to completely organize my thoughts and articulate an idea, he would have already guessed what I was going to say. Despite our differences we did build a Heathkit computer together during his teen years. Steve mastered it immediately, whereas I am still trying to figure it out. As he matured we have found many common interests in science and philosophy.

In a family practice postgraduate program, Steve became a compassionate and thorough physician in spite of the emotional price he was paying for his perceived failure to meet his own expectations. His wife, Cathy who he had married in 1996 expressed concern that Steve was reluctant to send in his application for a Tennessee medical license. While on the telephone, I tried to reassure him that such feelings are normal in new physicians; one can only do his best in caring for patients, but realistically, one cannot cure or save everyone. I wish I had pushed harder to understand his concerns. Steve and Cathy had no children together and divorced several years later. Because of his desire to improve patient care and because of his technical expertise Steve is now pursuing a PhD degree in biomedical engineering with an emphasis on Artificial Intelligence and its application in medical diagnosis.

※

"Mame," Sally's mother, at 85, had been failing somewhat for several years, but by early 1995 the downhill slide accelerated. Sally stayed in Columbus several months until March when Elizabeth VanDervort died at home with her three children by her side. Often one person seems to be the glue that holds a family together, and so it was with "Mame." Sally and her sister, Sue, remain close, but JD has not spoken to Sally since.

Shortly after, my mother's sister, who was always "Sissy" to me, Donna McKay Kimberly, died at age 99. Then my first cousin, Frank McKay, succumbed to esophageal carcinoma in September 1996.

Tragedy continued when Neil Ross, my sister-in-law's husband, disappeared, later to be found in a wooded area, having been murdered by a field hand on his farm. Then, his daughter Lisa Dahn Ross died after a diagnosis of ovarian cancer, the same disease that claimed my wife, Lisa, in 1970. Not much later Pam VanDervort, Sally's sister-in-law, died of colon cancer. Compounding her tragedy, Ann Ross's second daughter, Evelyn, my niece, died of uterine cancer within two years.

All of this inevitable loss around us, although painful, does not stop a new day from dawning. Life's continuum triumphs. Amidst all the tragedy, our second Justis grandchild, Katie Lee Justis, was born on October 17, 1996. Jeff and Liz had returned to Memphis so we got to hold our second Justis grandchild within hours of her birth.

After a few false starts trying to find the ideal retirement location, Sally and I settled upon a rather progressive island in a rabidly conservative state, Oxford, Mississippi. The choice of our good friends, Doris and Jerry Boone, to retire there in 1995 was instrumental in our decision to buy land just outside the city in 1997.

In thinking back on my developing philosophy, I've always been a bit progressive, early on eschewing organized religion and the endemic racial prejudice in my family and in the south. But for years I considered myself a Republican because of its appeal to individualism and individual responsibility, even if I ignored the rather regressive party platform. Eventually, however, my interest in the environment, evidence for human-induced ozone depletion and climate change and the scientific method, convinced me that I no longer had anything in common with the GOP. Sally, I learned later in our marriage had always been a Democrat except for the aberrant time in which Goldwater swayed too many with his rhetoric.

So it was that Oxford, Mississippi would become our retirement community and in which we have developed many friendships with people of similar philosophy.

By this time I had already stopped doing surgery and had started a limited office practice; this allowed much more free time. Before starting the Oxford project in earnest I restored the Horseshoe cottage by adding a bedroom wing and a new kitchen and den. A local carpenter, Jimmy Cox, and I did the work. I can remember laying flooring in the new kitchen area together until late in the evening; we were both dragging but as always, I was happiest when building or fixing something. I usually spent two to three days at a time working at Horseshoe, and before my Dad became increasingly infirm in the last two years of his life, he and I had enjoyed working together. He especially enjoyed cutting the grass with the Ford tractor until his vision became so poor that he ran over the weed-eater.

The years, 1997 and 1998 were bad for Dad, and hospice care became necessary. He was 99 years old. Weeks before his death, the third Justis grandchild, Sara Elizabeth, was born July 11, 1998, and he was able to hold her in his arms. When he held her, he brightened, smiled, and gently kissed her on the forehead. Several days later I stopped by late in the afternoon after returning from working at Horseshoe. Dad was having difficulty breathing, and the head of his bed had been raised. I sat down beside him, holding his hand; his breathing became more labored; I moved my fingers to feel his pulse which was becoming thready, weaker and weaker, and with a final quick gasp my Dad died. I lowered the bed, closed his eyes as my Mom sobbed gently. They had shared sixty-seven years together. During Dad's decline I had come to terms emotionally with the inevitability of this last day. Nevertheless, when the memories of a lifetime faded into finality, I realized with deep sorrow that I had lost the source of those treasured memories.

My Dad and I had always had a special relationship. In spite of his initial disappointment in my not having chosen dentistry as a profession, he seemed quite proud of my accomplishments in medicine, and he was an early supporter of my flying, much to the chagrin of my mother. Because of his mentorship during my childhood, I emulated his can-do and do-it-yourself attitude, which contributed to my lifelong love of science, mechanics, and construction. I still miss him.

Sara Elizabeth brightened us during this time, helping my mom cope with her loss. Saddled with two men in her family, my mother doted on the girls, especially this youngest addition.

The fourth Justis grandchild, a boy, was born on April 28, 1999. Justis Jefferson Brooks Eikner, was born and given a name that should compensate for his mother Kim's lack of a middle name. Kim and Flip had been trying to have a child for at least six years and had suffered through several miscarriages so this success was celebrated by all. Just how this child of mine can now be a mother herself is a mystery, since she was only born yesterday -- in another life.

By this time we were committed to eventually living in Oxford, and Sally had traded her last rental house in Memphis for a comparable place near the University of Mississippi in Oxford and within walking distance of the University Oxford Airport. Tom Garrott and I had completed a trade in which I bought back his share in the Aztec and he bought back our part of Mountain Air. We loved the times we had spent in the mountaintop villa overlooking the airstrip at this unique fly-in community in the Appalachians, but increasing expenses and limited use prompted the decision to change. In addition, I was planning to move the airplane to a hangar in Oxford, so Tom would not have had convenient access to the plane. After working all day in the office on Tuesdays in the spring and summer of 2000, I drove the sixty miles to Oxford helping John Huerta build my 50 x 60' hangar, large enough to house the Aztec and eventually the RV 6 I had been building since 1987. John, a talented metal building and concrete contractor, and I worked well together. I had finished the Horseshoe project and was ready for another construction job. I rented a ditch digger to bring a power cable and water line to the hangar and did much of the wiring.

Meanwhile, Sally and I continued to work on plans for our house. I had tried several approaches, including a computer program (unsuccessfully), manually drawing plans to scale, but being frustrated by changes Sally suggested that required starting the drawing over again. Finally, with the help of Macel Juergans, our ideas were finalized and I built a model to better visualize the structure. At Jeff's suggestion I investigated and eventually became convinced that steel frame construction would offer many advantages, not the least of which was that we would not have to contaminate the ground and possibly our water supply with poisons to control termites.

Although obviously busy with my few days in the office, work on the hangar and beginning partial clearing of our land at Longmeadow, there was still time for flying to San Francisco for a meeting of the American Academy of Orthopaedic Surgeons and a return to Woodberry Forest for my 50th high school reunion that, once again, reinforced memories of my intellectual journey that continues to this day.

While we were in Virginia, we learned that Ebony had developed symptoms that later proved to be the result of a uterine cancer; after several months she died quietly at home at the age of twelve. Three days after her death I returned to Oxford to work on the hangar. When I went to our College Hill home for lunch, a little black poodle greeted me at the door, jumping up on my leg and shortly capturing my heart. On her way to Oxford on highway 78, Sally had seen the panicked puppy running along the highway and rescued her. She could find no identification and subsequently was unable to find anyone who might claim Holly as she was named (she was found near the Holly Springs exit), so we kept her.

With Holly in tow, we found ourselves in Wickenburg, Arizona, near Phoenix, on September 11, 2001. We experienced an emotional roller coaster while dealing with the events in New York, Pennsylvania, and Washington. Initially, US airspace was closed to all aircraft, but by Saturday, September 15, general aviation flights on instrument flight plans were allowed, and we were able to return home through eerily quiet skies.

On October 27, 2001, I was again in Oxford working on the hangar when Sally called to tell me that my mother who was 97 had died. This was not unexpected because she had been declining for several months. She had been so burdened first by her sister's long illness then by my dad's death in 1998. With a sad heart, I returned to Memphis. I sat by her bedside and held her hand one last time as she lay silent and still and peaceful at last.

A MOTHER'S HAND

*Tiny fingers are cradled
In a Mother's warm, protective palm—
Until Life demands independence
And the child reluctantly pulls away.*

*Always, though, a Mother's hand
Reaches through the years to comfort.*

*And now, no longer a child's hand
But a hand, aging in itself,
Holds a Mother's hand
And, seeking comfort,
Tries to comfort
Until Death demands independence
And a Mother's hand
Falls gently away.*

Jeff Justis
2001

THE NEXT TO THE LAST CHAPTER

Memoir is a recounting of one's life as it is remembered and felt through the fog of time.

As we come closer and closer to the present, we begin to recite events that have not been clothed in the significance that the passage of time gives to memory. So my plan is to end this narrative (but not this life) at a milestone.

With our house plans finalized, at least to the extent possible, considering that we had no architect (Macel is a draftsperson, albeit an excellent designer), they were given to the steel frame company in Cullman, Alabama, and fabrication of wall sections with windows and door cutouts, roof sections, and floor joists was soon underway—in essence, a very large kit for erection on-site was being assembled.

Of course, we still lived in Memphis where I continued work in the shop, building a wooden plenum for the heating and air-conditioning unit that would be installed in my new hangar. In addition, Kent and Jean Peterson had asked me to build an 18th century Knife Box for their dining room; I began this project in Memphis, completing theirs in my old shop but leaving two more partially finished, the very last project for this workshop that had always been so much a part of my life.

During my frequent trips to Oxford I continued clearing the hill for our new home using "Junior" with his educated horse. After felling a tree, accurately placing it between others, he attached a chain, signaled his horse who promptly dragged the log down the hill to the waiting truck. This was so much better than using a bulldozer to clear an area in that one can be more selective, leaving the more desirable trees. This is not to say that I did not enjoy using John's bulldozer to clear a driveway and move dirt into low areas. Oh, the power of trampling anything in the way as I manipulated the controls of this machine!

During the very hot summer of 2002, John, his crew, and I worked to lay footings (extra wide and deep because of the sandy soil) and build forms for our well-engineered foundation (12-inch reinforced concrete walls). As part of the process, I rubberized the outside of the walls, used a draining mat and perforated PVC piping to carry any water that might reach the foundation away to lower parts of the property. I enjoyed this work even though I almost had a heatstroke late one afternoon; Sally found me half conscious in the truck. Ebony usually had the luxury of sleeping in the air-conditioned truck while I worked, so there was no problem for her.

I was never at a loss for something to do, even when the weather interfered with outdoor work because by this time I had moved the RV parts to the new hangar. The wings, tail assembly, and the engine had been completed in Memphis; the fuselage construction required a wooden jig, built in the back of the hangar, to keep the formers aligned so that the longerons and skin could be attached accurately. Before retirement, whenever I was not working in Memphis at the clinic (one or two days a week) or at our home site, I could be found at the airport. Work was, and is, my recreation.

In September 2002, the first shipment of steel arrived at our building site. When Javier, the construction supervisor, tried to hoist a bundle of rafters with a fork lift, the flexible steel bent. I lost my composure, cussed, and felt betrayed by the contractor who was rarely on the job. He was from Memphis, had other jobs and, although he initially came down once a week, by the time the house was nearly finished I would not see him for a month or more. I canceled his contract and took over contracting with subs myself for the last year or so of construction.

Since I was living in the house on College Hill road most of the time following my full retirement from the Campbell Clinic in March 2001, I was able to be on site every day that the building crew was working. I was amazed to find how many mistakes would have been made had I not been there. Sally came down from Memphis on occasion and spotted a problem I had missed.

"Aren't those holes supposed to be lined up?" She said pointing to the steel floor joists that were being placed across the basement walls of my workshop which was an integral part of the house.

The joists had multiple holes designed to lighten the structure and provide channels for plumbing, wiring and ducting. If the holes were offset from each other it would be impossible to have straight runs of the utilities. I'm sure that if we had not caught this problem early even more problems would have developed later.

One day, after 12 inch I-beams had been installed over the main basement, joist hangers had to be welded in place. The problem was that the workman who knew how to weld was not available. Since I had learned to weld while restoring the Aeronca Champ with Jeff several years before, I proceeded to crawl out onto the I-beams to weld each of the hangers in place. I laughingly tell people that I was 40 years old (actually 69) when I started the house building project. Now look at me! The work was hard but gratifying. As soon we had roofing on the house, I was able to bring many of my power tools from Memphis. Thus, I was able to build the arches in our living room and dining room area and to prepare the kitchen for hanging cabinets. With Jeff's help, I was able to move all of my shop equipment and all of the furniture that I had built over the years in my trailers or U-Haul. We only had to hire professional movers to bring the piano and a large green hutch that Sally had purchased and that could not be disassembled.

There are advantages and disadvantages in contracting one's own home construction. The primary advantage is that I could be on site whenever the subs were working. When we were installing windows, for example, I cautioned my workers to be sure to place waterproofing membrane over the flanges before laying the brick. I walked around the house to check on something else and when I came back they had not done what I wanted so I made them take some of the brick off to properly seal the windows. They didn't forget again. I held back some money from the drywall contractor even though he promised to return the following week to finish the job and was hoping I would pay him the full amount. He never returned, and I ended up using the money I had held back to hire another drywall man to finish and correct some problems. The disadvantage of self contracting is that the subs realize that I will have just the one job, whereas a professional contractor may use them for many jobs. Often I would wait weeks for a subcontractor to return.

Except for the drywall, I did most of the finish work in my workshop. I had the electrician bring a primary line over to the third circuit breaker box and from there I did all of the wiring in the shop. I installed the flooring, narrow tongue and groove maple salvaged from a LeMoyne Owen college basketball court, and I engineered the dust control system.

It seems that building a house is a never-ending process and when we move in we begin considering changes to correct unanticipated problems...and so it continues.

In 2003 another first cousin, Edwyll Tindall died at her home in Stuttgart, Arkansas. She had been a teenager when I was in grade school and, mischievous as I was, I delighted in teasing her, especially when she was recovering from an appendectomy. "Don't make me laugh, Jeff," she pleaded and, of course, I promptly made a face and danced around her bed. She held her side and pleaded again as she laughed painfully. In spite of that, we remained good friends over the years.

Later the same year my aunt Mabel died at 103 years of age. She was my mother's sister-in-law and in spite of her age, she flew

DR. E. JEFF JUSTIS

with me several times from Dewitt, Arkansas to to Memphis for Thanksgiving and Christmas. She was always a good sport and kept me supplied with wonderful angel food cakes for many birthdays.

In January 2005, Sally and I became official residents (for tax and voting purposes) of Oxford, Mississippi, although we were outside the city limits by two miles.

Being in Oxford certainly didn't keep us from celebrating the birth of our youngest granddaughter, Nora James Evelyn Eikner (another compensation for NMN) on February 15, 2005.

We continued flying the Aztec to Flying Physicians Association meetings in Charleston, San Diego and Asheville. It was in Asheville that we saw our long-time friend Mike Downey for the last time. We had met Mike and his first wife, Nancy, in the early 70s, and Sally had become a second mother to his children who usually accompanied him to the meetings. We befriended his second wife, Jeanette, and a later significant other, Amy. A great friend and pilot, he was killed in a midair collision in Montana while flying as co-pilot with another flying physician. Over the years that I have been privileged to fly airplanes, I have lost many friends in aircraft accidents. When our hominid ancestors dared to cross rivers, climb mountains, or traverse the jungles, there was always risk and some died, but those who continued were rewarded by what they found on the other side. So it is that we fortunate few will continue to climb above the clouds and find our heaven there.

The Flying Physicians Association, founded shortly before I joined in 1957, has been an important organization in my life from the early days when I was the youngest member to the present when I am among the oldest. The adventure of flying to new places and the shared camaraderie being with old friends has always been an attraction for physician pilots. Unfortunately, the cost of flying and lack of interest in aviation among young people is negatively affecting general aviation and the Flying Physicians Association in particular. We may be in the last days of an air transportation system that allowed a young person to use his birthday money to learn to fly and buy an airplane ($350 in 1954).

With capability comes opportunity and a return trip to Grand Bahama Island and later to the Dominican Republic, again with the Flying Physicians highlighted 2009 and 2010.

Meanwhile, since the house was finished, I worked on the RV6 project regularly and continued building furniture in my shop, often gluing up an assembly, then, while waiting for the glue to dry, going to the airport to rivet a panel on the RV6. Finally, after 23 years everything was coming together. The engine and propeller had been installed and checked, the instrument panel completed, and taxi tests performed. We flew the Aztec to Texas for my transition training with an instructor in his RV6. While there we were able to spend time with our granddaughter, Sara Beth, an accomplished violinist. She is the oldest daughter of Susan Strain Carmichael who is Sally's stepdaughter with Fred Strain.

Returning to Oxford, I waited for perfect weather and on November 9, 2010 I pushed the throttle full forward and, for the first time since its creation, N921SJ (named such in honor of our anniversary) accelerated briskly down the runway, generating lift, and climbed into the clear blue sky. I was busy monitoring the instruments and maintaining a safe flight profile, so exhilaration at this accomplishment was fleeting, but palpable. Twenty-five hours of test flying followed before the experimental aircraft was considered safe for normal operation.

In July 2011, Jeff and I flew the plane to Oshkosh, Wisconsin for the EAA, Airventure fly-in. Cathy drove to Oshkosh from Memphis where she was education director for the Wolf River Conservancy, with Sara and Nora James. We stayed at the Heidel House Hotel in Green Lake, Wisconsin and had a great time. Jeff had to fly out commercially on business, so I flew the RV6 home alone, dodging weather and getting within four miles of the airport before having to turn around and land in Holly Springs because of a storm that was sitting right over the Oxford airport.

I was honored in 2012 when one of my furniture pieces (the half scale Queen Anne side chair) was chosen for exhibit at the

Connecticut Historical Society in Hartford Connecticut along with other pieces produced by members of the Society of American Period Furniture Makers.

At the end of this narrative I can say with some confidence that our adult children and members of our extended family are all positively contributing to our world, and that their children, Sarah Beth (36), Amy (34), Lisa Ann (20), Katie Lee (17), Sara (15), Brooks (14) and Nora James (9), will, in their time, make it a better place for their having been here.

In September of 2012 after obtaining a visa for travel to Russia, which was somewhat of a hassle, we enjoyed a river cruise from Moscow to St. Petersburg, and in March 2013 we toured Tuscany. I suppose we've reached that time in life when comfort sometimes preempts adventure, but certainly not *all* adventure, for, as promised, this narrative ends at a milestone.

The little white, blue, and grey experimental airplane speeds down runway 27, accelerating molecules of air until their combined effort generates sufficient lift that the craft and its now 80-year-old pilot are freed from earthly constraints and search for new adventures in life..

Made in the USA
San Bernardino, CA
27 October 2014